THE GIFT OF GIVING LIFE

THE GIFT OF
Giving Life

Rediscovering the Divine Nature of
Pregnancy and Birth

By Felice Austin, CHt

Lani Axman, Heather Farrell, CD(DONA)

Robyn Allgood, AAHCC, and Sheridan Ripley, HCHI

Foreword By Lynn Callister, PhD, RN, FAAN

MADISON & WEST PUBLISHING

This book contains information and stories about spiritual approaches to birth care. This book should not be substituted for the personal care of a qualified physician or midwife, but should be used only to consider and become familiar with the full range of birthing options. The authors and publishers are not responsible for any adverse effects resulting from the use of information contained in this book. Individuals are cautioned to consult their health care professional in all matters concerning their specific needs.

 Published by MADISON & WEST PUBLISHING

The Gift of Giving Life: Rediscovering the Divine Nature of Pregnancy and Birth. © 2012 by The Gift of Giving Life, Inc. Foreword © 2012 by Lynn Callister. All rights reserved. Printed in the United States of America. No part of this book may be used or reproduced in any manner whatsoever without written permission except in the case of brief quotations embodied in critical articles or reviews. For information, address The Gift of Giving Life, Inc. c/o Madison & West Publishing, 10866 Washington Blvd., Suite 518, Culver City, CA 90232.

Book Design by Marie Reese
Cover Photograph by Shannon Flores / Shannon Flores Photography

For photograph credits, see page xxx.

www.thegiftofgivinglife.com

Library of congress Cataloging-in-Publication Data
Austin, Felice
The gift of giving life: rediscovering the divine nature of pregnancy and birth/ Felice Austin, Lani Axman, Heather Farrell, Robyn Allgood, and Sheridan Ripley
Includes bibliographical references and index.
1. Pregnancy, physical and spiritual preparation 2. Spirituality of birth 3. Mormon birth book 4. Parent preparation 5. Postpartum 6. Birth stories 7. Prenatal care 8. Childbirth

ISBN 978-0615622521

PRINTED IN THE UNITED STATES OF AMERICA

We humbly dedicate this book
to our little ones
who have opened the gates for us to discover the
divine nature of pregnancy and birth
and to our Savior
who gives life freely.

Contents

The book contains essays and personal stories.
Personal stories are indented below and can be indentified
throughout the book on shaded pages.

10   The Atonement   339

11   Unity   401

Key

When you see this symbol throughout the book, it means that more
resources on that subject can be found on this book's website:
www.thegiftofgivinglife.com.

Stories that may contain loss or graphic material are marked with a ribbon.
If you are sensitive, make sure you surround yourself with a cushion
of light as you read.

Foreword

It has now been forty-six years since I joyously gave birth to my first daughter, Carolyn, four days after Christmas. What a rich physical, emotional, and spiritual experience that was! That day and the subsequent births of my other four children are indelibly etched in my mind and heart. I lived through my first pregnancy in two distinctly different worlds: that of a nurse caring for critically ill patients in a highly technological medical center, and the growing world within me that I could visualize in my mind's eye. My own mother had died of breast cancer when I was seven years old, and how I longed to have her describe her feelings about my birth. How I yearned to listen to other women share their feelings about giving birth. Where were the mother-texts? Where were the voices of childbearing women?

Because of this paucity of mother-texts, I began my professional life work of collecting birth narratives from culturally diverse women, from the highlands of Guatemala to birth houses in Russia; from women espousing Christian, Jewish, and Islamic religious traditions and those espousing no particular faith but still describing the spiritual dimensions of giving birth. Themes generated regarding spirituality in childbearing women include childbirth as a time to grow closer to God, the use of religious beliefs and rituals as powerful coping mechanisms, childbirth as a time to make religiosity more meaningful, the significance of a Higher Power in influencing birth outcomes, and childbirth as a spiritually transforming experience. Childbirth is the ideal context in which to enrich spirituality, as I have learned during more than two decades of listening to birth stories.

I gained tremendous respect for the strength and wisdom and courage of women who chose to bear and rear children. For example, one Orthodox Jewish woman spoke of giving birth as one way to transcend herself: "I finally did something worthwhile in this world. I, everyone, comes here for a purpose, especially the woman. She comes here to continue the generations." A Muslim woman said about giving birth, "During childbirth the woman is in the hands of God. I felt like a miracle might happen—that there was something holy around me, protecting me, something beyond the ordinary, a feeling, a spirit about being a part of God's creation of a child."

The diverse and profound perspectives of childbearing women are detailed in this remarkable book, *The Gift of Giving Life*. These narratives were collected by a group of amazing young mothers who edited this book. The narratives are alive with the richness and creativity of "meaning making," by childbearing women experiencing one of the most profound experiences of their life. These mother's perspectives demonstrate how birth is shaped by deeply held values and cherished dreams. Sue Bender, writing in *Everyday Sacred*, invites us to know that each step in life's journey, including bearing a child, is miraculous and that it is the small acts that make our days sacred.

As you read this book and reflect on its contents, you will never view giving birth as you did before. It is my hope that this work will inspire you to collect birth stories, writing about your own births and interviewing your grandmothers, mothers, daughters, and grand-daughters about their births: generations of women over time articulating the meaning of having a child.

Lynn Clark Callister, PhD, RN, FAAN

Acknowledgments

Many wonderful people helped us along the way in the creation and publication of this book. From the purest and deepest parts of our souls, we would like to thank everyone who contributed their birth stories, even if their story wasn't used.

We are so grateful for Meleah Ekstrand for her countless hours keeping us organized and efficient, and for others who gave their time, talents, or support, including: Rixa Freeze, Elizabeth Day, Katy Rawlins, Marie Reese, Shannon Flores, Lynn Callister, Suzy Bills, and many others.

We would like to thank Sister Julie Beck, for encouraging us to ask the hard questions; Anna Harrison for her interest and support from the beginning; faithful home teachers and visiting teachers; all of our blog readers; our bishops and church leaders, a few wonderful temple workers, and the sister missionaries for their insights, interest, and help cleaning the house.

For their thoughts and advice on publishing, we would like to acknowledge: Carol Lynn Pearson, Randy Gibbs, Rebecca Overson, Tamara Johnson, and Dennis Danziger. We thank Bonnie Ballif-Spanvill for reading the manuscript before it was perfect.

We are grateful for all of our husbands and children for waiting patiently while we wrote just one more page or read one more birth story. We honor and give thanks to our mothers for first giving us the gift of life so that we could in turn share that gift with others. We would also like to acknowledge: our midwives, doctors, doulas, friends, and others who contributed to our spiritual birth experiences; all of our close friends who listened to us ramble about birth for several years; and many angels and ancestors in the spirit world.

We are also deeply indebted to all the modern women who have gone before us who have paved the way for spirituality and birth such as Lynn Callister, Gurmukh Kaur Kalsah, Ina May Gaskin, and many many others.

We are grateful to our Father and Mother in Heaven for giving us this challenge and opportunity and for all the blessings we have received from it. We are grateful for our Savior whose birth reminds us that God and His angels attend birth everywhere, from stables to hospitals to bathtubs. Our Savior can guide us and support us not only through our lives but through our births, and has attended us through the writing of this book.

Introduction
and How to Use This Book

In "The Family: A Proclamation to the World,"[1] the prophet and his apostles reiterated the emphasis the Lord has placed on childbearing: "We declare that God's commandment for His children to multiply and replenish the earth remains in force."

Not only does God want us to bring children into this world, but He also has an ideal structure for families. He emphasized this structure in the proclamation on the family (children are to be born to a loving mother and father who are married, the father is to preside and provide, the mother is to be the primary nurturer, parents are to be equal partners, etc.). Though this ideal isn't possible for everyone, it is still something to strive toward as much as we can within our individual circumstances.

In addition to providing the ideal family structure, the proclamation addresses how children are brought into this world: "We declare the means by which mortal life is created to be divinely appointed." This means that not only conception but also the physical and spiritual processes of pregnancy and birth are divinely appointed. Elder David A. Bednar said:

> Nothing is more holy; nothing deserves more reverence; nothing is more central to the plan of happiness.[2]

In Satan's attempts to frustrate the plan of happiness, he uses diverse and subtle ways to tempt us to abuse or disregard our sacred powers. In the case of sex, many of us are wise to his tactics, but he has undermined the sacredness of pregnancy and birth in more subtle ways.

As Latter-day Saint women, we know that our bodies were created in the image of our Heavenly Mother and are, therefore, perfectly designed for their divinely appointed purpose. Just as there is an ideal structure for the divine institution of the family, God also has an ideal for pregnancy and birth (labor starts on its own, the woman has support from a loving husband, etc.). However, this framework, like the family, is an ideal and variations need to be made for individual circumstances.

This book does not advocate any one type of birth or approach to prenatal care; rather, it intends to unify our families and communities in regard to the sacredness of birth. We also aim to provide you with resources, information, and inspiration that you may not have had access to all in one place before.

Our Heavenly Father has commanded us to "teach one another words of wisdom, and learn wisdom out of the best books" (D&C 88:118). Many women have contributed to this book. Some have written essays on spiritual topics related to childbearing in which you will find much wisdom from the best books, including the scriptures, general conference addresses, early Latter-day Saint history, and other sources. Women and men have also contributed their personal stories. We have included personal stories because we believe it is through stories that we can learn possibilities we weren't aware of; feel more connected and inspired; and, when necessary, be healed from our personal experiences, fears, and attitudes about pregnancy and birth.

You can use this book in several ways. You can read it straight through; refer to it by topic as your needs/interests arise; or say a little prayer, asking to be guided to what you need to read in the moment.

Though we have written the book unabashedly for a Latter-day Saint audience, we hope that birthing women, birth attendants, and birth advocates of all faiths will find the book useful and informative. If you have any questions about any of the terms used in this book or about The Church of Jesus Christ of Latter-day Saints, we invite you to visit mormon.org or e-mail any of the authors through The Gift of Giving Life website.

Special Note to the Reader

Nothing in this book should be considered medical advice. Couples should always consult with their health care providers and pray about health care decisions as a family.

Though we have made every attempt to be consistent with the doctrine and teachings of The Church of Jesus Christ of Latter-day Saints, this book is an expression of many of our own thoughts and reflections from pondering the truths of the gospel that we treasure. This book is not an official declaration of doctrine in regard to The Church of Jesus Christ of Latter-day Saints to which we belong and cherish our membership. Please make sure to pray about and ponder everything you read.

Author's Note:
The Power of Words

A word fitly spoken is like apples of gold.

PROVERBS 25:11

In the third verse of the Bible, at the very beginning of the Christian cannon, we learn the importance and power of words: "And God said, Let there be light: and there was light" (Genesis 1:3). The organization of the world was accomplished not with hands but with words. In fact, words are so powerful that one of the names used to refer to Jesus Christ is "the Word."

> In the beginning was the Word, and the Word was with God, and the Word was God. . . . And the Word was made flesh and dwelt among us (and we beheld his glory, the glory as of the only begotten of the Father,) full of grace and truth. (John 1:1, 14)

It is also by His words that we are forgiven and by our words that we are judged. Christ explained, "Ye are clean through the words which I have spoken unto you" (John 15:3), and "the word that I have spoken, the same shall judge him in the last day" (John 12:48).

As we know, the inaccurate translation of just one word can cause confusion, contention, and disbelief for generations. In fact, when God wanted to frustrate the building of the Tower of Babel, he confounded the people's language. Being able to speak the same language is a gift.

I second Job's exclamation to the prophet Eliphaz, "how forcible are right words!" (Job 6:25). In fact, the "right" words are so important that God promises: "For it shall be given you in the very hour, yea, in the very moment, what ye shall say" (D&C 100:6).

In Pablo Neruda's beautiful poem "The Word," he wrote of language as an inheritance:

this is the wavelength that connects us
with dead men and the dawning
of new beings not yet come to light.[2]

Language is indeed an inheritance, and as birthing women, we are in the position to affect the value of the inheritance we pass on to the next generation. The words we listen to, read, think, and allow others to say to us have a great influence on us at all times, and they are especially powerful during childbearing and postpartum. During this time, a woman's mind is very open and vulnerable to positive and negative words.

Just as God "spake, and it was done" (Psalm 33:9), our words have similar power as goddesses-in-training over our own kingdoms—the kingdom of the body. As you will read in "The Spirit-Mind-Body Connection" chapter and in many of the birth stories, the words we think and believe often become our physical realities.

You may notice that a few of the childbirth education programs mentioned in the birth stories in this book have changed the common terminology of birthing to make birthing positive and empowering. For example, some women refer to labor as their "birth time," and babies are not "delivered" but are "born," giving the power back to the mother. Other women use the more common terminology—contractions, labor, and so forth. We have chosen to leave all language in the birth stories unchanged. Within the essays and articles, we have attempted to use positive language and never to affirm anything as true for *all* women, unless it is true, such as that we are all children of God. When it comes to birth, there is no *always*. We can each have a unique experience.

We hope that each woman will chose to surround herself with positive words, stories, and images, remembering, that "the words of the Lord are pure words" (Psalm 12:6) and we should have them ever before us (see Deuteronomy 11:18).

---

1   See Isaiah 51:16; 59:21; Jeremiah 1:9; 2 Nephi 8:16.
2   Pablo Neruda, "The Word," *Fully Empowered*, (New York: New Directions Books. 1975), 5.

CHAPTER ONE

Our Legacy

Yea, they had been taught by
their mothers, that if they did not doubt,
God would deliver them.

ALMA 56:47

We Are Each Eve

By Heather Farrell, CD(DONA)

*Mother, who willingly made that personal
journey into the valley of the shadow of death to take us by the hand
and introduce us to birth—even to mortal life—deserves
our undying gratitude.[1]*

THOMAS S. MONSON

No matter who we are, where we live, or what we believe, all women on this earth share a common and powerful heritage; we are all daughters of Eve. We know that by choosing to eat of the tree of knowledge of good and evil, Eve brought pain, sorrow, and death into the world. Throughout history, she has been vilified and condemned for her choice, and much of the world's sorrows have been blamed on her supposed poor judgment and gullibility. Yet, as Latter-day Saints, we have an enlightened and different picture of this great woman and the choice she made in Eden.

Elder Dallin H. Oaks has said, "Some Christians condemn Eve for her act, concluding that she and her daughters are somehow flawed by it. Not the Latter-day Saints! Informed by revelation, we celebrate Eve's act and honor her wisdom and courage in the great episode called the Fall."[2] In truth, given what Latter-day Saints know about Eve's eternal character, it is hard to imagine Eve as a passive actor in the great drama of the Fall or as someone who could be easily deceived by any of Satan's lies.

Dr. Nehama Aschenasy, a Hebrew scholar, said that in Hebrew the word which is translated as *beguiled* in the Bible does not mean "tricked" or "deceived" as we commonly think. Rather, the Hebrew word is a rare verb that indicates an intense, multilevel experience evoking great emotional, psychological, and/or spiritual trauma. As Aschenasy explained, it is likely that Eve's intense, multilevel experience, this "beguiling" by the serpent, was the catalyst that caused Eve to ponder and evaluate what her role and purpose in the Garden really was.[3] We don't know how long she sought for understanding, but we know she found it because we read that "the woman saw that the tree was good for food, and that it became pleasant to the eyes, and a tree to be desired to make one wise" (Genesis 3:6).

Eve *saw*. She wasn't deceived—she made a conscious choice. Her choice is even more powerful when we remember that Eve wouldn't have known about the Atonement or about the Savior until *after* she had eaten the fruit. In what was one of the bravest acts ever done, Eve ate—thinking that she was going to die but willing to suffer those consequences if it meant being able to bring children into the world. In view of her sacrifice, one can only imagine her incredible joy when God revealed the plan of salvation. How she must have clung to and respected the garment that was given to her. The garment, symbolic of Christ's sacrifice, was her reminder and promise that even though she had chosen death, there would be continuing life for her and for all the generations that would come after her.

As daughters of Eve, modern women must make similar choices. We each get to decide whether we will "partake of the fruit" by choosing to welcome children into our homes or whether we will remain in a figurative Eden. The choice today is no less difficult than Eve's because Satan is still trying his hardest to beguile Eve's daughters and confuse them about their divine missions. General Relief Society President Julie B. Beck has said:

> Satan knows that he will never have a body; he will never have a family. He will target those young women who create the bodies for the future generations and who should teach the families. They don't even know what they're being taught in the messages. It's just seeping in, almost through their pores. Because Satan can't have it, he's luring away many women, and also men, and they're losing confidence in their ability to form eternal families.[4]

Satan is doing all he can to make young women fear the process of birth, diminish their faith in the importance of having children, and paint motherhood to appear as oppression.

As modern women, we, like Eve, need to ponder, pray, and meditate about the decisions we make concerning childbearing, pregnancy, birth, and motherhood. There is no decision too small with which to concern the Lord when it comes to creating and nurturing His precious spirit children.

"To the first man and woman on earth, the Lord said, 'Be fruitful, and multiply.' This commandment was first in sequence and first in importance. It was essential that God's spirit children have mortal birth and an opportunity to progress toward eternal life. Consequently, all things related to procreation are prime targets for the adversary's efforts to thwart the plan of God." [5] —Dallin H. Oaks

Ultimately, Eve ate the fruit because she *saw* and understood what God wanted her to do, not because she was swayed by the serpent's popular arguments. As Eve's daughters, let us learn from the example of our first mother and have the courage to do God's work; not because we are afraid or deceived but because we see and understand who we are and our responsibilities as women in God's eternal plan.

1   Thomas S. Monson, "An Attitude of Gratitude," *Ensign*, May 1992, http://lds.org/ensign/1992/05/an-attitude-of-gratitude.
2   Dallin H. Oaks, "The Great Plan of Happiness," *Ensign*, November 1993, http://lds.org/ensign/1993/11/the-great-plan-of-happiness.
3   Beverly Campbell, *Eve and the Choice Made in Eden* (Salt Lake City, UT: Bookcraft, 2003), 71.
4   Julie B. Beck, "Teaching the Doctrine of the Family" (talk given for the Seminaries and Institutes of Religion Satellite Broadcast, Salt Lake City, UT, August 4, 2009), 5.
5   Dallin H. Oaks, "The Great Plan of Happiness," *Ensign*, November 1993, http://lds.org/ensign/1993/11/the-great-plan-of-happiness.

DIVINE NATURE

By Catherine Kemeny Gambrell

WHEN MY DUE DATE CAME AND WENT, I started to feel a bit panicked. It wasn't a surprise, as I had gone past my due date with my son as well, but it was still worrisome. We had planned a hospital birth with a certified nurse-midwife in attendance. I knew that, based on the policies of the doctors in her practice, my midwife would release me from her care if I did not consent to an induction at 41 weeks. After having a painful and fearful induction with my son, I knew what to expect if this happened. More than I had wanted anything in my life, I wanted to feel spontaneous labor. I wanted to go into labor on my own.

I pleaded many nights with my Father in Heaven. Many times I was reminded of the Psalm: "Delight thyself also in the Lord; and he shall give thee the desires of thine heart" (Psalms 37:4). I told Him, "I have tried to be obedient, to delight in You. Will You give me this, the one desire of my heart?"

I asked my husband to give me a priesthood blessing. I needed guidance about what to do about an induction, but mostly I wanted the Lord to tell me, through the blessing, that I would not need to be induced, that I would go into labor on my own, that I could have the birth I so desired. I did not hear this. What I heard instead was that I did not need to fear. Things would work out, regardless of the circumstances. The blessing brought an immense sense of relief and peace to our home. My husband and I decided to stay with our midwife even if that meant being induced, and I resigned myself to the possibility of an induction.

This didn't stop me from continuing to bring my plight before the Lord. Each night, I poured out my soul to my Heavenly Father. I cried. I continued to beg and plead: "Please, please, let me have this. I want to know what it feels like. I want to know I am not broken. I want my body to do what it was designed to do."

Finally, on a Tuesday, I had the last appointment with my midwife. She scheduled the induction for Friday, at a time when she had no other appointments and could be the most available to me. She requested a nurse she knew was experienced in natural birth. I left the appointment feeling defeated and sad, but the priesthood blessing my husband had administered was always in my mind.

I had been having contractions for several weeks, so when they started again that Wednesday night, I wasn't concerned or excited. When I crawled into bed at 1:30 in the morning, I had almost forgotten completely about them. It wasn't until I woke up feeling sick to my stomach around 6:30 the next morning that I remembered how strong the contractions had been early that morning. Despite the nausea, I went about my day as normal. I made breakfast for my son. We played with toys. I read him books. When the contractions got stronger, I put a movie on for him, and we sat together, he on his hoppy ball and me on my birth ball.

I called my husband around 8:30 and told him that my contractions were getting stronger. While I didn't think I was in labor, I told him that I did need some help taking care of our son. When he got home a few hours later, the contractions had definitely increased in intensity but were still very erratic. My husband made lunch, rubbed my back, played with my hair, distracted our son, and did anything else that needed to be done so I could focus on my body.

While our son played at the neighborhood park, I swayed in the sunshine, leaning when I needed to on the playground ladder or the swing set for support. I swung on the swings, imagining the baby in my womb swinging down into position, trying to imagine what the baby would look like. Was it another little boy, or was it a girl? Would it look like our son, or would it have a different look altogether? Would it have hair?

After spending some time together at the park, my husband put our son down for a nap, and I took a bath. I enjoyed the relaxation that soaking in the bath afforded, but the lack of sleep from the previous night was starting to catch up to me, and I was suddenly feeling completely exhausted. I got out of the bath and decided to try to take a nap.

The instant I laid on my bed, my contractions changed. Suddenly, I couldn't find a comfortable position when lying down, so I got up again. I started to get antsy. I couldn't sit still. I walked around our bedroom. I sat on the toilet. I bounced on the ball. I kneeled in front of the recliner. My husband had been timing my contractions, getting me water to drink, rubbing my back and shoulders and arms. The contractions, only twenty minutes after getting out of the bath, had gone from erratic to very regular, and they were now coming two and a half minutes apart and lasting about a minute and a half.

We continued to work through the contractions. Sitting on the toilet was excruciating. Lying in bed was torture. Sitting up on the birth ball felt nice, and kneeling over something, like the edge of the bed where I could let my belly hang and arch my back, helped the most. A few minutes after call-

---

To give birth in any way is life-changing, earth-shattering, momentous. Becoming a mother, for the first time or the fourteenth time, is powerful.

---

ing my sister to watch our son, my husband told me he thought we should go to the hospital. I wanted to wait for my sister to arrive, but he was afraid we didn't have time. He called my visiting teaching companion who came and sat with our son while he napped. During the six minute drive to the hospital, I had three strong contractions. By the time we pulled into the parking lot and got out of the car, my contractions were bringing me to tears.

When we reached our room, I was still smiling between contractions but crying during them. I was informed that I needed to be strapped to the external fetal monitor for thirty minutes. After only ten minutes of sitting in bed being monitored, I told my nurse that I couldn't handle any more; I needed to get up. I needed to let my belly hang. I wanted to stand with my husband, leaning on his arms for support. I was lucky to have an understanding nurse who was happy to support my birth plan. She unhooked the monitors, and I was able to move about freely, as I wished.

My husband was my rock during this time. Whenever I felt a contraction coming on, I cried to my husband. He reassured me that I was strong, powerful, brave. He reminded me that I didn't need to handle it forever, just for about a minute at a time. I could handle a minute at a time. He was right.

Suddenly something felt different. I didn't feel so passive. I felt like I needed to do something. I decided to give a little experimental push. It felt like such a relief. I was tired and wanted some support, so between contractions I moved to the bed and sat down. It was at this time that my midwife arrived, dressing in her gown and gloves as she entered the room. My husband helped me pull my legs to my chest. The next contraction started, and my body took over. My midwife was rushing to get ready, but my body's reflexes couldn't resist the urge to push. Even as my midwife begged me to push slower so she could apply pressure to the perineum to prevent tearing, I couldn't. I had no control. My body was totally and completely in control.

Pushing was one of the most satisfying parts of labor. It made my contractions feel so much better to push through them. In just two pushes, my baby was out, breaking the water as she emerged. A baby girl! A perfect baby girl. My Eve. She was calm and alert, and the love I immediately felt for her was quiet and unassuming but strong. I also felt a loud, frantic thrill in my body. I felt empowered, strong, womanly, godlike. I now understood what "divine nature" really meant. I was in awe of God's flawless design of our mortal bodies. I better saw the perfect wisdom in His plan. I admired my baby for knowing what to do to be born.

I suddenly realized how fitting our daughter's name was as I felt a deep gratitude and kinship with Eve, the original mother. The Lord told Eve as He cast her out of the garden of Eden that "in sorrow thou shalt bring forth children" (Genesis 3:16). Later, after Adam and Eve had born children and felt both sorrow and joy, Eve realized the magnitude of her choice in the Garden and felt glad, saying, "Were it not for our transgression we never should have had seed, and never should have known good and evil, and the joy of our redemption, and the eternal life which God giveth unto all the obedient" (Moses 5:11). There were times both in pregnancy and during labor that I felt I couldn't go on. But after feeling the sorrow and the pain, I was able to recognize the joy.

I also felt a deep kinship with every woman who has ever lived, but especially with the women on my family tree, my ancestors. I felt connected to them, knowing that I had done the very thing that all mothers through all ages of time have done. My body birthed my baby. I didn't need anyone telling me what to do. My body, in its divine design, knew just what to do to safely bring my baby into the world. I have never loved or appreciated my body, God's creations, Eve and my ancestor mothers, and all women as much as I did then, in the afterglow of naturally birthing my daughter.

To give birth in any way is life-changing, earth-shattering, momentous. Becoming a mother, for the first time or the fourteenth time, is powerful. But, for me, giving birth to my daughter, without medical interventions or medicines, was an intensely spiritual, empowering, defining moment in my life that has changed me fundamentally, given me beautiful memories, and taught me many lessons that will never leave me. And for that I will be eternally grateful.

A New Woman

By Jessi H.

WHEN OUR DUE DATE CAME AND WENT, I knew our son would be born exactly one week after. Everyone was still holding their breath all week long, thinking he could come at any time once the due date passed, but I really just kicked back and enjoyed that last week without any angst.

We were planning to get induced at forty-one weeks, but during our dinner on the way to our induction, my labor started. I didn't know at first and just kept eating, but when we headed out to the car I had a contraction that left me no doubt that this was it. Luckily we were only about five minutes away from the hospital.

We got to the hospital right on time for our scheduled induction only to explain that I was already in labor. We were escorted to our room, experiencing several contractions along the way, and tried to get as comfortable as possible. By this time, contractions were coming about every three minutes, but I was only dilated to 2 cm. I really wanted to try to make it to 4 cm before I got an epidural because I wanted to experience laboring, and I wanted to rely on my husband for emotional, spiritual, and physical support. I also didn't want to be bedridden for an entire day, so we put the epidural off. John gave me a beautiful blessing that really set the tone for the incredible night. It was so special to me.

After about four hours of laboring naturally, I was ready for my epidural. I could not have asked for a better epidural experience. I did not feel a thing when the needle went in, and I could still move my legs and feel a teensy bit of painless pressure from most of the contractions which is the sign of a perfect epidural. I was still very proud of myself for sticking it out as long as I did.

My water broke at 11:30, and about fifteen minutes later I noticed in my half sleep that every time I contracted the baby's heart rate would drop. I figured that the nurses could see this on the monitor at their station and that if it were a problem they would come in and check it out. Five seconds later, in walked my nurse. I told her my observation and she said she had noticed the same thing. She said that she wasn't planning on checking my cervix again so soon, but that she wanted to see how much further along I had gotten, just to be safe.

I was 10 cm and we were ready to start pushing! Around 1:00 a.m. the on-call doctor showed up. We called our moms to come, and they rushed right over arriving around 1:15 a.m. My darling husband and glorious mother held my legs while my saintly mother-in-law rubbed my shoulders and my talented sister took pictures of the incredible event. We met James for the first time at 1:32 a.m., just seven short hours after my first contraction.

I could not have asked for a better experience. John was so incredible the entire time, and we were both so relieved that our moms and sister could be there. Everything went perfectly. At one point during the delivery I literally yelled out, "I love birth!" The nurses chuckled and said they hadn't ever heard that one before. But I just couldn't contain my joy and awe over the whole process.

I'm so glad I labored naturally for as long as I did. I'm so glad I got such a successful epidural. I'm so glad we had the nurses we had. I'll never forget what it was like when Dr. D placed James right onto my chest. I was a new woman from that moment on. "My baby! My Baby!" I kept yelling out. He was so perfectly cute and so perfectly John's, with his little puffy eyes, juicy lips, and gobs of dark hair.

My labor and delivery was the most sacred, precious, impressionable experience I have ever had. It was like an entire seven hours with my Savior right by my side, ending with Him personally giving me my son. My son. Our son. Our sweet baby James.

Heavenly Mother

By Rixa Freeze, PhD

In the heavens are parents single?
No, the thought makes reason stare!
Truth is reason; truth eternal
Tells me I've a mother there.[1]

ELIZA R. SNOW

Our belief in Heavenly Mother sets The Church of Jesus Christ of Latter-day Saints apart from many other Christian faiths. Not only do we reject the idea of a substanceless, bodiless God, we also believe that Deity is not solely male, but rather a united, eternal couple. Our belief in Deity as a male-female couple can give us courage and confidence as we navigate through our childbearing and mothering years. We can glean significant insights about the nature of Mother in Heaven from a careful reading of the scriptures; from the words of modern-day prophets and Church leaders; and from our own personal meditation, pondering, and prayer.

One way that we can draw closer to Heavenly Mother is to read her into scriptural passages that mention God. Heavenly Father and Mother are united as an eternal couple, sharing a mutual interest in the welfare of their spirit children. As you read the scriptures and the words of latter-day prophets, you can replace "Heavenly Father" and "God" with the phrases "Heavenly Father and Heavenly Mother" and "our Heavenly parents." In fact, the apostle Erastus Snow recommended doing this:

> "What," says one, "do you mean we should understand that Deity consists of man and woman?" Most certainly I do. If I believe anything that God has ever said about himself, and anything pertaining to the creation and organization of man upon the earth, I must believe that Deity consists of

man and woman. . . . [T]here can be no god except he is composed of the man and woman united, and there is not in all the eternities that exist, nor ever will be, a God in any other way.[2]

Some Latter-day Saint scholars have suggested that Heavenly Mother is not as absent from the biblical record as we might initially think. Kevin L. Barney, for example, has identified allusions to Heavenly Mother in the Old Testament, including her close connection with healing and with the symbolism of sacred trees; and her interest in childbirth, fertility, and lactation.[3] Barney suggested several ways to honor Heavenly Mother: honoring her role by planting a tree or by showing reverence for nature; creating our own artistic representations of Her; paying careful attention to scriptural passages alluding to wisdom, happiness, and tree symbolism; and most importantly, attending the temple.

We can also learn more about our Heavenly Mother by studying the attributes of Jesus Christ. As the spiritual son of Heavenly Parents—though born to an earthly mother—Jesus personifies all of the attributes of both God the Father and God the Mother. Ida Smith gave a talk at a 1980 Brigham Young University Women's Conference, later reprinted in the Ensign, entitled "The Lord as a Role Model for Men and Women." She pointed out that the Savior possessed attributes that both sexes should strive to emulate:

> Some women complain that they have no strong role models in the scriptures. That is not true. We have many models there. And our main one is the Savior, himself. Nowhere is it written that he is a model for men only; and nowhere is it written that men and women should each be allowed only half of his traits! . . . Nowhere, for example, does the Lord say that tenderness, kindness, charity, faithfulness, patience, gentleness, and compassion are strictly female traits and should be utilized by women only. And nowhere does he say that courage, strength, determination, and leadership should be the exclusive prerogative of men.[4]

The best way to learn more about the nature of Heavenly Mother is to exercise our gifts of personal revelation, inspiration, and spiritual guidance. Thoughtful prayer, scripture study, and meditation can give each of us personal insights about her.

Heavenly Mother knows firsthand what we are going through as our bodies and spirits change and stretch to accommodate new life. She will give us support and encouragement through our years of pregnancy, child-bearing, lactation, and mothering. Our earthly experiences of childbearing and mothering are "internships" for the divine work we will be doing in the next life. One sister reflected on the importance of these tasks:

> Birth is really and truly goddess work. When a woman creates a human body it isn't just mortal; it is immortal. Because of the Atonement, the body she creates will never ever die. It will be eternal and it has the possibility to become a god or a goddess. In the same way that men are "apprentices" to their Heavenly Father and have been granted his priesthood power to "practice" with, women are "apprentices" to their Heavenly mother and our creative work here on earth is "practice" for our eternal job of being goddesses.

> When we look at it that way it makes a lot of sense why so many of us feel women's experiences in the birth process matter immensely. It is our apprenticeship, our training—the most important lessons we can be learning here on earth (including mothering and nurturing the spirit we create). Our Heavenly Mother grants us some of Her power and gives us authority to "create" in Her name, just like men have been granted some of Heavenly Father's power to "act" in his name.[5]

Although we do not formally pray to Heavenly Mother, we can still communicate with and draw strength from her in many other ways. Foremost, remember that your prayers *are* going to both Heavenly Father and Mother. She hears and understands your concerns and joys alongside Heavenly Father. One woman recalled the following from a recent stake conference:

> Yesterday at our stake conference, my ears perked up as our stake president spoke of prayer. He said if you feel like your prayers are bouncing off the ceiling, then go to a private room and picture Heavenly Father seated

in front of you. See the love and concern in His eyes and then imagine next to Him your Heavenly Mother with just as much love and concern in Her eyes as you pray. Direct your words to the Father. [6]

We can also draw close to Heavenly Mother through meditation. Spend some quiet time reflecting on her qualities and attributes. Imagine how you might relate to her, what you might talk about if she were in the room. Draw strength from her presence, knowing that she has accompanied countless other women during their journeys through motherhood.

We can honor Her role by appreciating the magnificence and intricate beauty of these biological processes. For example, the hormones of labor (oxytocin and endorphins) dull pain, create a feeling of euphoria, give the

---

"Sisters, I testify that when you stand in front of your heavenly parents in those royal courts on high and look into Her eyes and behold Her countenance, any question you ever had about the role of women in the kingdom will evaporate into the rich celestial air, because at that moment you will see standing directly in front of you, your divine nature and destiny."[7] —Glenn L. Pace

---

mother an intense natural "high," and prime both mother and baby for falling in love with each other. The more intense the labor, the higher the levels of the body's natural painkillers. The hormones of breast-feeding (prolactin and oxytocin) foster feelings of love, security, attachment, and contentment in both mother and baby. In addition, naturally high levels of endorphins are transferred through the mother's milk, giving the baby feelings of pleasure and satisfaction every time the baby nurses.

These hormones are released more easily when we feel safe, loved, and secure. In contrast, fear, anxiety, and stress lead to lower levels of the hormones necessary for giving birth and breast-feeding. Love and trust literally allow the biological processes to work as they should. The scripture 2 Timothy 1:7 comes to mind: "For God hath not given us the spirit of fear; but of power, and of love, and of a sound mind." When we approach childbearing from a *spiritual* perspective and exercise love rather than fear, we also facilitate the *physical* process. This is a wonderful demonstration of how the spiritual and temporal dimensions are interconnected.

It can be incredibly reassuring to know that a woman was involved in the planning of our physical bodies. Pregnancy, childbirth, and lactation are miraculous in both their simplicity and their complexity. As we see these these processes through the eyes of Heavenly Mother, we gain a glimpse of the feminine divine.

1   Eliza R. Snow, "O, My Father," in *Hymns of the Church of Jesus Christ of Latter-day Saints* (Salt Lake City, UT: Deseret Book, 1985), no. 292.
2   *Journal of Discourses* 19:269-270, 3 Mar. 1878.
3   Kevin L. Barney, "How to Worship Our Mother in Heaven (Without Getting Excommunicated)," *Dialogue: A Journal of Mormon Thought* 41, no. 4 (2008): 121–146.
4   Ida Smith, "The Lord as a Role Model for Men and Women," *Ensign*, August 1980, http://lds.org/ensign/1980/08/the-lord-as-a-role-model-for-men-and-women?lang=eng&query=%E2%80%9CThe+Lord+Role+Model+Men+Women,%E2%80%9D.
5   Heather Farrell, e-mail message to the Gift of Giving Life (GOGL) Google group, June 16, 2010.
6   Robyn Allgood, e-mail message to the GOGL Google group, October 11, 2010.
7   Glenn L. Pace, "The Divine Nature and Destiny of Women" Brigham Young University Devotional, Provo, UT, March 9, 2010. http://www.byub.org/talks/Talk.aspx?id=3936 (accessed Nov. 29, 2011).

HEALING THROUGH MOTHERHOOD

By Meghan Raynes-Matthews

I NEVER THOUGHT MUCH ABOUT BEING A MOTHER. I was focused on graduate school and the brilliant career I was going to have as a feminist historian. And then I got married, and graduate school didn't happen, but pregnancy did.

I was so conflicted, knowing that I should have been happy but feeling so incredibly inadequate. I couldn't be a mother; I had no mothering skills at all and I didn't like babies. More than anything, I was afraid that I would pass on all my insecurities to this child. Pregnancy released painful memories from my childhood that I had worked so hard to forget about. The loneliness and fear I had felt as a child came crashing down on me. I felt myself falling into a darkness that consumes. The hopelessness inside me was overwhelming, almost as if I was being buried alive.

The waves of hopelessness pounded me for months until one Sunday, sitting in sacrament meeting, I heard the Lord speak. "The child will heal you." I felt a wriggle in my womb as if the baby I carried was trying to assure me of this truth. Something other than myself knew that being this child's mother would provide the balm to my weary soul. A calm in the storm came, and so I waited.

The day of my delivery arrived. It was long and exhausting. I had chosen to have my baby in a birth center. I wanted to feel every contraction, every movement. I wanted to touch the power of womanhood. As I transitioned, the pounding waves came again, but this time they were physical and primal. I pushed for two hours; wondering through each contraction whether this would be the one to snuff out my life. And then I felt Her. The love was unbelievable. I was surrounded by my husband, mother and father, sister and two midwives, but theirs was not the only love I felt. My unnamed Heavenly Mother. The one that I had so often longed for was with me, stroking my damp hair and holding me through the pain. I could not voice Her presence, but I know She was there.

That night, as my husband lay sleeping, I tried to calm my beautiful newborn son. As he fussed and cried, I felt the familiar panic rise up in my throat. I saw the sadness in his big, blue eyes and I did not know how to comfort him. Tears came to my eyes as I felt my inadequacy. Then a simple tune escaped my lips. My crying child quieted.

As I sung those cherished words of the realization of a Mother, my son, the child sent to heal me, looked at me with the deep perception that only newborns posses, as if to say, "I know, Mama. She is with us." I felt Her presence and Her overwhelming love for me and my son. She has been with us ever since, whispering in my ear, lovingly instructing me how to be a mother. And that has healed me.

Our Early Latter-day Saint Birthing Legacy

By Heather Farrell, CD(DONA)

After having been forced out of Nauvoo by increasing mob violence, Zina D. H. Young, wife of Brigham Young and the third president of the Relief Society, gave birth to her second son on the banks of the Chariton River in a pouring rainstorm. It was March 22, 1846. In her diary, Zina wrote:

> We reached the Chariton River between 3 and 4 weeks after leaving Nauvoo. I had been told in the Temple that I should acknowledge God even in a miracle in my deliverance in woman's hour of trouble, which hour had now come. We had traveled one [morning] about 5 miles, when I called for a halt in our march. There was but one person with me— Mother Lyman. There on the bank of the Chariton River, I was delivered of a fine son. Occasionally the wagon had to be stopped that I might take a breath. Thus I journey on.[1]

After the birth, Zina and her new baby boy (whom she named Chariton, after the river) were placed on a feather bed and propped up against some wooden barrels. She wrote that every time the wagon bounced she could feel the iron hoops of the barrels dig into her bed. Yet, as she noted in her journal, "I did not mind the hardships of my situation, for my life had been preserved, and my babe was so beautiful."[2]

WOMEN IN THE WILDERNESS

As Latter-day Saint women, we have an incredible legacy of strong and faithful women to draw strength from as we venture on the journey to motherhood. Even women who don't have ancestors who crossed the plains with the early Saints still share a heritage with these women—a common faith in the same God, the same prophets, and the same divine plan.

It is important to remember that these early Latter-day Saint mothers weren't the rugged frontier women we sometimes imagine them to be. Many of the women who crossed the plains to the Rocky Mountains came from well-to-do families and were used to living in better circumstances. Eliza R. Snow wrote the following about these women:

> Let it be remembered that the mothers of these wilderness born babes were not savages accustomed to roam the forest and brave the storm and tempest—those who had never known the comforts and delicacies of civilization and refinement. They were not those who in the wilds of nature nursed their offspring amid reeds and rushes or in the recesses of rocky caverns. Most of them were born and educated in the eastern states. . . had gathered with the saints . . . had lovely homes decorated with flowers and enriched with choice fruit trees just beginning to yield plentifully.[3]

Early Latter-day Saint women were much like us. Taking a leap of faith into the literal wilderness and giving up their homes, their security, and sometimes their families was likely as frightening to them as it would be for us. Yet they endured and overcame in the same way we do today: through exercising faith, praying, trusting the power of the priesthood, and supporting and loving one another.

In September 1846, eight months after the first group of Saints left Nauvoo, mob violence intensified so much that the remaining Saints were forced to flee for their lives. Among these Saints were nine pregnant women, who (according to midwife Jane Johnson Black) all delivered on the same night they made their forced exodus from Nauvoo. Later in life, Black recounted:

> Before crossing the Mississippi River. A posse of the mob rode up and surrounded our wagons and demanded we give up our firearms. I had a pistol in my bosom and I drew it out and told them "Here is my pistol, but I will use it before I give it up." They did not take it from me but

threatened to throw me in the river that night. Then we were ferried across the Mississippi River into Iowa and remained there a short time. I buried what arms I had in a quilt in a hole under the wagon wheel.

I borrowed a tent from Brother Johnston and had women that were being delivered at childbirth put in it. I was the mid-wife, and delivered nine babies that night. We had nothing to eat but a half bushel of corn meal and a half-dozen cucumbers that were given to me by Martin Little-wood. There were a great many sick among us and nothing to comfort and nourish them but corn meal, until the Lord sent quails among us which supplied our wants. Blessed be the name of the Lord. We had nothing to sweeten anything with until the Lord sent honey dew, which we gathered from the bushes until we had all the sweets we wanted. I also boiled maple juice and got cakes of maple sugar.[4]

Even though the mob persecutions ceased after the Saints left Nauvoo, life didn't become easy for Latter-day Saint women. Eliza R. Snow, reflecting upon the hardships suffered by the women on their exodus to Salt Lake City, wrote:

As we journeyed onward mothers gave birth to offspring under almost every variety of circumstances imaginable, except those to which they had been accustomed—some in wagons, in rain storms, and in snow storms. I heard of one birth which occurred under the rude shelter of a hut, the sides of which were formed of blankets fastened to poles stuck in the ground, with a bark roof through which the rain was dripping. Kind sisters stood holding dishes to catch the water as it fell, thus protecting the newcomer and its mother from a shower-bath as the little innocent first entered on the stage of human life.[5]

The journal of Patty Sessions, who is the most famous of the early Latter-day Saint midwives, recorded that she attended the births of more than one hundred babies as she made the trek to Zion. Among the women who gave birth on the plains was one for whom Patty had to ride two miles, through mud and belly-high water to reach. She recorded the following:

About 2 o'clock in the morning I was called for. . . . I found the sister that I was called to in an old log cabin. Her child was born before I got there. She had rode 13 miles after she was in travail, crossed the creek on a log after dark. Her husband carried over such things as was necessary, left his wagons and teams on the other side as the water had carried off the bridge."[6]

Anna Marie Sorenson, a Scandinavian convert, was expecting a baby when she arrived with the Saints at Wood River, Nebraska. Someone recorded that when her time came she "retired from the camp, and under some willows gave birth to a baby girl. In the morning she appeared with the baby in her apron. . . . [T]he baby survived, as well as the mother."[7]

Like the women who traveled in the wilderness with Lehi's family in the Book of Mormon, these faithful Latter-day Saint women "suffered all things, save it were death" (1 Nephi 17:20). They walked and rode the thirteen hundred miles to Zion with morning sickness, swelling bellies, postpartum bodies, tender breasts, and newborn babies strapped to their sides. They colonized and cultivated a vast wilderness while carrying their children beneath their hearts and in their arms. These Latter-day Saint women truly understood the meaning of *labor* and *travail*, and with God's help they bore their challenges well. They did not let the hardships of their situation stop them from continuing to bear children or fulfill their divine callings as mothers. Perhaps if Nephi had lived among them he would have exclaimed, as he did of the women in his day: "our women . . . were strong, yea, even like unto the men" (1 Nephi 17: 2).

MIDWIFERY AS A SPIRITUAL CALLING

Once the early Saints arrived in the Salt Lake Valley, women had no other choice but to support and attend to one another in childbirth. These early Latter-day Saint women had great faith in spiritual healing, and it was common for women to be blessed, washed, and anointed by their midwives or other female birth attendants before they were delivered (see "Mother's Blessings in the Early Church," on page 165). In fact, in the early days of the Church, midwifery was a Church calling. A woman was called to be a midwife by priesthood authority and set apart by the laying on of hands. She was set apart by a general authority of the church, if available, and the calling was for life.

The first woman we know of who was set apart as a midwife was Patty Bartlett Sessions, who delivered at least 4,000 babies. As a young girl, Patty received a strong spiritual confirmation about her calling as a midwife, and she had been working in that capacity for many years before she joined the Church. When she arrived in Nauvoo, she was set apart by Elders Brigham Young and Heber C. Kimball as a "doctor of women" and went on to deliver thousands of babies for the Latter-day Saint community. She had great faith in women's spiritual gifts and often encouraged young women to study to become midwives.[8]

During the early days of the Church, hundreds of women were set apart as midwives. Some had formal training before their calls, but others did not. For example, when Josephine Catherine Chatterly Wood was twenty-nine years old and the mother of several children, her bishop called her to be the midwife for the community. At first she refused, saying, "I am green as a cucumber and I don't know how babies are born." The bishop gave her a blessing, telling her that the Lord would guide her and that great wisdom would be hers. Still feeling inadequate, Josephine read all the books she could find on women's health and studied and prayed tirelessly. Before her first call to a mother in labor, she asked her husband to give her a blessing. Then she went to the bishop's house and made him come with her to the birth because she was so nervous. The birth went well, and she did not need the bishop's assistance. Yet, for several years afterward, Josephine would occasionally call the bishop to come be with her at a birth.[9]

In general, however, most Latter-day Saint midwives had some sort of formal training. Latter-day Saints were unique in this respect because in most of nineteenth-century America, very few midwives had any sort of formal training. One reason Latter-day Saint women were so highly skilled in midwifery was because some of the early coverts to the Church came to Salt Lake City from Europe and had studied midwifery at schools in Scotland and France. In addition, Brigham Young felt strongly about properly caring for prospective mothers and was particularly impressed by the trials and tribulations that women suffered when they had to "go down to the valley of death" to bring forth the new citizens of Zion. Brigham

Young had a real mistrust of doctors, which was probably very warranted considering most of them didn't have any sort of training at that time, but he eventually changed his mind. In the 1880s, he started sending women to medical school to learn obstetrics. As a result, Utah had one of the largest groups of women doctors in the nineteenth century.[10]

Dr. Ellis Shipp was one of the first women sent by Brigham Young to the Woman's Medical College in Philadelphia, Pennsylvania, to study medicine and obstetrics for four years. Despite being pregnant in her last year of school (she gave birth to her fifth baby the day after her last exam), she excelled in all her classes. After she returned from studying medicine, she traveled all over the Mormon territories, training hundreds of women as midwives and in the basics of home nursing. At that time, it was considered wrong for a man to attend a woman in childbirth, and so it was imperative that women be trained to be competent doctors and midwives.

The need for midwives in the newly established Zion was so great that Brigham Young suggested that three woman from each ward be selected to study obstetrics. Eliza R. Snow, the general Relief Society president, encouraged women to get medical training. She said, "We want sister physicians that can officiate in any capacity that the gentleman are called upon to officiate and unless they educated themselves the gentlemen that are flocking in our midst will do it."[11] So under the guidance of Eliza R. Snow, each ward Relief Society nominated women to be trained and set apart as midwives. These prospective midwives would usually travel to a place where Dr. Shipp or another traveling doctor was holding a temporary midwifery clinic. Since the time commitment was great (at least three months) and the cost very expensive (the book cost was $20, which was a small fortune back then), the Relief Society of each ward would pay for the women's books and feed and watch over their husbands and children while the women were away.

Most of these early midwives viewed their responsibility of guiding new spirits into this world as one of their most important spiritual missions. Many of them would kneel in prayer before leaving for a birth and ask for God's guidance and strength to help them know what to do. Dr. Ellis Shipp said that the one thing she tried to instill in all the women she trained was this: "When called to maternal duty, pray unto God for his blessing. Pray in your soul as you hasten to your duty . . . to usher a new life into the world—that life so precious to the suffering mother and most sublime in the sight of God."[12]

Women and midwives often called upon brethren to give priesthood blessings before, during, and after a delivery; this was especially true if a labor was difficult or long. There are also several accounts of midwives who spoke of themselves as "presiding" or "officiating" at births.[13] *Presiding* is an interesting word in a Latter-day Saint context because it is most often used to describe a man who holds the Melchizedek priesthood and who oversees a church meeting. The man presiding isn't always the one who is in charge of conducting the meeting; commonly he doesn't say anything, but he is there representing the priesthood authority of Heavenly Father. It is a beautiful and intriguing image to think of a midwife as not delivering or catching a baby, but rather presiding over the birth. Her job wasn't to do the work—that was in the hands of God, the mother, and the baby— rather, she was there to oversee the process and to represent the power of Heavenly Mother. One midwife, Annie Bryceon Laker, once told a friend that "the strength that comes to us is from the Priesthood, and the power we receive through the Priesthood is from our Father in Heaven."[14]

ANNIE CLARK TANNER'S STORY

Despite the exceptional level of care early Latter-day Saint women received, many women in Utah still found themselves giving birth in unexpected and difficult circumstances. Due to anti-Mormon persecution in her area, Annie Clark Tanner was forced to go into hiding while she was pregnant. When she gave birth to her second child, she was living alone with her two-year-old daughter in Franklin, Idaho, under an assumed name. As the birth of her child drew near, she wrote the following in her journal:

August 23, 1890

Mother left me and it was a sad parting. I was really homesick after she left. The next day was Sunday and I could but cry most of the time. But Monday I could go to work again and soon felt contented. . . . The satisfaction of having so noble a husband, my home and sweet baby with the blessing of God that attended us during the sacrifices that I had made and must make, are sufficient for my happiness and should cause me to rejoice. After mother left, I finished a rug that I had begun, made some frames for my pictures and photos. I suffered a great deal from cramps and at time could scarcely get around. A friend of mine, who was a doctor, said this condition was caused by pressure on a nerve. I discovered that by taking warm baths I could get relief.

September 20, 1890

At about ten in the evening I gave birth to my little son, Myron. I felt to claim the blessings that had been promised me in the Temple. Although suffering alone, I was greatly blessed. No one was near to assist in the baby's birth but the Lord heard my prayers. It was such a quick labor, due to the relaxation from warm baths, that I could not get on the bed, so the child was born on the floor. I had called to Sister Fox. Finally, the old lady we call Grandmother came, and she went for another neighbor who asked a man to go for the midwife. The midwife lived about three mile up the canyon. . . . My husband came about a week after the baby's birth.[15]

Annie later wrote: "There seems to be times when we cannot see our blessing, but after the evil of darkness is lifted they shine forth with double splendor. . . . I feel to thank the Lord for this deliverance and especially that he granted the desire of my heart to have a son."[16]

Like these early Latter-day Saint women, we may also take leaps out into the darkness, journey into the wilderness, and face the unknown as we labor to bring forth God's children. As we take our own birthing journeys, we can remember the sisters who ventured into the wilderness before us. God has given us a work that may push us to our utmost limits physically, emotionally, mentally, and spiritually. Yet these early Latter-day Saint women show us that God is aware of the sacrifices all of His daughters make to bring forth His children, and He will fortify us with the strength and courage we need to do our divine work.

1   Janet Peterson and LaRene Gaunt, *Elect Ladies: Presidents of the Relief Society* (Salt Lake City, UT: Deseret Book, 1990), 50–51.
2   Ibid.
3   Edward W. Tullidge, *The Women of Mormondom* (New York, 1877), 307.
4   Carol Lynn Pearson, "Nine Children Were Born": A Historical Problem from the Sugar Creek Episode." *BYU Studies Journal* 21, no. 4 (1981): 441.
5   Edward W. Tullidge, *The Women of Mormondom* (New York, 1877), 307.
6   Patty Bartlett Sessions, "Mormon Midwife: The 1846–1888 Diaries of Patty Bartlett Sessions," ed. Donna Toland Smart (Logan: Utah State University Press, 1997), 41; punctuation added.
7   Linda Dekker, "Some Must Push and Some Must Pull," *Ensign*, July 2006, http://lds.org/ensign/2006/07/some-must-push-and-some-must-pull.
8   Patty Bartlett Sessions, "Mormon Midwife: The 1846–1888 Diaries of Patty Bartlett Sessions," ed. Donna Toland Smart (Logan: Utah State University Press, 1997), 31.
9   Claire Noall, "Mormon Midwives." *Utah State Quarterly* 10 (1942), 133.
10 Claire Noall, "Mormon Midwives." *Utah State Quarterly* 10 (1942), 116.
11 Chris Rigby Arrington, "Pioneer Midwives," in *Mormon Sisters: Women in Early Utah*, ed. Claudia L. Bushman (Cambridge, Massachusetts: Emmeline Press, 1976), 57
12 Ellis R Shipp, "While Other's Slept: Autobiography and Journal of Ellis Reynolds Shipp, MD" (Salt Lake City, UT: Bookcraft, 1962), 283.
13 Claire Noall, "Mormon Midwives." *Utah State Quarterly* 10 (1942), 144.
14 Claire Noall, *Guardians of the Hearth: Utah's Pioneer Midwives and Women Doctors* (Bountiful, Utah: Horizon Publishers, 1974), 83–84.
15 Annie Clark Tanner, *A Mormon Mother: An Autobiography of Annie Clark Tanne* (Salt Lake City: University of Utah Library, 1969), 126–127.
16 Ibid.

THE FAMILY TREE OF KNOWLEDGE

By Felice Austin, C.Ht.

When I was a few months into my pregnancy and feeling pretty alone, I came across this quote by Harriet Lerner:

> We are never the first in our family to wrestle with a problem, although it may feel that way. . . . Learning how other family members have handled their problems similar to our own down through the generations, is one of the most effective routes to lowering reactivity and heightening self-clarity.[1]

I thought, *Yeah right. Who does this happen to? No one else in my family has been abandoned three months into a planned pregnancy.* I kept reading:

> If we do not know about our own family history, we are more likely to repeat past patterns or mindlessly rebel against them, without much clarity about who we really are, how we are similar to and different from other family members, and how we might best proceed in our own life.[2]

I had been into family history before I became pregnant, so I decided to test out this idea and have a look at my family tree to see if there were, in fact, any single mothers and what, if anything, I could learn from them. I had no idea where this test was to lead me.

I was surprised to find that there were more than a few single mothers and amazed at what I learned about them. On my mother's side, I learned the story of my great-grandmother, Ellen. She was married, and lived for a time in the Mexican colonies. She had four daughters by her husband. After the fourth, he accused her of cheating on him, saying that Violet was not his child. He left her and moved back to the Unites States.

That was also a time of great political unrest in Mexico. Pancho Villa was threatening to kill the white settlers if they did not leave. So Ellen and her four daughters, with the rest of the colony, fled Mexico with a few days' notice, on foot, and returned to the United States. Ellen went back to her parent's home in Cedar City, Utah, and lived with her family. From what I can gather, she worked hard picking fruit and taking care of her girls until sometime later when she re-met a man she had known in childhood, married him, and had four sons—one of whom is my grandfather.

Another story I pieced together was from my father's side. My father was adopted by his stepfather, and I had been trying to trace his biological father's line for some time. I had discovered a few years before, to my great surprise, that they were of slave ancestry.

To cut to the good part, I found a census that listed my third-great grandmother, Maria, as a single black woman living with her young daughter, who was listed as Mulatto, in Pennsylvania in 1860. Her occupation was "washer woman" and she was listed as owning property.

Maria was born in Virginia, so she was almost certainly born into slavery. Her child was mulatto and she was never married, so I can only speculate about what master impregnated her and whether or not she was a willing participant. Then I can only speculate about how she somehow escaped or earned her freedom (1860 was pre-emancipation proclamation) and made it to Pennsylvania and owned property. It was rare even for a white woman to own property then.

What this tells me about Maria is that she was an incredibly strong woman. There are also clues that she was a Quaker (Society of Friends), because they were the only group that would be accepting enough to embrace a black woman into their community and let her own property.

The result of all of this discovery was that I felt much less alone. I felt connected to these powerful ancestors and inspired by them. I looked to what they did in their time of trial and saw that both of them turned to their family or their faith. That is what I knew I would do, too.

Through meditating on these and other strong women in my life stream, I felt them draw nearer to me. When my daughter was born, I felt them all surrounding me—my mother, my grandmother, Ellen, Maria and many more I didn't even know, but who knew me and knew my daughter.

Our Mothers, Our Daughters

By Felice Austin, CHt

"Know the mother that you may know the child."

QUAN YIN, BUDDHIST GODDESS OF COMPASSION

———————————————

Mother is our first true love. Much of our behavior and personality is formed by or in response to the way our mothers mothered us. Many studies are showing that this influence begins in the womb—or maybe even earlier. Like Russian dolls that stack inside each other, female fetuses have a uterus, ovaries, and all of their eggs before they are born. That means that the egg that became you existed inside your mother while she was still growing inside your grandmother. This also means that, if you have a girl, she is carrying the eggs that could become your future grandchildren.

As I watch my daughter grow and nurture her baby dolls, I see how she imitates me and even my mother, who died before she was born. This is what the poet Rilke described as "gesture rising from the depths of time."[1] Studies show that despite a woman's birth plan, many women birth like they were born. This happens even in women who don't know their own birth stories—the mind and body remember. However, God has given us a way to change "the traditions of our fathers" if we so choose.

Learning your own birth story early on can give you time to ponder your legacy. And if you can learn your mother's birth story, it will give you even more heritage to study. You can then decide whether it is a legacy that you want to cherish and carry on, like Jayne (whose story follows), and, if not, you can decide how you will become a "repairer of the breech, a restorer of paths to dwell in" (Isaiah 58:12) and create a new legacy for your children. Your birth choices and experiences will become a new legacy for not only your daughters but also your sons. Sons grow up to marry daughters,

THE GIFT OF GIVING LIFE

and a husband's view on birth will affect his wife, as we see in Jaime Wagner's story on page 415. If you want to change your story, you might find the "Spirit-Mind-Body Connection" and "Meditation" chapters helpful.

MOTHERLESS MOTHERS

Even though mother is our first true love, she may not always retain that status. Mothers are mortal, which means that they are subject to fears, flaws, temptations, vulnerabilities, and death. For the purposes of this book, a motherless mother is a woman who lost her mother before she herself had a child. Mother loss can happen from death, abandonment, suicide, mental illness, abuse, or other kinds of estrangement.

Losing one's mother can have a profound effect on pregnancy, labor, postpartum and lifelong mothering skills. Pregnancy can magnify unresolved issues or unmourned losses from the past. Also, in natural times of uncertainty, like pregnancy, some adults regress and need mothering themselves.[2] I remember when I was pregnant and my husband left, I did not feel as sad about the loss of my marriage as I did about birthing without my mother, whom I had lost 16 years prior.

If you don't have a mother who is physically or emotionally available, it is important to surround yourself during pregnancy and birth with other nurturing women and substitute mothers who are positive examples for you. Hope Edelman, author of Motherless Mothers, wrote, "Women with a history of mother loss, or a highly complicated mother-daughter relationship, may need extra support throughout labor and delivery if sadness, fear, and grief episodes come and go."[3] At my daughter's birth, it was important for me to be surrounded by a midwife and friends who were supportive and loving.

If your mother is alive and wants to be with you during labor but is not loving or supportive, make this decision prayerfully. Even women with excellent, loving mothers sometimes chose not to have their mothers at their births. You are the last word on what is right for you and your child, and you don't have to explain your reasoning to anyone.

Postpartum recovery for a motherless mother may also involve unexpected emotions, such as hyper self-reliance, resistance to grandmothers, difficulty bonding, fear of being a bad mother, and depression.[4] However, the more a person deals with mother issues during pregnancy, the better the postpartum transition is likely to be.

There may also be unexpected positive results. For example, the greatest blessing I experienced graduating from motherless daughter to motherless mother was healing. When I lost my mother at 11 years old to cancer, it left a hole in my heart that I thought would never be refilled. However, after I had my daughter, that dark spot in my heart went away. It is difficult to explain how it happened, but slowly, over time, as I loved and mothered my little girl, I was also receiving love and mothering myself until I was completely healed.

Some women who have experienced mother loss worry about their mothering skills, especially if they had an abusive or neglectful mother. Studies show that women tend to pass on their mothering styles or repeat the way they were mothered; however, the influence of other nurturing women in a motherless daughter's life can positively change that legacy.[5] Hence, the importance of a support system like the Relief Society.

It is also never too late to heal your inner child through therapeutic processes and through the Atonement. The Atonement is how all healing takes place, even if we don't recognize it as the source. Pregnancy is long enough to give us plenty of time for both healing the past and preparing and learning new skills that will change the future. Luckily, there are millions of books and classes available once you decide on which parenting style might work for you. You also have the divine gift of personal revelation and an extra measure of the Spirit that may be responsible for what is referred to as "mothers intuition."

Becoming a parent is life altering—but the changes happen in stages. As a motherless mother, you may have growth opportunities with each phase of your child's development. As part of your preparation, I invite you to learn more from other motherless mothers about such things as how to better bond at birth (see Building a Better Bond on page 185), how to handle the "missing grandmother," what Edelman called the "neon numbers" (strong emotional reactions that sometimes occur when you turn the age your mother was when you lost her and also when your child turns the age you were when you lost your mother)[6], and how to handle rejection by your children.

Though I have used the term motherless mother liberally here, it is not a completely accurate term because no mother is truly motherless. Every daughter of God has a Heavenly Mother who knows her individually and nurtures her in just the right way, if she will allow it. I testify that our Heavenly Mother is especially interested in mothers. Though we do not pray directly to her, remember that Heavenly Father and Mother are a united, eternal couple. Whenever you pray to Him, She hears also and may well be directing the angels who attend you and your little ones.

1. Maria Rainer Rilke, *Letters To A Young Poet* (New York: Vintage Books, 1984), 62.
2. Hope Edelman, *Motherless Mothers* (New York: Harper Collins, 2006), 36–37.
3. Ibid
4. Ibid., 94–121.
5. Louann Brizendine, *The Female Brain* (New York: Random House, 2006), 110–111.
6. Hope Edelman, *Motherless Mothers* (New York: Harper Collins, 2006), 94–121.

A TALE OF TWO BIRTHS

By Jayne K.

WHEN I WAS TEN YEARS OLD, my Dad woke me up in the wee hours of the morning and asked me to come see something in their room. As I timidly entered the dimly lit room, I saw my mother in her big armchair, sweaty and glowing in the last stages of labor. The midwife, Chris, was sitting near her, quietly coaching her, and I sat on the bed wide-eyed and silent and witnessed the birth of my youngest sister.

This was the way that births happened in our family. There were no beeping monitors, no blinking lights or nurses rushing in and out. It was so quiet and still, and the beauty of my mother was overwhelming. Chris swaddled the brand new little girl and handed her to me to hold while she took care of my mom.

The baby slept, and I gazed and felt things I had never felt before. The spirit was thick in the room, so thick it was almost like you could reach out and touch Heaven. Here she was, and there she had been only moments ago.

Twelve years later, when it was my turn to give birth, I knew exactly what I wanted. Incredibly, Chris, the midwife, was still delivering babies and was thrilled when I called. Along with my husband, she cared for me throughout a beautiful pregnancy.

When I told people that we were planning a home birth, I never once got a favorable reaction. All we heard was "You don't know how you labor, anything can happen!" "What if you can't handle the pain?" "What if you need medication?" "What if your baby gets stressed?" "Who will do the episiotomy?" But my husband and I had prayed and truly felt that what were doing was not only safe, but better for us.

I had seen my mother do it, and I knew that I could too. When mid-February came, we were ready for the baby to come. My parents were living in Italy at the time, so my husband and I were house-sitting for them and living in their home. Because my due date was nearing, my mom had flown home to be with me. Valentines Day came, and in the evening my husband and I were on our way to dinner when the contractions hit hard. He turned the car around, and we headed home.

We called Chris, and she headed our way. By the time we got home, the contractions were harder, and I barely made it up the stairs to the bedroom. My incredibly calm mother was quickly arranging the bed and all the birth stuff. As I went into the last stages of labor and my body began to take over for me, I experienced the most amazing peace. It was like a wave of calm came splashing over me and my mind was as clear as it has ever been.

While my labor raged on and the pain made me scream, it was as if I was watching it all happen from the corner of the room. I was thinking to myself *Wow. Is that me screaming? I bet they think I'm a crazy woman. I wonder what my baby looks like? Is she almost here?*

Then my mom said, "Jayne, maybe you should stop pushing."

I said "Are you kidding me? That's not me doing that!" And soon the baby crowned. My husband was as nervous and scared as I have ever seen him. So was my mom, she later told me, but I was not. I felt like maybe I should be, but I wasn't. Finally Chris arrived and slipped on her gloves and eased my little girl out. As I felt her slide down, it was as if I felt life pass through me. I don't know how else to describe it. There she had been inside me, and now here she was, looking up at me from my chest, wiggling and kicking just like she had in my womb. She felt exactly the same, only now she was on the outside. Chris laid a warm towel over us and this tiny little squirmy slimy being began to nurse. She closed her eyes and relaxed against me, and we were, still one.

Here I was, in the same house in the same room that I had been in twelve years before. Only this time I had done it, and she was mine. I have since had another baby at home, this time a feisty little boy who came to this life with an agenda. I hope to have a few more, and I can only imagine that, as many more times as I do this, I will never cease to be amazed at it all.

For one thing, I'm amazed that Heavenly Father could trust me with something so pure and perfect and want me to keep it as close to that state as possible so that one day He can have it back. I am also amazed that my body is so fully equipped to do all this mothering stuff. My body created a new little body, with arms and legs and toes in the right place, and then out that little body came. I am able to care for it through the milk that my body creates to feed it and the love that my heart has to give it. They say that children don't come with a handbook of instructions, but I'm a firm believer that they don't have to. Everything we need has already been given to us and will be given to us if we just ask.

Heavenly Father is the ultimate parent. He has created us in His own image, and with the ability to create and raise children. Through prayer, we can ask even the hard questions, and we will get answers that are true. If getting to the Celestial Kingdom means that I can keep doing this for eternity, then there is nothing that I want more.

We Are Daughters: Preparing Young Women for Pregnancy and Childbirth

By Brittany Cromar, CD(CBI)

Every Sunday, twelve to eighteen-year-old girls all over the world stand and recite a very beautiful and powerful statement:

We are daughters of our Heavenly Father,
who loves us, and we love Him.
We will "stand as witnesses of God at all times
and in all things, and in all places" (Mosiah 18:9)
as we strive to live the Young Women values, which are:

Faith
Divine Nature
Individual Worth
Knowledge
Choice and Accountability
Good Works
Integrity and
Virtue

We believe as we come to accept and act upon these values,
we will be prepared to strengthen home and family,
make and keep sacred covenants,
receive the ordinances of the temple, and enjoy
the blessings of exaltation.[1]

Learning to live the values in this theme is an important part of the Young Women's program, and the Personal Progress program is designed to give young women opportunities to learn about and develop these values in their lives.

As stated in the theme, the purpose of living the Young Women values is to prepare young women for the future, including the responsibility to "strengthen home and family." The phrase "strengthen home and family" was added when I was in the Young Women program. Part of strengthening home and family involves our participation in "the means by which mortal life is created,"[2] the process of conception, pregnancy, and childbirth. It makes sense to me that living the Young Women values can be a preparation for the important experiences of being pregnant and giving birth.

I would like to explore how each of the values applies to the great work of childbearing the Lord gives to His daughters. I will include with each value the scripture and short explanation of the value from the 2009 edition of the Personal Progress book.[3]

FAITH

Faith is not to have a perfect knowledge of things; therefore if ye have faith ye hope for things which are not seen, which are true (Alma 32:21).

I am a daughter of Heavenly Father, who loves me. I have faith in His eternal plan, which centers on Jesus Christ, my Savior.

Faith is the first principle of the gospel. If we have faith, we can ask the Lord for guidance in our lives and trust that the inspiration we receive is from Him. Then we must exercise faith to act upon it. As women of faith, we know in whom we must place our trust. With our faith in the Lord, we can be guided to make the decisions that are best for us and our individual children.

DIVINE NATURE

Be partakers of the divine nature. . . . Giving all diligence, add to your faith virtue; and to virtue knowledge; and to knowledge temperance; and to temperance patience; and to patience godliness; and to godliness brotherly kindness; and to brotherly kindness charity (2 Peter 1:4–7).

I have inherited divine qualities, which I will strive to develop.

Divine nature is the knowledge that we are created in the image of God (Genesis 1:26–27) and that we are His children and have within us divine potential. The processes of pregnancy and birth are things that our Father designed our bodies to do. It can be harmful to interfere with the natural birth process when it is going according to Heavenly Father's design. These processes are a beautiful, sacred, godly purpose of our creation. As Boyd K. Packer has said, "The woman, by her very nature, is also co-creator with God."[4]

INDIVIDUAL WORTH

Remember the worth of souls is great in the sight of God (D&C 18:10).

I am of infinite worth with my own divine mission, which I will strive to fulfill.

God wants us to know that He loves us each individually, with our own unique attributes and purposes. This is why the value of individual worth is distinguished from the value of divine nature. Knowing that our Father loves each of us helps us recognize that He cares about our experiences enough to guide us in them.

He also loves each of our babies. I had difficulty enjoying my second pregnancy because the experience was not new and therefore not as exciting as my first pregnancy. But then I realized that my new baby was his own unique soul. This realization helped me significantly to bond with my child, who I know the Lord loves and created to be an individual with infinite worth. As the Lord told His prophet Jeremiah, "Before I formed thee in the belly, I knew thee" (Jeremiah 1:5).

KNOWLEDGE

Seek learning, even by study and also by faith (D&C 88:118).

I will continually seek opportunities for learning and growth.

The Lord desires for his daughters to cultivate a spirit of learning. In a speech to Brigham Young University students entitled "The Journey of Lifelong Learning," Elder Robert D. Hales specifically addressed opportunities for learning in motherhood:

> Just think of the learning process of a mother throughout the lifetime of her children. . . . For example, in the process of rearing her children, a mother studies such topics as child development; nutrition; health care; physiology; psychology; nursing with medical research and care. . . . The learning examples could continue endlessly. . . . My point is, my dear sisters . . . a mother's opportunity for lifelong learning and teaching is universal in nature.[5]

In something as important as the divinely created process of bringing God's children into this world, I believe that the Lord is pleased when his daughters desire to learn more about it. We are acting on the value of knowledge when we learn about how pregnancy and birth typically unfold according to His plan, as well as the benefits and risks of various tests, procedures, and medications commonly used in pregnancy and birth.

CHOICE AND ACCOUNTABILITY

Choose you this day whom ye will serve; . . . but as for me and my house, we will serve the Lord (Joshua 24:15).

I will choose good over evil and will accept responsibility for my decisions.

41

The basic principle of choice and accountability is that we have choices and our choices have consequences. From the account of the war in heaven, we know that it is part of God's plan for us to have choices and that Satan's rebellion was based on the belief that he could accomplish universal salvation by taking away agency (Moses 4:1–4).

It is common in American maternity care for women to defer all decisions, and therefore all responsibility for the consequences, to their doctors. I believe that our Heavenly Father desires for us to make our own decisions, with His guidance. If we learn about all of our options and the possible consequences of various choices we may make, we are in a position where we can be accountable for our choices.

GOOD WORKS

Therefore let your light so shine before this people, that they may see your good works and glorify your Father who is in heaven (3 Nephi 12:16).

I will help others and build the kingdom through righteous service.

Good works is the value of giving of one's self for the benefit of others. Many years ago, the First Presidency referred to motherhood as "the highest, holiest service . . . assumed by mankind."[6] The sharing of the body's resources with our babies during pregnancy and other hardships we may endure in order to give our children life constitute very important forms of service.

INTEGRITY

Till I die I will not remove mine integrity from me (Job 27:5).

I will have the moral courage to make my actions consistent with my knowledge of right and wrong.

Integrity is having the courage to act on what you know is the truth. In pregnancy and birth, this applies to holding strong to what the Lord has guided you to do to best take care of yourself and your baby. Sometimes your choices may not be popular, but integrity means holding fast to your principles—even in the face of opposition from those who may disagree with your choices, whether they are friends, family, or medical professionals.

VIRTUE

Who can find a virtuous woman? for her price is far above rubies (Proverb 31:10).

I will prepare to enter the temple and remain pure and worthy.

My thoughts and actions will be based on high moral standards.

The eighth value, virtue, was added in November 2008. Virtue encompasses chastity in thought and deed, as well as modesty in dress, speech, and actions. A virtuous woman knows the true holy purposes of her body and does not seek to misuse her body for ungodly purposes. Striving to be virtuous before marriage will bless a women in her marriage as she uses her divine body for two of its most divine purposes: the binding together of husband and wife and the creation of physical bodies for children to join her family.

I encourage our young women to consider that while being worthy to enter the Lord's house is a very good reason to be pure, it is not the only reason. Virtue is not a means to an end of obtaining a temple marriage but rather a lifestyle of respect for Heavenly Father's plan and our appropriate place within that plan. We use our divine, mortal, God-given bodies to fulfill His purposes, of which pregnancy and birth are a very important part.

1. The Church of Jesus Christ of Latter-day Saints, "Young Women Theme," *Young Women Personal Progress* (Salt Lake City, UT: The Church of Jesus Christ of Latter-day Saints, 2009), https://lds.org/young-women/personal-progress/young-women-theme?lang=eng.
2. The Church of Jesus Christ of Latter-day Saints, "The Family: A Proclamation to the World," *Ensign*, November 1995, http://lds.org/ensign/1995/11/the-family-a-proclamation-to-the-world.
3. The Church of Jesus Christ of Latter-day Saints, *Young Women Personal Progress* (Salt Lake City, UT: The Church of Jesus Christ of Latter-day Saints, 2009), https://lds.org/young-women/personal-progress?lang=eng.
4. Boyd K. Packer, "For Time and All Eternity," *Ensign*, November 1993, http://lds.org/ensign/1993/11/for-time-and-all-eternity.
5. Robert D. Hales, "The Journey of Lifelong Learning," *BYU Magazine*, Winter 2009, http://magazine.byu.edu/?act=view&a=2338.
6. James R. Clark, comp., *Messages of the First Presidency of The Church of Jesus Christ of Latter-day Saints*, 6 vols.(Salt Lake City, UT: The Church of Jesus Christ of Latter-day Saints, 1965-75), 6:178.

Circle of Women

By Velinda Mitchell, RN

BORN IN THE MID-FIFTIES, my generation arrived at a time when many babies were born in "Twilight Sleep." Birthing women were put under anesthesia and woke up to meet their babies. Babies were born limp, blue, and with forcep marks on their skulls. Mothers bought into the modern convenience of bottle feeding their babies and putting them on strict regimens of feeding, napping, and even bowel routines.

My mother had six children. We moved from one community to another when my youngest sister was a baby, and we were cautioned not to let out the family secret that she was still nursing my baby sister. I remember the seriousness with which I guarded this fact. Only later did I do the math and calculate that she was less than a year old!

By the time I was a teenager in the 1970s, the revolution in birthing had begun. You began to hear the words "natural childbirth" and "breast-feeding." Fathers were beginning to attend their baby's births. I remember being around when Relief Society sisters were talking and raving about how wonderful breast-feeding was. Something of all this worked its way into my subconscious because, when it came time for me to make my birth choices, there was something inside me that knew that I wanted a natural childbirth and that I would nurse my babies.

For several generations in my mother's family there were women who were midwives. My mother was a registered nurse with some OB experience, and I became a nurse too.

As an OB nurse, my favorite mothers to work with were first time mothers because they didn't have a previous experience to compete with and were willing to be putty in my hands. I could work with them and help them to have a positive experience. As a nurse, I felt like it was my job not to be judgmental of a woman's choices and support her in having the most positive experience she was ready to receive. I felt like whatever it took to help her feel willing to return was her best course.

I have come to believe that birth and death are sacred ordinances, and both should be treated with respect and dignity. Some of the most spiritual moments I had as a nurse were when I attended the death of a patient or when we delivered a miscarriage or stillborn babe—when birth and death are the same event. Those were heartbreaking deliveries but it seemed as though the veil thinned a little and the Holy Spirit descended to comfort the mother too.

Nothing I learned in my nursing training prepared me for my own natural childbirths. I was blessed with relatively short and rapid labors. While I was grateful for my rapid labors, having been an OB nurse and having observed many women in labor, I do know that the contractions for such deliveries are intense. So I always felt it was a miracle that I was sustained during my births. I always felt like I was in the Lord's hands as I labored. I never felt so close to Him as when I was depending on him for every breath I drew to maintain my breathing and focus on my laboring. As the miraculous moment arrived when the baby was born, I always felt like the Lord had mercy on his handmaid, and I basked in the glow of that moment when eternity and mortality are one.

I always felt primeval in my births, at one with the circle of women, beginning with Eve. From the woman in the rice paddy to the Queen in her palace, throughout all history, all women shared the commonality of birth. I truly feel sorry that men do not ever get to know what it feels like to give birth. Although I have never met a man that felt as bad for himself as I feel for him. They don't know what they don't know.

I had seven babies in hospitals, two were among the first to be delivered in what was then considered to be revolutionary—birthing rooms. I had one birth in a free-standing birthing center (my personal favorite), and one at home with a certified nurse-midwife. I had the privilege of bearing nine children, which to many seems like a lot. But to me that is only a few precious times to experience such a glorious thing as birth. If a person likes to ski, it would not seem excessive to ski a dozen or more times in their life. Most women are able to experience birth just a very few times; all the more reason to be careful about creating the best birth possible.

CHAPTER TWO

The Importance of Giving Life

Children are an heritage of the Lord:
and the fruit of the womb is his reward.

PSALMS 127:3

The Spirit of Elijah

By Lani Axman

Behold, I will send you Elijah the prophet
before the coming of the great and dreadful day of the Lord:
And he shall turn the heart of the fathers to the children.

MALACHI 4:5–6

Seven months into our marriage, my husband and I went to the temple seeking the Lord's guidance. We wanted to know when we should start having children. Standing in the crowded celestial room, we each prayed to know the Lord's will. As I listened for an answer, I felt a strong, uncontrollable surge of feeling; tears started streaming down my face; and I struggled to restrain my sobs. I couldn't really understand what was happening to me or why, but I couldn't stop smiling in between my sobs. It felt like a massive release, an uncontrollable rejoicing, an overwhelming exultant feeling unlike anything I had ever experienced before. It wasn't until recently that I pieced together what that unfamiliar, uncontrollable surge of feeling was—it was the Spirit of Elijah.

Fast-forward a few years. Again my husband and I had gone to the temple—with empty stomachs, open hearts, and a question: "Is it time for us to welcome a second child into our home?" The answer arrived in prayer as four words penetrated—individually and simultaneously—into our bosoms and burned within us: "The Spirit of Elijah." Tears came to my eyes. In a sudden stroke of insight, we both understood that Elijah's spirit motivates more than just family history and temple work. Then, in the sacred space of the celestial room, we shared the insights that had come to us. Our hearts were turned to the spirits of our waiting children, and within a few weeks I conceived.

Elder Russell M. Nelson has explained that the Spirit of Elijah is "a manifestation of the Holy Ghost bearing witness of the divine nature of the family."[1] Never has this world needed the Spirit of Elijah more than in our day. Satan's deceptions have turned parents away from their children and children away from their parents. Increasingly, men and women are turning their hearts away from traditional roles—calling these roles the foolish traditions of their fathers.

Men and women are also turning their hearts away from their unborn children in increasing numbers. Elder Robert D. Hales has said, "Because of the importance of the family to the eternal plan of happiness, Satan makes a major effort . . . to discourage parents from placing the bearing and rearing of children as one of their highest priorities."[2] Birth rates are plummeting around the globe, particularly in industrialized nations where, in some groups, they are falling below replacement level. I ache when I read Elder M. Russell Ballard's words: "Each year an estimated 46 million abortions take place worldwide. Indeed, some estimate induced abortions end one-fourth of all pregnancies."[3] If you are struggling with the decision of whether to keep your baby, you may find strength and comfort in the essay "The Decision to Have Your Baby," on page 74.

God's purposes cannot be fulfilled without mortals willing to multiply and replenish the Earth. We cannot fulfill the mission of the Church—to proclaim the gospel, perfect the Saints, and redeem the dead—without first giving the gift of life to eagerly waiting spirits. As President Spencer W. Kimball has said, "This is the great, irreplaceable work of women. *Life cannot go on if women cease to bear children.* Mortal life is a privilege and a necessary step in eternal progression. Mother Eve understood that. You must also understand it."[4] These words from the Savior can remind us of the importance of receiving these little ones into our arms and homes: "And whoso receiveth one such little one in my name receiveth me" (Matthew 18:5).

Some women want to be mothers but still find themselves terrified to take that leap or to take that leap a second, third, or many times. Fears about finances, emotional well-being, the challenges of pregnancy, the intensity of childbirth, and the overwhelming responsibility of caring for another human being can be paralyzing. As the world increases in turmoil and uncertainty, rational and irrational fears can lead us to hesitate. With each subsequent child I have conceived, I have felt the strength of the adversary's anger, opposition, and terrorizing efforts intensifying toward me. Satan uses every tool and tactic in his arsenal to try to prevent us from using our innate creative powers to give bodies to God's children.

One of John the Revelator's visions could be interpreted as a vivid description of these efforts of the adversary. While the woman in chapter

---

"Exercising faith in God's promises to bless them when they are keeping his commandments, many LDS parents have large families. Others seek but are not blessed with children or with the number of children they desire. In a matter as intimate as this, we should not judge one another."[5] —Dallin H. Oaks

---

12 of the book of Revelation has traditionally been considered symbolic of the Church, most prophetic visions have layers of meaning and many messages for us to distill. How might this excerpt give us deeper understanding and perspective as life-giving women in the last days?

> And there appeared a great wonder in heaven; a woman. . . . And she being with child cried, travailing in birth, and pained to be delivered. And there appeared another wonder in heaven; and behold a great red dragon, . . . and the dragon stood before the woman which was ready to be delivered, for to devour her child as soon as it was born. . . . And when the dragon saw that he was cast unto the earth, he persecuted the woman which brought forth the man child. . . . And the serpent cast out of his mouth water as a flood after the woman, that he might cause her to be carried away of the flood. . . . And the dragon was wroth with the woman, and went to make war with the remnant of her seed, which keep the commandments of God, and have the testimony of Jesus Christ. (Revelation 12:1–4, 13, 15, 17)

President Boyd K. Packer recently said, "The adversary is jealous toward all who have power to beget life. Satan cannot beget life; he is impotent. 'He seeketh that all men might be miserable like unto himself.'"[6]

While Satan certainly seeks the misery of all mankind, I believe he holds a special hatred for women, particularly women who use their life-giving powers in righteousness. John's vision of Satan's vehement, desperate attempt to destroy the childbearing woman can give us a glimpse of just how much the adversary is desperate and ever striving to tear down the mothers of the latter days.

Our Savior also knew these difficult days would come. Some of His last words spoken in mortality were to women. As He was led by His crucifiers to Golgotha's hill, crowds of people gathered to follow after Him. Among them were many women, weeping in despair. We read:

> But Jesus turning unto them said, Daughters of Jerusalem, weep not for me, but weep for yourselves, and for your children. For, behold, the days are coming, in the which they shall say, Blessed are the barren, and the wombs that never bare, and the paps which never gave suck. (Luke 23:27–30)

Christ told His women friends to weep for our day. He had just endured the agonies of the Garden of Gethsemane and had felt deeply all the suffering and grief that women would shoulder on the earth through Satan's potent onslaught. He had seen our day—and even beyond our day—where modern women are more and more inclined to leave their wombs empty. Society's attitudes are gradually coming to resemble Christ's description: blessed are the women who don't have to endure the physical, spiritual, and emotional pains that come with being a mother.

However, Christ's words are not an indication that we should refuse the call of motherhood. Just as Christ walked willingly into His loving sacrifice, He calls us to follow Him. We follow in His footsteps as we become saviors for our waiting spirit children by creating bodies for, raising, nurturing, and teaching them.

When I think of a mother choosing to become a savior for her children in the face of sorrow and fear, I think of our great Mother Eve. I imagine that Eve, aching from the pain of losing her first sons to murder and evil, struggled within herself to find the courage to give life again. Rodney Turner honored Eve's great faith with these words: "If ever a woman would have been excusable in refusing to bring more pain and sorrow upon herself, it was Mother Eve. But she set the example for all of her daughters down through time. She continued to bear children."[7] We can follow the Savior's and Eve's examples and choose to give life, despite the darkness and difficulty around us. It may not be easy, but we will reap the immeasurable joy that children bring and the blessings that come from following the Lord's commandments.

"You sisters . . . belong to the great sorority of saviorhood. . . . You are born with an inherent right, an inherent authority, to be the saviors of human souls. You are the co-creators with God of his children. Therefore, it is expected of you by a right divine that you be the saviors and the regenerating force in the lives of God's children here upon the earth."[8] —Matthew Cowley

---

Just as we can take hope from the Savior's and Eve's courageous gifts of life, John's revelatory vision of the childbearing woman can also bring us hope. She was not without help in the face of the dragon's persecutions:

And to the woman were given two wings of a great eagle, that she might fly into the wilderness, into her place, where she is nourished for a time, and times, and half a time, from the face of the serpent. . . .

And the earth helped the woman, and the earth opened her mouth, and swallowed up the flood which the dragon cast out of his mouth. (Revelation 12:14, 16)

We, too, can be blessed with spiritual rescue. The Lord is intensely aware of mothers and the difficulty of the tasks before us. No matter how daunting it may become to choose to give life through motherhood, we *will* be given assistance from both seen and unseen forces in our holy work.

The spirits of our waiting children cannot progress further without our help. We could not have progressed had not our mothers and fathers, grandmothers and grandfathers, and all others who came before us chosen to give us the gift of life. God has sent us the Spirit of Elijah to turn our hearts to those *behind* us, those *around* us, and those who will come *after* us. The more we stand in holy places, the deeper the Spirit of Elijah will penetrate into our hearts. President Ezra Taft Benson has promised, "When you attend the temple and perform the ordinances that pertain to the House of the Lord, certain blessings will come to you: You will receive the spirit of Elijah, which will turn your hearts to your spouse, to your children, and to your forebears."[9]

The Spirit of Elijah will come to all of us. The tendrils of his spirit reach far and wide—into the hearts of married couples, birth mothers, adoptive parents, foster parents, grandparents, aunts and uncles. He calls on the highest and best within each of us to turn and welcome, protect, teach, and nurture the children waiting to be and those already among us. It may not be easy, but the Lord has promised to help us. Procreation is crucial. Pregnancy, birth, and motherhood are holy. Children are life's greatest blessing.

The Church of Jesus Christ of Latter-day Saints' Stance on Birth Control and Surgical Sterilization

In the The Church of Jesus Christ of Latter-day Saints' Church Handbook 2: Administering the Church, it states: "It is the privilege of married couples who are able to bear children to provide mortal bodies for the spirit children of God, whom they are then responsible to nurture and rear. The decision as to how many children to have and when to have them is extremely intimate and private and should be left between the couple and the Lord. Church members should not judge one another in this matter. Married couples should also understand that sexual relations within marriage are divinely approved not only for the purpose of procreation, but also as a way of expressing love and strengthening emotional and spiritual bonds between husband and wife."[1]

The handbook also contains counsel about surgical sterilization (which includes tubal ligation, hysterectomies, and vasectomies) as a form of birth control: "The Church strongly discourages surgical sterilization as an elective form of birth control. It should be considered only if (1) medical conditions seriously jeopardize life or health or (2) birth defects or serious trauma have rendered a person mentally incompetent and not responsible for his or her actions. Such conditions must be determined by competent medical judgment and in accordance with law. Even then, the persons responsible for this decision should consult with each other and with their bishop and should receive divine confirmation of their decision through prayer."[2]

1   The Church of Jesus Christ of Latter-day Saints, *Church Handbook 2: Administering the Church*, 21.4.4, http://lds.org/handbook/handbook-2-administering-the-church/selected-church-policies?lang=eng#214.

2   The Church of Jesus Christ of Latter-day Saints, *Church Handbook 2: Administering the Church*, 21.4.15, http://lds.org/handbook/handbook-2-administering-the-church/selected-church-policies?lang=eng#214.

1   Russell M. Nelson, "A New Harvest Time," *Ensign*, May 1998, http://lds.org/ensign/1998/05/a-new-harvest-time.

2   Robert D. Hales, "The Eternal Family," *Ensign*, November 1996, http://lds.org/ensign/1996/11/the-eternal-family.

3   M. Russell Ballard, "The Sacred Responsibilities of Parenthood," *Ensign*, March 2006, http://lds.org/ensign/2006/03/the-sacred-responsibilities-of-parenthood.

4   Spencer W. Kimball, "Privileges and Responsibilities of Sisters," *Ensign*, November 1978, http://lds.org/ensign/1978/11/privileges-and-responsibilities-of-sisters.

5   Dallin H. Oaks, "The Great Plan of Happiness," *Ensign*, November 1993, http://lds.org/ensign/1993/11/the-great-plan-of-happiness.

6   Boyd K. Packer, "Cleansing the Inner Vessel," *Ensign*, November 2010, http://lds.org/ensign/2010/11/cleansing-the-inner-vessel.

7   Rodney Turner, *Woman and the Priesthood* (Salt Lake City, UT: Deseret Book, 1973), 173.

8   Qtd. in *Preparing for and Eternal Marriage Teacher Manual*, by The Church of Jesus Christ of Latter-day Saints (Salt Lake City, UT: The Church of Jesus Christ of Latter-day Saints, 2003), http://institute.lds.org/manuals/preparing-for-an-eternal-marriage-teacher-manual/marr-prep-13.asp.

9   Ezra Taft Benson, "What I Hope You Would Teach Your Children about the Temple," *Ensign*, August 1985, http://lds.org/ensign/1985/08/what-i-hope-you-will-teach-your-children-about-the-temple.

Waiting For Asheleigh

By Matthew

SINCE BEFORE MY WIFE AND I WERE MARRIED, I've known that we would have a daughter. I vividly remember the moment I knew she was there. I was at my wife's parents house, at a time during our dating when things were looking like we were going to split up and go our own ways. I was sitting on her bunk bed, while she cleaned and vacuumed her room, badgering her about us getting back together and finally getting engaged for real. We had been in that "broken up but still close friends" stage for a few months. My wife was doing a good job of pretending I wasn't there to the point that I got angry and started the thought process to just give up and walk away. And that is when she let me know what she thought of that idea, and I don't mean my wife.

As clear as day, I heard a little girl say, "Daddy, don't go. If you and Mommy don't stay together, then I won't be able to come, so Daddy please stay." I looked around the room to see if someone else was there and wondered if someone down the hall was watching T.V. or listening to the radio, but nothing. And my wife kept right on cleaning (ignoring me) as if she didn't hear a thing. I start to get back up, thinking I'd just imagined it, when again I heard this little girl say again, "Daddy please don't go." And so I stayed.

Years later, after we'd been married for a while, we found out we were expecting our first child, and I was overcome with joy at the thought that I might get to finally meet that special little girl who'd spoken to me and convinced me to have patience with my wife's stubborn streak. And so we started picking out names for a girl. Then we had the ultrasound. Much to our surprise, our little girl was actually a little boy. With each subsequent pregnancy, we would start to get excited thinking, "Surely this time it is her," only to be surprised again and again that we had another little boy on the way.

Three little boys later, we got the news we'd been hoping for at the ultrasound: a little girl, our Asheleigh. As the months went by, we kept trying to come up with a middle name that we felt fit her. Then we started to realize that for some reason the name Asheleigh didn't "feel" right. It wasn't until my wife had an experience that we knew the little girl she carried was indeed not Asheleigh, but her older sister. We knew that she was still patiently waiting for her turn (especially since Daddy had gotten it into his head that with his little princess on the way we could finally stop having kids). And thus it was that we came up with the name Aeryn for her older sister.

Much sooner than we'd expected, we found out we were expecting yet again, and again that moment of anticipation at finding out the gender came and floored us to find out we had yet another silly little boy to add to our growing family. At least at this stage we felt confident we knew how to handle another boy. He came. And Asheleigh continued waiting.

About a year ago, my wife had what we thought was a bad case of the stomach flu, which our whole family had been going through that week, but hers did not pass. Fearing that there might be something else going on, she went to the doctor. Doing a work-up to try and determine what was causing the abdominal pain, they discovered that, "Surprise, you're pregnant." But they feared it might be ectopic because of the pain location. So off she went to get an ultrasound, but at only about five weeks along, nothing was conclusive. We were told to follow-up with her normal OB and symptoms to watch for. Time went by, and things seem "normal," but that cloud of unfounded doubt continue to hang over us.

And then we started to feel and see signs of her at home. My wife kept thinking she saw one of the kids, only to find them all sitting at the dinner table. She kept counting heads to see where everyone was and getting the feeling that someone was missing, even when they were all present and accounted for. Even one of the boys said he thought he saw a little girl over by Mommy and the little kids' bedrooms.

Then I got my own firsthand experience as I went through my usual late night routine, trying to soothe all the aches and pains and get ready to sleep. Out of the corner of my eye, I saw a little girl walk from our bedroom at the end of the hall to Aeryn and Liam's room next door, but I shrugged it off initially. A few minutes later, I saw her again, a little more clearly, dressed up in a little spring/summer-style white Easter dress, her skin very fair with a head full of curly strawberry blonde hair. I rubbed my eyes, still thinking it was a late night hallucination or perhaps Aeryn getting back in bed with my wife. But Aeryn wasn't that tall, and she certainly wasn't sleeping in a dress. One more time I saw her walk from our bedroom to the kids room, and I finally got up to go see what was going on. Ethan and Aeryn were sound asleep in the kids' room, Liam and my wife in our bed.

And so I went and sat on the floor next to my wife and gently awakened her to relate what I'd just seen. We both felt strongly that it was most likely our Asheleigh, perhaps making an appearance to let us know that all was well. Obviously not knowing the logistics of whether the spirit of an infant in the womb is tied to that body all the time upon conception or if it is still allowed freedom to travel around, I can't help but stop and wonder how she could be in both places at the same time. I remember the last thing I said to my wife before climbing into bed and succumbing to sleep myself was, "I just want to hear her call me Daddy again..."

The night passed in a flash, and my wife awakened me in the morning at 9 a.m. Before taking the kids to school, she had started bleeding a little. On her way home from dropping the kids off, she felt impressed to stop and get a pregnancy test. Before I could even awaken enough to open my eyes, the world came crashing down around me as she told me that the test came up negative. As I type this, the tears start again. She wasn't coming. My little Asheleigh wasn't coming.

Between the moments of supreme grief and heart-wrenching numbness, I found brief moments of peace. Perhaps her making the appearance was to let us know she was still patiently waiting for her turn, just that it wasn't yet that time. Part of me wonders if she was going from room to room to let us each know that things were going to be okay, that she would join us in her own time. I love my unborn child just as much as those who have already joined our wild and crazy monkey tribe, and I suppose I'll just have to draw upon her example of patience and wait for her time to join the crew. And deep in my heart and soul I just want to hear her call me "Daddy" again.

Two Veils

By Heather Farrell, CD(DONA)

*Clearly God's greatest concerns regarding mortality are how one
gets into this world and how one gets out of it.[1]*

JEFFERY R. HOLLAND

In the fifth paragraph of "The Family: A Proclamation to the World" we
read, "The means by which mortal life is created are divinely appointed."
The way in which mortal life is created is a four-step process beginning
with sexual intimacy, followed by conception, then pregnancy, and culmi-
nating in the birth of a new human soul. All four of these things—intimacy,
conception, pregnancy, and birth—are parts of the same process; each is
necessary to create mortal life, and all four take place *within* a woman's
body. A woman's body is the means by which mortal life is created and, as
such, her body has been divinely appointed to do God's sacred work.

Elder Jeffery R. Holland has taught that the first step of the procreative process, sexual intimacy, is a sacred and holy event—a literal sacrament. He said:

> If our definition of sacrament is that act of claiming and sharing and exer-
> cising God's own inestimable power, then I know of virtually no other
> divine privilege so routinely given to us all—women or men, ordained
> or unordained, Latter-day Saint or non-Latter-day Saint—than the
> miraculous and majestic power of transmitting life, the unspeakable,
> unfathomable, unbroken power of procreation. . . . I know of nothing so
> earth-shatteringly powerful and yet so universally and unstintingly given
> to us as the God-given power available in every one of us from our early
> teen years on to create a human body. . . . I submit to you that you will

THE IMPORTANCE OF GIVING LIFE

never be more like God at any other time in this life than when you are expressing that particular power.[2]

It stands to reason that if God designed the first part of the procreative process, intimacy and conception, to be deeply and powerfully symbolic of a man and a woman becoming "one flesh," then He may have also designed the second half of the process, pregnancy and birth, to be deeply and powerfully symbolic as well. In order to discover the possible symbolism and meaning behind pregnancy, labor, and birth, and to better understand why the process of creating mortal life may be considered a type of sacrament, we have to go back to Eve and the Garden.

TWO TREES

When God placed Adam and Eve in the Garden of Eden, He planted two trees: the tree of knowledge of good and evil and the tree of life. He told Adam and Eve that there would be consequences if they ate of the tree of knowledge but "nevertheless, thou mayest choose for thyself, for it is given unto thee" (Moses 3:17). We know that Eve exercised the agency God gave her and chose to eat of the fruit of the tree of knowledge of good and evil. Through modern-day revelation, we know that what we she did was for the benefit of mankind and that by partaking of the fruit she was fulfilling her divine mission as a woman. President James E. Faust said:

> We all owe a great debt of gratitude to Eve. . . . The choice was really between a continuation of their comfortable existence in Eden, where they would never progress, or a momentous exit into mortality with its opposites: pain, trials, and physical death in contrast to joy, growth, and the potential for eternal life. In contemplating this choice, we are told, "And when the woman saw that the tree was good for food, . . . and a tree to be desired to make her wise, she took of the fruit thereof, and did eat, and also gave unto her husband with her, and he did eat." And thus began their earthly probation and parenthood. . . . If it hadn't been for Eve, none of us would be here.[3]

Eve was fulfilling her divine purpose when she partook of the tree of knowledge. From the foundations of the world, she had been chosen and named as "the mother of all living" (Genesis 3:20), so she partook of the fruit, enabling her body to become a fountain of life. Eve knew that she wouldn't be able to fulfill her divine role without Adam's help, so she got Adam to partake of the fruit. The scriptures don't say she had to deceive or trick Adam; rather, it seems that Adam hearkened unto his wife so that Eve would be able to fulfill her divine calling.

Just as Eve was set apart to be the "mother of all living" from the foundations of the world, Adam was set apart to be the first high priest of the earth. Joseph Smith taught, "The Priesthood is an everlasting principle, and existed with God from eternity. . . . Christ is the Great High Priest; Adam next. . . . The priesthood was first given to Adam; he obtained . . . . it in the Creation, before the world was formed."[4] It was Adam's divine responsibility to hold the keys and perform the saving ordinances that would bring the children of God back into His presence.

God has designed a beautiful partnership in which Adam helped Eve fulfill her mission to bring God's children into the world, after which it was Eve's turn to help Adam fulfill his mission to bring those children unto Christ, the tree of life, and back into God's presence. President J. Reuben Clark Jr. said:

> So came Eve, an helpmeet to the Priesthood mission of Adam. . . . The Only Begotten had fashioned the world, had filled it with beautiful flowers and lofty forests, with grasses and grains, and multitudes of living creatures; Adam had had some part in this. But the key to the glorious arch of temporal, earthly creation for man was still missing. So Eve came to build, to organize, through the power of the father, the bodies of mortal men, to be a creator of bodies under the faculties given her by the Priesthood of God, so that God's design and the Great Plan might meet fruition.[5]

It doesn't seem like a coincidence that God placed two people, male and female, in the garden and also planted two trees in the garden; two people, two trees, two divine responsibilities.[6]

TWO VEILS

The trees that God planted in the Garden of Eden have multiple levels of meaning. One way in which they might be interpreted is as representing the two veils that all mankind must pass through on their journey toward exaltation. These two veils are described in Moses 6:59, which reads:

> That by reason of transgression cometh the fall, which fall bringeth death, and inasmuch as ye were born into the world by water, and blood, and the spirit, which I have made, and so became of dust a living soul, even so ye must be born again into the kingdom of heaven, of water, and of the Spirit, and be cleansed by blood, even the blood of mine Only Begotten; that ye might be sanctified from all sin, and enjoy the words of eternal life in this world, and eternal life in the world to come, even immortal glory.

The first veil that all mankind passes through is the veil of birth, in which we are born into the world by water, blood, and the spirit. Women have a stewardship over this first veil. When Eve partook of the tree of knowledge, she became more like God, knowing good from evil and gaining the capacity to bear children. Eve's transgression "opened the matrix," as it says in Exodus 34:19, meaning the womb—the gateway through which the souls of all mankind would pass into the mortal world. The only gateway into this mortal world is through the strait and narrow way of a woman's body and the shedding of her blood. There is no other way.

The second veil is the veil that we must pass through in order to reenter the presence of God and continue on our eternal journey. Men have a stewardship over this second veil. Like Adam, righteous men hold the priesthood keys and administer the ordinances that cleanse us from our sins and enable us to walk back into the presence of God. Like the first veil, the second veil also requires a sacrifice of blood, water, and spirit, a sacrifice that Christ made for each and every mortal.

Christ taught that the salvation He offers—entrance into His Father's kingdom—is a type of birth. When speaking to the Pharisee Nicodemus, Christ said: "Except a man be born of water and of the spirit, he cannot enter into the kingdom of God. That which is born of the flesh is flesh; and that which is born of the Spirit is spirit. Marvel not that I said unto thee, Ye must be born again" (John 3:5–7). Through His Atonement, Jesus Christ performed this great and last sacrifice for all mankind. Just as the sharing of a woman's body and accepting her sacrifice is the only gateway into the mortal world, symbolically partaking of Christ's body and accepting His sacrifice is the only gateway into the eternal world. There is no other way.

We are also taught in Doctrine and Covenants 76:24 that, "by him [Christ], and through him, and of him, the worlds are and were created, and the inhabitants thereof are begotten sons and daughters unto God." While the process of creation is still very mysterious to me, after having given birth to two children, I have a better understanding of how creation is by, through and of God and how we are his literal children. My own two children were created *by* my body, they came *through* my body, they are literally *of* my body because my body gave pieces of itself to create them. Because my children went through this process, they are now my begotten son and daughter.

Understanding this relationship between mortal birth offered by women and eternal birth offered by Christ has transformed the way in which I view the sacrament. I now understand that when I partake of the emblems of His body and His blood, I am becoming *of* him, symbolically taking pieces of Him into myself in the same way my babies took blood and nutrients from me in the womb. I am becoming *by* Him for He is my mediator with the Father. Finally, I know that it is only *through* Christ that I gain physical access to the presence of my Heavenly Father and become reborn. In 2 Nephi 9:41, we read:

> O then, my beloved brethren, come unto the Lord, the Holy One. Remember that his paths are righteous. Behold, the way for man is narrow, but it lieth in a straight course before him, and the keeper of the gate is the Holy One of Israel; and he employeth no servant there; and there is none other way save it be by the gate; for he cannot be deceived, for the Lord God is his name.

As we are born into this world through the strait and narrow way of a mother's birth canal, the way into God's world is just as narrow and strait and there is only one way to enter. Christ is the Way.

TWO DIVINE STEWARDSHIPS

I know many men and women who express pain regarding their belief that the Church of Jesus Christ of Latter-day Saints is male centered. Indeed, only men hold the priesthood keys, there are fewer women in the scriptures than men, and while we know we have a Heavenly Mother we don't hear much about her. These are facts that eat away at some faithful Latter-day Saint men's and women's hearts. Yet when we remember that we have already passed through the first veil, over which women have a stewardship, and are now working toward the second veil, over which men have a stewardship, it makes much more sense why things like Church administration, priesthood ordinances, and even the scriptures are so male centered. Besides, who knows; if we could only glimpse into the premortal world and see the other side of the veil, might we see a world that is very female centered because the focus is on preparing children to go through the first veil? Would we see women working with their Heavenly Mother to prepare the souls of mankind to receive their mortal bodies, teaching them their premortal lessons, and guiding them to their earthly homes? Maybe.

We don't know much about the premortal world. Yet one thing we do know is that before we were born we received instruction that would prepare us for our individual labors. Prophet Spencer W. Kimball said the following about women's divine roles:

> Remember, in the world before we came here, faithful women were given certain assignments while faithful men were foreordained to certain priesthood tasks. While we do not now remember the particulars, this does not alter the glorious reality of what we once agreed to. You are accountable for those things which long ago were expected of you just as are those we sustain as prophets and apostles![7]

Also, in Doctrine and Covenants 138:56, we read about the "noble and great ones" and that "even before they were born, they, with many others, received their first lessons in the world of spirits and were prepared to come forth in the due time of the Lord to labor in his vineyard for the salvation of the souls of men."

Given how incredible it is that women's bodies are able to create complete human beings, without their conscious minds directing this process, it seems possible to me that part of the first lessons women received in the premortal world was how to create bodies. While our conscious mortal minds don't remember how to do it, perhaps it is a woman's eternal spirit that directs and guides her body and mind in the construction of a baby and oversees the process of labor and birth.

It is interesting to note, and I don't think it is purely coincidence, that the placenta (the organ the mother's body creates to sustain her baby's life), with all its blood vessels, looks like a tree. It is a literal tree of life, supplying the baby with blood, nutrients, and oxygen, and the "fruit" of this placental tree is human life. It is a beautiful testament to me that even within the very organ a woman uses to create mortal life, there is symbolism of her divine mission.

We also know that in the premortal existence, Satan and a third of the host of heaven rejected God's plan to come to earth and receive mortal bodies. Because they were not faithful in keeping their first estate, Satan and his third will never pass through the first veil; no women will ever create bodies for them or shed blood by bearing them into the world, nor will Satan and his third ever have children. This is one of the reasons that many of Satan's tactics are directed at women and at the structure that is meant to protect them: the family. He tries to convince women that their bodies, which are the gateway through the first veil, are dirty, ugly, imperfect, dysfunctional, common, and of no importance. If he can destroy women's faith in their bodies and make them lose sight of the sanctity of intimacy, conception, pregnancy, and birth, then he is well on his way to thwarting God's plan.

Satan is also trying to convince women that men's stewardship over the second veil is more important than women's stewardship over the first veil. Brigham Young University professor Valerie Hudson Cassler explained:

Pregnancy, labor, delivery and breast-feeding are concealed as far as their full drama and their full glory are concerned. The sacrifice of blood and water—sometimes even the very sacrifice of life itself by caretakers of light [women]—is usually not seen by the family or the community, but rather by a birth professional—a doctor or a midwife. . . . We no longer see the drama and we value less the gateway and the sacrifice that brought us here. Even caretakers of light begin to view their works as mothers as ordinary, menial, and dirty instead of the glorious stewardship it really is. Only young children seem to recognize the importance of the work of the caretakers of light and reward it with complete devotion.[8]

It is important for women to know that their stewardship is not less important in the plan of salvation than the administration work men do. Intimacy, conception, pregnancy, and birth are moments when we unite our will with God—they are divine sacraments—and I believe God expects us to treat this process with the same type of reverence and faith with which we would approach other sacraments and priesthood ordinances. God has given both men and women great gifts and powers that must be respected and used with wisdom and righteousness.

THE EQUALITY OF THE STEWARDSHIPS

In any discussion of the divinity of motherhood it is important to clarify that all women, no matter their ability or opportunity to become mothers, possess the same divine stewardship and qualities. Sheri L. Dew, a former counselor in the general Relief Society presidency, said:

> While we tend to equate motherhood solely with maternity, in the Lord's language, the word mother has layers of meaning. Of all the words they could have chosen to define her role and her essence, both God the Father and Adam called Eve "the mother of all living"—and they did so before she ever bore a child. Like Eve, our motherhood began before we were born. Just as worthy men were foreordained to hold the priesthood in mortality, righteous women were endowed premortally with the privilege of motherhood. Motherhood is more than bearing children, though it is certainly that. It is the essence of who we are as women. It defines our very identity, our divine stature and nature, and the unique traits our Father gave us.[9]

It may be that priesthood authority and motherhood are equal and complimentary roles. Just as there are women on this earth who are unable to bear children, there have been men on this earth who have been unable to bear the priesthood. For example, in the Old Testament, out of all the twelve tribes, only the Levites were authorized to hold and use the priesthood. In the New Testament, there was a time when the Gentiles were not allowed to partake of priesthood blessings. In modern times, it wasn't until the last thirty years that all men were given the privilege to hold the priesthood in the Church of Jesus Christ of Latter-day Saints. We don't know why the Lord put these restrictions on priesthood authority, except that God has His own reasons that we don't always understand them. In a similar manner, we don't really know why some women aren't able to bear children in this life. Yet it is a beautiful promise that just as now all worthy men are able to hold the priesthood, some day all worthy women will be able to become mothers—it is part of their eternal nature and birthright.

When we come to fully understand and appreciate the divine stewardship that God has given his daughters, it is obvious that He loves them just as much as He loves His sons and that both His sons and daughters have important roles to play to make His work possible. It is only when these two powers—male and female, motherhood and priesthood—are united that mortal and eternal life are possible.

The more I come to understand the miraculous process of birth and study its scriptural significance, the more I see that God cares deeply about how women birth and how children come into this world. I know from my own experience birthing my children that no child comes into this world unaccompanied and that God sends angels to be with His children as they enter this world. The veil is thin for a woman in labor, and if she is listening she is able to feel the power of God in an incredibly powerful way. For a few hours she becomes a wide-open portal into heaven, foreordained from the foundations of the world to bring the children of heaven into this mortal world. She is the means by which mortal life is created—she is divinely appointed.

1   Jeffery R. Holland, "Of Souls, Symbols, and Sacraments" (talk given at Brigham Young University, Provo, UT, January 12, 1988), 2.
2   Jeffery R. Holland, "Of Souls, Symbols, and Sacraments" (talk given at Brigham Young University, Provo, UT, January 12, 1988), 5.
3   James E. Faust, "What It Means to Be a Daughter of God," *Ensign*, November 1999, http://lds.org/ensign/1999/11/what-it-means-to-be-a-daughter-of-god.
4   Joseph Smith, *Teachings of the Prophet Joseph Smith*, ed. Joseph Fielding Smith (Salt Lake City, UT: Deseret Book, 1938), 157–158.
5   J. Reuben Clark Jr., in Barbara B. Smith and Shirley W. Thomas, *Words for Women: Promises of Prophets* (Salt Lake City, UT: Bookcraft, 1994), 70.
6   I am indebted to Valerie Hudson Cassler and her essays in *Women in Eternity, Women of Zion* (Springville, UT: Cedar Fort, 2004) for these insights.
7   Spencer W. Kimball, "The Role of Righteous Women," *Ensign*, November 1979, http://lds.org/ensign/1979/11/the-role-of-righteous-women.
8   Alma Don Sorensen and Valerie Hudson Cassler, *Women in Eternity, Women of Zion* (Springville, UT: Cedar Fort, 2004), 149.
9   Sheri L. Dew, "Are We Not All Mothers," *Ensign*, November 2001, http://lds.org/ensign/2001/11/are-we-not-all-mothers.

PARTING THE VEIL

By Jennifer

EARLY IN MY LABOR, as I sat on my overstuffed chair, I had the only cry that I would have all day long. The Spirit made it very clear to me how thin the veil between heaven and earth would be that day. I thought of the significance of the event, and my eyes filled with tears as I realized that my son was making his transition from immortal to mortal that day, that it was finally his turn to come to earth and be tested, that the veil would be parted to allow one of my Heavenly Father's choice spirits to come to *my* home and enter mortality as *my* son.

I'm glad I took a minute to soak in that moment, as the nature of my labor in itself made it very difficult for me to make spiritual connections later on. To me, the character of my home has become more sacred, as the events that occurred there that day were some of the most spiritual that God offers us as His children. It was a blessing to be able to welcome that event in my home. I know now that those few small moments between contractions—while I was sitting on my overstuffed chair late in the morning—were a distinct blessing from God. It was an experience that I would call upon throughout the rest of the day for strength and purpose.

Not once during my labor did I feel fear. I'm quite sure that I even *tried* to be afraid. But I couldn't. Joseph gave me a blessing prior to my labor and another blessing as labor was beginning, and in that blessing I was promised that all would be well. I had a Heavenly promise that everything would be okay, and while my body was going down an unknown road, my spirit remained assured that I need not fear. For that I am so grateful.

I was reminded by another recently-postpartum mother of how close to God one finds herself when laboring to give birth. There were so many times throughout my labor when the only One upon whom I could call was my Heavenly Father. It was He who designed my body to do this seemingly impossible thing of transitioning one of His children to mortality. He is the perfect architect of childbirth. When my body wanted to shrivel and retreat, it wasn't anyone but God Himself that I could turn to for fortification.

And while Heavenly Father didn't once take away the pain or the discomfort or even the fatigue of my body, I felt, on several occasions, the relief of the fatigue of my spirit. It was certainly true, as Moroni wrote, that "it is by faith that miracles are wrought, and it is by faith that angels appear and minister unto men." And I believe that statement by the ancient prophet to be absolutely true. The pain of my body was overwhelming, but I had such relief of spirit. I often felt the distinct and clear presence of my sister—it was as if Blake was being escorted from one side of the veil to the other. And while Allison never gave birth in this life, she did experience pain—often—and probably understood the physical situation in which I found myself.

In the months since Blake's birth, I've wondered why our Father in Heaven designed our bodies to experience such pain when we give birth. Being a perfect and loving God who created women as His crowning creation, I can't help but assume that He *could* have designed a way for children to be born without pain, discomfort... *agony*. I cannot speak for all women, but the whole physical process of bringing Blake into the world was an uncomfortable, painful, physical challenge. My pregnancy was challenging, as was Blake's birth. After much thought and pondering, I can only presume that women have the opportunity to *gain* something from the experience.

For me, Blake's birth was the single most spiritual experience of my entire life. I felt closer to my Father in Heaven during those nineteen hours of labor and the hours following the birth than I ever have before. Speaking only for myself, of course, I know that this was my opportunity to learn about God Himself. I learned what it means to be truly dependent on Him. I learned the true strength of my body and what a gift my body is. And when we learn about the true strength of ourselves, we can therefore know that we have learned something about God—for are we not created in His image?

My labor brought me through the valley of the shadow of death. Knowing that I was giving *life* and giving *mortality* has reminded me that I was taking part in Heavenly Father's plan. It makes me happy that I was able to undertake this experience. God made me perfectly with a perfect plan. That knowledge gave me confidence—even at the lowest, most difficult parts of my labor—that I was made to do this. I was created with the ability to bring a child from one side of the veil to the other.

It has also been made very clear to me that giving birth brings us closer to Jesus Christ than nearly anything else I have experienced. The simple act of experiencing pain for the sake of another brought me closer to the Savior than I've been in a long, *long* time. Christ's act of Atonement was not for Himself but for others. In this instance, I can understand the Savior's lesser-used title of Father. The Atonement was, in essence, an act of a loving parent—sacrificing Himself for the benefit of His children, just as mothers sacrifice the comfort of their bodies for their children while giving birth. Jesus Christ is the Father of our salvation, and I didn't really make that connection until I, myself, gave birth.

Puah and Shiphrah:
Delivering the Deliverer

By Heather Farrell, CD(DONA)

While it may sometimes appear that it is always the men in the scriptures or in the Church who do the important work—the delivering out of bondage, the saving, the rescuing, the administering—the truth is that many of God's plans start with women. For example, in the first chapter of the book of Exodus we read about the story of Puah and Shiphrah, who were midwives to the Hebrew women in Egypt. We read that the children of Israel "multiplied and grew" and that Pharaoh feared they would soon overpower the Egyptians.

When slavery and hard work failed to dissuade the Hebrews from having more children, Pharaoh called Puah and Shiphrah and told them, "When you do the office of midwife to the Hebrew women, and see them upon the stools, if it be a son, then ye shall kill him: but if it be a daughter, then she shall live" (Exodus 1:16). Yet these two brave women feared God more than Pharaoh and continued to deliver children and keep them all alive, boys and girls.

When Puah and Shiphrah were called before Pharaoh and asked why there were still so many male babies running around the Hebrew camps, they told him, "Because the Hebrew women are not as the Egyptian women; for they are lively, and are delivered ere the midwives come unto them" (Exodus 1:19). It is unlikely that all the Hebrew women had quick and unassisted births, but it seems that they were significantly different enough from their Egyptian counterparts that Pharaoh believed the midwives when they told them that Hebrew women gave birth differently than Egyptian women did.

As a result of the actions of righteous women like Puah and Shiphrah, and presumably many other midwives, there were 603,550 Israelite men

"When the real history of mankind is fully disclosed will it feature the echoes of gunfire—or the shaping sound of lullabies? The great armistice made by military men—or the peacemaking of women in homes and in neighborhoods? Will what happen in cradles and kitchens prove to be more controlling than what happened in congresses? When the surf of the centuries have made the great pyramids so much sand, the everlasting family will still be standing, because it is a celestial institution, formed outside telestial time. The women of God know this."[1] —Neal A. Maxwell

who were over the age of twenty years old at the time Israel was delivered out of bondage (Numbers 1:46). Many of those men probably owed their lives to women who valued life above all else and had the courage to protect it even at great risk to themselves. In fact, Moses himself would probably not have survived infancy without these women's courage. So, in a way, one could say these midwives were the first deliverers of Israel because they delivered the deliverer.

As modern Latter-day Saint women, we might be characterized as these Hebrew women who were "not as the Egyptian women" because we have a unique perspective on life, motherhood, and eternity that makes us different from other women in the world. In 1979, President Spencer W. Kimball said the following about the role of righteous Latter-day Saint women:

> Much of the major growth that is coming to the Church in the last days will come because many of the good women of the world (in whom there is often such an inner sense of spirituality) will be drawn to the Church in large numbers. This will happen to the degree that the women of the Church reflect righteousness and articulateness in their lives and to the degree that the women of the Church are seen as distinct and different—in happy ways—from the women of the world.[2]

One "happy way" that Latter-day Saint women can distinguish themselves is in how they approach their sacred role and make decisions about childbearing, pregnancy, birth, and motherhood. Just like Puah and

Shiphrah (and the Israelite women they served), righteous women of God can choose to conceive, deliver, and protect life above all else.

1. Neal A. Maxwell, "The Women of God," *Ensign*, May 1978, http://lds.org/ensign/1978/05/the-women-of-god.
2. Spencer W. Kimball, "The Role of Righteous Women," *Ensign*, November 1979, http://lds.org/ensign/1979/11/the-role-of-righteous-women.

The Decision to Have Your Baby

By Felice Austin, CHt

I was reading a pregnancy book when I came across the following phrase in a somewhat ordinary paragraph: "When you decided to keep your baby . . ." I was shocked when I first considered the implication of those words, but later realized their truth. Every woman who has a child makes this decision. Even women who want a baby desperately and don't believe in abortion still reach a point in their pregnancies when they mentally accept their unborn children and decide to go through with it. For many, this happens in the background, outside the range of awareness. For others, this decision may create a conscious struggle.

Pregnancy can elicit a chaotic range of emotions. The first trimester may be especially difficult because a woman may experience sudden changes in her body, yet she can't feel her baby—making it easy to believe that the baby has no feeling either. Maybe you're reading this and you still haven't made the decision to keep your baby. Whatever you are feeling, I would like you to know that you are not alone.

Even though I had planned and wanted a baby, in my first trimester I came to understand, for the first time ever, the "it's my body" argument that I had heard so many times. It was my body, and it was being violently taken over by something I had no control over. Or did I? I knew that I actually did have a choice.

I thought about that choice. I was so sick I could barely walk a few feet. The sickness wore down my body and also my ability to reason. I also became angry. My natural instinct for survival made me want to stop whatever it was that was causing me so much suffering. I didn't believe in abortion, but there were moments I wished I did and moments I wished for a miscarriage, especially given my rocky marital situation. I thought it might be better not to bring a child into it.

I struggled daily. I began to question why abortion was wrong. Then

I read something in the *Ensign*—I don't remember what, but it gave me a brief surge of faith. Soon after, a friend told me with some confidence that babies choose the wombs they enter and have all the right tools to deal with the lives they choose.

Finally, I realized and accepted that whenever there is a birth, there is also a death. I had been fighting with the baby inside of me, but also with myself. I knew that part of me had to die—the selfish, free, and independent part of me—in order to grow into the mother I was to become. I had to rely on God and my body and my baby to each do their part. That is when I was finally able to feel love and friendship for my baby, and even though I couldn't feel her yet, I felt a great spiritual comfort from within, and I knew that the comfort partially came from her. Then, the nausea didn't bother me as much. There wasn't a question about abortion. We were friends, and I'm willing to suffer a lot for my friends when they need me.

An important truth I learned from this experience is that emotions don't define us. They are merely signals. When we hold space for them without judgement, like one very good friend did for me, it is easier to see what we or another person may really be crying out for.

If you are struggling with whether to keep your baby, or if you are not sure why abortion is wrong, I encourage you to read the information and stories that follow. If you have had an abortion and are struggling with repentance or forgiveness questions, I invite you to read Kristin Hodson's story in the chapter titled "The Atonement" (page 339).

WE AFFIRM THE SANCTITY OF LIFE

The doctrine of The Church of Jesus Christ of Latter-day Saints affirms the sanctity of life, and members are counseled not to submit to or perform an abortion except in rare cases.[1] Elder Russell M. Nelson explained that abortion "matters greatly to us because the Lord has repeatedly declared this divine imperative: 'Thou shalt not kill.' Then he added, 'Nor do anything like unto it.'"[2]

Concern for the health of the mother is obviously one exception. My own mother had to have an abortion when she discovered that she had stage three cancer when pregnant with her fifth child. However, even with this diagnosis, I know that she followed this counsel: "Even then it should be done only after counseling with the local presiding priesthood authority and after receiving divine confirmation through prayer."[3]

Another concern applies to pregnancies resulting from rape or incest: "This tragedy is compounded because an innocent woman's freedom of choice was denied. In these circumstances, abortion is sometimes considered advisable to preserve the physical and mental health of the mother. Abortions for these reasons are also rare."[4]

Some people or caregivers, out of genuine concern, may argue for abortion because of fear that a child may have a disability or malformation. Elder Russell M. Nelson stated that "life has great value for all, including those born with disabilities. Furthermore, the outcome may not be as serious as postulated."[5]

Elder Nelson told the story of a couple who were advised by doctors and family members to get an abortion because the developing baby would almost surely be damaged. The couple were consoled by the following scripture: "Trust in the Lord with all thine heart; and lean not unto thine own understanding. In all thy ways acknowledge him, and he shall direct thy paths" (Proverbs 3:5). Elder Nelson then related how the story ended:

> They chose to follow that counsel and allowed their child to be born—a beautiful little girl, normal in every respect, except for total hearing loss. After their daughter's evaluation at a school for the deaf, the parents were advised that this child had the intellect of a genius. She attended a major university on a scholarship. Now some 40 years later, she enjoys a wonderful life.[6]

ALTERNATIVES TO ABORTION

Abortion is often thought of as a problem of unwanted children. However, as one birth mother explained in Mary Firth's documentary *The Giving*, "in reality, they [the children] are just as wanted." Many mothers and fathers who may be considering abortion may feel that their overwhelming circumstances are less than ideal for a child. In this case, the Church recommends adoption as a wonderful opportunity: "Adoption is an unselfish, loving decision that blesses the child, birth parents, and adoptive parents in this life and throughout the eternities. We commend all those who strengthen children and families by promoting adoption."[7]

As you read this, thousands of worthy couples out there are desperate to have children, but for whatever reason they can't do it in the traditional way. Current studies show that roughly one in six couples who try to conceive have fertility issues.[8] For some of these couples, adoption is exactly what God has in mind for them, which means that giving a baby to an adoptive couple is exactly what He has in mind for someone else.

"Fred Riley, commissioner of LDS Family Services, says that [adoption] is a profound gospel principle. He point[ed] out that when the prophet Elijah restored the sealing keys, these keys encompassed adoption."[9] Adoption is a holy alternative that is as old as time. Anciently, women who could not conceive used a surrogate or "handmaiden" (see Genesis 29:21–28; 30:4, 9, 26; 30:12–13; 1 Chronicles 7:13). At baptism, each of us, if not born into one of the tribes of Israel, are "adopted in" and given all the same rights, responsibilities, and privileges (see Romans 9:4).

The stories of two mothers on different ends of the blessing of adoption can be found on the following pages.

1   Gilbert W. Scharffs, "The Case against Easier Abortion Laws," *Ensign*, August 1972, http://lds. org/ensign/1972/08/the-case-against-easier-abortion-laws.

2   Russell M. Nelson, "Abortion: An Assault on the Defenseless," *Ensign*, October 2008, http://lds. org/ensign/2008/10/abortion-an-assault-on-the-defenseless.

3   Gilbert W. Scharffs, "The Case against Easier Abortion Laws," *Ensign*, August 1972, http://lds. org/ensign/1972/08/the-case-against-easier-abortion-laws.

4   Ibid.

5   Gilbert W. Scharffs, "The Case against Easier Abortion Laws," *Ensign*, August 1972, http://lds. org/ensign/1972/08/the-case-against-easier-abortion-laws.

6   Russell M. Nelson, "Abortion: An Assault on the Defenseless," *Ensign*, October 2008, http://lds. org/ensign/2008/10/abortion-an-assault-on-the-defenseless.

7   Ibid.

8   "Age and Female Fertility," The American Fertility Association, http://www.theafa.org /library/ article/age_and_female_fertility.

9   Rebecca M. Tayor, "Why Adoption," *Ensign*, January 2008, http://lds.org/ensign/2008/01/why-adoption.

Choices

Name Withheld

HOW DO YOU CHOOSE someone else to raise your baby? It seems an impossible task, yet this is exactly the choice I now had to make. Nine months previously, after breaking up with my boyfriend, I had begun to experience strange symptoms. I had a pretty good idea what was going on, but I refused to accept the reality. I was just starting my freshman year of college and enjoying my independence.

As my body began changing, however, I could no longer ignore what was happening. I went to the doctor and took a simple test that turned my perfect world upside down. I was pregnant. Confronting reality was extremely painful. I cried for what seemed like days as I made another choice. Would I allow the pregnancy to continue or have an abortion? The idea of having an abortion definitely appealed to me, as my problem could just "go away." It only took me about one day, however, to know that I could never go through with it. I had helped create this life, and it deserved to be born. But I did not feel ready to raise a child on my own. I was part way through my first term of college and working part-time for minimum wage. I was barely surviving. Marrying the father was not an option. I saw no other viable option except to place my baby for adoption.

I had not gone to church for months and had not prayed or felt the promptings of the Holy Ghost for even longer. Yet, as I made the decision to place my baby for adoption, I immediately felt peace. That, along with the encouragement of a returned missionary I had met and was now dating, gave me the courage to go to my bishop and tell my family—two of the hardest things I have ever had to do. I was slowly returning to the things I knew to be true, and to activity in the Church, in the same way that I had originally gone away—through a series of small choices.

I began attending sacrament meeting. This was difficult to do, as my mistakes were there for everyone to see. I knew that many people were judging me, so it took courage to keep going. In addition to my growing abdomen, there was also the embarrassment of having others see me not partake of the sacrament. But I couldn't let what others thought of me hinder my eternal progression. I also began praying again, even though I had felt for so long that I was not worthy to pray.

I began attending group therapy sessions with other unwed mothers at LDS Social Services. I came away every week with increased gratitude for my family's support. So many of the other girls who attended the group were still struggling to decide whether to keep their babies or place them for adoption. In contrast, I felt such peace, continually confirmed by the Holy Ghost, that the choice I had made was right. I was truly experiencing the healing power of the Atonement for the first time in my life.

So, there I was, in the last month of my pregnancy, reviewing the anonymous profiles of several prospective couples. It seemed an overwhelming task, so I prayed for guidance. With that, I was able to narrow it down to three couples, but I still could not decide on one. As I returned the profiles to my social worker, apologizing that I could not choose one, she explained to me that I had misunderstood the instructions. I was only asked to choose three, then a group of social workers would pray for guidance to know which was the one God intended. What a relief I felt! No wonder I was having such a hard time choosing one—it wasn't my decision to make. So, as I left my social worker's office, I left the decision in God's hands.

It was only a few days later that I gave birth to a healthy baby girl. I held her briefly in the hospital before saying good-bye forever. Even though I knew that I had made the right decision, it was so difficult to leave the hospital knowing that I would never see her again. In addition to the physical recovery, I shed many tears over the next few days and weeks as I attempted to heal emotionally. Had I truly done the right thing? My body was aching to hold her again while my mind filled with doubts. Thankfully, I was continually assured through the Spirit that I had made the right choice.

A few weeks later, I knew that I had completed the repentance process when I began to feel remorse for adding to the Savior's suffering in Gethsemane. It was a long night as I sobbed and begged for forgiveness. I felt peace wash over me once again as the healing power of the Atonement was working on my behalf. Not long afterward, my bishop and I agreed that I was worthy to again partake of the sacrament. That was one of the happiest days of my life!

Later, as I prepared to attend the temple for the first time, I met again with my bishop and stake president. I had such a smile on my face as I was able to answer the recommend interview questions. I felt similar joy as I dressed in white, the symbol of purity, and knelt across the altar to be married, knowing that the Atonement had erased the poor choices I had made and that I was truly pure and worthy to be there.

It has been many years since I made all of these choices. As I've grown spiritually and continued to progress, it seems that these experiences happened to someone else, because I am no longer the same person I was then. I have never regretted the choice I made to place my baby for adoption, and I felt strongly that she was never mine to begin with. I pray that she feels loved by her parents and that the choice I made has resulted in a happy life for her. Even though I would gladly give up the trials I faced as a result of my poor choices, I would not give up the spiritual learning and growth that I gained from those experiences.

The power to choose is an amazing gift from God. As I watch my children make choices, I understand better how difficult it must be for our Heavenly Father to allow us to make poor choices that result in painful experiences. I know, however, that having the power to choose is an integral part of His plan. I thank God for giving us this amazing gift and for enduring the agony that comes from allowing us to use this gift freely.

BIRTH THROUGH ADOPTION

By Mandi F.

I received my patriarchal blessing when I was fifteen. At the time, there were two big questions in my heart: Would I marry, and would I have children? As the patriarch placed his hands upon my head, I felt the Spirit very strongly. And then he spoke these words that brought so much comfort to my soul:

> Mandi . . . there will be children born into your home, born under the covenant, and you, along with the husband you do choose, will have a great responsibility in rearing them, and teaching them the gospel.

After receiving that blessing, I could have told you exactly how my life was going to play out. Not everything went according to plan, however. I didn't meet my husband until I was almost thirty. We started trying to conceive right away, but nothing happened. I got help with some health problems. My headaches went away, and I started having regular periods. But still no baby.

We fasted month after month. I would cry and plead with the Lord to give us a baby. We prayed and prayed and prayed. There were women in my ward that were my age. They had fifteen-year-old daughters. They had three to six kids. They were done. They looked at me and wondered why I "didn't want children." They thought I was wrapped up in my career or had chosen something else. If only they knew.

We wondered if we should adopt. We wondered if the Lord would heal my body and allow me to conceive. I was so tired of waiting. I wanted a little baby to love. I wanted to change poopy diapers and get up for midnight feedings. My patriarchal blessing did say that we'd have children "born into our home, born under the covenant." That sounded pretty straightforward, right? Should we just cling to that with faith that it would one day come true? Or did we have to *do something* to get there? Was that the real test? We just didn't know.

On New Years of 2008, Jack and I toasted the New Year with a bottle of sparkling cider and promptly crawled into bed. But I couldn't sleep. All I could think about was another year without a baby. The pillow quickly became soaked with my tears. It felt like my heart would break. I seriously considered leaving Jack so he could remarry and have a family with some-one else—a real woman that could have children and make him a father. I was completely hysterical that night. I had had trials in my life before but nothing like this. This was the hardest thing I'd ever been through.

We're not sure when/if we ever got a concrete answer about adoption, but all of sudden we had the paperwork and were turning it in to LDS Family Ser-vices. It took several months to get all the paperwork completed and to do the required background checks, fingerprinting, etc. It is quite a lengthy process.

Over a year and more trials later, on June 23, 2009, were contacted by a birth mother named Melissa. She had found our profile on LDS Family Ser-vices website and asked if we were still working with LDSFS. (We had given up on them and gone with another agency we hoped would be faster.) We felt such a connection with her. Later, we met Melissa and were so impressed by her strength and wisdom and selflessness. She was a beautiful young woman, inside and out. We loved her immediately. Then I flew out to Utah the first week of September for Melissa's twenty week ultrasound. It was very emotional to see that precious little baby for the first time.

That Christmas, after spending time with Jack's parents in Utah, we were supposed to fly home, but the day before our flight we got a text message from Melissa saying that she was at her midwife appointment and that she was dilated to 4 cm, and 70% effaced. (She wasn't due until January 16.) We decided to stay and just wait it out.

About a week later, on January 8, Melissa went into labor. Melissa's mom and I held her legs while she pushed for about an hour. Then there he was! I got to cut his cord. He had big brown eyes and lots of dark hair. He was perfect. Our hearts swelled with love for our new baby boy, and we felt like the luckiest people on earth. We named him Leo.

Forty-eight hours later, we waited in another room while Melissa was signing the relinquishment papers. The case worker came in and said that Melissa wanted to talk to me, so I went in. She was crying hysterically and said to me, "Promise me he's going to be okay. Promise me. I know that I could be a single mom. I could do this. But I know that what he needs is a mom and a dad. He needs Jack. He needs a dad. I know his birth father just can't do that for him."

We were both bawling by that point. My heart was breaking for her. I hugged her tight and told her how much we loved her and how much we loved Leo and that we were going to be the best parents to him that we could be. We talked for a few minutes more, and she said that she was okay and was ready to sign.

A few minutes later, we signed our paperwork with the other case-worker, and then presented Melissa with a gift—a locket, so she can carry a photo of Leo with her always. We told her how much we honor her and love her. It was very emotional for all of us. Melissa and I helped dress Leo in his little outfit and got him ready to leave. She breastfed him one more time, and then she bundled him up and handed him to me. It was time to go. We had tearful goodbyes with everyone, and then Jack put Leo into his car seat. This was it. He was all ours. I couldn't believe it. He was the most beautiful, precious thing I had ever seen.

One month from the time of this writing, Leo will be sealed to us for time and eternity, "as though he had been born under the covenant." That will be a joyous, happy day.

I wish I were a writer or a poet, so I could find the words to convey the joy I feel when I look at my sweet boy's face. He is an angel. A miracle. I feel so privileged to be his mom. He was worth the wait. The pain of infertility has been washed away. I am so grateful for the Lord's tender mercies, and I wonder why I did not trust Him. Once again, the Lord has proven that He knows what is best for me. He loves me. The plan and timeline He has for my life is always right, is always best.

CHAPTER THREE

Personal Revelation

Trust in the Lord with all thine heart;
and lean not unto thine own understanding.
In all thy ways acknowledge him,
and he shall direct thy paths.

PROVERBS 3:5-6

Counsel with the Lord

By Lani Axman

Have ye inquired of the Lord?

1 NEPHI 15:8

The scriptures teach us, "Let your hearts be full, drawn out in prayer unto him continually for your welfare" (Alma 34:27). Perhaps at no other time is our welfare more important than when we are carrying a new life within us. No one knows our bodies and their natural processes better than our Father and Creator, and He has not sent us to earth without instructions.

One morning I opened my scriptures to the second half of Matthew chapter 7 and soon found myself mentally singing the old Primary favorite: "The wise man built his house upon a rock . . . ." At first I smiled fondly at the song, oblivious to the message God was trying to deliver. Then, as I opened my mind, in an instant the Holy Spirit flooded my mind with the following:

> Therefore whosoever heareth these sayings of mine, and doeth them, I will liken [her] unto a wise [wo]man, which built [her] house upon a rock: And the rain descended, and the floods came, and the winds blew, and beat upon that house; and it fell not: for it was founded upon a rock. And every one that heareth these sayings of mine, and doeth them not, shall be likened unto a foolish [wo]man, which built [her] house upon the sand: And the rain descended, and the floods came, and the winds blew, and beat upon that house, and it fell, and great was the fall of it. (Matthew 7:24–27)

As this new insight washed over my heart and mind, I could see my own experience in those words.

When I was pregnant for the first and second times, it never occurred to me to consult with the Lord about my pregnancy or birth plans. I suppose, in my mind, they were physical and temporal matters, so I consulted worldly sources—library books, baby reality TV shows, and websites. In my third pregnancy, I approached everything differently—consulting with the Lord in almost every detail. Including Him changed my childbirth and postpartum experiences in profoundly positive ways. My third pregnancy and birth were built upon the rock—the Lord.

While pregnancy and birth are physical processes, they are (or can be) simultaneously deeply spiritual. So how can we be like the wise woman who built her pregnancy and birth house upon a rock? The Doctrine and Covenants is full of helpful wisdom:

> Seek ye out of the best books words of wisdom; seek learning, even by study and also by faith. Organize yourselves; prepare every needful thing; and establish a house, even a house of prayer, a house of fasting, a house of faith, a house of learning, a house of glory, a house of order, a house of God. (D&C 88:118–119)

> Study and learn, and become acquainted with all good books. (D&C 90:15)

> But behold, I say unto you, that you must study it out in your mind; then you must ask me if it be right, and if it is right I will cause that your bosom shall burn within you; therefore, you shall feel that it is right. (D&C 9:8)

God is eager for us to seek and hear His counsel in all matters, both temporal and spiritual. Sister Julie B. Beck, general Relief Society president, declared in general conference, "The ability to qualify for, receive, and act on personal revelation is the single most important skill that can be acquired in this life."[1] When we counsel with the Lord regarding our pregnancies and childbirth, He expects us to do our part. First, we must prayerfully study and learn all that we can from good sources.

Most bookstores and libraries have an expansive array of pregnancy and birth books, but any two given books are likely to offer conflicting

"We're in danger today, it seems to me, of our members of the Church looking to worldly priorities in their decisions about childbearing. Instead of making those decisions in faith on the Lord's promises and in reliance upon what we know of the great plan of happiness and the purpose of life, they look to other sources—television or prominent ideological gurus in the world today or even the pressure of their neighbors—to make decisions that are fundamental and eternal and need to be made prayerfully before the Lord."[2]

—Dallin H. Oaks

advice regarding tests, nutrition, procedures, medications, and even what is "normal." How are we to determine what is right or which are the "good books" that ought to be studied?

In the Doctrine and Covenants, the Lord gave the Church direction regarding the Apocrypha—a group of ancient writings not included in the Holy Bible. He counseled: "There are many things contained therein that are true. . . . There are many things contained therein that are not true, which are interpolations by the hands of men. . . . Therefore, whoso readeth it, let him understand, for the Spirit manifesteth truth; And whoso is enlightened by the Spirit shall obtain benefit therefrom" (Doctrine and Covenants 91:1–5). We can think of all those books on the library shelf as the apocrypha of pregnancy and birth. Some of what they contain is true, but some of it is not. As we prayerfully study and let the Spirit enlighten our minds, He will manifest the truth to us. As we determine what is true and weigh our options, we must select what feels right and then take our choices to the Lord for confirmation.

The Lord will answer us, but even with the Lord's confirming assurances, we may still encounter opposition and difficulty—whether from family, friends, care providers, or life circumstances. During my third pregnancy, after receiving a clear answer from the Lord of the unusual path my family should take, I still found my faith wavering on occasion as I allowed my fears to cloud my faith. I struggled to do as Proverbs 3:5 urges us: "Trust in the Lord with all thine heart and lean not unto thine own understanding."

In such moments, we may sympathize with the children of Israel as they prepared to cross the Red Sea. If they were to trust in logic or their own understanding, fear would most certainly have kept them rooted on the water's edge, incapable of stepping forward into the parted sea. Elder Jeffrey R. Holland has urged us to do the following:

> After you have gotten the message, after you have paid the price to feel His love and hear the word of the Lord, go forward. Don't fear, don't vacillate, don't quibble, don't whine. . . . Nobody had ever crossed the Red Sea this way, but so what? There's always a first time. With the spirit of revelation, dismiss your fears and wade in with both feet.[3]

Perhaps the Lord will instruct you to cross your own Red Sea as you navigate your pregnancy and birth journey. This could mean following a seemingly illogical prompting to seek emergency medical attention when your gut tells you something is wrong with your baby (see "The Cesarean Choice," on page 107). This could mean choosing to give birth without pain medication when all of your friends and family say it's impossible. This could mean breast-feeding exclusively despite pressure from "experts" to supplement (like Meleah, on page 473). Or your Red Sea could be a planned, elective cesarean prompted by revelation (like Robyn R., on page 190). The right path isn't always the logical path, or the easy path, or the path we had envisioned, but God's guidance will always be in our best interest. I pray that we may all become wise women, building our houses upon the rock of the Lord's perfect counsel.

---

1   Julie B. Beck, "And upon the Handmaids in Those Days Will I Pour Out My Spirit," *Ensign*, May 2010, http://lds.org/ensign/2010/05/and-upon-the-handmaids-in-those-days-will-i-pour-out-my-spirit.

2   Dallin H. Oaks, Jeffrey R. Holland, Julie B. Beck, Susan W. Tanner, and Cheryl C. Lant, "Round-table Discussion," *Worldwide Leadership Training Meeting: Building Up a Righteous Posterity*, http://lds.org/library/display/0,4945,8027-1-4404-1,00.html.

3   Jeffrey R. Holland, "'Cast Not Away Therefore Your Confidence'," *Ensign*, March 2000, http://lds.org/ensign/2000/03/cast-not-away-therefore-your-confidence.

PROMPTED

By Rebecca R.

MY EXPERIENCE GIVING BIRTH TO MY SON Grayson was one of the most spiritual experiences I have ever had. First, Grayson was a baby that came after nearly eight years of infertility. So that in itself made his birth very special.

I was eight days past due when I went in to be induced with my son. Since about thirty-four weeks, I had a feeling that I would not be having the unmedicated birth I had planned on. However, I was given a blessing the evening before by my husband and father that promised a "natural delivery." (I still am not sure what this means.)

When I went in to be induced, before they started the Pitocin drip, they hooked up the monitors. Grayson's heart rate began to drop into the nineties (it should be between 120 and 160 beats per minute). It would take a few minutes for it to go back up. The nurse prepared for a C-section in case my OB decided to automatically take the C-section route. The on-call OB felt that we were not in an emergency situation at this point so we could wait for my doctor to arrive. When my OB arrived, Grayson's heart rate had been steady for an hour or so. He went ahead and broke my water and then began a Pitocin drip thirty minutes later.

As I would get up here and there to use the restroom, Grayson's heart rate would still dip but would return pretty quickly. An internal heart monitor was placed to see if he was just moving away from the monitor. The next time I used the restroom, it dipped again. The nurse decided from then on I would be using a bed pan.

By this point, the contractions were getting closer together, and I was having back labor. I was still breathing through the contractions pretty well though. The nurse asked me at this time if I would like an epidural. I told her I was fine. She said she was going to leave the room and be back in fifteen minutes.

As soon as the nurse left the room, I had a *very strong* prompting to get the epidural. Because of the words that had been spoken in the blessing the night before—that I would be guided by the Spirit, that I needed to heed those promptings, and that the nurses and doctors would be led to make suggestions to me by the Spirit—I knew I needed to heed this prompting. The nurse came back in and I told her I would like the epidural.

As the epidural was being placed, the only thing I could think to ask was, "Will this be used in the case of a C-section?" I knew the answer to this due to my childbirth preparation classes, but for some reason I wanted that reassurance. They told me that it would. They were kind enough to grant my wish for a low dose so that I could still feel contractions and tell if they were progressing.

About an hour after the epidural was placed, I was lying on my left side. I was not comfortable in that position. Even though Grayson's heart rate had been fine for hours, I felt like I should not move without the nurse in the room. When she entered the room, I told her that I wanted to readjust my lying position but wanted her there when I did. She said she was sure everything would be fine, and I didn't need to wait for her. I moved to get comfortable, and at that time Grayson's heart rate dropped to thirty-three beats per minute. The nurse helped me move around, pushed on my stomach, and gave me oxygen to try and raise it. My husband had been sleeping and woke up to several nurses rushing into the room, calling my OB on the phone. He was trying to figure out what was happening. My nurse told him to go change into the scrubs they had placed in the room early that morning.

My OB came into the room. He looked at me and said this baby was giving him a heart attack. At that moment, I felt more calm then I had all day, and I looked right at him and said, "I know what you have to do, and I trust you to get him here safe and healthy." I was rushed into the OR as my husband was still changing. They began cutting me open before he even entered the room.

My C-section was called at 11:35 a.m. and at 11:48 a.m., Grayson was born. Had I not gotten the epidural, I would have needed to be put under general anesthesia during the C-section and would not have been awake for the birth. He was perfectly healthy and weighed 7 lbs 3 oz. He scored a 9 on his APGAR. He had no health issues.

I can count on one hand the number of times I have felt the Spirit as strongly as I did that day. I know that I was guided my entire pregnancy to start preparing for a birth experience that may not have been my ideal or preferred birth for Grayson. I know that the Lord was watching out for my son that day. I am so grateful that I was able to have that guidance as did the medical staff. I may not have had the birth experience I had hoped for, but the experience I had was perfect for Grayson and me. It only increased my testimony of the Holy Ghost and our Heavenly Father and Savior. I still do not understand what was meant in my blessing when I was told I would have a "natural birth," but I know that I was told the things I needed to hear and that the Lord had a plan in place to bring this little man to my family.

A SURPRISE BREECH

By Cherylyn

BY THE TIME I RECEIVED the surprising news that I was pregnant with my fifth baby, I had given birth to two of my babies in the hospital completely medicated and to the other two in the hospital without any medication. At the time I was reading everything I could get my hands on about pregnancy and birth. I felt like a sponge. I had discovered a deep passion, and I was soaking up every bit of information I could.

In my studies, I had learned about the option of home birth. It was something I had never considered before in my life. As I thought about my options, the idea of a water birth at home gave me great peace. The peace I felt surprised me, but I welcomed it. I prayed about planning to birth my baby at home, and that resounding peace filled my soul. That peace stayed with me throughout my entire pregnancy. I never felt fear about my choice to birth at home.

Along my journey, I had been blessed to meet people with wonderful skills. Through his work in massage therapy, my husband had gotten to know a midwife who specialized in home birth and had been working in that field for fifteen years. We started meeting regularly for prenatal visits and monthly forum meetings at her home. She did all of the clinical work that my obstetrician had done at the prenatal visits, but she also offered emotional support that I had never experienced with a birth care provider before. Over the months, my midwife and I developed a close bond and friendship that I had never expected.

About four days after the due date, my midwife brought the birth tub to our house and we set it up in our bedroom. My midwife checked the baby's heartbeat and the kids all got to hear it, with grins and wide eyes. She also checked my cervix and found it was dilated to 4 cm, almost 5, and 80% effaced.

After she left, my contractions gradually started to build in intensity and frequency. I stayed busy doing things around the house, doing whatever I could think of to prepare and keep my mind off of the growing pressure. I called my midwife to let her know what was happening, and she suggested I go for a walk and call her back if things changed. I walked through the neighborhood around midnight and the contractions started coming every two minutes. I called my midwife, and she started on her way to our home.

My midwife arrived, and my husband helped her set up her things as I moved about the house doing what I could to help and get comfortable. She checked me and found my cervix was at 5 cm. I was completely calm, able to move about freely as I wanted to. I had my birth ball in our front room and would lean my torso against it in a kneeling position during each contraction. I was using focused breathing through them at this point but was managing well without needing additional support. At some point, my midwife checked me again and I was dilated to 7 cm. She called her attendant to come assist—another midwife whom she had felt prompted through prayer to invite.

As I stepped into the warm water of the birth tub, the pressure seemed to completely melt away, and I felt instant relief. My husband sat behind the tub as I leaned against the back of it. He held my hands to support my arms and pressed some acupressure points to alleviate the pain. It worked wonders. The next time my midwife checked, I was dilated to 9 cm. We were elated and anxious to have a baby! She stepped out to talk with her attendant, and my husband and I talked about how this was the easiest birth by far, and how wonderful it was to be at home and for everything to be so calm and comfortable.

When my midwife came back in to see if it was time to push yet, she found that my cervix had started to close back up! I was back to a 7, and my cervix was swollen and hard. We were perplexed and disappointed. We had no idea why my body had gone backwards. I was tired, so we all decided to lie down and try to rest. My husband lay down behind me to press on my sacrum during contractions to help relieve the pressure in my back. It felt good to breathe deeply in and moan as I exhaled. I slept between the contractions.

We called Grandma and asked her to take the kids (who had awoken). We promised to call the oldest two back home when the baby was ready to come out. I got back into the birth tub in an upright position, and my husband pressed on my back. It was only about twenty minutes after the kids left that my midwife checked me and found I was again dilated to 9 cm. So the older two kids came home. I was finally able to push, and my kids stood at the side of the tub while my husband sat behind my head and supported my back. It felt good to stretch my body out as long as I could and arch my back.

With the first really good push, it felt to me that the baby's head was about to come out, but it went back in. My midwife asked me to stop while she cleaned some stool out of the water. She soon realized it was meconium from the baby and wondered why there was so much of it. When she checked, she found that it wasn't the baby's head that was about to come out, but his bottom! I knew from personal revelation that I needed to plan a home birth, but I didn't know why. When the midwife told me he was breech, the words came to me: "This is why we needed to be at home." Since then I've had countless more confirmations of that very fact.

I knew my baby would be fine, and I waited to be instructed on the next step. My midwife told me to stop pushing and was about to have me get out of the tub. She didn't have a lot of experience with breech babies, but her attendant who was there had experience birthing more than twenty breech babies, including three of her own grandchildren, which explains why my midwife had felt prompted to invite her. The attendant knew exactly what to do. She quickly stepped in and said, "No, it's alright. Let's just keep her here and keep going."

They instructed me to push and not stop; just keep on pushing! I forced myself to push harder than my body wanted to as the baby's bottom came out, then one leg, then the other leg. As my midwife reached to help the baby I heard the attendant say "No. See how he's kicking? He's doing just fine!" I closed my eyes, focused, and kept on pushing. They told me when his torso came out, then one arm and then the other arm. It was good for me to be in the water and allow the baby to feel the weightlessness similar to the womb and be able to manipulate his own body in ways I never would have imagined possible. I felt every movement as the pressure eased with each body part that came out. Then, as my six-year-old described it, the baby "put the feet and the hands on the bum cheeks and pushed his head out." They immediately lifted him out of the water and placed him in my arms. He was beautiful and perfect, and I just held him against my body in the warm water. He let out two little cries and instantly started to pink up.

My husband and I both felt calm through the whole thing, even with the surprises that came up, and we are both very happy we made the decision to have this baby at home. We're not sure why we didn't know the baby was breech beforehand. The midwife is still wondering if she could have detected it earlier. I don't fault anyone for not knowing he was breech. We didn't know, but God knew and provided us with what we needed to handle it.

Each time I'm prompted to share my birth story with someone, I feel the Spirit reconfirm to me the importance and beauty and blessing of it all. With my next pregnancy, I'll pray about how to plan for it and move forward again. I may be required to have faith once again, trusting that the Lord knows all and will bless me for my obedience, but I believe it will be easier to do that after what the Lord has shown me already.

Between Life and Death

By Valerie Christensen

MY FIRST CHILD, BENJAMIN, took me seven years, two bouts of induced menopause, five surgeries, and the power of temple blessings to finally conceive. I chose a natural birth because my babymaker had been medicalized to the max. Aside from spiritual reasons, I simply did not want my birth to be just another procedure in a long line of procedures. I prepared heavily, read extensively and took an excellent childbirth education class. I hired a doula. I prayed about having a home birth and got a "no," so I planned a hospital birth.

I labored at home for almost seven hours, spent time in a hot bath until my doula begged me to get out and leave, drove the mile to the hospital in full transition and was in my hospital room all of ten minutes before I started pushing. And there he was—a gorgeous blond, blue-eyed 6 lbs, 13 oz. He ended up having severe hypoglycemia and needed the NICU for five days which explained the "no" on the home birth. Other than that, it was an utterly transcendent, enlightening, highly spiritual experience. That day, I found that mystical "Laborland" and realized that I really was made to do this. I learned a fundamental spiritual lesson in Ben's birth—that submission and trust in God are not just the keys to labor, but the keys to life.

My second child, Sophie, was born two years later. I knew that I was a fabulous birthing machine, and I could easily brush off the constant attempts at needless interventions, but having to do so was stressful. I never found my way into "Laborland," and I never got that rush of endorphins. I was out of my element and fully cognizant of every stark detail of that short, but violent, five-hour birth. After she came, a beautiful, dark-haired 8 lbs. 3 oz., she didn't stop screaming for a long time, and I remember hugging her and repeating over and over, "I know, I know, that was so hard!" We both cried while I tried to console us.

After that birth, I felt stupid. Why did I put myself through that? If I'm going to choose a medical birth in a hospital, why fight everything? Why not just kill the pain? I was lucky to have a very rare L&D nurse who told me I'd done the right thing. She said she had seen her share of medicated moms and babies and that, although it's rarely said, she did see a significant, positive difference in unmedicated births.

When I learned I was pregnant a third time, I went to a group of certified nurse midwives in the Los Angeles area. I'd never felt myself in better hands. When I went in at twenty-two weeks and my CNM couldn't find the heartbeat with her stethoscope, I just thought to myself, "We just need better

---

I hope that as Latter-day Saint women, we seek to make our birth experiences truly sacred, where our heart is laid open before the Lord so we can discover all He is able to teach us.

---

equipment." Looking back, the midwife was a fifteen-year veteran and already knew exactly what had happened, but she allowed me to hold onto my illusions and accept it on my own terms. She told me to go do the ultrasound and give her a call. Of course, the ultrasound told the same story.

Little Eden, stillborn at five months, taught me the greatest lesson in the spiritual side of birth. I sat in the same labor and delivery ward where I had given birth to Sophie, but this time the nurses all spoke softly, and I took every painkiller offered.

My bishop came quickly. I told him how scared and horrified I was to have to go through all the pain of labor only to hold a dead baby. He thought for a very long time, and the Spirit was strong as he started to talk. I could tell his counsel was coming straight from the Lord. He said:

> Valerie, this is your opportunity to come to know the Savior in a new way, a way you haven't before. Jesus Christ suffered and sacrificed to give us eternal life, just as mothers suffer and sacrifice to bring life to their children. He suffered for those who would accept His sacrifice, and He suffered even for those who wouldn't. Like you will experience today, some of His suffering and sacrificing was to no avail. If your heart is open to it, through this trial, the Lord is going to help you be closer to Christ and glimpse a little more of what His sacrifice means.

I received a blessing that it would go as smoothly as possible, and the birth ended up being only a moderately painful yet heartbreaking, extremely spiritual experience. After that day, I firmly believe that for mothers our sacrifice in birth, especially if we do not shrink from the bitter cup, can serve to strengthen our love of the Savior and our understanding of His Atonement. I don't believe in needless suffering, but I do think that in this case, our pain has a purpose and the potential to teach us a great deal.

Despite the intense love and presence of the Spirit I felt during this time, I was still understandably broken with grief after burying a tiny body next to grandparents and great-grandparents in the old cemetery. As a result, I was nothing but tears when I learned I was pregnant two months later. It turned out to be anembryonic—a fertilized egg that stops growing after a few divisions but forgets to tell your body it's not pregnant anymore. I was strangely relieved. I was not ready. After one more cycle, I was pregnant again, but I had been renewed. I prayed about doing a home birth and received a very comforting assurance.

On a Sunday in October, during sacrament meeting, I started contracting. During Relief Society, I was practically in active labor. I was asked why I stayed, and I said, "I can stay here and be distracted or I can go home and think about my contractions." When church was over my husband, David, ran home to start filling the portable birth tub in our bedroom. I got home and fell into "Laborland," but this time, I was entirely in my own space and on my own terms. In the hospital, I needed constant support from my husband. In my own home, I was in my own element and didn't need to rely on anyone for safety. I sat on the edge of the bed as if in a trance. There was rushing to get midwives there, the tub filled, and Ben and Sophie off to a neighbor's. My sweet, not-so-little 9 lb., 4 oz., Noah was born just about two hours after we arrived home from church.

It was my most magnificent birth experience, and I felt safer and more peaceful than I ever imagined, aided by wise, competent women working in tandem with me, not just working *on* me. They did just what knowledgeable women like them have successfully done for millennia. Studies have shown that women birth faster with a woman in the room, even if the woman is just sitting in the corner, uninvolved. After this experience, I came to believe sisterhood definitely plays a significant, spiritual role in childbirth that we have yet to fully understand.

My final baby, little Lucy, was to follow suit with the same midwives, but I felt prompted to switch to an OB at twenty-seven weeks. Thank heaven I listened to that prompting. Lucy was born in an emergency C-section one week later at twenty-nine weeks because my placenta gave out. All the surgeries and six pregnancies in a row had done me in. I was hemorrhaging, and her amniotic fluid was being replaced with blood. My amazing OB, awe-inspiring world-class NICU doctors and nurses, an amazing facility, and a half a million dollars all had an active hand in making sure my sweet, 2.5 lb baby grew into a healthy, little (very little), but very active girl.

I have come to see that birth can truly be a conduit to heaven, where we walk in the valley of the shadow of death with none but Christ at our side and come to know things about ourselves and about Him that were unknown before. Actively participating in the birthing process, we act in partnership with God in the creation of life. I can think of no better way that we as women can fill the measure of our creation. I hope that as Latter-day Saint women, we seek to make our birth experiences truly sacred, where our heart is laid open before the Lord so we can discover all He is able to teach us. I truly believe there are lessons that can only be learned in that holy place between life and death.

And God Remembered Rachel

by Natalie Holbrook

MY HUSBAND AND I STARTED OUR "Summer Project" in June. Oh we had high hopes, and then somehow summer turned to fall and then to winter, and by early spring I was ready to crawl into a hole and die. There is a certain kind of sting in the failure of the body to perform what for most species is its most basic function. While it has never bothered me that I can't really do long division, or that I don't know how to sail, or that I can't do the splits, this failure to conceive somehow cut me so low, made me doubt myself so much, and I just felt completely lost, humiliated, and heartbroken. Horribly, horribly heartbroken.

I consulted friends and loved ones for advice. Always I heard the same: *Relax. Don't stress out. Go on vacation. Try some red wine. Lay off the caffeine. Try this doctor. Eat more avocados. Just stop trying. Trust the Lord's timing.* But every night as I prayed I heard it: *Keep looking.* So I saw doctor after doctor after doctor: two OB/GYNs, one naturopath, one highly specialized and highly expensive reproductive specialist. They all told me the same things. *Your body is healthy. There is nothing wrong with you. Everything works. Just wait it out. Try to be patient.* Still I received the same prompting, the same nudging deep in my heart. *Keep looking*, it said. Over and over I heard it. *Keep looking.*

The prominent women of the book of Genesis are as follows: Eve, Sarah, Rebekah, Rachel. Of these prominent women in the book of Genesis, only Eve does not suffer from infertility. Genesis is chock full of God's chosen women suffering from want of children. In each case, she is a woman whom God directed a prophet to find and marry. She is a woman who was promised that her seed would bear rulers and kings. She is a woman who was loved by God.

First there is Sarah. Sarah is the wife of Abraham, the eventual mother of Isaac. Sarah is easily the most severe of the Infertile Myrtles. At the age of ninety, she has yet to conceive and is menopausal (Gen 18:10). As Abraham prays considering an eventual heir, God continually tells him that Sarah will conceive. Every time, Abraham and Sarah laugh. In Genesis 18:14, the Lord's messengers rebuke Sarah, saying, "Is anything too hard for the Lord?"

This was the question which kept me up at night for months and months and months. Surely nothing is too hard for the Lord. But how much can I expect from Him when I pray? Could I ask for a miracle, and would I receive? Could I ask for guidance, guidance so specific and direct, like a road map? Should I just ask for comfort? Is that the "faithful" thing to do? So, I asked. I was told to *Keep looking*. I had to look for a long, long time.

When Rebekah, wife of Isaac, and eventual mother of Esau and Jacob was experiencing infertility, Isaac went to the Lord and demanded answers on her behalf. Rebekah had been blessed to be the mother of thousands of millions, so why was nothing happening? Like Rebekah, I had been blessed to know that my life's calling would be found in motherhood (although at the time I remember feeling entirely disgusted about it). So what was the hold up? Further reflection and prayer on my part led me to know what I always knew. That I was to *Keep looking. Keep Asking.* Sometimes we are blessed with miracles. That wasn't my path.

I think Rachel, wife of Jacob, is the woman in Genesis I relate to the most. If you remember, Rachel is the daughter of a proud and sneaky man who tells Jacob he can marry her after seven years hard labor and then pulls a trick by slipping Leah in at the wedding instead. Jacob loves Rachel most, and for Rachel he continues to work for his father-in-law. When Leah has children easily and Rachel cannot, well Rachel starts to dispair and says to Jacob, "Give me children, or else I die."

It was during my second November of wanting that I started to feel like Rachel. *Give me children, or else I die.* It was also around November that I felt prompted to throw myself into my own fertility charting. After just two cycles, I knew exactly my problem: My Luteal Phase was precisely one day too short. *One day.* I showed my doctor the results, and by the end of the appointment I held a tiny little pill that promised to sort me all out.

I asked my husband if he would maybe give me another blessing. This time I was blessed to know that I would get pregnant soon. That my body would be able to receive a spirit child of Heavenly Father. That I would have a healthy pregnancy. That month the pregnancy test blinked a word at me that was so foreign it nearly took me off my feet and I needed a minute before I could even tell if it was in English.

When I told an older lady in the ward I was "finally" expecting, she screwed up her mouth at me and said, "Now, don't go insulting the Lord. This was his timing after all." I believe that, of course, but there has to be so much more to it. The thing is, I've talked with Him, pleaded with Him, listened for Him for far too long to really think I was a just passive participant faithfully awaiting my time. Those long months when I poured my soul out in prayer, the Lord whispered to me that it was in my hands, that with faith and obedience He would lead me to my baby, but that I would have to do the work. It was such a teeny, tiny, small thing, how could I have found that on my own? We figured it out together. That was my path to this baby. I believe the Lord wanted me know that I had power with Him, that He heard my prayers. In my obedience I learned I can ask and receive, and that together we can make wonderful things happen. Alone I will be left to struggle.

What I take from Genesis, and what I take from my own experience, is this: If you work with God, God will work with you. It is like a delicious cheat sheet. We can be co-creators with our God. We can create our lives with Him, if we let Him show us the path he means for us to blaze. All we have to do is ask.

Genesis 30:22 And God remembered Rachel.

THE HOURGLASS THEORY

By Courtney J. Kendrick

It looked like an egg dissected down the middle. But instead of a slimy and shapeless center, the yolk was beating. Hump. Hump. Hump. "Fast and healthy!" said Katie as she moved the ultrasound baton over Lucy's belly.

My baby had a male appendage, and Lucy's had a heartbeat. All was well at the doctor's office that winter afternoon. Until later that night when Lucy called me crying, "I'm bleeding." She bled all that night and for weeks after. That lively, beating yolk disseminated into tissue and left her body via labor-like cramping. Her baby was gone and her heart was broken.

For weeks I wondered why I felt so strongly that Lucy should come with me to find out the gender of my baby. My husband was out of town, and our cousin Katie had an opening in her schedule. It didn't seem right to find out the news all alone, there in a dark basement room, and the thought of inviting my little sister reoccurred in my mind. She was eight weeks pregnant, sick and worried. Normal.

"Call Lucy," I heard all morning. I called. She came. Katie had time to check both of us. Our babies were alert and strong. We celebrated at dinner that night. Japanese food with our father. Her miscarriage started a short time later.

This experience shocked not only Lucy and me but Katie as well. For some time after, we traded theories, all viable, all plausible. Miscarriage is common, we understood, but the timing perplexed us. Finally, I knew of no other way to satisfy Lucy's grief and my confusion then to ask my Heavenly Father *why. Why were we supposed to see her baby alive only hours before she lost it?*

I wasn't given an answer, but another question. The same question every mother has ever asked since the beginning of this earth. When does life begin? Peace would come in the answering, I was assured. Not only peace for the given situation, but requisite for my own baby whose secure entry into this world was not guaranteed either.

One night, in a state of insomnia induced by pregnancy, I searched the doctrines of the Church for an answer. They ranged from Brigham Young's insistence that life begins when the mother feels the baby move, to ideas that—just like Adam—life is not received into the body until there is a breath. From the Church's Public Issue's website, it is declared that, "The Church of Jesus Christ of Latter-day Saints has no official position on the moment that human life begins."

In answering this question, I was left with my own resource, the promise that prayer and study would resolve my concerns. So I began to ask that I might receive. My answer came in three parts as I meditated on this unpublished doctrine.

I. At first Nana was just confused. I'd sit in the living room with her and listen as she told the same story three, sometimes four, times in a row. Then she'd ask, "Did I already tell you that story?" As my mother had already rehearsed me for this moment, I'd reply, "No! What a funny story!" To which she'd reply, "Well, it reminds me of another story." And the tale would start again.

As Alzheimer's conquered more of her brain, she became less amiable. Part of her soul was missing. She'd have panic attacks and ask us, "Where am I?" And I'd wondered too, *where was she?*

Later, she was moved to a home where she could get twenty-four hour care. We'd visit and surround Nana's beside. The nurse would enter the room telling my mother, "She was talking to Angus last night. She was laughing." "Ah yes," Mother would explain, "Angus is her father. He's already gone. She's starting to go."

On Thanksgiving night we received the phone call. Nana was gone.

II. I recalled a memory of walking on the frozen Utah lake with my mother the previous year. I was almost thirty, almost five years invested into wanting a baby, almost five years of no return.

"I feel that I should tell you about when you were born," my mother said as the dogs chased out on the white lake before us. "I wanted another daughter. Poor Page, stuck in the middle of four brothers. You can't imagine how excited I was to find out that I was pregnant again!"

Really? I thought. *Even after five babies? Is it never just routine?*

"One night, when I was about twelve weeks along, I started to cramp and bleed. I knew I was miscarrying. Your dad took me to the hospital where I stayed for awhile. I sat in the hospital bed, overwhelmed by sadness. I prayed and prayed for hope, and it came. I was visited by you. You didn't say anything, but I knew it was you, and I knew that you had decided to leave, but you promised to come back." Then she added, "When you came, a year later, I saw that you had such a fickle personality. I was assured that we had met before."

III. I awoke one morning with a vision. It was an hourglass. The top sand was slipping through the skinny waist into the bottom. And I knew my answer.

Perhaps life doesn't begin or end at a single moment. Maybe our souls slip from one side to the other until we are all *here*, or we are all *there*. My Nana spent time dwelling on both sides until heaven pulled stronger. Simi-

---

I thought about a heaven full of spirits yearning for bodies, and an earth full of bodies longing to be spirits. This was peace for me.

---

larly, I started out in my mother's womb partially there, but cognizant enough to pull the plug when I wasn't thrilled about the body being created for my spirit.

I thought about a heaven full of spirits yearning for bodies, and an earth full of bodies longing to be spirits. This was peace for me. I liked the residual emotion of transition, better than the harshness of finality. It made enough sense to ease my confusion and offered hope into my heart. Lucy's baby would come again.

Perhaps most importantly, I learned that the Church's absence of an official position regarding this doctrine has a purpose. Each mother is allowed to search for herself the enlightenment that is promised to those who seek. And for each mother there is an interpretation. An answer that transcends official positions and public discourse to reside only in a quiet, maternal heart.

The Cesarean Choice

By Sheridan Ripley, CD(DONA), HCHI

My first and second births were both guided and supported by the Lord, but the experiences couldn't have been more different. When I was thirty-four weeks pregnant with my first baby—after being on bed rest for nine weeks—I woke up one day and after a while noticed he hadn't moved that morning. I had an impression that there was something wrong with him. I called the doctor, who told me to drink juice and call back in an hour to report. But I already knew there was something wrong.

I had my husband give me a blessing. He said that the baby would be okay and would come when he was ready. As soon as my husband said he would be okay, I felt a large weight come off of my shoulders. I knew that my baby was going to be okay.

We went in to get the baby monitored, and it quickly became apparent that the baby was under distress and needed to be born immediately. My husband asked whether I wanted another blessing before the cesarean section, and I said, "No, you said he would come when he was ready, so he must be ready now!" I went into the surgery knowing that it was something needed to save my baby's life, and I was happy to sacrifice going through a major surgery to save him. That blessing helped me have peace during and after the surgery.

When it was time to welcome our second child, after much learning and research, I was guided to plan a VBAC (vaginal birth after a cesarean). My husband pointed out to me that it was *because I chose to learn* that the Lord could give me a particular answer in regard to planning a VBAC versus an elective repeat cesarean section. My choices would have been different if I had not taken the time to learn my options. Ultimately, I achieved my goal and gave birth to my second son vaginally.

Cesarean sections can be a controversial topic. There is risk in life, and there is risk in birth. Cesarean sections can be a gift when they are medically necessary to save either a mom's or baby's life, but many cesarean sections performed today are not medically necessary. In the United States, the cesarean section rate is now at an alarming all-time high of 34 percent.

Having a cesarean delivery is neither right nor wrong; it is a choice. We need to research available options and follow our intuition in making choices. It is crucial that the Lord be included. Counseling with the Lord can bring peace of mind concerning our decisions. We will be guided to the best choices for us.

WHY IS THIS DECISION SO IMPORTANT?

A cesarean section is a major abdominal surgery that can affect your future family. Studies have found that a woman who has a cesarean section for her first baby is likely to have fewer children than a woman who has a vaginal birth.[1] Two of the most common surgeries performed on women (cesarean sections and hysterectomies) permanently affect women's reproductive anatomy—the gateway into this world.

Smaller family size isn't the only long-term impact of cesarean deliveries. In addition, a woman's risk of accreta (and other placental abnormalities and postpartum complications) increases dramatically the more cesarean sections a woman has. Placenta accreta is when the placenta grows through the uterus and can cause hemorrhage potentially leading to a hysterectomy. The incidence of placenta accreta has been increasing at an alarming rate, especially in Utah, where women tend to have more than two children.

Dr. Robert Silver, a professor of obstetrics and gynecology at the University of Utah, has studied cesarean deliveries, placenta accreta, vaginal birth after a cesarean section, and recurrent pregnancy loss and stillbirth for nearly two decades. In 2006, Dr. Silver published a study on the risks of multiple cesarean deliveries. He and his research team concluded, "Women planning large families should consider the risks of repeat cesarean deliveries when contemplating elective cesarean delivery or attempted vaginal birth after cesarean delivery."[2] Multiple cesareans can affect the safety of bringing more children into the world. It is important to protect our wombs and powers of procreation from unnecessary harm.

PREVENTING AN UNNECESSARY CESAREAN DELIVERY

There are certainly times when cesarean deliveries are medically needed to save mom or baby, but some cesarean sections are avoidable. Many women are told: "Your pelvis is too small" or "This baby is too big for you to birth." Some women wanting VBACs are told it isn't safe or that they can never have a vaginal birth: "It didn't work last time, and it won't this time either." Women carrying twins and breech babies are often told that vaginal birth isn't an option. However, in these situations, by doing more research, counseling with the Lord, and finding competent and supportive care providers, many moms can go on to have safe, successful vaginal births.

Making choices with limited information or out of fear is not empowering. Tad Callister explained: "No principle in the celestial realm is more sacred than the right to agency. It is the keystone upon which heaven and earth are governed. Without informed decisions, agency would be but a mockery. The Savior was informed and knowledgeable of his impending ordeal."[3] Become informed and exercise your agency. The choices you make can help lower your cesarean risk.

How can we further protect ourselves and our wombs from unnecessary surgery? There are some things you can do before giving birth to help avoid a cesarean delivery:

- Choose your care provider wisely. Select someone who is dedicated to maintaining low cesarean section rates, performing them for only true medical needs.

- Choose your birth location carefully. Tour more than one hospital/birth center. Find out their cesarean section rates. Prayerfully consider the best location for your birth.

- If your care provider suggests a cesarean delivery, do research, make sure you are fully informed, and make your choice based on facts and your intuition rather than fear. Get a second opinion!

- Avoid induction. Inducing labor can also significantly increase your risk of a cesarean delivery. Being patient and allowing your baby to choose the birth day is a great way to improve your chances of a vaginal birth.[4]

There are some things you can do during your birth to help avoid a cesarean delivery:

- Stay unmedicated as long as possible. Move as your body feels the need to. Being in an upright position can help your baby descend more easily.

- If a cesarean section is suggested, there are two great questions to ask: "Is mom OK? Is Baby OK?" If the answers are yes, then you can ask for more time. One study found that when women who experienced "failure to progress" waited two extra hours, one-third were able to have vaginal births. So patience has proved to be a good way to avoid unnecessary surgery.[5]

- Consider how to change the situation and increase your chances of a vaginal birth, such as trying new positions, getting an epidural so you can rest, and addressing fears or emotional barriers that might be holding you back.

IS A VBAC RIGHT FOR YOU?

Are VBACs safe? What about the risk of uterine rupture? You need to do your own research on the safety of VBACs and weigh the risks and benefits. Don't let the opinions and fears of other people determine your choice. Local childbirth educators and doulas are dedicated to helping moms have the best birth experiences possible. Childbirth educators and doulas are great resources for finding local care providers and information on choosing a repeat cesarean delivery or a VBAC. I did my research and found that elective repeat cesarean sections have risks of their own. I wanted the experience of having a vaginal birth and decided that was the best choice for me. With the Lord's help, you can make the best decision for you and your baby.

I have had two great VBACs. These are some things that I feel contributed to my success:

- Preparation: There are many methods and means of preparing for birth. I feel that hypnosis really helped me to get over my fears from my first birth and to develop a positive "I can do it" attitude. I felt very confident that I would be successful birthing my baby, and I was able to recover a trust that my body could carry a baby full-term and have a vaginal birth. I love the Hypnobabies® program because it has a fear release CD you can listen to as many times as you need.

- Supportive care providers: My obstetrician was supportive, and the hospital staff were also supportive. The support helped a lot because I didn't have to fight for my rights. My care provider was on my side and fighting for me. It is worth the hard work to find a supportive care provider.

- Doula support: Doulas can be invaluable. I didn't have one for my first VBAC but did for my second one. It is wonderful to have an extra person to give you support. I know my first VBAC would have gone more smoothly had I used a doula.

- Husband support: My husband believed I could do it. His belief helped me.

I have had the privilege of attending many VBACs as a doula. It is wonderful to witness the strength, determination, and empowerment of other women. Shannon shared her story:

When I found out I was expecting my third child after two previous cesareans, I was determined to get my VBAC, especially since I knew this would be my last pregnancy. I desperately wanted that natural birth experience. At the time, my doctor had said she wouldn't allow it. It was also at this time that ACOG [American Congress of Obstetricians and Gynecologists] published their new guidelines for VBAC and VBA2C. This definitely helped us and added needed ammunition to our fight.

This is where the turning point occurred. Once my doctor discovered I was switching to another OB, she suddenly changed her tune. I decided to stay with her after she promised to allow me to try a VBA2C.

Twice I was told by my OB that my fluid was low, but this time I had learned enough to ask for a second opinion. Both times the fluid was found to be fine. I was told I would be allowed to go to 41 weeks but no longer. We had a C-section scheduled for Friday morning at 9 a.m. At 2 p.m. on the day before the scheduled C-section, my water broke and contractions started. I began timing them and called my OB and Sheridan (my doula) to let them know. This was the first time I had ever felt contractions. We arrived at the hospital by 4 p.m.

Once we were in the room, Sheridan began coaching me and offering suggestions to help keep the labor going. It was comforting to know I had someone in my corner. Hospitals are intimidating enough, and it helped to have her knowledge, support and advice. At around 10 p.m. we were given permission to walk laps around the halls. As we walked, the contractions began to come closer and closer. We walked for 20 minutes or so and it was enough to do the trick.

At that point, the contractions were getting pretty intense for me. I was really having a hard time focusing on my scripts and practicing my meditation techniques. I was so exhausted at this point. I chose to have an epidural and have never regretted it. I was able to take an hour nap, pushed for an hour, and delivered my son five hours before our C-section was scheduled.

IS A PLANNED CESAREAN DELIVERY RIGHT FOR YOU?

When I find out someone is planning a cesarean section, I start a conversation with them. "I had a cesarean section with my first baby. Why are you having one?" Then I listen to their reasons. I ask how they feel about having a cesarean delivery. Some women feel really good about it. They have already done their research and know it is the best choice for them.

In those cases, I fully support them in their decision and help them prepare to have the best possible cesarean birth. A cesarean birth can be a positive experience, a celebration of the wonder of a baby entering this world! (See "Creating a Sacred Cesarean Section," page 190.)

Other women facing planned cesarean deliveries are on the fence and seem to want more information. If a woman is open, I share information with her. We explore her real choices. I offer places she can go to do some research.[6] If you are in a situation where you are choosing between a cesarean delivery or a vaginal birth, ask a lot of questions. Get a second opinion from a care provider supportive of vaginal birth in your particular situation (previous cesarean delivery, twins, breech, etc.). Tour multiple birth locations. Pray about it.

Women who take time to question what they are being told and to do their own research will be able to make the choices that are really best for them. They are making informed decisions rather than coerced decisions. Many women, upon doing further research, will realize that a vaginal birth is a good option for them. Some women will choose or need to have a cesarean section. These women have taken all the information and combined it with their intuition to make the best choice for them. This choice should be respected and supported. Women know what is best for them when they have all the information and have prayerfully made a choice.

1   Mette C. Tollånes, Kari K. Melve, Lorentz M. Irgens, et al., "Reduced Fertility after Cesarean Delivery—a Maternal Choice," *Obstetrics and Gynecology* 110, no. 6 (2007): 1256–1263.
2   Robert M. Silver, Mark B. Landon, Dwight J. Rouse, et al., "Maternal Morbidity Associated with Multiple Repeat Cesarean Deliveries," *Obstetrics and Gynecology* 107, no. 6 (2006): 1226–1232.
3   Tad R. Callister, *Infinite Atonement* (Salt Lake City, UT: Deseret Book, 2000), 151
4   Henci Goer, "Informed Choices in Childbirth," http://www.hencigoer.com/articles/elective_induction.
5   Dana E. Henry, "Perinatal Outcomes in the Settings of Active Phase of Arrest of Labor," *Obstetrics and Gynecology* 112, no. 5 (2008): 1109–1115.
6   Resources include the International Cesarean Awareness Network website (http://www.ican-online.org) and the Childbirth Choices website (http://www.childbirthchoices.com).

Bottom First

By Katrina Barker Anderson

DURING MY SECOND PREGNANCY, I practiced self-hypnosis, spending many hours learning to relax and visualizing my ideal birth. I would go into labor in the morning after a good night's sleep, have a quick, peaceful, comfortable labor, and then birth my daughter in a pool while kneeling, catching her myself.

At the start of the third trimester, my daughter turned breech. And she stayed there. No amount of coaxing would convince her to turn. I tried everything I had ever heard of to turn a breech baby: breech tilt, inversion, chiropractor, acupuncture, massage, "Turn Your Breech Baby" Hypnobabies® CD, music, ice, flashlight, headstands, homeopathics, priesthood blessings, and of course lots and lots of prayers.

And yet she remained breech.

Finally, at 38 weeks, we went to visit an OB to see about doing a version. When my fluid levels were discovered to be very low, the version was out of the question, and I was advised that a C-section would probably be the best choice. An emergency C-section at that. But first we needed to check out the baby and make sure she was okay. We decided not to stay at the hospital for that, and I went to my midwife's office to do the non-stress test. My baby girl was happy as can be. No cesarean for us!

Despite the low fluid levels and breech position, I continued to feel like Miriam's birth was going to go well. We needed to change to a new midwife who could attend a vaginal breech birth, so we worked on doing that. I felt a lot of peace as we continued to monitor her every other day for the next week, and she was always very responsive and happy. I knew she was doing just fine in there. I trusted her, and I trusted my body. But we felt, based on all the circumstances, it would be a good idea for her to come sooner rather than later. So my midwife stripped by membranes and gave me labor-stimulating herbs to see if it would be Miriam's birthday.

Indeed it was. Within a few hours, I was holding my sweet, beautiful, perfectly healthy baby girl in my arms. She came exactly as I had visualized she would, with just one tiny difference—her bottom came out first!

LISTENING TO THE SPIRIT:
A SPIRITUAL CESAREAN

By Jennifer Y.

I HAD SIGNS OF PREECLAMPSIA starting early in my second trimester. As warnings increased, my doctor's concern did as well. My patriarchal blessing said that I wouldn't have complications in pregnancy or childbirth. I fully believe this to be true. I continued to take care of myself and our son (our firstborn) to the best of my ability during pregnancy.

As I approached my due date, I was tested and checked often. With all the swelling, they couldn't tell how big my boy was. They thought 8 *maybe* 8.6 lbs. The day before my due date, I was scheduled for a non-stress test. That morning I woke up a little anxious. In the moments before my husband woke, I prayed to my Heavenly Father, and I sat and pondered what might take place in the next few days. I knew full well that, after the non-stress test, I might be induced depending on my blood pressure, swelling, and slight pain in my side.

Within minutes of my prayer, I had an overwhelming feeling of peace, and the still, small voice whispered bluntly yet sincerely, "A C-section is not a complication." I dismissed the thought immediately. There was no way in my mind that I would ever need a C-section. I mean, I hadn't even read those chapters in the books because *I surely would never have a C-section.* I was meant to have many children, and it would be easy and so rewarding.

After my non-stress test, it happened as I suspected. I was induced. More than twenty-four hours later, I had slowly progressed. I was finally able to get my epidural (as my husband and I had prayerfully decided on months earlier). I continued to progress but so slowly. I spent over nine hours

---

I had an overwhelming feeling of peace, and the still, small voice whispered bluntly yet sincerely, "A C-section is not a complication."

---

dilated to 6 cm. Seventy-two hours, after I had entered the hospital for the non-stress test, I was faced with a decision. I could try for two more hours for something to happen and have a C-section if I continued to make no improvements, or I could do the C-section then.

The prompting, or reassurance, I had two days earlier flooded my mind. I started crying. The doctors thought immediately that I was scared, but that wasn't it at all. They were tears of joy for the comfort and peace I had making my decision. I signed the paperwork and within forty minutes my little boy was safe and sound in this world. He was 9 lbs 10 oz and had never even entered the birth canal.

Because of prayer and promptings, he and I were both safe. We avoided any possible complications that could've come from preeclampsia by listening to the Spirit, and thus fulfilled the words promised to me in my patriarchal blessing.

I know that every mother (and father) can turn to the Lord when faced with difficult decisions. Though we may feel that the promptings we're receiving couldn't possibly really be promptings, if we follow them in faith, we will truly be blessed.

CHAPTER FOUR

Patience

Wait on the Lord: be of good courage,
and he shall strengthen thine heart.

PSALMS 27:14

They Who Wait upon the Lord

By Heather Farrell, CD(DONA)

The Lord did strengthen them
that they could bear up their burdens with ease,
and they did submit cheerfully
and with patience
to all the will of the Lord.

MOSIAH 24:15

Birth is a time of waiting. A woman may wait to conceive. She waits nine to ten months with a tiny soul growing beneath her heart. She waits while that soul makes its entry into the world, and she waits in great awe for her baby to take its first breath. Waiting for something as wonderful, exciting, and life changing as a baby can be difficult physically, emotionally, and spiritually. Yet, the Lord has promised that if we will come unto Him that He will make our weakness become strengths. In Isaiah 40:31 we read, "But they that wait upon the Lord shall renew their strength; they shall mount up with wings as eagles; they shall run, and not be weary; and they shall walk, and not faint." What a beautiful promise for a woman who is waiting for a child—to know that when she is feeling weak in body, mind, or spirit, if she will have patience, the Lord will renew her strength and cause her to "run, and not be weary; and . . . walk and not faint" (D&C 89:20).

In Hebrew, the word for "wait" is also the word for "hope" and denotes spiritual expectation and anticipation. Dr. Lynn Callister, a professer of nursing at Brigham Young University, explained:

Waiting denotes an active process . . . requires continual self-examination, constantly trying to become more worthy, and ever-deepening and progressive discipleship of a broken heart, a contrite spirit, a yielded will and consecration of self. When we know that the guidance is of the Lord and the answers to our prayers are spiritual gifts, we cannot control or demand. We must be content and peaceful.[1]

Isaiah promised that those who wait upon the Lord "shall mount up with wings as eagles" (Isaiah 40:31). In the scriptures, eagles often represent the Lord, and eagles' wings almost always refer to the Lord delivering His children out of a difficult situation. For example, the Lord described the deliverance of the children of Israel out of Egypt by saying, "I bare you on eagles' wings, and brought you unto myself" (Exodus 19:4). Deliverance has a rich and deep meaning to a pregnant woman. Just as the Israelites felt relief and joy when they finally rested in peace in the promised land, so a woman, holding her newborn child, feels joy and relief at having been delivered by the power of the Lord.

Learning to wait upon the Lord's timing can be difficult, particularly when we lean on our *own* understanding. A woman waiting for a child, whether she is waiting to conceive, waiting to go into labor, or waiting for the imminent birth of her child, has a unique opportunity to put her faith and trust in the Lord and demonstrate her willingness to wait on Him. When she is patient and hopeful, she opens herself up to receive miracles, great truths, and spiritual gifts.

WAITING FOR PREGNANCY

The trial of being unable to bear children is one that God gave to some of His strongest and most beloved daughters. Great women such as Sarah, Rebekah, Rachel, Hannah, Samson's mother, and Elisabeth struggled with fertility. A significant portion of the stories we have about women in the scriptures are about women who struggled with barrenness for long periods. Yet the beautiful thing about these stories is that all the women who are mentioned as being barren in the scriptures eventually bore children.

Consider the story of Rachel who, after almost twenty years of infertility, wanted children so badly and was so jealous of her sister, Leah—

who had borne four sons—that she cried out to her husband, "Give me children or else I die" (Genesis 30:1). Resigning herself, Rachel turned to the ancient version of adoption. She gave her handmaid Bilhah to her husband, Jacob, so that Bilhah would "bear upon my knees, that I may have children" (Genesis 30:3).

Through Bilhah, Rachel had two sons, Dan and Naphtali, whom she named and whom she probably raised as her own. Yet the hope for her own child never left her. At one point, she bargained with Leah to get mandrakes, the ancient version of fertility drugs. The mandrakes didn't work. To make matters worse, Leah bore three more children while Rachel's womb remained empty. Yet, eventually, the Lord "remembered Rachel and . . . hearkened unto her and opened her womb" (Genesis 30:22). After more than twenty years of bareness, she bore two sons, Joseph and Benjamin, who would change the face of history.

We don't know why Rachel had to wait more than twenty years to bear children or why some women have the trial of barrenness and others do not. It is important to know that it is not a punishment and it is not forever. Remember that Eve received her call as "the mother of all living" (Genesis 3:20) before she came to this earth and that God and Adam both considered her a mother before she ever physically bore a child. All women have the same seeds, with the power to create life, inside of them and have been foreordained to be mothers, in this life or in the next.

The scriptures are full of stories of women who bore children despite previously appearing unable. Consider Sarah, who laughed when the Lord told her she was going to bear a son because she had "ceased to be . . . after the manner of women" (Genesis 18:11), meaning she had already entered menopause. Yet, we read that the Lord "visited Sarah" (Genesis 21:1) and that she conceived and bore a child, Isaac, who later became a prophet. Her story teaches us that God is in control of how and when children come into this world. If we learn to have faith in the Lord and wait upon Him with hopeful anticipation, He can and will work miracles on our behalf, no matter what our circumstances. Remember what the angel Gabriel told Mary, the mother of Jesus, when she asked how she, a virgin, would be able to bear a child: "For with God nothing shall be impossible" (Luke 1:37).

WAITING FOR BIRTH DAY

The last weeks of pregnancy can be difficult to endure, and scheduling an early birth day for your baby can sound very appealing, but there are some real benefits that come from waiting on the Lord's timing. During the last several weeks of pregnancy, your baby's lungs mature and he or she puts on the weight needed to be a healthy and strong newborn. Scientists estimate that critical brain development continues through forty-one weeks gestation and that between the thirty-fifth and the forty-first week that there is a five-fold increase in brain development.[2] When a baby's organs and brain are mature, the baby's body releases a small amount of a hormone that signals the mother's pituitary gland to secrete the hormone oxytocin and begin labor. Essentially, your baby signals when it's time to be born.

Due dates are notoriously imprecise, and your baby's size isn't indicative of how developed he or she is. Your doctor or midwife is only able to make a guess at your baby's development, and these guesses usually have a margin of error of plus or minus two or more weeks.[3] This means that if you are induced "early," say around thirty-eight weeks, your baby might only be thirty-six weeks old. Babies born at thirty-four to thirty-six weeks gestation are considered late-preterm babies and have more problems with breathing, jaundice, feeding, infection, and body temperature.[4] Induction also doubles the chances that a woman will have a cesarean section[5] and often leads to other interventions that may interfere with the natural process of birth and detract from the sacred spirit of the event. Just as with all pharmaceuticals, labor-inducing drugs have potentially negative side effects. Even so, sometimes a woman might receive strong promptings or revelation that an induction is necessary or there may be a real medical need, and she should be encouraged to follow such feelings and guidance. We know that no matter what we do or what difficulties may arise, God's work will always find a way to move forward.

From a spiritual perspective, it may be that in these last few weeks your baby's spirit is being prepared physically and spiritually for the mortal journey. President Joseph F. Smith taught, "Man, as a spirit, was . . . reared to maturity in the eternal mansions of the Father, prior to coming upon the earth in a temporal body."[6] Also, of his vision of the spirit world, President Joseph F. Smith said, "I observed . . . the noble and great ones. . . . Even before they were born, they, with many others, received their first lessons in the world of spirits and were prepared to come forth in the due time of the Lord to labor in his vineyard for the salvation of the souls of men" (D&C 138: 55–56). If your baby is taking his or her time to come to this earth, it's possible your baby might not be spiritually mature yet and may need every last bit of time in the spirit world to prepare for his or her important mission in this life. In the eternal scheme of things, it is very worth the wait.

When I was pregnant with my first child and getting impatient because I was nearing my due date, my visiting teacher shared a story with me that made it much easier for me to be patient. She said that her niece had an especially difficult pregnancy and was a week past her guess date. She'd had several false labors and had been sent home from the hospital multiple

---

"Birth is God's time. It can't be rushed or programmed to suit anyone's clock. It is a time to simply be there, respecting the woman's space and the natural rhythms of her body. Think of how time ceases to have relevance when you are caught up in the presence of God worshipping Him or when you are in love and spending time with your beloved. Time flies by, and you barely notice. Birth time is the timing of nature. Who knows when spring will come? Can a budding flower be found open? Yet in time, these things unfold. So does birth."[7] —Julie Bell

---

times. Her patience and strength were beginning to wane. Her father gave her a priesthood blessing, telling her that she needed to be patient a little bit longer because her son was having a hard time saying good-bye to those in the premortal world and was not yet ready for his mortal life. My visiting teacher said that the baby took his time and didn't come until more than two weeks past his guess date. Yet after gaining an eternal perspective on her pregnancy, this mother was able to wait with a glad and willing heart for her baby to be fully ready and prepared to come to her.

God has put events in place long before your little one is ever born that will determine his or her mission and course of life. Elder Neal A. Maxwell said, "Recall the new star that announced the birth at Bethlehem? It was in its precise orbit long before it so shone. We are likewise placed in human orbits to illuminate. Divine correlation functions not only in the cosmos but on this planet, too."[8] Just as the appearance of the star of Bethlehem was orchestrated to coincide perfectly with the birth of Jesus Christ, so are other events, probably unknown to you, perfectly orchestrated to coincide with the birth of your child.

One summer I was waiting for one of my doula clients to have her baby. It was her first, and she was almost forty-two weeks pregnant. Her care provider told her that she would have to be induced if she went past forty-two weeks gestation. She didn't want to be induced because she was hoping for a natural birth experience. She was feeling anxious and called me often for support and encouragement. One afternoon after getting off the phone with her, I went to the backyard to check on my son. I found him with a mouth full of raspberries. He was so excited because he had been waiting weeks for the raspberries to be ready. Just the day before when we had checked on them, they were white and hard. I was surprised to see that only a day later, the bush was now covered with tons of beautiful ripe, red fruit.

As I picked the beautiful raspberries, my thoughts turned to my client and the precious fruit she was carrying. I immediately called her and told her about my raspberries. I told her to be patient and to have faith in her body and in her baby. For just like my raspberries, one day might make all the difference in her baby's readiness to be born. Remember that the end of pregnancy is as miraculous and sacred as its beginning.

When we are called to wait, we can rest assured that we do not wait alone. God is aware of us, and He will sustain us. As we learn to trust His timing, we allow God's work and glory to be carried out in His perfect, beautiful way. We may not always understand why we must wait. Yet we can have faith that God is in perfect control of the universe, and that, in His own time, He will deliver us "with wings as eagles" (Isaiah 40:31).

1   Lynn Clark Callister, "They That Wait upon the Lord," *BYU Magazine*, Spring 1999.

2   Hannah C. Kinney, "The Near-Term (Late-Preterm) Human Brain and Risk for Periventricular Leukomalacia: A Review," *Seminars in Perinatology* 30, no. 2 (2006): 81–88.

3   William A. Engle, "A Recommendation for the Definition of "Late-Preterm" (Near-Term) and the Birth Weight-Gestational Age Classification System," *Seminars in Perinatology* 30, no. 1 (2006): 2–7.

4   K. M. Tomashek, C. K. Shapiro-Mendoza, M. J. Davidoff, and J. R. Petrini, "Differences in Mortality between Late-Preterm and Term Singleton Infants in the United States, 1995–2002," *The Journal of Pediatrics* 151, no. 5 (2007): 450–456; C.K. Shapiro-Mendoza, K. M. Tomashek, M. Kotelchuck, W. Barfield, A. Nannini, J. Weiss, et al., "Effect of Late-Preterm Brth and Maternal Medical Conditions on Newborn Morbidity Risk," *Pediatrics* 121, no. 2 (2008): e223–e232; Marvin L. Wang, David J. Dorer, Michael P. Fleming, and Elizabeth A.Catlin, "Clinical Outcomes of Near-Term Infants," *Pediatrics* 114, no. 2 (2004): 372–376.

5   J. Chris Glantz, "Elective Induction vs. Spontaneous Labor Associations and Outcomes," *The Journal of Reproductive Medicine* 50, no. 4 (2005): 235–240; Henci Goer, Mayri Sagady Leslie, and Amy Romano, "The Coalition for Improving Maternity Services: Evidence Basis for the Ten Steps of Mother-Friendly Care. Step 6: Does Not Routinely Employ Practices, Procedures Unsupported by Scientific Evidence," supplement, *The Journal of Perinatal Education* 16, no. S1 (2007): 32S–64S.

6   Joseph F. Smith, *Teachings of Presidents of the Church: Joseph F. Smith* (Salt Lake City, UT: The Church of Jesus Christ of Later-day Saints, 1998), 335.

7   Jenifer Vanderlaan, *The Christian Childbirth Handbook* (Colonie, NY: Birthing Naturally, 2008), 59.

8   Neal A. Maxwell, "Encircled in the Arms of His Love," *Ensign*, November, 2002, http://lds.org/ensign/2002/11/encircled-in-the-arms-of-his-love.

TO ALL MY SISTERS WHO STILL HOPE

By Courtney J. Kendrick

THE VERY FIRST MONTH THAT WE TRIED for a baby and did not conceive, I was devastated. I went to my parent's house, slunk into a fetal position and wailed. It wasn't just a missed cycle that I grieved, it was the unshakable feeling that this was the first of many to come. It was a manifestation of a personal revelation that said, "Infertility is your life's burden."

The second month I thought I might be pregnant. I was late by two hours. In trying for a baby everything is so calculated, you know, timed for best results. Caught up in my tardiness, I had forgotten the lesson that accompanied the previous month's period. This time I was reminded, and given more specific instructions, "It will be five years before your conception."

When we married, my husband and I decided to leave birth control up to the Lord's timing. In all disclosure, I felt that such obvious faith would be rewarded with ample fertility. My husband, on the other hand prayed that the Lord would know that a baby-right-off wasn't prudent for us. In this I learned that giving control to the Lord sometimes feels like chaos. But not necessarily directionless chaos.

Twelve barren months later, I gave into the current belief that infertility after a year is reasonably a medical issue rather than a spiritual one. I called a specialist, and while the phone rang, my head echoed, "Don't do it. Don't do it." Five thousand dollars, a couple month's worth of deflated pride and some strange, fruitless procedures later, we decided to quit.

About that time a friend came to visit a friend whom I wanted to meet. She had also carried the banner of INFERTILE, came to understand that she would be blessed through adoption, and had become a mother to a beautiful daughter some time later.

"I knew I was supposed to adopt," she declared.

And when she said the word "knew" my heart started to flip like a pancake on a hot griddle. I also knew, but I had never declared it to anyone.

Instead, I listened to years of advice and misdirection. Then she asked me, "Do you know?" I nodded.

"I am going to conceive," I said. And when that statement hit the atmospheric pressure of this earth, it transformed itself into light, so I felt like sunshine was figuratively bursting out of my body.

Not only did I know I was going to conceive, but there was no explanation for our situation other than Heavenly Father was in complete control. The same control that we thought we gave him by choice in the first place. He was exercising our right to agency. The baby was coming—coming via my body—all in good time.

Then, for the rest of the time that remained of the initial five years, I swam in the cycle of stability, frustration, and doubt. Close friends and family often questioned my seemingly lackadaisical approach. It was heavy on the spirit and non-existent on the body. Fine, fine, fine. We understand what Heavenly Father is saying, but what is the doctor saying? When in those moments, the Lord would visit me with encouraging inspiration, and I would start the cycle all over again. Many times I had to review what had been said. "You will conceive." "In five year's time." "Your body is perfectly healthy." These statements became more and more specific until, finally, I not only knew that I would conceive, but I knew how old I would be and the actual month it would occur.

Only, on the last month—as a tactic of survival—I decided to give up all hope for motherhood. I poured every last drop back out into the ether and replaced it with current contentment. I needed to be able to say that my happiness was contingent on nothing. I had given my will to the Lord, and His will was done. The hardest thing I had ever done. Or hope to ever have to do.

It has been almost a year since my stalled infertility. I came to know that pregnancy carries with it it's own special bag of insecurities and anxieties. Should I be blessed with that once-assumed ample fertility from here on out, I will be ever so grateful. If not, and my months of wishes return, I will also be grateful. And this is why: Something still grows inside a woman who doesn't conceive a baby. In her grows character that is consumed with confidence, humility, and desire. A symbolic embryo that is hers to nurture and others to behold.

And its birth is phenomenal.

Rejoicing after Recurrent Miscarriages

By Meghan

EVER SINCE I WAS A LITTLE GIRL, I knew that I wanted to be a mom. I loved playing with dolls and couldn't wait to have children of my own. So, when I went off to college, I was eager to meet the man of my dreams, get married, and become a mom. It took longer then I thought it would, and it got very frustrating at times, but I found an amazing man.

When we first found out I was pregnant, it was the most wonderful feeling. I was beyond excited, however that excitement was short lived. At eight weeks, I lost that sweet little life. No one could tell me why. No one could explain it to me.

So we got up the courage to try again. With in a month, I was pregnant again and again so happy. However, once again, this one ended at ten weeks. I remember going to the doctor, and they did an ultrasound and said, "Sorry, you are having a miscarriage. There is really no explanation for it." Once again, the depression set in—the crying and the blaming, but somehow I got through it. I was able to pull on my faith and knew that I would be a mother, but not in my time frame.

After a while, we got up the courage to try again. Again we were successful in getting pregnant. I was so happy when I made it past ten weeks. I thought for sure that this little one would join our family. However, at twelve weeks, this one was also lost. It took all my strength to not give up. That one was the hardest because it was the farthest I had gone. I was able to see her and tell her I loved her. Again they said they could find no reason why I lost the baby or why my body didn't want to stay pregnant. At this point, I didn't think I could take it anymore.

After much prayer and much debate, we tried again. When we got the positive test, I was terrified. I went right into the doctor who informed me that all would be well and that everything was just fine. After I got to about sixteen weeks, I started to relax. I knew that the Lord had finally given me a precious little life. When we had the ultrasound and saw it was a girl, we were overjoyed.

Then, at twenty weeks, I went into preterm labor. After ending up in the hospital, I was put on medication for the rest of the pregnancy to stop the contractions. It wasn't easy, and I was so angry. Why was this happening to me? Why was it so hard for me to be pregnant?

At thirty-nine weeks, and after nineteen weeks of contractions, the doctor induced me. It was so wonderful to know that our little angel was finally coming. I was put on Pitocin, and at about 4 cm I received an epidural. It was amazing. I was able to then enjoy what was going on around me. I was able to be present. I only pushed a few times, and my little angel was there.

Seeing through eyes of trial and tribulation, I truly knew what a wonderful gift she was to me. They gave her to me immediately, and I remember her lying on my tummy and just looking at me. The feeling that I was altogether complete was so overwhelming that I couldn't stop the prayer of thanks to my Heavenly Father who had brought this most amazing gift to me. She was the most beautiful thing that I had ever seen. The love was there instantly. I couldn't imagine a better feeling in the world.

When she was about two years old, we decided to try again to have another baby. We then suffered two more miscarriages. Once more we mustered up the courage, prayed, and figured we would try again. After becoming pregnant, something didn't feel right, so I asked the doctor to do an ultrasound at eight weeks. We found that my uterus had grown, but that there was no baby. They explained that it was a blighted ovum. I was given medication to end the "pregnancy" and then just had to wait. After about three weeks, I started to bleed very heavily (it was Easter Sunday), so severely that I kept collapsing. We went to the doctor the next day and received a D&C.

After that, I thought I was done. I didn't want to go through it again, and I didn't think I could take it anymore. So we decided that we wouldn't try for a while. We went on vacation later that summer. When we got home, we had a surprise: I was pregnant again. Figuring I would lose this one also, I didn't get attached at all. Until we hit about fifteen weeks, and I figured things were OK. We found out it was another girl and again got very excited. However, again at nineteen weeks, I went into labor. I was put back on medication to stop the contractions and made it till thirty-nine weeks, when I was again induced.

I couldn't wait to see this little one. So, when they set me up, I was giddy. My older daughter was with her uncle and aunt who brought her to see me while I was hooked up to everything. I had already received my epidural, so I made sure that I was covered up, and she came in. The excitement in her eyes made me even more excited. She had to leave pretty quickly because things were progressing fast.

My labor with the first went for about four hours. This one I went from 5 to 10 cm in about twenty minutes. It made me sick at first because she dropped so fast. I didn't even push—she had pretty much done all the work herself. Again, as they laid her on my tummy, I was filled with the wonderful sense that I was looking into the eyes of the most precious gift that could ever be given. The love that I felt was amazing. When her sister came to see her, the interaction between them was powerful. I have a picture that was taken, showing them looking at each other like they have known each other for so long. It is one of my favorite pictures.

Now we are on baby number three after having two more miscarriages. I was able to find a doctor who actually looked for a reason and found one. I am in my second trimester and cannot wait to see what the future holds for me with this one.

It's difficult to explain how I was able to make it through eight losses and not fall apart. But there is nothing that can compare to the feeling of self worth and divine purpose I have felt when I have seen my little angels for the first time. Truly each child is a gift from our loving Heavenly Father. Maybe I was given these trials so that I could have more patience with the children that I have and be a better mother? Whatever the reason, I am glad that I have been able to have these experiences.

LATE, BUT NOT YET RIPE

By Cindy Maw

MARTY WAS THE FOURTH of my five children. His due date (which I now think had been miscalculated) was the end of June or the first of July. When the end of July was approaching, and I was still pregnant, I was struggling. This was back in the 1970's when inductions weren't common, and women were allowed to go more than two weeks past their due date.

The three weeks of waiting for his birth had brought some weariness to my soul, but I knew deep down that Marty wasn't ready to come yet. I kept having the impression that this little baby was taking his time coming to earth because he was doing important missionary work in his premortal life. I especially felt like he was spending time with my inactive grandmother who had died a couple of years before Marty's birth. He was enjoying many special spaces with her and sharing the wisdom of his soul.

Yet I mistakenly allowed my weariness to surface at the last appointment with my physician, and he couldn't deal with my tears. He virtually took my choice away about waiting "for the apple to drop on its own." I told the doctor, "It's OK. I can wait for him to come when he is ready." My words fell on deaf ears. Marty's birth was induced on July 21, not without distress for his mother.

My labor was fairly short, six or seven hours, and everything went smoothly. Yet it was obvious, after Marty had been with us for a few hours, that his liver was immature. He was quite jaundiced. Even though according to his "due date" he was long past due, in reality his little body had not been ready to be born. As his life continued, we could see no desire in him to live by the clock. He just wanted to be and do without being moved upon

---

As his life continued, we could see no desire in him to live by the clock. He just wanted to be and do without being moved upon from the outside. He came from a place where there is no time, and I guess he just wanted to keep it that way.

---

from the outside. He came from a place where there is no time, and I guess he just wanted to keep it that way. As I look back, it is no wonder I had to wait so long for him to be born, the concept of time means something different to him than it does everyone else.

He was a precious, tender child. Our spirits, mother and son, were very close. He spent most of his first year on my hip. I didn't want to be without him, and he enjoyed the closeness too. A friend of mine once said to me, "I can't tell where your body ends and his begins." He was my sweet Marty, and it has been a moving and revelatory experience to raise him.

In Good Hands

by Sierra Cory

BEFORE I BECAME PREGNANT, I heard the name Lydia and knew it would be my daughter's name. A few months later, I had a dream where I saw a beautiful little girl with blond pigtails and the widest, most contagious smile. While still dreaming, I thought, "That must be Lydia." I awoke with a start, "Who is Lydia?!" I thought it might be a good time to take a pregnancy test. Positive.

I always knew I wanted a natural childbirth, and so I began researching care providers whose birth philosophies aligned with my own. An ultrasound provided an estimated due date of December 26. I felt so bad, not wanting Lydia to feel gypped having her birthday so close to Christmas. I consoled myself with the silver lining of after-Christmas shopping. I also guessed I would birth post-dates, as my mom had with all five of her children. I decided to aim for a New Year's baby. I thought a birthday of 1/1/11 would be cool. As the days progressed, and New Year's Day came and went, friends joked that I could just go for Plan B, 1/11/11. I thought that certainly I wouldn't still be pregnant by then.

When I was twelve days post-due, I was feeling discouraged, not because I was uncomfortably pregnant but because I was concerned that I had taken that week off work with no sign of a baby. My husband laid his hands on my head and pronounced a blessing of comfort, peace, and patience. I went into labor two days later, waking up with slight cramping in my lower back. The sensation felt promising so I spent the day walking around the neighborhood, kicking a soccer ball, and trying to remain active because it was still early labor.

At exactly forty-two weeks, we took the last of the weekly "belly bump" pictures and set up the birth tub. My doula, Marcie, arrived and had me walk up and down stairs and bounce on an exercise ball. I was shocked that a laboring woman would have to move so much! Marcie stayed with me all night, holding my back when it seemed it would burst. She recommended a hot bath, which eased the contractions and allowed me a bit of sleep. Sadly, I was not progressing much, and my midwife stopped by to monitor Lydia's heart rate. Marcie left with promises to return when things picked back up again. I was left to stay in John's loving hands.

My mom flew in that Monday afternoon. She thought that certainly I would have had the baby by then, but it appeared that Lydia wanted her Grandma there to see her grand entrance. When my mom walked into our bedroom, tears welled up in my eyes. There was no one I wanted to see more than my mom—this woman who had brought me and four other children into this world naturally. Her presence reminded me that her strength ran in my blood, that we women were built for this hefty but surmountable task, and that the legacy of powerful women would be continued with this birth. As more waves of contractions came, my mother's gentle hands gained strength and rubbed the pressure out of my low back. John's fingers found mine and supported me through each new surge.

April, my midwife, arrived that night to check on things and offer encouragement. When I asked when they thought Lydia would arrive, Marcie and April guessed times—admittedly unsure—but settled on: "She will be born before the sun rises."

Again, at Marcie's suggestion, I took a bath to help my body rest. Marcie stayed up with me all night again. The next morning, April returned, worried that she had slept through a phone call saying I had delivered. I had no sense of time during labor, so the fact that I was entering day three of labor was lost on me. At this point, April asked if I wanted to be checked to see how things were progressing. I agreed, and she let me know I was at 4 cm and 80% effaced. She said it takes the longest time to get to that point

THE GIFT OF GIVING LIFE

and that labor should start to progress more quickly. She felt Lydia's head and found that she was indeed in the correct position. I was overjoyed! I had never known such hope.

When I was indeed in active labor, I was allowed into the birth tub. What relief! At one point, I was hugging (and hanging onto) John, feeling so much gratitude and love for those in the room. I couldn't help but kiss John and told him I loved him. I was on an oxytocin high. There was no screaming—merely gentle words of love expressed.

With each surge, I had to stand. April said, "I'm noticing that you're standing. Why is that?" I replied, "Well, I feel like I have to poo!" She asked if she could check me again, and I consented. I was shocked when she said, "Why don't you try giving a few pushes—you're at 9 cm." I remember April telling me that I had demonstrated not simply an act of strength, but strength of character in doing what I knew to be best for my baby. That was one of the greatest compliments I had ever received.

My mother returned to the room. John held one leg while my mom held the other as I pushed for the first time. It was so surreal. At this point, I remember more acts performed by each pair of hands—April brushing my hair back into a ponytail, Allyson applying chapstick to my lips, and John getting into the tub and supporting me from behind. I remember April suddenly having a commanding tone telling me how to push and when. The power in her voice brought me such reassurance. Once I finished a push, she told me to take a big breath and push again. She asked for three pushes, but I would give four because the contraction was still lasting. I had no idea how I was going to get Lydia's head out of me, but I kept listening to the coaching and cheering to guide me.

Finally, my water broke just as Lydia's head shot through and the sensation was incredible. I reached down between my legs and felt her head—it was so soft and so tiny. Finally, with one last surge, the rest of her body slid out into the warmth of the water tub at 5:15 p.m. on January 11. In awe, my hands reached into the water and lifted the most beautiful, precious, and robust baby to my chest. My hands were the first that lifted my baby into this world. Everything about her was perfect.

The birth was exquisite—more than I could have imagined. After all my efforts, no one whisked my healthy baby away. Rather, I could sit peacefully in the tub, supported by my husband, holding this precious new person.

Lydia could hold her head up the moment I placed her on my shoulder, and she stared deeply into her daddy's handsome face. My dad arrived shortly after Lydia was born. I remember his face broadcasting his amazement as he entered the room. He said, "This is sacred! This is how every baby should be born!" With April's guidance, John gingerly cut the cord, and I delivered the placenta with one final surge. April showed me the placenta, which showed no signs of calcification, meaning Lydia's "life support" was functioning beautifully even though she was sixteen days post due date.

As John showered, my wonderful birth team guided me in nursing Lydia. There was so much love in our home that night. Three days of exhausting work, and I received the grandest prize—my beautiful baby girl. Gazing at her tiny, perfect face, I saw that little Lydia was indeed "trailing clouds of glory." John and I, curled around our new baby girl, never knew greater happiness than that night. I could not have done it without my amazing husband and those powerful women surrounding me.

During labor and birth, I remembered being so grateful for the *five women* guiding me through, but re-counting those present only added up to *four*—my mom, with her loving and serving hands; Marcie, with her strong and healing hands; April, with her capable and guiding hands; and Allyson, with her caring and compassionate hands. It was then that I realized that my husband's mother, Karen, who had passed away twenty-two years before, was there watching from the other side of the veil, passing Lydia from one grandma to the next. What a powerful experience to guide my daughter into this world with my hands, shaky but full of love, after being guided through labor and birth by others' loving hands.

CHAPTER FIVE

Preparation

If ye are prepared, ye shall not fear.

D&C 38:30

Choice and Accountability

By Robyn Allgood, AAHCC

I have set before you life and death, blessing and cursing: therefore choose life, that both thou and thy seed may live.

DEUTERONOMY 30:19

I remember waking up the morning after the birth of my first child. I had quickly fallen in love with my beautiful baby girl, but it was difficult to enjoy the moment. I was groggy and weak. I later saw the pictures and realized that my body had not reacted well to many of the medications I was administered. My body was swollen to the point that I had black eyes, and I could barely move without wincing in pain from the stitches across my abdomen. What I did not realize at the time was that there were choices I could have made before my delivery to help prevent this outcome. Though we can't control everything in regard to our birthing experiences, we can increase our power to choose through carefully preparing, seeking the Lord's guidance, and obeying the promptings of the Spirit.

Agency—the right to choose between good and evil and to act for ourselves—is the cornerstone of the plan of salvation.[1] Another way of defining *agency* is "the freedom to choose." I recognized after my first birth that I had given away my agency in some ways and had to live with those consequences. I chose to only prepare myself for one kind of birth. I ignored the other options. I would now have a label attached to my records—"high risk"—and would have limited options for future births. It became apparent to me that I could either give away my agency or increase my agency according to my willingness to take responsibility for being informed regarding my options.

For my next birth, I prepared with a kind of zeal that surprised me. I decided to test the promise that our weaknesses could become strengths

Agency, Choice, and Consequence

By Rixa Freeze, PhD

There are three basic situations in which we must exercise our agency: our individual choices, institutional policies and care providers' actions, and uncontrollable circumstances.

INDIVIDUAL CHOICES

We are free to exercise our agency in our individual preferences regarding pregnancy, birth, and breast-feeding. These are choices that we have the most control over. Along with this right to choose comes the responsibility to accept the consequences of our actions.

INSTITUTIONAL POLICIES AND CARE PROVIDERS' ACTIONS

Most women interact with both institutions and care providers during the course of their pregnancies and births. Choices that other people make have consequences for us—for example, how a certain care provider might act at a birth. We have some control over this, in that we can do research, prepare, and choose care providers carefully, knowing that there may be times that we are at the mercy of others' agency.

No matter the institutional policies or care providers' preferences, we have the divine right and responsibility to exercise our agency. We can stand up for these rights—often supported by the law—if we are told that something is not allowed. We can familiarize ourselves with our legal rights and insist upon informed consent and informed refusal.

UNCONTROLLABLE CIRCUMSTANCES

Finally, there are uncontrollable circumstances, which are random events unrelated to agency, such as miscarriage, premature labor, birth defects, and disease. We can still use our agency by choosing how to react to these situations. Even though you cannot control all the outcomes of pregnancy and birth, you can prepare yourself for challenges that may arise physically, emotionally, and most important, spiritually.

(see Ether 12:27). Before I was even pregnant again, I was devouring birth books, weighing options, and searching for answers through study and prayer. When I did become pregnant, my husband and I accelerated our preparations to include a comprehensive childbirth class that taught exercises to prepare me for birth, nutrition, informed decision making, and relaxation. The instructor provided materials that helped me to confront my mental and emotional roadblocks and caused me to search even deeper for personal revelation regarding the options available to my husband and me.

In contrast to our first birth, our focus moved from temporal matters, such as having all of our baby stuff, to a more complete approach that included our physical, mental, emotional, and spiritual needs. I felt this approach increased my freedom to choose. We were more aware of the options available to us and were then able to access the Lord's help in exercising our agency as it related to our growing family.

CATEGORIES OF AGENCY AND CONSEQUENCES

Rixa Freeze, PhD, identified three basic categories of how agency and consequences relate to childbearing in our lives:

- Individual choices
- Institutional policies and care provider's choices
- Uncontrollable circumstances

In all of these categories, we can mitigate the negative consequences and seek out the positive consequences by researching, praying, pondering, seeking blessings, and following the Spirit.[2]

THE COMPONENTS OF FREEDOM

In order for us to fully exercise our freedom, there are four components that need to be present:

- An intelligent being
- Knowledge of good and evil
- Availability of choices
- The power to execute or carry out such choices[3]

We are intelligent beings who can act and not be acted upon. I often hear women tell me that their births have to be a particular way because their caregivers told them a certain way is in their best interests. Whether the particular course of action is needed, I don't know. What I do know is that a woman can and should be aware that she can act, whether or not that action is in agreement with her caregiver. It is risky to go into a birth and expect that our caregivers and hospital staff will take care of everything. Our approach to childbearing should be one of accountability.

Knowledge is the second principle in increasing our freedom and makes it possible for us to find out if a course of action is right or wrong for us. God encourages us to increase our spiritual and temporal knowledge. One without the other is limiting. For example, we could study everything there is to know about childbirth, but without seeking the Lord's guidance about what we learn, we will be limited. Oliver Cowdery was chastised for neglecting to do his own study before asking God:

> Behold, you have not understood; you have supposed that I would give it unto you, when you took no thought save it was to ask me. But, behold, I say unto you, that you must study it out in your mind; then you must ask me if it be right, and if it is right I will cause that your bosom shall burn within you; therefore, you shall feel that it is right. (D&C 9:7–8)

God can only help us according to our willingness to seek out knowledge. He expects us to do our own research and then come to Him in prayer. Our willingness to increase our knowledge unlocks the powers of heaven. This leads to the next component of freedom.

The third component necessary for us to exercise our agency is the availability of choices. Choosing not to learn about our options leaves us with fewer options. For example, I have heard women say that their caregivers or hospitals do not allow VBAC (vaginal birth after cesarean) deliveries, so the women do not have a choice. The reality is that there are other options. Women can go to different caregivers or hospitals. Some women even choose to birth at home or at a birth center. Such routes may take extra work, but exercising our agency requires effort. President Thomas S. Monson reminded us of the following: "Decisions are constantly before us. To make them wisely, courage is needed—the courage to say no, the courage to say yes. Decisions do determine destiny."[4] If you are uncomfortable with the way that your caregiver manages your care, look for other choices available in your area. The truth is that if you do not know your options, you do not have any.

The last principle of freedom is the power to carry out or execute the choices available to us. As Elder Tad R. Callister explained, "We may have knowledge of good and evil; we may even have choices placed before us; but unless we have power to fulfill, then our freedom is but a facade."[5] We have been told in the scriptures that we are powerful beings that should be "anxiously engaged in a good cause, and do many things of [our] own free will, and bring to pass much righteousness; for the power is in [us], wherein [we] are agents unto [ourselves]" (D&C 58:27–28). In order to increase our power, we are to increase our knowledge of earthly and heavenly things. The more you study about birth from secular and spiritual standpoints, the more your power to choose is strengthened. While earthly power alone has its limits, God's power does not:

> Both earthly and spiritual power (which ultimately are but one power) constitute the power of godhood for gods 'have all power' (D&C 132:20). With each new power acquired, we develop greater control not only of the elements but of our destiny. In this way we become the driver, not the driven—the cause rather than the effect. We act for ourselves rather than be acted upon.[6]

OBEDIENCE

To most people, the idea of obedience might seem to take away our freedom when in reality it increases it. One way of looking at it is in the context of our health. Someone who obeys the laws of good health—such as maintaining good nutrition, avoiding harmful substances, and exercising regularly—is free to experience life more fully because of their good health. They are unfettered by addictions and less likely to experience illness and disease. They are promised blessings:

> And all saints who remember to keep and do these sayings, walking in obedience to the commandments, shall receive health in their navel and marrow to their bones; And shall find wisdom and great treasures of knowledge, even hidden treasures; And shall run and not be weary, and shall walk and not faint. (D&C 89:18–20)

What blessings wait for you as you exercise your agency? Elder Russell M. Nelson has reminded us, "Obedience allows God's blessings to flow without constraint. He will bless His obedient children with freedom from bondage and misery. And He will bless them with more light."[7]

I have felt the truth of this statement as I have obeyed the counsel to study my scriptures daily. I look forward to the "light" and "great treasures of knowledge" that will be opened up to me each morning. As I have studied birth from secular and spiritual standpoints, my eyes have been opened and my faith strengthened. I have felt my ability to choose increase as I rely more fully on God than man for wisdom in making choices for myself and my babies. Any time we submit our will to God's will, we actually increase our freedom. This act of faith helps us develop self-mastery and restraint, no longer being subject to the whims of the "natural man."

INFORMED CONSENT

As a childbirth educator, I teach my students the importance of informed consent. Informed consent is "a patient's consent to a medical or surgical procedure or to participation in a clinical study after being properly advised of the relevant medical facts and the risks involved."[8] Is there true informed consent when your provider only offers one kind of information? For example, if you were only told about the benefits of a test and not the risks involved, you are likely to consent to taking the test. This limits a person's agency. Another example could be when a caregiver only provides one option. You will only have one option available to you unless you choose a different caregiver. It is a good idea to study as much as you can about the tests and procedures offered to you. It is also helpful to interview more than one caregiver and tour more than one birth location. You will find a wide variety of "required" procedures and opinions related to pregnancy and birth. Searching out your options with the help of the Lord will help you to identify what risks and benefits you are most comfortable with.

BIRTH PLANS

The term *birth plan* can be misleading because it sounds as if we can simply write out a plan for our birth and it will be followed. In actuality, it is good to think of a birth plan as a birth preferences list. It is not a list of demands. It is meant to give your birth team an idea of your desires regarding your experience while remaining open to the priority of a healthy mom and a healthy baby. Sometimes we exercise our agency in a way that we did not expect, like choosing an intervention we would have preferred to avoid but was needed. A couple planning a home birth may not think they would need a birth plan, but it is important to be prepared for the possibility of a transfer to a hospital. It is a comfort to me that when we are unsure, we can pray for the Lord's help in making decisions that involve our pregnancy, birth, and postpartum experiences.

There are many resources online to help you understand your options. Simply do a search for *birth plan* to get started. In addition to listing your wishes in regard to interventions and childbirth options, do not forget to list the preferences you have in regard to your faith. For example, because I am a Latter-day Saint I do not like to hear the Lord's name taken in vain or used flippantly. Had I known that the midwife assisting in one of my births would repeat the Lord's name over and over, I would have included my preference in my birth plan so that she would have known to respect my beliefs. If you plan to have a blessing or prayer during your birth, you could mention that also.

Lynn Clark Callister, RN, PhD, FAAN, a professor of nursing in Brigham Young University's College of Nursing, coauthored a study on spirituality and childbearing. She stated, "Our research illustrates that for most women, childbirth is a deeply spiritual experience. As health care providers, we need to recognize and support this evidence, and listen to women's voices to guide their care." This same study also recommends caregivers ask, "Do you have any spiritual beliefs that will help us better care for you?"[9] Most caregivers want you to feel respected while under their care; they may just not know how to do that as it concerns your religion. Don't wait for them to ask—it is a sign of respect to let them know. (The "Unity with Care Providers" essay, on page 433, also provides some great advice on birth plans.) A birth preferences list can help you prepare for your birth as you prioritize your feelings about the available options.

You have the Lord's assurance that "if ye are prepared ye shall not fear" (D&C 38:30). Agency is a gift. Giving life is a gift. Knowledge is power to execute these gifts. It is my hope that as women we can make choices that enable us to "choose life, that both thou and thy seed may live" (Deuteronomy 30:19). Let us not forget these words of President David O. McKay: "Next to the bestowal of life itself, the right to direct that life is God's greatest gift to man."[10v]

---

1   The Church of Jesus Christ of Latter-day Saints, *Gospel Principles* (Salt Lake City, UT: The Church of Jesus Christ of Latter-day Saints, 2009), 17.

2   E-mail message to the GOGL Google group.

3   Tad R. Callister, *Infinite Atonement*, (Salt Lake City, UT: Deseret Book, 2000), 252.

4   Thomas S. Monson, "The Three Rs of Choice," *Ensign*, November 2010, http://lds.org/ensign/2010/11/the-three-rs-of-choice.

5   Tad R. Callister, *Infinite Atonement*, (Salt Lake City, UT: Deseret Book, 2000), 256.

6   Tad R. Callister, *Infinite Atonement*, (Salt Lake City, UT: Deseret Book, 2000), 257.

7   Russell M. Nelson, "Face the Future with Faith," *Ensign*, May 2011, 34–35.

8   Dictionary.com, s.v. "informed consent," http://dictionary.reference.com/browse/informed+consent.

9   "New Data Show Connection between Childbirth and Spirituality," May 27, 2010, Lamaze International, http://www.lamaze.org/IntheNews/NewsReleases/NewDataShowConnectionBetween-ChildbirthandSp/tabid/878/Default.aspx.

10   David O. McKay, in Conference Report, April 1950, 32.

If Ye Are Prepared, Ye Shall Not Fear

By Valerie Walker

WHEN I SAW THE POSITIVE PREGNANCY TEST, I was excited and nervous. Not really nervous about having my first child, but nervous about the giving birth part of that equation. I began to throw my efforts into studying all about the birth process because I wanted to be as prepared as I possibly could so that I could turn the nerves into complete confidence.

Growing up, we weren't much of a doctor-going family. My mom had learned from her mom that the body needs time to heal on its own, and doctor intervention could sometimes prevent your own immune system from learning how to heal itself. Of course there are instances where a doctor is needed, and for those times we are grateful for them. In my reading about the standard hospital birth, I found that many of interventions used weren't necessary and could lead to an unnecessary C-section. I was appalled to find out that the local hospital's C-section rate was at 30%.

I knew in my heart that giving birth did not have to be major surgery, so I decided to take matters into my own hands. In addition, I've always had a needle phobia, and cold, smelly hospitals have never appealed to me. So, I was already leaning toward a natural home water birth, even before

I found out that my own mother and grandmother had birthed all of their children naturally.

When I told some friends of my desire to have a natural birth, they thought I was crazy. "Your mom is a strong woman. I'm not surprised she could do it, but you? You really think you can handle all the pain?" This was one response I got, and it made me question my strength and ability to go through with it.

This scripture ran through my mind at that time: "If ye are prepared, ye shall not fear" (D&C 38:30). I soon realized that I was cut out to do this, and that Heavenly Father had created me to do this. From then on, I moved forward in my research with confidence, knowing that with the right preparation, I could indeed have the natural birth I so desired.

With my husband on board, we took a twelve-week Bradley Method® course. We also read several books on natural birth as well as countless positive natural birth stories. We practiced the different relaxation techniques we were taught. Throughout the pregnancy, I ate as healthy as I could and exercised regularly. I wanted to do everything I possibly could to have a healthy birth.

As my due date drew closer, I did not fear. I was only excited and confident. The phrase "knowledge is power" rang true for us. In my heart, I knew Heavenly Father was happy with my efforts and preparation. I knew that having a drug-free home water birth was going to be the best choice for me and my so-anxiously-awaited baby girl.

The week leading up to my due date, I started having contractions at about the same time every night. I knew that this "prelabor" was getting my body ready for the big event. Friday, May 22nd started out like a normal day. With my due date approaching in just two days, I wanted to do everything I could to get this baby coming out on time. As early evening approached, my husband and I decided to do a little walking. We went to an outdoor mall and every minute or so I had to sit down and put my feet up. After I couldn't bear to walk another step, my husband got the car and picked me up. We ate some dinner at home and started a movie. That's when the contractions started. I figured they would go away after a while, just like every other night that week. Instead, they seemed to be a little more intense and getting a little closer together.

Needless to say, I didn't watch much of the movie because I couldn't sit still. I knew that if I changed activity and the contractions were still just as strong, then it could be real labor. So I walked around the apartment, ate some canned apricots, and sure enough they were getting stronger and closer together. After the movie, my husband timed them with me. I got to the point where I couldn't stand through them anymore, so I assumed my labor "sleep" position on the bed.

The knowledge I had gained in my classes and personal reading not only helped me be more confident leading up to the birth, but during the labor I was able to visualize and understand what my body was going through and to not be afraid of it. I was also able to know the signs of the different stages of labor (which would later help us in deciding when to call the midwife). During contractions, my husband would try the different techniques we had practiced. It only took a few contractions for me to realize what I needed from him: a strong back rub and peacefully describing a beautiful place we had been to in Europe or on a beach. I stayed pretty relaxed, although the pain was getting very strong. It was at this point that we both realized that our baby would be coming soon.

Between contractions, my husband frantically got things ready. He had to inflate the water birth tub, fill it with water, lay out all of our birthing supplies for the midwives to use, and gather the towels and sheets we would need for after the birth. In addition, he dimmed the lights, lit all the candles, and played the soft music we had chosen weeks before. Finally at around 4 a.m., my husband called our midwife. After assessing the situation and realizing I was pretty far along in labor, she made her way over.

At this point I was still on the bed, very seriously trying to relax and let things happen. Between contractions, the midwife checked the baby's heartbeat with a Doppler and checked to see how far dilated I was—the only exam I would receive through the entire labor. Thankfully, I was already 7 cm dilated. Soon after, the two student midwives arrived and assisted with the preparations.

After laboring awhile longer, things were getting extremely intense so I was helped into the water birth tub, just steps away from my bed. The warm water immediately relaxed me on a whole different level. However, the contractions that ensued once I was in the tub were indescribable. It was the most intense pain I had ever experienced. But I knew this meant I would see my little girl very soon. I was encouraged by the midwives and my husband to keep relaxing and to let my body do its work. Soon, I couldn't fight the urge to push anymore. With my husband in the tub with me, ready to catch the baby at any moment, I started the forty-five minutes of pushing. I was relieved to find that pushing for me was so much easier than relaxing. The moment I could feel the hair on her head was one I will never forget. Knowing this pain was ending and that there was a light at the end of the tunnel was so extremely comforting.

When she came out, my husband caught her in the warm water and gave her to me. I couldn't believe that I had actually given birth to this beautiful baby girl. This precious moment in my life was one of the most sacred and spiritual I had ever experienced. I felt so connected to our Father in Heaven and Jesus Christ. The fact that I had just participated in creation and giving of life was a humbling thought. This little baby was sent to me directly from Heavenly Father.

The fact that she was born without pain medication in her system is something that I am proud of. The fact that I was able to fully participate in the birth of my baby without being numbed physically and mentally is also something that I am proud of. And the fact that my husband was able to participate in the birth was something we both knew would be really special. The eight hour labor was intense but well worth it. I truly felt that Heavenly Father was with me, giving me the strength to do what I needed to do to bring Ava Cheyenne into the world. We are truly blessed.

Growing Faith

By Nicole

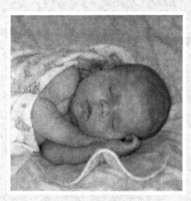

WITH THE BEGINNING INKLINGS of my first pregnancy, all the decisions that had to be made weighed heavily on me. I knew I wanted a natural birth and thought I could get that in my local hospital if I was assertive enough. When my pregnancy ended in a miscarriage made traumatic by the treatment by the hospital staff, I started looking for other options.

With the next pregnancy, although nervous at first, I chose a free standing birth center three hours from home. I knew this was my answer. That is where I delivered my first-born son.

My second child, a daughter this time, was supposed to be born at the same birth center. My husband had given me a blessing towards the end of my pregnancy that promised I would be calm and know what I needed to do throughout my labor. When I went into labor, I was very centered and able to focus. Throughout my five-and-a-half-hour labor, I kept telling my husband and midwife that it was time to go. In spite of being only twenty minutes from the birthing center, I delivered my daughter into my husband's hands on an off-ramp of a major interstate!

Through all my pregnancies, I had been adamantly against home birth (for me). While I had read a lot about home births, and even attended one of a friend's, the idea was still very scary to me. After delivering our daughter in our truck, it suddenly seemed more doable. Gradually, over the next year and a half, the idea kept floating around my head.

Then I was pregnant and terrified because I didn't feel comfortable with my hospital nor with my previous midwife at the birthing center. But I had to birth somewhere, right? I couldn't get home birth out of my head.

After discussing it with my husband and praying about it together, we decided to make an initial appointment with a home birth midwife to see how we felt. I remember sitting with her in her living room and just feeling this sense of rightness come over me. We all felt it and knew that we were to make this journey together. This pregnancy ended up being different on so many levels. The weight of the responsibility for this birth hit our shoulders like never before, as we were totally in charge. My second daughter began having a lot of challenges, leading us to suspect Autism, and I developed antepartum depression.

On the one hand, I had such personal care; my midwife held my hand whenever I needed it. However, on the other hand, even though I had received my answer and knew this baby needed to be born at home, there were moments of fear, anxiety, and of being overwhelmed. While I have never minded standing out in a crowd before, I became overwhelmed with the idea of telling people that I was birthing at home. I didn't want to explain my choice, and I didn't want what felt like a very sacred and personal decision talked over by everyone I knew. I also had a tough time fulfilling my Church calling—teaching a very difficult and large Primary class. After church each Sunday, I would come home and have contractions from stress and anxiety.

After much prayer, we asked that I be released. I felt so guilty, so overwhelmed, so alone. It was through priesthood blessings, prayer, and promptings that I learned that the Lord doesn't give us the entire picture at once. He gives us just enough to help us do it ourselves and go on down the path He has laid before us. I didn't know what would be around the bend, but I trusted that, with His help and the support of my husband and midwife, I could make it through.

As these promptings and impressions would come, and when I was given a blessing, I would write them down in my journal. This was such a blessing to me! I could go back and pour over them and be reminded and uplifted again and again. These became my references, my guides that I could read to regain direction when I again become lost in the fear or the anxiety of my depression. I learned that, as we exhibit our faith, it will grow. It will grow strong enough to carry us through the trials that inevitably come. Our second daughter, our third child, was born at home. It was a Mary Poppins birth—practically perfect in every way.

Then came another chance to try our faith. The Lord told me it was time for another spirit to enter our home. Suddenly I was overwhelmed with fear that my depression would again surface with pregnancy. Yet I knew there was a baby boy who was anxiously waiting to join us in our family. Still I balked; I was scared. I wanted to take a few months more to do all I could to ensure a depression-free pregnancy and postpartum period. It was then that the Lord gently admonished me in a blessing. I was told that, while the health of the mother is important, the mission of motherhood (at least for me) superseded my health. I was then promised that, as I obeyed, the way would be made for me to be made whole again.

That pregnancy was my best pregnancy. I felt good. I had energy. I didn't have depression, and I haven't since. I have my bad days, but nothing like the all-encompassing anxiety that I lived with for so long. My fourth child, a second son was born at home almost a year ago. My birthing journey from hospital to birthing center to truck to home all led me to step out from my safe places and rely on the Lord's plan for my births. I have learned that the Lord truly can direct us in all of our paths.

154

Mother-Centered Baby Showers

By Robyn Allgood, AAHCC

Having their hearts knit together in unity and in love one towards another.

MOSIAH 18:21

―――――――

For twelve years, I was the only daughter in my family. I had wished for a sister over and over as I blew out candles on my birthday cake or watched a shooting star. I said many heartfelt prayers, asking Heavenly Father to please grant me a little sister. This was before routine ultrasounds revealed the sex of the baby, so I literally jumped for joy the day my sister was born. I grew up feeling very protective of my long-awaited sister—almost like another mother to her, but at the same time her best friend.

As we passed through different stages in our lives, my sister and I remained close even though there were so many years between us. I was so excited when she told me she was expecting. As she prepared for her first birth, I yearned to give her something of the hope and desires I had for her. I had loved this girl before she was even conceived in my mother's womb, and I desired to infuse her with the kind of wisdom and strength that I knew would help her in her transition to motherhood.

Instead of a typical baby shower, I planned a mother's blessing for her, also called a blessingway (not to be confused with the Native American blessingway ceremony,[1] which is sacred and is not represented in the context of this essay). Every day, not only are babies born but mothers are too. Unfortunately, very little is done to acknowledge the new mother's passage. While baby showers honor the new little life entering a home, a mother-centered shower is intended to honor the transition of a woman as she leaves behind maidenhood and embraces motherhood. So what exactly is a mother's blessing or blessingway?

A *rite of passage* is defined as "any important act or event that serves to mark a passage from one stage of life to another."[2] A mother's blessing honors this transition. This concept really is not that foreign. Latter-day Saint history is laden with examples of women blessing other women in a variety of ways. Early Latter-day Saint midwives were even called and set apart to bless the mothers whom they assisted in childbirth. (See "Mother's Blessings in the Early Church" and "Our Latter-day Saint Birthing Legacy," on pages 165 and 19.) In addition, in the New Testament we read of the Savior being honored as He prepared to pass from one stage of life to the next. Birth is a powerful symbol of Christ's Atonement, death, and resurrection, and we can learn from reading about how He prepared for these life-changing events. As women gather to honor a woman as a part of a mother's blessing, the hope is that the mother's blessing will turn the hearts of those in attendance to the Savior.

A mother's blessing can be planned in place of or in addition to a traditional baby shower. The two events can also be carefully and thoughtfully combined. A new mother may need many of the essentials that a baby shower provides yet still benefit from the empowering experience of a mother-centered shower. However, women should not overlook the importance of honoring a mother whether this is her first, fifth, or tenth baby. Each pregnancy, birth, and child is unique and presents itself with different challenges and blessings. A blessingway can enable a mother to connect with her unborn child, pondering her own needs and the needs of this special baby. When planning a mother-centered shower, it is important to set the tone, invite honored guests, use a sacred space, and plan empowering activities to honor and serve the mother.

"A blessingway is a special ceremony designed to acknowledge, honor, and celebrate a woman's journey into motherhood. In contrast to a baby shower, the main goal of a blessingway is to provide a loving place where an expectant mother can explore the challenges and joys that lie before her as she approaches childbirth and motherhood. Surrounded by the most important women in her life, she will gain a sense of power, confidence, and support that will help her before, during, and after the birth of her child."[3]

SET THE TONE

In planning a mother's blessing, it is important to take into account what kind of spirit or mood the gathering will have. You might consider the following questions as you and the mother determine the tone you desire for the event:

- Is this the first, fifth, or tenth (etc.) baby?
- Is she expecting multiples (twins, triplets, etc.)?
- Are there special circumstances about the birth to take into account (VBAC, planned cesarean section, difficulties with pregnancy, fears, desires, etc.)?
- Does the mother prefer a more upbeat or serious mood?
- Will this baby join the family through birth or adoption?
- Is there a scripture, quote, or song of special meaning to the mother on which to focus?

INVITE HONORED GUESTS

A *ritual* is defined as "a ceremonial act or action."[4] In preparation for His Atonement, the Savior began by gathering with His Twelve Apostles in a carefully chosen space to eat their Passover feast (Mark 14:12). This event was to be an intimate moment for ritual and ceremony among His closest friends and confidants, "and he said unto them, with desire I have desired to eat this Passover with you before I suffer" (Luke 22: 15). They ate together, and then the Savior taught them of the sacrament to be instituted in remembrance of His great atoning sacrifice. The sacrament is a sacred ordinance. It is a ceremonial act that is meant to turn our hearts and minds to the Savior. Childbirth is also a sacred event that is intended to turn our hearts and minds and even bodies to the Savior.

Jesus took great care in choosing who would be with Him for this ceremonial event. It was an opportunity for Him to teach and prepare those He loved for the change that was about to take place in His life. One of the most important components of a mother's blessing is who is invited. It should be an honor to be invited because those who are asked to attend are considered to be the women closest to the mother and are also likely to have influenced her life for good. The tone you set for the event will help determine who will be invited. This may not be the kind of gathering to which you invite every neighbor, as you might for a tradi-

---

Just as birth is not a requirement to become a mother, a mother's blessing could be appropriate in a variety of situations: adoption, foster care, gaining a child through marriage, pregnancy or infant loss, or death of a child.

---

tional baby shower. The individuals invited to a mother's blessing are the women considered to have had a hand in preparing the mother for pregnancy, childbirth, and motherhood. They should be comfortable with the idea that this is a spiritual and empowering event. Most of the time, a blessingway is exclusively for women, but it can include couples, if desired. Above all, it is the mother who will decide who is included on the guest list.

USE A SACRED SPACE

In preparation for His rite of passage, the Savior sent his disciples to find a sacred space in which they could take part in their Passover feast (Luke 22:8–13). Christ also knew that in this space, He would share with His disciples important teachings of the sacrament and service. He therefore cared very much about where this event was to take place.

> A number of houses featured a permanent structure on the second story. These upper rooms were sometimes called summer rooms, and hosts often used them as guest chambers. When a family entertained a large number of guests, the most honored were assigned the upper chamber.[5]

Next to the temple, the home is considered to be most sacred. The home of the mother-to-be is the ideal, but not required, location of the mother-centered shower. Wherever you plan to carry out the event, it should be private, welcoming, and comfortable, especially to the mother you are honoring. Hopefully there is enough space and seating to be in a circle. Removing chairs and being seated nearer to one another on the floor may contribute to the intimacy of the gathering.

PLAN SACRED ACTIVITIES

The first event in the preparation for the Savior's passage is found in Mark 14:3–9 and John 12:3–8. Christ's feet and head were anointed with a very precious ointment called spikenard. This anointing was a very tender moment for the Savior. When others complained of the expense of the ointment, Christ lovingly said of Mary, "Why trouble ye her? She hath wrought a good work on me" (Mark 14:6). He further explained, "She hath done what she could: she is come aforehand to anoint my body to the burying" (Mark 14:8). Mary offered the Savior what she could. It was an act of profound love that brought our Lord great comfort before He was to suffer and die for us. Would not the Savior deserve to be so honored before He was to offer his life in our behalf? The Bible Dictionary tells us that "anciently anointing was done for reasons both secular and sacred." We can read further of the customs in Christ's day:

> Not only were weddings elaborate, but so were banquets and meals to celebrate holidays or to entertain special guests. A host would welcome each guest with a kiss and would place wreaths upon the heads of the most honored. A servant would anoint the heads of the special guests with oil, and the host would escort the guests to the table, seating them by age or importance.[6]

After Mary honored Jesus in a very private manner, He was then honored in a more public manner as He entered Jerusalem for the Passover feast: "On the next day much people that were come to the feast, when they heard that Jesus was coming to Jerusalem, took branches of palm trees and went forth to meet him, and cried, Hosanna: Blessed is the King of Israel that cometh in the name of the Lord" (John 12:12–13). The people laid palm branches in His path to honor Him. Palms were necessary for the survival of people during Christ's time. The use of palms for this event was a powerful symbol: "Strewing palm branches at Jesus' feet was, then, a symbol of the giving up of worldly goods, both necessities and luxuries."[7] This event was known as the triumphal entry and was symbolic of the Savior's triumph over sin and death. Although the Atonement had not yet come to pass, the triumphal entry was a powerful preparation for the life-changing transition to come. A mother's blessing is a celebration that honors the triumph of childbirth before the event takes place. It is a symbolic gesture to honor the mother-to-be before she is crowned with the glory of her child.

As a part of the Last Supper, the Savior also took the time to wash the feet of His Apostles. This was a very intimate moment that He used to teach His disciples: "So after he had washed their feet, and had taken

---

Don't let the idea of a mother's blessing intimidate you. You can easily bring in this sacred feeling to a normal baby shower by implementing one or two of the ideas.

---

his garments, and was set down again, he said unto them, know ye what I have done to you? Ye call me Master and Lord: and ye say well; for so I am. If I then, your Lord and Master, have washed your feet; ye also ought to wash one another's feet" (John 13:12–14). Washing the feet of guests was a common ritual in Christ's day performed by the servants of the house.[8] During the Last Supper, the Savior washed His disciples' feet, leaving them with a powerful lesson of service.

Before retiring to the Garden of Gethsemane, the Savior sang a hymn with His disciples: "And when they had sung an hymn, they went out into the mount of Olives" (Matthew 26:30). I do not know which hymn the Lord chose to sing; however, I'm sure it brought Him comfort and maybe even echoed through His mind as He pled for strength to endure His sufferings.

These examples from the Savior's life reveal elements that can be used to plan a mother-centered shower. A mother-centered shower can be as elaborate or simple as you want it to be. The tone of the event will help determine the kind of activities that will be most appropriate. You may want to discuss with the mother-to-be her comfort level with the activities you are planning. For example, some mothers would love to do a belly cast and others would not. As I was planning my sister's special day, I kept in mind that this would be a new kind of experience for everyone involved, including myself. As a result, it was fairly simple but still very meaningful. The following are some ideas for activities:

- Have each guest introduce herself and share a statement honoring the women who came before. This could include saying something like, "I am _____, daughter of _____, granddaughter of _____, great-granddaughter of _____," and so forth. It is a good idea to let guests know that they will be introducing themselves in this manner so they can be prepared. In addition, each guest could also recognize her relationship to the other guests by saying something like, "My name is _____, I am the sister of _____, friend to _____, and niece to _____." The mother for whom the shower is given could introduce the guests, sharing a little bit about each person and how the mother has benefitted from the person in her journey through maidenhood, marriage, pregnancy, birth, and/or motherhood.

- Ask each guest to take a turn sharing a blessing, wish, thought, poem, quote, or scripture for the mother. These notes could be compiled in a folder, binder, or scrapbook for the mother to keep.

- Make a bracelet or necklace for the mother. Many of the mother's blessings that I have attended have included each guest sharing her note and providing a bead to accompany it. The bead is to be symbolic of the note in some way. After each note has been shared, the guests can create a bracelet or necklace. (Even individuals who cannot attend may send their beads and notes to be read.)

- Make a blessingway quilt. Ask each guest to bring a square for a quilt to be made for the baby. The quilt could be made at the gathering or at a later time, depending on time constraints.

- Wash the mother's feet in water scented with essential oils. (Be aware that some essential oils are not recommended for use during pregnancy, such as oregano. Lavender and jasmine, among others, will work.) Washing the mother's feet could be followed by a foot massage. Some women even enjoy having their hair brushed and styled. The idea is that the mother be pampered in one way or another.

- Adorn the mother with a wreath of flowers or a lei.

- Tie one another together in a circle. Pass around yarn or string as you stand or sit in a circle. Wind the string around each person's wrists to bind everyone together. As you do this, you can repeat, "From women we are born," or something else that has meaning to the mother. After the binding is completed, cut the string, leaving a bracelet for each guest to wear home. This is the guests' reminder of the unity of womanhood and to keep the mother in their thoughts. After the birth of the baby, the bracelet can be cut off.

- Give a candle to each guest to take home as a reminder of the mother. If the mother so desires, form a phone tree so that after the mother goes into labor, each guest can be notified to light her candle, letting it to burn until the baby is born.

Would you love to have a blessingway but few family and friends are near you? Consider a virtual blessingway, mailing wishes and beads via the postal service.

- Sing a hymn, lullaby, or other song that is of special meaning to the mother. The mother may even have a song in mind that she has chosen to sing throughout her pregnancy, during her labor, and when nurturing her little baby.

- Serve food that will enhance the experience—the food doesn't have to be elaborate. Keep in mind the nutritional needs of the pregnant mother and any allergies or preferences she may have.

- Gifts can be an optional part of a mother-centered shower. You might consider asking that gifts be for the mother instead of the baby, that gifts be handmade, or even that a freezer meal be given to the mother to use after her baby comes to help her ease into her normal routine. Again, gifts are not required, especially if a baby shower has already been held for the mother in which she has been given many of the essentials.

There are certainly many other activities you could include. Be creative, and look for more ideas on the Gift of Giving Life website. When making plans for the appropriate activities to include, you might ask, "How would Jesus honor this woman as she prepares for this child?"

So how did my sister, Rachelle, feel about her mother's blessing? Looking back on the experience after giving birth to her little boy, Eli, she shared with me her thoughts,

> My mother's blessing was something I will always cherish. It was a beautiful highlight in my preparation to become a mother. As these women that I admire took turns sharing their Mother's blessing or birth wish, I felt surrounded by love and overcome with support and empowerment. Childbirth and motherhood is so meaningful. As you can imagine, many eyes were emotional as each woman shared her wisdom or desire for me and my baby. Each birth wish became so meaningful for me, not just in childbirth, but also in difficult life situations. I have gained strength as a woman, confidence as a daughter of God, and wisdom as a mother. I am so grateful for the strong women who have preceded me. In honoring me in this way, these women had done more for my child than a traditional baby shower could have.

USING SYMBOLISM

There are many powerful stories in the scriptures that reference childbirth. The scriptures are rich with the symbolism of birth. Trees, vines, fruit, seeds, water, blood, baptism, and resurrection are just a few examples of symbols that may refer to birth. One symbol that is especially important is that of a circle. It is ideal to form a circle among the guests and mother because "the circle is an ancient and universal symbol of community, unity, and feminine power."[9] The circle also is a symbol of having no end, being in one eternal round, bringing to mind the eternal nature of life. When a mother takes part in the miracle of birth, she is contributing to the eternal circle of life. In a circle, "we open ourselves to each other, working together instead of working alone. We make trusting connections with one another in our circle and contribute in mutually supportive ways."[10] Mother-centered showers enable the mother to feel "encircled about eternally in the arms of his love" (2 Nephi 1:15) because of the women who surround her. As we join as sisters to honor one another in our journeys through motherhood, may our "hearts [be] knit together in unity and in love one towards another" (Mosiah 18:21).

1 Yana Cortlund, Barb Lucke, and Donna Miller Watelet, *Mother Rising* (Berkeley, CA: Celestial Arts, 2006), 4.
2 Dictionary.com, s.v. "rite of passage," http://dictionary.reference.com/browse/rite+of+passage.
3 Yana Cortlund, Barb Lucke, and Donna Miller Watelet, *Mother Rising* (Berkeley, CA: Celestial Arts, 2006), 19.
4 Merriam-Webster.com, s.v. "ritual," http://www.merriam-webster.com/dictionary/ritual?show=1&t=1289589750.
5 Richard D. Draper, "Home Life at the Time of Christ," *Ensign*, September 1987, http://lds.org/ensign/1987/09/home-life-at-the-time-of-christ.
6 Ibid.
7 Dorothy D. Warner, "Palms for the Lord," *Friend*, March 1996, http://lds.org/friend/1996/03/palms-for-the-lord.
8 Richard D. Draper, "Home Life at the Time of Christ," *Ensign*, September 1987, http://lds.org/ensign/1987/09/home-life-at-the-time-of-christ?.
9 Yana Cortlund, Barb Lucke, and Donna Miller Watelet, *Mother Rising* (Berkeley, CA: Celestial Arts, 2006), 3.
10 Ibid., 9.

Mother's Blessings in the Early Church

By Heather Farrell, CD(DONA)

In the early days of The Church of Jesus Christ of Latter-day Saints, it was common for women to give each other blessings before childbirth and to wash and anoint an expectant mother's body. These blessings were often referred to as "mother's blessings" and were different from the temple ordinances. *In Women of Covenant: The Story of the Relief Society*, the authors explained:

> Washing and anointing prior to childbirth . . . was the "blessing of one sister to another," intended to provide comfort and reassurance in ways inappropriate to priesthood administration. "Washing of the parts of the body to be affected, and anointing them with sacred oil, then pronouncing a mother's blessing," as general Relief Society president Louise Y. Robinson would explain in 1936, was to be "very quietly performed." This was not a priesthood ordinance; sisters were not specifically set apart to perform this office and there was no set form for the service.[1]

Since there was no set form for mother's blessings, they must have varied much from sister to sister. We do have one recorded blessing that was given sometime between 1901 and 1909 in the Oakely, Idaho, Second Ward Relief Society. The blessing reads:

> We anoint your back, your spinal column that you might be strong and healthy no disease fasten upon it no accident befall you, Your kidneys that they might be active and healthy . . . your bladder that it might be strong and protected from accident, your Hips that your system might relax and give way for the birth of your child, your sides that your liver, your lungs, and spleen that they might be strong . . . your breasts that your milk may come freely and you need not be afflicted with sore nipples as many are, your heart that it might be comforted.

And, at the close, we read:

> We unitedly lay our hands upon you to seal this washing and

anointing . . . for your safe delivery, for the salvation of you and your child and we ask God to let his special blessings to rest upon you, that you might sleep well at night that your dreams might be pleasant and that the good spirit might guard and protect you from every evil influence spirit and power that you may go your full time and that every blessing that we have asked God to confer upon you and your offspring may be literally fulfilled that all fear and dread may be taken from you and that you might trust in God. All these blessings we unitedly seal upon you in the name of Jesus Christ. Amen.[3]

Mother's blessings were given commonly up until the 1920s, when the practice began to get confused with temple ordinances and priesthood authority. Many women felt confusion about the purpose of these blessings, so the practiced slowly started to die out. In 1946, President Joseph Fielding Smith circulated a letter to Relief Societies that said, "While the authorities of the Church have ruled that it is permissible, under certain conditions and with the approval of the priesthood, for sisters to wash and anoint other sisters, yet they feel that it is far better to follow the plan the Lord has given us and send for the Elders of the Church to come and minister to the sick and afflicted."[4]

While women are no longer encouraged to bless or to wash and anoint each other before childbirth, the gift to heal is a gift of the Spirit and as Jesus said, "shall follow them that believe" (Mark 16:17–18). This gift has never been taken away from women. The only thing that has changed is the way the gift is administered, and as Moroni said, "there are different ways that these gifts are administered; but it is the same God who worketh all" (Moroni 10:8). Today, Relief Society sisters can still administer a mother's blessing to an expectant mother through their united faith, prayers, and fasting on the mother's behalf. Sisters can also administer to the mother through writing or sharing words of blessing, encouragement, and wisdom; giving her physical support in the form of hugs, massages, or other types of healing touch; providing and caring for her family; and sometimes even being with her in labor to comfort her and give her strength. Just as in the early days of the Church, there is still great power when a group of faithful women unitedly administer their faith and pour out love upon a new mother.

---

1   Jill M. Derr, Janath R. Cannon, and Maureen U. Beecher, *Women of Covenant: The Story of the Relief Society* (Salt Lake City, UT: Deseret Book and Brigham Young University Press, 2000), 221.

2 Linda King Newell, "Gifts of the Spirit: Women's Share," in *Sisters in Spirit: Mormon Women in Historical and Cultural Perspective*, ed. Maureen Ursenbach Beecher and Lavina Anderson (Urbana: University of Illinois Board of Trustees, 1987), 130–131.

3 Ibid.

4 Claudia L. Bushman, "Mystics and Healers," in *Mormon Sisters: Women in Early Utah*, ed. Claudia L. Bushman (Cambridge, Massachusetts: Emmeline Press, 1976), 18.

Showered with Love

By Whitney J. Panton

ON A FALL AFTERNOON, my midwife finished up my prenatal visit and we prepared for my guests to arrive. I was well into my seventh month of pregnancy with my fourth child. My oldest sister was busy in the kitchen putting the finishing touches on the pumpkin spice sheet cake we baked. The welcoming aroma of autumn foods filled the house. Smells create very vivid imagery, especially for pregnant women. This was the perfect opportunity for those in my close-knit circle of friends and family to meet my midwife and gather in a circle of love and sisterhood to celebrate our upcoming birth.

In our culture, we rarely celebrate the symbolism of giving birth or focus on the mother being born. I looked forward with anticipation to this gathering and was excited about the new mindset I had found. As I prepared mentally for this occasion, I pondered how I had already been pregnant three times and given very little thought to the rite of passage this life event was. Would I baptize a child, arrive to go through the temple for the first time, or show up on my wedding day without great spiritual study or instruction?

My visiting teacher and friend who was hosting the event arranged a halo of stephanotis for my hair. It was modeled after a gift I had been given at my mission farewell which a dear friend from Tonga had his mother send from Hawaii—a halo of real jasmine flowers and colorful flower leis for myself and my mother. Not really appreciating the meaningfulness of this experience fourteen years earlier, I now embraced this tradition into my mother blessing experience.

My feet were bathed in pure essential oil water and massaged. My hands were rubbed by my guests as they entered the room, passing on positive energy to me. With them, they each brought a bead/charm and an accompanying hand-written blessing. My mother-in-law wrote the following prayer and sent it in the mail, "May the baby pram charm 'bless' you with safety in all of your travels. Just as a baby is kept warm, snug and safe inside. May you also be kept safe and snug and feel of the love and warmth of my blessing for you." These written prayers are such a treasure for me to read today.

All of the beads and charms were strung into a mother blessing bracelet for me to wear in labor to draw on the support and strength of my loved ones. I still wear the bracelet from time to time, however, more often I wear a necklace chain in which I strung the sterling silver charm of a stretched out heart symbolizing how your heart is capable to stretch allowing one more spirit child into our lives. Our body also has the magnificent ability to stretch to carry a baby and then stretch some more to birth the baby—a reminder that, as mothers, we have the capacity to love the fourth baby as much as the first.

I put together a mini scrapbook album of the legacy of women in my family including my beautiful mother and grandmothers dating back to 1786. I also framed a special photograph taken in 1909 of my great great grandmother on my maternal side with her fifteen children—all born in a one room log house about forty miles from where I live. Each of her children lived to adulthood, and her story inspires me daily. The presence of my ancestors was very tangible throughout my pregnancy. I felt their strength deeply at this time, particularly from two of my great grandmothers. The veil is tissue thin in life events such as this.

Paintings and hand made gifts were suggested to present as gifts in place of store bought gifts. Votive candles wrapped in cello were given as party favors with an attached thought: "May this little flicker be an added source of strength and comfort to Whitney as we light it as soon as we hear labor has begun."

In the childbirth preparation book, *Birthing from Within*, by Pam England, there is an extensive section on honoring childbirth as a rite of passage. I have participated with others in the following ways: belly casting, breaking clay pots, baking a warrior cake, brushing the mothers hair, dancing, painting, and singing. Whatever your fancy may be. I hope your experience preparing to give birth showers you, the mother, with love and strength. Jane Austen once said, "Remember one can never have too large a party." CELEBRATE.

SURROUNDED BY ANGELS

By Lani Axman

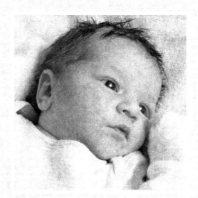

WHILE ALL MY OTHER CHILDREN came five to ten days early, my fourth baby chose to make her appearance five days "late." I like to think that waiting was her first act of love to me. In the weeks leading up to her birth, lots of people asked me, "Are you so ready for this baby to come?" My response was often an immediate and adamant, "No. I wish I had two more months!"

I had been nesting for quite awhile and crossing things off my before-the-baby-comes to-do list every day, but I still felt unsettled. Each night, as I went to bed, wondering whether contractions would be waking me soon, I felt an overwhelming lack of surety—a feeling that not everything was in place, a yearning for something to bolster me and give me the foundation I needed to give birth in peace in confidence. Then it came.

Thirteen days before my daughter's birth, I received an unexpected package on my doorstep, opened it, and found a beautiful bonsai tree. My book collaborators (the lovely women responsible for this book) held a vir-tual "mother blessing" for me as I prepared to give birth, and my bonsai tree was the first of their gifts. It was followed a few days later by a package with a handful of beads and written messages from each of the women. As I sat reading their words, big fat happy tears began streaming down my face. I had spent the previous days and weeks feeling so apprehensive and unready, but the tension melted away as those loving words enveloped me. I was totally overcome with joy, empowerment, peace, strength, and confidence. Robyn's words, in particular, went straight into my heart and soul:

> As the birth of this little one nears, I would like to remind you that you will be blessed with the aid of angels. I have been touched as I have read of your loved ones who have passed through the veil. Surely they have and will be present during your earthly sojourn. They are surely rejoicing at the arrival of your sweet baby. . . . My hope is that this bead will remind you of the errand of angels and their nearness to us especially as heaven opens to bring you this little spirit.

My friends had given me the choice to use the beads as I wished, suggesting maybe I could hang them on the bonsai tree. But I knew I wanted to have the beads right with me as a constant reminder as I labored. So I decided to make a spur-of-the-moment birthing necklace.

My husband and children each chose a bead from our crafting supplies, I took beads from a necklace that belonged to my grandmother before she died and a bead from a necklace my deceased sister-in-law gave me for my birthday (just weeks before she died). I found some charms to represent Mother Eve (an apple) and Jesus Christ (a lamb), beads and charms given to me by special women in my life in the past, a handful of filler beads, and a large glass pendant my father and stepmother brought back from Egypt.

I had also chosen seven beads to represent seven women in the world of spirits—three of my baby's great-grandmothers, a sister-in-law, a cousin, an aunt, and a dear friend. I felt hopeful that these seven women would be spiritually present at my baby's birth, lending us their love, strength, and protection. The beads were mostly clear, sort of spiral-shaped, with a swirl of white in the middle. I had used them to make Christmas ornaments a few years back and had plenty leftover.

As my daughters excitedly watched my bead collection grow, they pleaded to help me make the necklace. I thought it was a fabulous idea. After their bath, we sat on my bed, turned on my birthing c.d., and made my necklace together. It was a really special experience, and I hope to repeat it someday with them as they prepare to give birth themselves.

Though I had gone to bed fearful and "not ready" to welcome my baby many previous nights, that night there was no fear. Peace and love filled and surrounded me. I placed my newly-created birthing necklace on my nightstand, finally emotionally and spiritually ready to welcome my baby whenever she chose to arrive. When we turned off the light, suddenly my husband said, "Whoah! Look at your necklace!"

Perhaps it was coincidence, but—coincidence or not—I was filled with joy and love and assurance as I stared in amazement at my birthing necklace in the dark that night. My seven spirit sister beads were glowing in the dark. Apparently, the white swirl inside of those clear beads had properties I was unaware of.

For the next ten nights, I laid my birthing necklace on my nightstand before going to sleep, turned off the light, and smiled—filling each time with love for God, my baby, and those seven women who I believe used a tender, creative, and playful way to let me know they would most definitely shine light and love into any darkness or difficulty in our birth journey ahead.

Then it was time. Ten nights after making my necklace, the Braxton-Hicks contractions I had grown accustomed to—tightening and releasing regularly multiple times every hour of every day—started to feel suspiciously like the real deal. At first I was hesitant to hope, but after they'd been coming (admittedly still far apart and mild) for a while, I started timing them—7:10, 7:34, 7:56, 8:07. After getting my kids to bed, I figured I'd call my midwife to give her a heads-up. She said to get snuggled up in bed and see what happened. The last contraction I recorded that night came at 10:16. Then I laid my birthing necklace on my nightstand, turned off the light, and tried to sleep.

Despite the contractions, I fell asleep fairly quickly. Sometime after 4:00 a.m., after getting up to pee, I decided to stay up for a bit. I sat on my birth ball in the dark at my desk and updated friends and family via the Internet. Then I realized how hungry and lonely I was. So I woke up my husband.

Those moments in the wee hours of the morning of February 24th were very sweet and special for me. My husband and I sat up together in our bed in the dark and talked for awhile. Then I told him how hungry I was, so he made me some toast. Before lying back down, cuddled together for some more rest, I asked him for a blessing. All the words of that blessing were a comfort to me, but it was these words that sent a wave of warmth and love through my body and tears streaming down my face: "God wants you to know that you are *surrounded by angels*." My friend, Robyn, and my glowing necklace had given me reason to hope, but in that powerful moment, *I knew*. I was surrounded by angels.

The next afternoon, as I waited for my midwives to arrive, 7 cm and astonishingly comfortable, my husband reminded me to put on my birthing necklace. Over the next ten minutes or so, my contractions started coming closer together. I spent a couple of them holding onto my husband with my ear against his chest, listening to his heart beat. As I listened to that strong, steady rhythm, I felt like the three of our hearts—my husbands, my baby's, and mine—were connected to each other by an invisible electrical impulse, each one prodding the next along, each heart strengthening the others. The discomfort seemed to melt away with each beat of my husband's heart. It was a peaceful, beautiful calm before the storm.

After only a handful of difficult contractions, and a crazy intense five minutes of pushing on hands and knees, my baby emerged with her hand up behind the top of her head. My midwife caught her and immediately passed her between my legs and into my hands. I quickly pulled her up to my chest and waddled on my knees to the head of the bed, turning and collapsing in relief onto the pillows with my baby on my chest. She made a few little gentle cries, letting us know she was breathing, and pinked right up.

As soon as she was in the crook of my arm, against my naked chest, she calmed right down. Slowly, she relaxed her face muscles and began blinking, testing out her eyes in this new place. As she fully opened her eyes for the first time, my face was the first thing she saw, and she stared straight into me. I don't think I audibly gasped, but I was momentarily stunned by her intense gaze. It was mere seconds, but it felt like our eyes were locked together for several enthralling minutes, saying, without words, "*It's you*."

I don't even know how to describe the power of that moment. Just thinking about it always bring me to tears. What a privilege to hold that fresh, precious soul in my arms, straight from God, escorted by loving angels. Could there be anything more marvelous? Since then, I've heard enough stories and enough heavenly whispers echoing through my soul to become convinced of one thing: Every baby enters this world and every mother is born (and re-born) surrounded by angels.

Emergency Preparedness

By Lani Axman

One Sunday in Primary, my children learned about the signs of the Second Coming. All that talk of wars, pestilence, famine, and other hardships provoked my five-year-old to crawl onto her Primary teacher's lap in fear. Her response is not uncommon. The coming disasters and difficulties of the last days can feel daunting and frightening. Thinking of man-made and natural disasters always gets me thinking about one particular group of people: pregnant women.

In Matthew, we read that in the last days there will be an "abomination of desolation" causing many to flee in search of safety. We also read, "Woe unto them that are with child, and to them that give suck in those days!" (Matthew 24:15, 19). In the Book of Mormon, Samuel the Lamanite warned the apostate Nephites similarly: "Yea, except ye repent, your women shall have great cause to mourn in the day that they shall give suck; for ye shall attempt to flee and there shall be no place for refuge; yea, and wo unto them which are with child, for they shall be heavy and cannot flee" (Helaman 15:2).

It could be easy to read those passages and be overcome with fear, much like my five-year-old was in Primary, but the Lord has not left childbearing women without hope. In the very first section of the Doctrine and Covenants, we read: "Wherefore the voice of the Lord is unto the ends of the earth, that all that will hear may hear: Prepare ye, prepare ye for that which is to come, for the Lord is nigh" (vv. 11–12). The Lord has also assured us that if we prepare, we "shall not fear" (D&C 38:30).

Regardless of what type of emergency may occur, there will always be pregnant women in need of special assistance. Pregnant women are among those most at risk in disaster situations, in part because severe stress can trigger premature labor, but also because women may need to give birth under precarious circumstances. With the possibility of hospitals overflowing with sick and injured survivors, roads or transportation being inaccessible, and electricity being unavailable, women who would otherwise have given birth at the hospital will have to seek alternatives. It is also a possibility that hospitals will only have resources for the most high-risk pregnant women, leaving low-risk mothers to give birth with little or no assistance from staff. Even on an ordinary day-to-day basis, sometimes a birth happens too quickly for the mother to make it to the planned location or before a qualified birth attendant can be present.

Robbie Prepas, a certified nurse-midwife, saw many such births first-hand during the Hurricane Katrina disaster. She delivered five babies in the New Orleans, Louisiana, airport; delivered twins in an ambulance; and provided impromptu care to hundreds of pregnant and postpartum women, checking fetal heart tones and so forth. She explained, "There were no policies or procedures in place to care for pregnant women or mothers and their babies after Katrina. We even lacked such basics as diapers, formula, baby bottles, and clean clothes."[1] Midwife Mary Callahan also assisted in the Hurricane Katrina relief effort, providing midwifery services to displaced women in a large shelter and assembling emergency birth and prenatal kits for use in other area shelters.[2]

While we may be fortunate to cross paths with a doctor, midwife, or paramedic with birth supplies in an emergency childbirth situation, we can't count on it. Given all of the possibilities, the best course is to do as the Lord instructs: prepare. Just as the Church has organized plans and supplies to assist victims of natural disasters all over the world, we too should have plans and supplies so that we can handle our own unique emergency situations.

The American College of Nurse-Midwives has made an important document available through their website: "Giving Birth 'In Place': A Guide to Emergency Preparedness for Childbirth," by Deanne Williams, CNM, MSN.[3] This five-page document includes a list of supplies for an emergency birth kit. Deanne Williams recommends keeping the kit in an easy-to-carry tote bag in case you have to leave your home quickly and must give birth elsewhere. You will find a link on our website to "Giving Birth 'In Place': A Guide to Emergency Preparedness for Childbirth," including the birth kit supply list.

These are some additional ways we can cover our emergency preparedness bases as pregnant and nursing mothers:

- Learn and practice techniques for comfortable childbirth. Even if you're planning a medicated birth, it's always a good idea to be prepared for birth without medication. In addition, many of the techniques used for comfort during childbirth will also help you to stay calm in a disaster situation (deep breathing, relaxation, hypnosis, meditation, etc.).

- Get or make yourself a good baby carrier, and keep it handy. Having your baby strapped safely to your body could save his or her life. Additionally, it will free up your arms to help your other children and/or carry supplies.

- Ensure you're equipped to feed your baby. If you're breast-feeding, you can easily "carry" your baby's food, but if you bottle-feed, make sure to include formula and clean water in your emergency kit.

- Prepare for a hospital transfer if you're planning a home birth. If you're planning a home birth, you likely have birth supplies handy, but what you may not have considered preparing for is a hospital transfer. One of the requirements for ensuring that home birth is safe is having the ability to quickly and efficiently transfer to a medical facility when needed. Packing a hospital transfer bag may be wise. Education about hospital policies and informed consent will also ease the transfer experience.

- Take classes in CPR and neonatal resuscitation. You never know whether your skills might save your own baby's or another's life. (You can read Rixa's story, "Resuscitating My Baby," on pages 182.)

In addition to being physically and temporally prepared to handle an emergency childbirth situation, it is also important to be spiritually prepared. The Holy Spirit can give crucial promptings to those who are listening and able to heed them. When we are spiritually in tune, we can better receive those important messages. *The Latter-day Saint Woman:*

Basic Manual for Women encourages: "We need to know specifically what to do for common injuries so that we can act with purpose and knowledge. It is helpful to have a constant prayer in our hearts during an emergency, in order to be better prepared to receive inspired guidance."[4] While this is making reference to first aid, the same is true for other potential emergency situations.

If we find ourselves giving birth in disaster or emergency circumstances, we can be assured that God and angels will help deliver us: "I will go before your face. I will be on your right hand and on your left, and my Spirit shall be in your hearts, and mine angels round about you, to bear you up" (D&C 84:88). Whether we must deliver a child alone, assist a friend, or simply encounter unexpected childbirth complications, we can expect and count on guidance from our loving Heavenly Parents and the angels who serve Them, and we can approach challenges with greater calmness and peace when we have done all that we can to prepare.

---

1   Qtd. in Katherine Camacho Carr, "Disaster Preparedness for Mothers and Babies: Getting Prepared," *Quickening*, September 2006, http://www.midwife.org/siteFiles/education/K_Carr_Sept._06_Quickening_article.pdf.

2   Mary Callahan, "Chicago Midwives Travel to Baton Rouge," *Quickening*, November/December 2005, http://www.midwife.org/siteFiles/education/November_December_Quickening.pdf.

3   Deanne Williams, "Giving Birth 'In Place': A Guide to Emergency Preparedness for Childbirth," supplement, *Journal of Midwifery and Women's Health* 49, no. 4, S1 (2004): 48–52, http://www.midwife.org/siteFiles/education/giving_birth_in_place.pdf.

4   The Church of Jesus Christ of Latter-day Saints, "Lesson 23: First Aid, Part 1: Preventing and Preparing for Injuries," *The Latter-day Saint Woman: Basic Manual for Women*, Part B (Salt Lake City, UT: The Church of Jesus Christ of Latter-day Saints, 2000), 185.

CHANGE OF PLANS

By Tami Foytik

WHEN I WAS PREGNANT WITH MY FIRST, my daughter Elizabeth, I never considered any other options other than going to the OB/GYN for my appointments, delivering in the hospital, and being drugged-up because that is what everyone I knew recommended. I can laugh now because, to our surprise, the hospital birth and drugs never happened.

It all started on Friday. I woke up around 4 a.m. having contractions. I headed to the bathroom and noticed my mucous plug and some bloody show. The contractions lasted most of the day, but they never got really strong or too close together. I called the hospital and my doctor's office, and they both assured me this was just the beginning and to stay off my feet and relax.

Round two of the story starts in the early morning hours of April 1st. My first thought on my contractions starting was: *I cannot have this baby on April Fool's day.* My second thought was: *My doctor is out of town until the 2nd. I have to wait until tomorrow.* Once my contractions got to every three minutes, we finally headed to my parent's house because we lived an hour away from the hospital and they were less than ten minutes.

Around 8:00 p.m., I was admitted for observation. The nurse checked me, and I had only dilated to 3 cm. She called the doctor on-call, and he said (being a first-time mom) I had a good twelve to fourteen more hours before I would deliver. I was sent home. I knew I would be.

The nurse said she didn't feel right letting me go. She loaded me up with juice and told me to work on breathing and focusing and that I would need it when it was time to push. We went back to my parents' house to get

---

It all happened so fast. One push, a gush of water, and there I was holding her.

---

our little dog. They tried to get us to say with them just in case. I was hard-headed and just wanted to take a hot bath in my own tub and sleep in my own bed.

We got home around 11 p.m. I took my bath and decided to sleep on the couch in the living room. My little dog was so worried about me he kept pacing and kissing me. Jeremy had to work the next day, so I told him to go to bed, and I would be fine. It had to be around 11:55 p.m.

Here's where the fun begins. The contractions were still just three minutes apart, and I really do not believe they were getting stronger. I was getting a three-minute nap between each contraction. Finally, after a while, I decided maybe I needed to empty my bladder. I was also thinking: *If this isn't labor, and it's only going to get worse, Elizabeth will be our only child.*

Once I got to the bathroom, I never left. I can remember the back labor being so painful I would dig my fingers in my back and massage it during the contraction and then lean over on the sink and take my little nap. I'm not really sure how long I did this. I just know there was a point when I suddenly woke up, the contractions had stopped, and I felt the urge to push.

I remembered reading pushing too early was a bad thing, so I tried to fight the urge to push. But my body took over. I had to push. I remember looking down, and my belly had dropped almost like it wasn't there anymore. I stood up to go get Jeremy, and that is when I noticed the bulge between my legs. The head was not out yet, but it was time for this baby to come. I made it to the door of the bathroom when I felt the urge to push again.

It was then that my water broke, and out came Elizabeth. It all happened so fast. One push, a gush of water, and there I was holding her. I flipped her over and the first thing I noticed was that she looked just like her daddy. Then I calmly called down the hall, "Jeremy, the baby is here." I heard him get up. He told me later that he thought I meant I needed him to take me back to the hospital. He turned the corner, and there was Elizabeth sitting in my lap wide eyed.

Jeremy called 911, and the EMTs were there in less than fifteen minutes. I had delivered the placenta while waiting for them. The EMTs cut her cord, put her in a little blanket bag, and we were off to the hospital. I got to hold her the whole way there. I was so exhausted, excited, yet relaxed and calm. I know that my unexpected home birth was a blessing from God. It was His way of showing me what I was capable of.

Resuscitating My Baby

By Rixa Freeze, PhD

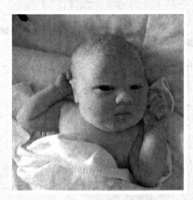

I WOKE UP TO STRONG CONTRACTIONS around 1 a.m. At 6:48 a.m., I got up to use the bathroom and decided it was time to get up and work with, rather than try to ignore, the contractions. Soon we were all awake and getting ready. I called the midwife first thing to give her a heads-up, letting her know I'd call again when I was ready for her to come.

I kept hurrying Eric and the kids on. Somehow I just *knew* that we didn't have the time for a leisurely morning. As soon as I got out of bed, the contractions starting coming much more frequently. I showered and dressed and started filling the birth pool. My logical brain was wondering if I was jumping the gun, but the instinctual part of me compelled me to act quickly.

Eric hurried to finish last-minute tasks, then gave me a blessing. I've asked for one during each of my labors, and they have always been incredibly reassuring. By this point, labor was really, really intense. I sensed the dizzy, spinny, buzzing feeling heralding the endorphins of advanced labor. But was I really that far along? I called the midwife a second time and told her to head over. I didn't want her to arrive too early, but if my instincts were correct, things were really cooking. There was no physical indicator, just an interior knowledge that the baby was on its way.

I was keen to film this birth, so Eric set up the video camera. I had a few contractions in the tub and started feeling a little bit pushy. *Already?* I needed something to grab onto, so Eric and I "arm wrestled" during contractions. Once the baby's head began to crown, I put my right hand down to support my tissues. For the third time, I experienced the impossible-yet-inevitable sensation of a baby's head emerging out of my body. My palm was cupped over the head. There was a slight pause after the head was born. Then the shoulders emerged. I lifted my baby out of the water. We discovered we had a girl! We didn't look at the clock until a few minutes after, so we're guessing the baby was born at 9:12 a.m.

Of all the people to have a baby born needing a little assistance, I was one who was prepared for it.

Soon after the birth, Inga lost muscle tone and color. I quickly realized that I needed to perform mouth-to-mouth. Fortunately, I became certified in neonatal resuscitation several years ago, so I knew what to do. It was tricky getting the angle right, since the cord was short. I gave her five breaths. After each breath, she coughed and perked-up a bit more. Within seconds of Inga being fully recovered, the midwife's assistant arrived.

Was I scared? Not really—more focused on the situation at hand. I do remember thinking, as Inga was losing color and muscle tone, "I have *not* done all this work for nothing—come on, baby!" I also feel that having the blessing in labor and the power of the Holy Ghost made all the difference. I don't want to dismiss the seriousness of some of those seconds as I was holding Inga and helping her come into her body, but at the same time I had received a blessing and I held to what it said. I knew it was serious, but I also knew that I had the appropriate knowledge and skills. Of all the people to have a baby born needing a little assistance, I was one who was prepared for it. I feel strongly that every pregnant woman should prepare herself for how to handle situations such as this, no matter where she is planning to give birth. Had I been planning a hospital birth, I seriously doubt I would have made it on time. And the midwife won't always make it on time either.

These words about Inga's birth video from Tatiana, an aspiring midwife, resonated deeply with me:

> That this one precious, tender, incredibly sensitive new little person could be born needing help and receiving that help from her mother in the warm safety of a tub is a transcendently beautiful departure of what neonatal resuscitation normally looks like. Nothing jarring, nothing painful or invasive, nothing panicked . . . No, just family, breath appropriately applied, and the rolling of time into life here among us other breathing people. . . . I'm so glad for her, and for that sweet baby girl who may have had the world's most tender resuscitation.[1]

---

1 http://becomingmidwives.blogspot.com/2011/03/i-dont-have-punchline.html

Building a Better Bond

By Lani Axman

Around the time I was eighteen months old, my parents took my siblings and me to see E.T. in the movie theater and told us they were getting a divorce. Soon afterward, my five older siblings and I packed into our family car with my dad and drove away from the most important source of security and love I had ever known—my mother.

This early loss can be put into perspective when we read the words of Elder M. Russell Ballard:

> A mother's nurturing love arouses in children, from their earliest days on earth, an awakening of the memories of love and goodness they experienced in their premortal existence. Because our mothers love us, we learn, or more accurately remember, that God also loves us.[1]

My earliest memories of this life are full of the ache of losing that peace Elder Ballard spoke of. I am the third in a line of "motherless" women. Motherless, not because our mothers passed away, but because our mothers were unable, for one reason or another, to provide their constant presence or the physical and emotional nurturing we needed. Fortunately, many wonderful women stepped in to help raise and "mother" me.

Because of the struggles with mothering in my family history, I have become intensely interested in ensuring that I establish as strong of an early bond as possible with my own children. I feel certain that those who are deceased now have a greater and deeper understanding of the circumstances of their own lives as well as a desire to assist their posterity to cease unhealthy or damaging patterns of behavior. I believe my ancestors (and my living mother) want me to break the negative cycle of motherlessness, and I feel confident that they are helping me to do so.

So, when I gave birth to my firstborn and waited to fall in love with her . . . and waited . . . and waited . . . I was understandably nervous. *What if I'm broken? What if I can't love my babies?* I don't remember how much time passed (days? weeks?) as I waited for that flow of love to spring forth. Meanwhile, I prayed my heart out. God told me the love would come. One day I was playing with my daughter, smiling and gazing at her, and "I love you" fell from lips so effortlessly that it took me a moment to realize what I had said. And then I said it again with tears streaming down my face.

With each of my four children's births, I have been shown line upon line how I might improve and intensify the initial bond I feel with my babies. When my second daughter was born, I knew that I wanted to hold her on my chest immediately after delivery (something I hadn't been able to do with my first daughter). My third baby I held skin-to-skin for the first thirty minutes of his life and delayed washing him. I've learned that skin contact and smell play an important part in the bonding process. Additionally, all of my children were breast-fed within the first hour of life, which has also been shown to improve bonding.

Later, as I prepared for the birth of my fourth child, battling very real fears that I wouldn't be able to love her, I sought the Lord's help. I wanted to know what I could do to enhance the love I would feel for my new baby. I knew there had to be more that I was missing. So I delved into my scriptures, pondered, received direction, and was able to identify some additional ways to maximize our initial bonding experience.

A LOVING LIFESTYLE

God taught me that I needed to show more love to my little family on a daily basis—more praise and gratitude, more random acts of kindness, more hugs, more kisses, more cuddling, more massages. I was reminded that when I live a lifestyle full of love, affection, and service for those around me, I further enhance my capacity to love more deeply, until eventually I am able to feel and give "perfect" love.

I found the following scripture particularly instructive: "If we love one another, God dwelleth in us, and his love is perfected in us. . . . God is love; and he that dwelleth in love dwelleth in God, and God in him. Herein is our love made perfect" (1 John 4:12, 16). It was that perfect, deep, God-like love that I hoped to experience as I gave birth to my baby and afterward.

God's advice made complete sense, of course. A person living a life-style of loving action is a person flooding herself constantly with the love hormone—oxytocin. The higher our oxytocin levels rise, the more intensely we are able to bond with others. Mothers can experience the highest oxytocin peak of their lives at the moment of birth and imme-diately afterward. A 2007 study in Israel found that women experience varying oxytocin levels throughout pregnancy, but those women whose oxytocin levels increased from early to late pregnancy experienced a higher maternal-fetal bonding.[2] God, who knows our bodies and their processes better than anyone, was essentially telling me to implement behaviors that would cause an increase in my oxytocin levels leading up to my child's birth.

FORGETTING MYSELF

Another lesson the Lord taught me was how my thoughts during child-birth could enhance or inhibit the loving feelings I hoped to feel for my child. I realized, with some degree of shame, how selfish I had been during my previous births. I was so wrapped up in the intensity of what was happening to my body that I essentially forgot about the baby coming at the end. God helped me to see that if I wanted to enhance the initial bonding moments, then I needed to keep my baby in focus throughout the entire birth experience. Though it seems pretty obvious to me now, it was a total paradigm shift for me.

So my goal was to lose myself, forget about *me*, and fill my heart and mind with my baby. Consequently, I thought a lot about what childbirth must be like for those sweet babies and their fledgling fresh-from-heaven spirits. Those babies and their spirits have never been born before. Child-birth is such a departure from everything they have ever experienced. It could potentially be extremely traumatic and frightening for them, espe-cially if we, their mothers, allow our own fears and discomforts to over-whelm our minds and bodies. I wanted to do whatever I could to ease and soothe my baby's transition into mortal life. Remaining calm, serene, and relaxed as I gave birth was no longer about improving my *own* experience; it became a labor of love for my baby.

187

I visualized a crowd of loving (and familiar) spirits who had prepared my child to come to earth. I pictured them encouraging and ushering my baby's immortal spirit across the veil between that premortal realm and our world, and then I visualized myself welcoming that newly created and unified soul into my arms. I imagined myself as a vessel, carrying and protecting a very special, sacred soul as we navigated an intense journey through water, blood, and fire. I visualized my baby descending through my body, completely aware of all of my emotions, thoughts, and sounds.

"The birth of my son was a life-changing experience. He made me a mother. The intensity of the experience will never leave me: that immediate rush of emotion, of pure and ecstatic and frantic love. From the moment I first looked upon him, I knew he and I were intricately connected, for eternity. From that very first moment, I knew I would do anything, give anything, for this little person. He was a part of my soul, and without him I would be incomplete. Though the circumstances of his birth were not what I had imagined, I will forever remember it with profound joy. And for that I will be eternally grateful." —Catherine Gambrell (See her daughter's birth story on page 5.)

I wanted to flood my heart and mind with reassurance and encouragement for my baby: *Everything is going to be okay, baby. You're safe. I'm okay. We're okay. You don't need to fear. We are doing this together. I will never leave you alone. I love you.*

Despite my expectations to the contrary, I didn't cry the first time I gave birth. I didn't cry the second time or the third time either. But, as I sat nursing my freshly born fourth baby, with my husband at my left and my sweet five-year-old at my right, tears came to my eyes. I couldn't even describe what I was feeling when my daughter asked, "Why are you crying?" I know from my thirty plus years on this earth that there are only two things that can get me to cry: intense emotional pain and God. So I guess the best answer to my daughter's question would have been: "I'm feeling God."

Seeing how deeply I love my fourth baby, it seems silly that I ever worried I wouldn't love her just as much as I loved the other three. Would I have fallen in love with her whether I had spent the last weeks of my pregnancy boosting my oxytocin levels, visualizing my baby during labor, and nursing her skin-to-skin for her first hour of life? Probably. Babies have a way of winning us over despite whatever difficulties may arise. Their Designer was a genius in that department. Deep loving bonds can be formed with our children regardless of whether we are able to implement all the practices I've discussed or whether those attachments take time to develop. This is a fact adoptive parents, foster parents, and all others who have ever loved a child are well aware of.

Yet I have seen from my own experience that the stronger and deeper our initial bond with our babies becomes, the more we will delight to serve and care for them. I was stunned by my own sheer joy in caring for my newborn son after falling deeply in love with him in his first days of life. I adored serving him both day and night. I had never felt anything like it before, despite already having two other children (whom I loved). I believe a deeper initial bond can enhance and ease our mothering experience. This is no doubt the kind of joy and love the Lord wants and yearns for us to feel as we care for our children, and I believe it is a small taste of the joy and love He feels in serving and blessing us as His children.

What a relief it has been to discover again and again with each new birth that I'm not "broken." I *can* be a loving and nurturing mother, regardless of my family history and childhood traumas. I am grateful to a loving Father in Heaven who has shown me the possibility and potential within those first moments, hours, and days of mortal life. Even more, I am grateful He has shown me a potential for love within myself that I didn't realize I was capable of. I stand all amazed.

1   M. Russell Ballard, "The Sacred Responsibilities of Parenthood," *Ensign*, March 2006, http://lds.org/ensign/2006/03/the-sacred-responsibilities-of-parenthood.
2   Ari Levine, Orna Zagoory-Sharon, Ruth Feldman, et al., "Oxytocin During Pregnancy and Early Postpartum: Individual Patterns and Maternal-Fetal Attachment," Peptides 28, no. 6 (2007): 1162–1169, http://www.ncbi.nlm.nih.gov/sites/entrez?cmd=Retrieve&db=PubMed&list_uids=17513013&dopt=Citation.

Creating a Sacred Cesarean Section

By Sheridan Ripley, HCHI, CD(DONA)

ROBYN R'S BIRTH STORY

I delivered my 9 pound, 10.5 ounce son by an unplanned cesarean after a long and difficult labor. When I got pregnant with my second child, I prayed about it and felt strongly about having another cesarean. In the back of my mind, though, I wondered—How would I feel if I delivered a baby that was smaller than my son? What if things could be different this time? But I kept going back to that certainty I'd had about the surgery and tried to remind myself that this was the answer I had received.

The day came for my baby to be born. I did my hair and makeup perfectly and put on my favorite Sunday maternity dress to wear to the hospital. I wanted to make the day as special as I could. The most important thing I did to get ready was to receive a priesthood blessing from my husband. He promised me that I would be calm and that things would go well during the surgery.

Later, as I was wheeled into the OR [operating room], I tried to pay attention to how carefully everything was prepared for my baby to be born. The OR was very cold so that germs couldn't grow there. The doctors and nurses were all carefully washed and dressed. While a regular delivery doesn't require all of these precautions, I saw them as preparations made for a very sacred event that is special in its own way.

As the anesthesiologist was putting the needle in my back, my nerves started getting to me. But as I thought back to the words of the blessing that I had received, I felt an intense overwhelming feeling of calm sweep over me. I knew immediately that I wasn't alone, that my Heavenly

Father was right there, that He was watching over me, and that the baby and I would be just fine.

Although I was totally numb and couldn't feel anything that was happening to me, as I laid there, I felt a magical, wonderful feeling. I believe it was a special gift that Heavenly Father sent to me to feel and to experience since I could not do so physically. I am so grateful for the presence of that strong, special spirit as my sweet baby was born. I can't fully put into words the mixture of anticipation, excitement, calm, joyfulness, wonder, and delight that it was. I was filled with gladness to be a woman and a mother and amazement at the blessing of being able to partner with Heavenly Father to bring one of his choice spirits to the earth. To anticipate and then witness that first breath and cry is a feeling unlike any other in the world.

The fun part was when the nurse announced that my sweet baby girl was 11 pounds and 3 ounces. She was so big that I couldn't dispute in my mind, when I was in pain and recovering, whether I should have had the cesarean. It was as if the Lord was smiling when He made my baby so big because He wanted me to know without a doubt that I had indeed received that important revelation about how I should deliver my baby.

It's up to us to recognize the miracle in each birth—the sweetness and the tender mercies that are still there for us, no matter how our babies come into the world, and especially when they come in a way we may not have originally planned.

This is a wonderful birth story. I love Robyn's positive attitude. She is a wonderful example of how following the Spirit regarding birth choices leads us to positive, spiritual birth experiences, regardless of how those births occur. Sometimes, despite all our preparation, planning, and the righteous desires of our hearts, things can't happen as we had hoped. Not many people get the exact birth they imagined, but we usually get the exact birth we (mother and baby) needed. The important thing to remember is that every birth is a miracle and no one should feel like less of a woman because her baby needed to come in a certain way.

Robyn's birth story illustrates some great ways to create a positive cesarean birth. The following are a few more ideas.

BEFORE BIRTH

Planned Cesarean Delivery

- Mentally preparing for a cesarean section is important. It takes as much mental preparation for a positive cesarean section as for a positive unmedicated birth. It requires a huge mind shift and focus.
- Having a doula, a woman trained to help and advocate for women through childbirth, can greatly improve a woman's experience. However, moms need to research their hospitals' policies about doulas and cesarean sections.
- Finding a good match in care provider and hospital is important. Hospital policies vary widely, and a mother can have more support in certain settings. For example, in some hospitals, the standard cesarean delivery has a three-hour separation of the mother and baby following the birth, and the baby is given glucose water and formula from a bottle. Contrast this with a hospital where the mother and baby are able to recover in the same room with skin-to-skin contact. Mothers shouldn't be afraid to change doctors/hospitals if their desires are not supported.

- Having a mother's blessing with loved ones can bolster a mother's spirits and surround her with love and joy as she prepares for her baby's birth. (See "Mother-Centered Baby Showers," on page 155.)

- Allowing labor to start on its own is sometimes an option for a planned cesarean delivery. This allows the baby to get the hormonal and squeezing benefits of labor.

Any Cesarean Delivery

- Remember that giving birth by cesarean section is a selfless sacrifice. A mother having a cesarean section is offering her body in behalf of another as she willingly undergoes surgery for her baby. Pondering this truth can connect her with the Savior and give her unique insight into His sacrifice. Pondering this truth will also help prepare her for many more sacrifices she will make for her children as the years go by.

- Use blessings and prayers to help mother and father feel more comfortable and confident in their cesarean-delivery decision. Have a prayer or blessing prior to the birth, specifically praying that the surgery will go well and for a spirit of peace.

DURING BIRTH

Physical

The following are some physical things to consider or research if planning a cesarean birth.

- Request a double suture of the incision, which can help with healing and increase options for VBAC in future.

- Consider the incision type. Depending on the circumstances, a bikini-line incision is preferable.

- Specify that you don't want narcotics, so that you can be more aware.

- State that you don't want your arms tied down.

- Request that your uterus remain in your body. In some hospitals (often in teaching hospitals), during the repair the doctor will flip the uterus out of the abdominal cavity to inspect it, massage it, or just to give the interns a tour around the mother's body cavity. This is typically unnecessary and can make a mother's recovery much longer and more difficult. When discussing an imminent or likely cesarean section, you can state that you strongly desire for your uterus to remain in your abdominal cavity and for your organs to be handled or moved around as minimally as possible.

- If bright lights are bothersome to you, bringing sunglasses into surgery may be helpful.

"I had four vaginal births and two emergency C-sections. I can honestly say that my C-sections were as spiritual as my other births. Having a baby is a sacred experience. I had four beautiful, routine, healthy births. But, when something goes wrong, when you feel virtual strangers doing all that they can to save the life of your unborn child, it is sacred. I felt overwhelming peace especially when things were unsure. I felt the love and service of hospital staff and doctors and friends and family. I would not intentionally choose a C-section. I wouldn't choose a 6-week recovery. I wouldn't choose NICU. But every day I thank God for my two C-section babies and for the miracles that brought them to earth. Planned, no. Sacred, for sure!" —Jennifer

---

Spiritual/Emotional

In a recent International Cesarean Awareness Network meeting, I was thrilled to hear from two trail-blazing doctors who are offering gentle cesarean sections.[1] The following are examples of some of the things the doctors discussed:

- Soft music and aromatherapy are allowed.

- A doula is allowed, in addition to the husband.

- The mother is elevated a bit to see her baby come out.

- The baby is given time to acclimate to the outside by being brought out gently and gradually, allowing for a gentle squeeze (which also helps to clear the baby's lungs).

- Clamping and cutting the cord is delayed.

- If the baby is in good condition (moving, crying, etc.), the baby is brought skin-to-skin with the mother, with all assessments done there.

- Breast-feeding is initiated in the operating room.

- No casual chitchat among the surgical team is allowed—all focus on the family.

- The surgical team communicates with the mother about what is happening during the surgery.

- Photographs and videos are allowed.

- The mother may use relaxation or hypnosis techniques to stay calm.

Immediately after Birth

Immediate skin-to-skin contact after birth is ideal. As a doula, I've had a couple of clients who were able to hold their babies skin-to-skin in the operating room. One of the hospitals I go to has a standard procedure of putting baby skin-to-skin with the father in the operating room. The father removes his shirt and puts on a hospital gown, open in the front, in order to receive the baby. I think bringing the baby skin-to-skin with the mother is best, but it would be good to offer the family a choice and perhaps to encourage the shirt-off preparation for the father in case the mother doesn't feel up to having the baby skin-to-skin while surgery is still in progress.

- If skin-to-skin contact is not possible, the mother can request to see her baby as soon as possible and to have her baby be within her sight while the assessments are completed.

- The mother may want to request a chance to kiss her baby, nuzzle her baby cheek-to-cheek, and sniff the top of her baby's head (the head is a major hormone release spot, and a newborn baby has a unique smell that fades if the medical team bathes the baby). These actions can aid in the bonding process and are best done as soon as possible, even while the mother is still in surgery.

- If the baby has to go to the nursery, the father can accompany the baby and stay with the baby for as long as the mother desires, making sure that the baby's in an incubator with hands-in access or even allowed skin-to-skin time with the father, if possible.

- If a separation is necessary and the father goes with the baby, a doula (or loving family member) is a wonderful help so the mother doesn't have to recover alone.

Postpartum Recovery

- I encourage family members to rotate staying with the mother after the cesarean section so that she can have the baby with her at all times and facilitate breast-feeding. One family negotiated with hospital staff to allow someone to be with the mother all night too, so she could still have rooming-in.

- The mother also needs more long-term help and support in the first months of her baby's life. Creating a schedule of postpartum helpers, child care, and meals can allow the mother to focus on bonding, breast-feeding, and healing.

- If the cesarean delivery was a change of plans or happened under emergency circumstances, having a completely nonjudgmental support network around the mother at this time can help turn a less than ideal situation into a more sacred event.

- Keeping a mental record of and/or writing down all of the events leading up to the cesarean section can make understanding and coping with it afterward much easier. Asking for input from others who were there and getting hospital records can also help a mother understand things better.
- A cesarean birth is not a failure. However, should a mother ever feel that way, she is not alone. There are many women who have been through what she has (including myself), and it will be of great benefit if she will seek someone supportive to talk to. (If needed, see "Healing from a Traumatic Birth," on page 396.)

Some great resources for planning a family-centered cesarean section can be found online at the website for the International Cesarean Awareness Network and the website for The Gift of Giving Life.

---

1. This approach is based on the writings of Dr. Nicholas Fisk.

CHAPTER SIX

Meditation

Be still, and know that I am God.

PSALMS 46:10

Meditation

By Felice Austin, CHt

We pay too little attention to the value of meditation,
a principle of devotion. In our worship there are two elements:
One is spiritual communion
arising from our own meditation; the other,
instruction from others, particularly from those who have authority
to guide and instruct us. Of the two, the more profitable . . .
is the meditation. . . . Meditation is one of the most secret, most sacred
doors through which we pass into the presence of the Lord.[1]

DAVID O. MCKAY

When I was four months pregnant with my daughter, my doctor's office invited me to a one-night childbirth education class that would meet upstairs in the loft. I said, "Sure, I'll come." I had no idea what to expect. The class itself was just introductory information, but the woman teaching it was a goddess. She looked sort of like my obstetrician. She was tall; gorgeous; and part African-American, part Native-American, and part European. She was stunning. Her energy, however, was different from my obstetrician. She had a spiritual beauty that radiated from within.

After the class, she agreed to be my doula, and I started attending her yoga class. It was a lovely group of women in a beautiful, healing space. As I continued going to yoga, and for the first time in my life, I learned to truly meditate. As a result, I began receiving a lot of personal revelation. Through the whole pregnancy, I missed my mother intensely. However, I found great peace in meditating on her and my other female ancestors and often felt their presence. Learning how to meditate changed my life.

I have pondered and wondered about why many faithful people "pay too little attention to meditation."[2] I think that perhaps the reason is because as members of The Church of Jesus Christ of Latter-day Saints, we feel the Spirit periodically or regularly at church, and so we assume that all is well. One retired Latter-day Saint institute director and meditation teacher related the following about his journey: "I realized that having spiritual experiences often has little to do with spiritual transformation."[3] I came to the same realization when I was pregnant. Despite my testimony and all my spiritual experiences, I was not becoming more Christ-like. I was not able to call forth compassion or other Christ-like behaviors in difficult circumstances. However, when I began a practice of meditation, I slowly transformed.

Many ancient and living prophets have counseled us to meditate. Meditation is one of the most important and sacred things we must learn how to do in this life. But what is meditation? How does it work, and how do we do it? Simply put, meditation is seeking the Spirit of the Lord. Whether they know it or not, all human beings crave the Spirit. President Ezra Taft Benson said, "Spirituality—being in tune with Spirit of the Lord—is the greatest need we all have."[4] While meditation is a form of prayer, prayer is not necessarily meditation. Today, many of our prayers are more like a monologue; as President Gordon B. Hinckley joked, we sometimes pray as if we are ordering groceries.[5] Perhaps the biggest difference between prayer and meditation is the attachment to an end result. Praying for an answer is a worthy undertaking, but meditation is not necessarily about receiving answers. A better word to describe the core of meditation is *intention*.

HOW DOES IT WORK?

Every time you think a thought or take any action, your brain creates a neuropathway. The more energy you attach to certain thoughts or actions, the deeper that pathway becomes. Let's make a comparison to a hose that is left on in the dirt—the water cuts a deeper and deeper groove. Let's say that the deepening rut is your negative thoughts. Pretty soon, other related thoughts and feelings start to fall in that groove, which means that you increasingly get into a similar emotional state. Meditation creates new neuropathways that will eventually allow for new feelings and thoughts.

Meditation can also be described as a hypnotic or receptive state that allows new thoughts/intentions to enter the unconscious without resistance. Spiritually speaking, however, meditation is a state of mind that allows you to access the power of the Atonement.

For example, let's say your intention for your meditation is patience, compassion, or a greater understanding of an answer to prayer you have already received. If you meditate every day with openness to that intention and to whatever else may come or not come, over time you will find that you become more patient, more compassionate, or more perceptive.

Even though we should not get attached to finding the answers while meditating, insights often come when our minds are calm and open. For

"Meditation on a passage of scripture . . . led a young boy into a grove of trees to commune with his Heavenly Father. That is what opened the heavens in this dispensation."[6] —Ezra Taft Benson

example, almost all of the revelations given in the Doctrine and Covenants came after or while the Prophet Joseph Smith meditated: "While we meditated on these things, the Lord touched the eyes of our understandings and they were opened, and the glory of the Lord shone round about" (D&C 76:19).

HOW DOES ONE MEDITATE?

In the scriptures, there are many different words that describe meditation: *ponder, consider, study, treasure up, muse, mediate, rest upon your minds, think, pray,* and *contemplate.* Elder Chauncey C. Riddle said that "meditation cannot be taught, because it is something personal and private: it is the venturing of the soul into the unknown."[7]

What works for me may not work for others. I love mantra meditation, Rebecca (see page 211) likes mindfulness, and President Hinckley's father used to sit on a wall in the thinker position. President Hinckley recommended pondering the stars or enjoying good culture. No matter what you choose, however, there are several elements that meditation should include.

- Faith: This faith can be as simple as a hope or a desire to believe you can commune with God.

- Intention or selective focus: Remember the hose cutting a groove in the dirt. It's easier if you stick with one intention at a time. Examples of intention include openness, patience, understanding, and peace. When you meditate, continually bring your mind back to your intention. This process will get easier with practice.

- Repetition: Daily repetition is important—it is just like exercise. I used to be able to do three pull-ups, but I stopped practicing and now have to build back up to three. Cognitive studies show that you need to exercise your brain daily to maintain the benefits achieved.

- Regulated breathing: Our breath is our life, and it is much more connected to our spirituality than we know. The word *inspiration* means "to breathe in." In Hebrew, the word for *breath* also means "spirit of God."[8] By deepening our breath, we can deepen our spirituality. Regulated breathing decreases metabolic activity in certain parts of the brain—such as the brain's center for fear and anger. By regulating our breath, we can control our mental and emotional state, which is at the core of a spiritual pursuit.

- A sacred grove: Joseph Smith set the pattern. President Thomas S. Monson taught:

Every [person] needs a sacred grove to which he can retire to meditate and to pray for guidance. Mine was our old ward chapel. I could not begin to count the occasions when on a dark night at a late hour I would make my way to the stand of this building where I was blessed, confirmed, ordained, taught, and eventually called to preside. The chapel was dimly lighted by the streetlight in front; not a sound would be heard, no intruder to disturb. With my hand on the pulpit I would kneel and share with Him above my thoughts, my concerns, my problems.[9]

WHEN AND HOW LONG?

Does it matter how long or what time of day you meditate? Yes and no. Most yogis rise early. The same schedule is followed by the general authorities of the Church. Elder Kikuchi recommended rising before 6:30 a.m. Scientific and behavioral studies agree. Early morning is a naturally receptive time, as is just before bed. But any time of day can work, especially if done at the same time every day. Start with three minutes a day, and add one minute every few days. Some say the magic number is twelve minutes. Some say it is eighteen. You can find your own magic number. Three minutes of focused meditation has more value than twenty minutes of unfocused meditation. If you have trouble focusing, try guided meditation or visualizations. If you have a difficult time finding alone time or space, try meditating in the shower. Lots of busy mothers have made the shower their sacred grove. In fact, a good portion of this book was inspired there.

Don't get so busy that you don't have time to meditate. Take the time. . . . Christ may be nearer than we have knowledge. "I am in your midst, but you do not see me." [10] —Harold B Lee.

THE BENEFITS

The following is a short list of some of the benefits of regular mediation:

- Brings freedom from unconscious conditioning: Daily mediation or communion with the Lord can free us from conditioned perceptions and responses, also known as "knee-jerk reactions." This freedom enables us to make conscious, loving choices.

- Awakens the divine within us: Meditation brings a closeness with our Heavenly Parents and nourishes our divine qualities. This divine nature unfolds in our thoughts, emotions, perceptions, and behaviors. We begin to act like the divine goddesses-in-embryo that we are.

- Increases our capacity to love: As we awake to our own divine nature, we begin to see everyone else as children of God. We are able to release attachment to how we want others to be and accept them for who they are, which is essential for true love.

- Nurtures unity with God, ourselves, and others: As the scriptures say, "Draw near unto me, and I will draw near unto you" (D&C 88:63) and "ye are all one in Christ Jesus" (Galatians 3:28).

- Develops emotional honesty: Meditation both allows and requires us to take inventory, to regularly ask God, "What lack I yet?"

- Brings calmness and gratitude: Regular mediation will reduce anxiety and create an awakening to all blessings.

- Brightens our countenances: When we meditate daily, "our very countenances radiate the influence of the Spirit."[11] When Moses came down from the mountain after fasting and communing with the Lord for forty days, his face shined so brightly the people could not look upon him, so he wore a veil (Exodus 34:34–35).

- Increases memory and cognition: Scientific studies show that meditation and contemplating on God can help prevent Alzheimer's disease and dementia.[12] Interestingly, I have never heard of an apostle or other general authority with memory problems.

- Increases power to resist temptations: The words of the hymn "I Need Thee Every Hour" illustrate how temptations lose their power "when Thou are nigh."[13]

- Decreases physical pain: Regular meditation has been shown to significantly decrease physical pain.[14] For example, patients with chronic pain who practice meditation require an average of 36% less treatment.[15] You can find more information and links to these studies in the Resources section of our website.

- Enhances physical healing: Meditation has been used for healing since ancient times, and medical meditation is growing in popularity in integrative medicine to treat all types of ailments, from asthma to blood pressure to AIDS. As one doctor and author said, medical meditation "is a veritable knifepoint of healing power."[16]

- Fosters emotional healing: Elder Kikuchi told the story of a mother of six trying to do her best but who sometimes felt discouraged, not good enough, and empty:

She had discussed her concern with her priesthood leaders and especially her husband but had yet to find relief. I suggested that after her husband left for work and their children were in school, she find a place in her home and there reverently and humbly visit with Heavenly Father. I suggested that she express her gratitude to God for her blessings and then wait for His holy inspiration. She committed to do this daily.

Sometime later I received a letter from her. She said that as she went to her knees in those quiet moments each day and dropped her burden at Heavenly Father's feet, He took her concerns away. She felt of her great worth to Him and learned more of "the healer's art" as He healed her soul.[17]

"My meditations fortified me during my pregnancy. In addition to the hypnosis practice, I listened to 30 minutes of daily pregnancy affirmations. Those affirmations and my meditation time became the best times of my day. I felt in tune with my body and in tune with eternal truths. I was relaxed. I was strong. I was confident. I was happy. Whenever pregnancy started to wear me down, I would slip into meditation. Soon I was rejuvenated and ready to continue my labor of love." — Name Witheld

OUR ULTIMATE EXAMPLE

Jesus Christ is the ultimate example of an advanced meditator. Regular daily communion with His Father enabled Him to say, "I and the Father are One"(3 Nephi 11: 27). President David O. McKay taught:

> As soon as he was baptized . . . Jesus [went] to what is now known as the mount of temptation. I like to think of it as the mount of meditation where, during the forty days of fasting, he communed with himself and his Father, and contemplated upon the responsibility of his great mission.[18]

Christ also meditated in solitude before he gave the beautiful Sermon on the Mount. If you search the life of Christ, there are many more examples of meditation. President McKay explained, "Again, after Jesus had fed the five thousand he told the Twelve to dismiss the multitude, but Jesus went to the mountain for solitude. . . . Meditation! Prayer!"[19] I echo President McKay's exclamation points. Meditation and prayer are miraculous.

"Be not conformed to this world, but be ye transformed by the renewing of your mind." —Romans 12:2

FORTY-DAY CHALLENGE

In a recent study, scientists selected people who had never meditated before and gave them a meditation to perform for twelve minutes a day. The scientists did baseline tests and brain scans of the participants and then scanned and tested the participants again after just eight weeks. The results surprised the scientists. They saw marked changes in the brain scans as well as the motor skills and memory tests of the participants in just eight weeks. I suspect that they would have found the changes as early as forty days. As you can read in "Forty Days of Rest," on page 459, forty is a significant spiritual number. It is the number of change. I challenge you to start meditating today. Read more about meditation on our website, download a free meditation MP3 there, choose a book on meditation from our resource list, or allow the Spirit to guide you as you invent your own meditation style. The stories that follow illustrate that there are many different and wonderful ways to commune with God, especially in the spiritually sensitive childbearing year.

1 The Church of Jesus Christ of Latter-day Saints, *Teachings of the Presidents of the Church: David O. McKay* (Salt Lake City, UT: The Church of Jesus Christ of Latter-day Saints, 2003), 31.

2 Ibid.

3 Phillip McLemore, "Mormon Mantras," *Sunstone Magazine*, April 2006, 20.

4 Ezra Taft Benson, "Seek the Spirit of the Lord," *Ensign*, April 1988, http://lds.org/ensign/1988/04/seek-the-spirit-of-the-lord.

5 Gordon B. Hinckley, "Q&A: Questions and Answers," *The New Era*, April 1996, http://lds.org/new-era/1996/04/qa-questions-and-answers.

6 Ezra Taft Benson, "Seek the Spirit of the Lord," *Ensign*, April 1988, http://lds.org/ensign/1988/04/seek-the-spirit-of-the-lord.

7 Chauncey C. Riddle, "Prayer," *Ensign*, March 1975, http://lds.org/ensign/1975/03/prayer.

8 Dharma Singh Khalsa, *Meditation as Medicine* (New York: Atria, 2001) 59.

9 Qtd. in "Opening the Heavens," by Yoshihiko Kikuchi, *Ensign*, August 2009, http://lds.org/ensign/2009/08/opening-the-heavens.

10 The Church of Jesus Christ of Latter-day Saints, Teachings of the Presidents of the Church: Harold B. Lee (Salt Lake City, UT: The Church of Jesus Christ of Latter-day Saints, 2000), 175-84.

11 Ezra Taft Benson, "Seek the Spirit of the Lord," *Ensign*, April 1988, http://lds.org/ensign/1988/04/seek-the-spirit-of-the-lord.

12 Andrew Newberg, *How God Changes Your Brain* (New York: Balantine Books, 2009), 1–63.

13 Annie S. Hawkes, "I Need Thee Every Hour," in *Hymns of the Church of Jesus Christ of Latter-day Saints* (Salt Lake City, UT: Deseret Book, 1985), no. 98.

14 Dharma Singh Khalsa, *Meditation as Medicine* (New York: Atria, 2001) 41–49.

15 Ibid., 42.

16 Ibid., 11.

17 Yoshihiko Kikuchi, "Opening the Heavens," *Ensign*, August 2009, http://lds.org/ensign/2009/08/opening-the-heavens.

18 The Church of Jesus Christ of Latter-day Saints, *Teachings of the Presidents of the Church: David O. McKay* (Salt Lake City, UT: The Church of Jesus Christ of Latter-day Saints, 2003), 32.

19 Ibid.

Pregnancy Visualizations

By Rixa Freeze, PhD

DURING MY FIRST PREGNANCY, I felt a strong closeness to Heavenly Mother. When I would pray, I would talk to Heavenly Father for a while and then say—much like I do when I'm on the phone with my parents —"Okay, now I need to talk to Heavenly Mother for a while." I needed a woman's presence and understanding as I drew closer to bringing life to this world. I asked her to lend me strength, wisdom, and support when I would labor to bring my baby into this world.

I listened to a HypnoBirthing® CD every day the last few months of my pregnancy. Both of the tracks, about twenty minutes each, contained guided meditations about your baby and your upcoming labor and birth. I found them incredibly relaxing and would often listen to them when I was having trouble falling asleep.

Every time I listened, a very detailed picture arose in my mind. I was walking down a long hallway, fully pregnant, in a long crimson dress. Alongside me walked Heavenly Mother. She wore midnight blue, her robes cut like mine. Her hair was straight, raven-black. We walked, side-by-side, until we came to a door at the end of the hallway. She left me there, and I entered the room.

The room had leaded diamond-paned windows, well-worn parquet floors, and wood paneling. It looked like the Loire Valley chateaux I knew so well (my husband and I worked in France for nine summers). I moved to a corner of the room with a fireplace, fur rug, and soft furniture.

This was the place where I would give birth. I was alone, yet not forgotten. There was another door in the room, opening into a great hall where there was a vast crowd of women waiting for me. I had to do this next part on my own. Only then could I pass over to the other side.

In the last scene of my meditation, I walked through that other doorway into the welcoming arms of those women. I held my baby, naked and new and wet, skin to skin against my chest. The umbilical cord still held the two of us together. I was a mother now.

During my second pregnancy, an entirely different vision arose as I was meditating (listening this time to the Hypnobabies® program). I was in a clearing in a deep forest. There was a stone cottage with a thatched roof, a simple wooden fence, and a sunny yard in front of the house. Again I was alone, but I could make out the forms of two people standing in the dim shadows of the woods. Heavenly Mother and Heavenly Father stood, side by side, silently watching and waiting. It was a late spring day, warm in the sun and refreshing in the shade. The cottage was comfortable and inviting: shelves of leather-bound books, padded window seats, faded tapestries. But I chose to stay outside. I knelt on a blanket on the grass. The sun warmed my back and shoulders. I was safe. In the still of the clearing, I gave birth to my baby, supporting its head and then its body as it emerged.

My Mindfulness Journey

By Rebecca Overson

I MUST CONFESS THAT UP UNTIL RECENTLY I used to think I knew what meditation was all about. After all, at age seventeen I was trained as a massage therapist and have spent my whole adult life teaching "this kind of stuff." I have read countless self-help books, attended workshops and trainings, and currently coach others in a process of contemplation and self-inquiry.

However, while in the process of studying personal transformation in school, it became clear that, despite my dabbling, I had no idea what this mindfulness stuff was really about. My brother-in-law, a licensed psychologist, handed me a copy of *Mindfulness in Plain English* by Bhante Gunaratana and said, "Read this before you read anything else." He was right. It was such a simple, straightforward introduction to the seemingly mysterious world of meditation practices, that, by the time I finished reading, I was sure I must have missed something.

After reading his book, I began attending a meditation class and practicing on my own. I will not endeavor to explain how to meditate; there are many methods, and numerous books have been written on the subject. I have found it a deeply personal journey, yet I will try to sum up the benefits.

Through sitting quietly with ourselves, we see how we are constantly trying to maintain our identity, how our thoughts act as a kind of glue that holds our identity structure together. As we witness the self-maintaining grip of the mind, without judging or blaming it, our sustained awareness can act as a gentle solvent that begins to dissolve the glue of the personality structure.

Of course, we often don't like what we discover when we see ourselves as we are. I experienced coming up against the tangled pattern of actions and reactions, conditioning, habit, unconsciousness, and fear. At this point,

---

I attribute much of the wonder of the experience to my commitment to birthing mindfully and being willing to experience whatever was before me.

---

it was not enough for me to just acknowledge what is; I needed to make a fuller relationship with it, which meant opening my heart to the situation in the moment. Feeling it, facing it squarely, and letting it touch me.

For example, during the birth of my second son, I observed the thoughts of dread going through my head. *I cannot do this. Do I really have to do this again? This is not happening already!* However, because of my mindfulness practice, I was careful to simply notice the thoughts, and I did not believe them; I did not get caught up in them and was able to stay relaxed. At one point I just said them out loud so I could hear what they were—just thoughts—and certainly not true. As I reclined against the wall of the birthing tub, I repeatedly whispered to myself, "Just feel this. Just feel what this feels like." I just observed my body in the process, doing what it knows instinctively to do.

I wouldn't say I "pushed" because it actually felt effortless, like I was being pushed. The experience was so ecstatic, so joyful, and so incredibly wonderful. I attribute much of the wonder of the experience to my commitment to birthing mindfully and being willing to experience whatever was before me. (Rebecca's complete birth story can be read on page 252.)

THE BREATH OF LIFE

by Heather Farrell, CD(DONA)

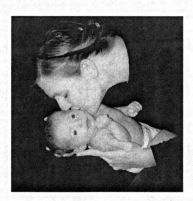

WITH MY FIRST PREGNANCY, I was really concerned about my ability to handle labor and birth. I knew that I didn't have a very high pain threshold, and so I began trying every relaxation and labor coping technique I could find. I read dozens of books, listened to numerous relaxation CDs, practiced yoga, attended a HypnoBirthing® class, and even took a doula certification course. As I immersed myself in these different techniques, I began to see that all of them had one thing in common—they all focused on using the power of your breath to help relax your body and take you deeper within yourself to find your inner strength.

I found this commonality interesting because in the book of Abraham we read that after God formed Adam's body from the dust of the earth, He took Adam's spirit (which had already been created) and put it into Adam. At this point, Adam's body and spirit were separate, but then we read that God "breathed into his nostrils the breath of life, and he became a living soul" (Abraham 5:7). It is our breath, the breath of life that God grants each of us, that unites our body and our spirit and allows us to become, like Adam, a living soul. When we die, we lose our breath, and our body and spirit again separate, waiting until the time when they will be resurrected and inseparably unified as a soul. Our breath is the glue that holds our body and our spirit together. The more conscious we are of it (and the more we are able to express gratitude for it), the more we strengthen the connection between the body and spirit and increase our soul's power. Breathing is truly one of our greatest gifts from God.

As I practiced my relaxation and breathing techniques regularly throughout my pregnancy, I found that I eventually began to reach a place within my soul that I hadn't previously discovered. It was like I'd found the place where my body and my spirit were joined, and it gave me a divine sense of unity not only with myself and with God, but also with my unborn son. I realized that at that point we were not quite two separate people yet. Our spirits were intertwined, and I found that my son would often teach me simple yet powerful divine truths. These teaching moments often came to me at times when I was focused on using my breath, such as while doing yoga, swimming laps at the pool, or practicing HypnoBirthing® scripts. In fact, one of the most powerful spiritual experiences I have ever had came during one of my HypnoBirthing® classes.

It was toward the end of the class, and the instructor was having us practice a relaxation technique. She asked us to breathe deeply and imagine ourselves in a peaceful place. I started envisioning myself on a sandy beach with the ocean lapping at my feet but quickly felt uncomfortable. Then, almost immediately, my mind shifted and I found myself sitting in the celestial room of the Bountiful, Utah, temple. This was the temple where I received my endowment, and it has always had special significance in my life.

As I sat there, I felt my soul become infused with peace and joy, and I received a vision (for there is no better word for it) of my unborn son. I saw him as a young man, tall, blonde, and clothed in white. He approached me and called me "Mother," and I felt in that one word all the gratitude and respect he had for me and for the sacrifice I was making to bring him to earth. I saw that in his eyes it was the grandest, noblest title he could call me by, and it made me realize the full scope of what I was undertaking. I don't know how long the vision lasted—it probably wasn't more than a few minutes, but it felt as if I had spent hours with him in the celestial room. Time stood still, and when I finally opened my eyes I was surprised to find myself still sitting in the HypnoBirthing® class, holding my husband's hand (who had fallen asleep during the relaxation). I felt as though I had been given a divine gift, and I knew that much of what I had been shown and taught was to be kept sacred within my heart.

A few weeks later, as I was giving birth to my son, I once again found myself accessing the power of my breath. It became my cadence, the rhythm to which I rocked, moaned, and whistled my way through each contraction. At first my breathing was easy, calm, and regular, but as labor progressed I began to panic and cry. It was at that point I remember the midwife telling me, "Breathe, Heather. Breathe life, breathe all the way down to your baby."

As I practiced my relaxation and breathing techniques regularly throughout my pregnancy, I found that I eventually began to reach a place within my soul that I hadn't previously discovered. It was like I'd found the place where my body and my spirit were joined.

Every time I lost it, she and my husband would help me focus on my breath, and I would feel peace flow into me again and calm my soul.

Hour after hour I took each contraction one breath at time and felt my body and my spirit merge closer and closer together, until suddenly, miraculously, I was holding my newborn son in my arms. As I looked into his little face, I recognized the spirit I had met in the celestial room. He was beautiful and perfect, and I marveled in awe as his little lungs took in their first breaths—and he became a living soul.

My Mantra Meditation Journey

By Felice Austin, CHt

THE FIRST TIME I CHANTED THE MANTRA "Ong namo guru dev namo" I was in a room full of pregnant women. The translation of the mantra was explained to me as: "I honor the divine teacher within me." It is an acknowledgement of one's status as both a child of God and a god/goddess oneself. As everyone began chanting, and the wavelengths of sound connected in graceful resonance, I looked around the room and wondered what was happening. I felt sure that something was happening to me, and that words were not adequate to describe it, yet words were the very thing creating it.

We tuned in with that same mantra every yoga class, and we tuned out with the mantra "Sat Nam" which means "I am truth, truth is my identity," another reminder of our spiritual nature.

For many weeks, I just went along with it because it felt nice, and the music was beautiful. Then I started doing some meditating at home—chanting and singing my favorite mantras. Most of the mantras were in Gurmukhi, an ancient language similar to Sanskrit in which every word most closely approximates the sound of the thing it describes. For example, Ong is the sound of creation (other traditions use Om). Something about the words being in a different language helped me get out of my looping thoughts which were all in English.

As I continued practicing, I became aware of something at the center of the sound vibration—a stillness, an openness. The best way to describe what happened is in metaphor. In the center of my mind, there was a still, clear lake, and into it I dropped, like a tiny pebble, the words and meanings of the mantra, such as God's wondrousness, or my own divine identity, and the ripples washed every shore. I began to change from the inside out. I was communing with God, and I was god. I began to literally shine. People asked me why I seemed so confident and happy, what face cream I used, how I handled my situation with grace.

I learned later that the word mantra means literally "mind vibration" or "mind tool." I think this is the best way to explain how it worked. Words were the tool, and by repeatedly chanting them, the vibration of these words penetrated the deeper levels of my mind and heart.

In Deuteronomy 11:18, God tells us to "lay up these my words in your heart." For me, in order to lay anything deeply in my heart, repetition is necessary, as is a strong emotional connection. Many of the meditations, which often included physically challenging mudras (hand/arm positions), broke down my emotional defenses and allowed me to conquer fear or embrace joy.

In addition to peace and access to inner resources I didn't know I had before, I began to have profound spiritual experiences every day. I can tes-

---

I can testify to the abundance of light and knowledge God is waiting to give us if we but tune in regularly.

---

tify to the abundance of light and knowledge God is waiting to give us if we but tune in regularly. It still blows my mind what can happen in just twelve minutes of meditation.

One morning, as the rain fell outside, I practiced a mediation for celestial communication that can best be described as a seated, joyous dance. As the music lulled and swayed to an end, I let my hands rest open in front of me as if inviting someone to put their hands in mine. In that moment I felt my mother come and take my hands and smile. My heart roused, and I smiled back. She then let me know that there was a line of people waiting for their turn. One by one, I felt many ancestors come and take my hands and then move on. Some of them I knew, and others I didn't know that I knew. Last was my unborn daughter who took my hands and started to swing them from side to side playfully. I instantly knew her. Her personality was playful and so familiar. We danced like this for a few minutes until it was time for them all to go. The best part was that I knew that I could call them back any time by meditating and then inviting them with open hands.

I enjoy reading my scriptures after I meditate because I am then prepared to receive the words into my heart. One particular scripture in D&C 121 became my personal mantra during my pregnancy: "My [daughter], peace be unto thy soul; thine adversity and thine afflictions shall be but a small moment" (vs. 7). I read it over and over until I felt it and believed it. And it came true. As I have continued my study and my practice of meditation, the Lord has blessed me with peace in my soul which has been my greatest resource in motherhood.

CHAPTER SEVEN

The Sprit-Mind-Body Connection

Thou shalt love the Lord thy God with all
thy heart, with all thy might, mind, and strength.

D&C 59:5

The Spirit-Mind-Body Connection

By Felice Austin, C.Ht.

*Behold, this is your work, to keep my commandments, yea,
with all your might, mind, and strength.*

D&C 11:20

The scriptures teach us to worship God with all our "might, mind, and strength" (D&C 4:2). In the dictionary, *might* is defined as "physical power or strength,"[1] which refers to the body. *Strength* is defined not just as physical but also "moral power, firmness and courage,"[2] which most accurately refers to our spiritual nature. Therefore, the aforementioned trio could be understood in modern terms as body, mind, and spirit. This trio appears together ten times in the scriptures[3] with different commandments. We are not just commanded to worship God with all our might, mind, and strength but also to serve, keep the commandments, work, and love God with all three parts as well. Though God does not specifically mention birthing in these verses, to give life is an act of service, work, and love, and it fulfills God's commandment to multiply. Therefore, any of these scriptures could be understood as I have interpreted Doctrine and Covenants 11:20: Behold, this is your work, to give life, yea, with all your body, mind, and spirit.

The restored gospel of Jesus Christ teaches that there is an intimate link between body, mind, and spirit.[4] For example, in the revelations containing the Lord's law of health (D&C 88 and 89), God has promised physical blessings of health and also blessings of the mind and spirit. In our worship services, we are also reminded of the need for constant nourishment of both body and spirit. As a hypnotherapist, I have the opportunity to help people understand how to use this powerful mind-body-spirit connection to transform their lives. (To learn more about hypnosis and it's long and distinguished history in obstetrics, please visit our resources section on this book's website.) Many people don't fully understand the mind-body connection, and many others confuse the mind and spirit, so I will address the mind-body connection first and then discuss the spirit's place in this trio.

"Man [is] the noblest work of the Great Designer . . . with a brain and a will, with a mind and a soul, with intelligence and divinity."[5]

—Thomas S. Monson

THE MIND-BODY CONNECTION

Knowledge of the mind-body connection has existed for eons. Thousands of years ago, ancient man left drawings on cave walls depicting shamanism—the oldest known tradition that used visualized images for healing. In the fourth century BC, the ancient Greek philosopher Socrates commented, "There is no illness of the body apart from the mind."[6] We can also find examples of the mind-body connection throughout the scriptures. In Proverbs 17:22 we read, "A merry heart doeth good like a medicine: but a broken spirit drieth the bones." In the Book of Mormon, we learn of a man named Zeezrom, who "lay sick at Sidom, with a burning fever, which was caused by the great tribulations of his mind on account of his wickedness" (Alma 15:3). And in the New Testament, we have a glimpse of Christ's infinite sacrifice. Although we don't know exactly how Christ took upon Himself the sins and sorrows of the world, we know that it caused Him great physical agony, such that "his sweat was as it were great drops of blood falling down to the ground" (Luke 22:44).

At present, the greatest scientifically documented evidence of the mind-body connection is called "the placebo effect." The placebo effect is a phenomenon in which patients given a pill (or other intervention) that is actually inert matter are healed or greatly improved. The placebo effect works on the psychological principle of expectancy. If patients believe the substance or procedure will help them, they improve. Alternately, if

patients believe that the treatment will do harm, the treatment has negative effects (the nocebo effect). The harm or healing effects can increase,
depending on other expectancy factors. In one study, the response to a
placebo increased from 44 percent to 62 percent when the doctor treated
patients with "warmth, attention, and confidence."[7] The placebo effect has
been documented thousands of times with similar remarkable results.

*A placebo described as a muscle relaxant will cause muscle relaxation
and if described as the opposite, muscle tension. A placebo presented
as a stimulant will have this effect on heart rhythm and blood
pressure, but when administered as a depressant, the opposite effect.[8]*

In my work we call the placebo effect the lowest form of suggestion, and some good complementary health care providers refer to it as
the highest form of medicine. It is an indisputable fact that our minds
accept suggestions all the time that affect our bodies. For example, when
watching an exciting or frightening movie, most of us will feel our hearts
beat faster. We are in no real danger, but our minds accept the suggestion
that something is scary, and so our heart rate changes. The unconscious
mind, or subconscious mind, is the largest part of the mind and controls
most of our behavior as well as our physical processes, such as heart rate,
respiratory system, nervous system, and immune system, and most of the
systems involved in the birthing process.

While we have some control over what suggestions our minds accept
or reject, there are certain times that the mind is naturally more receptive and
vulnerable. Pregnancy, birth, and the postpartum period are times when a
woman's mind is wide open to suggestions, both positive and negative.

Interestingly, however, not all suggestions have the same impact.
Suggestions work best when they are in accordance with a person's beliefs.[9]
For example, patients improve when they believe they are getting medicine
that will help them. Beliefs are often evident in expectations. In a study
comparing expectations with labor, "the proportion of women expecting
pain to those who actually received medication were nearly identical."[10]

In the Book of Mormon, Alma likened belief unto seeds. I also like
to compare a suggestion to a seed. If it is a good suggestion, it will begin,

as Alma said, to "enlarge [your] soul . . . enlighten [your] understanding" (Alma 32:28), and "your mind doth begin to expand" (Alma 32:34). Many of the stories in this book that describe physical, mental, or spiritual transformations follow the pattern Alma described. They begin with a woman or man accepting a suggestion—like Kamille Larsen (see "Close to Heaven," page 258) when she read, "If ye are prepared, ye shall not fear."[11] She nourished the seed, and through steady, incremental growth, her birth experience was transformed.

Just as the mind can profoundly affect our bodies, changes to the body can affect the mind. For example, nutrition, exercise, and breathing can have a huge effect on the mind. In my practice, I often have to educate clients about how a drop in blood sugar, poor nutrition, and lack of sleep cause difficulty in coping with stress and general emotional instability.

Conversely, regular physical exercise can increase a person's tolerance of mental and emotional stress.[12] In the body's ability to effect the mind, however, there is no example as profound as breathing. The simple act

---

"Retire to thy bed early, that ye may not be weary; arise early, that your bodies and your minds may be invigorated." —D&C 88:124

---

of breathing deeply releases a chemical that relaxes the body, including the brain-body, which in turn calms the mind.[13] This is why adequate and complete breathing is such a focus in childbirth education classes. To read more about breathing, I invite you to read the Meditation chapter (page 199.)

THE MIND-BODY CONNECTION
IN PREGNANT AND BIRTHING WOMEN

Because our minds are most receptive to suggestions when we are open and vulnerable, I can think of no other group of people who are as vulnerable as pregnant women and new mothers. Ina May Gaskin, one of our nation's most honored midwives, said the following about the mind-body connection:

My midwife partners and I . . . learned by observation and experience that the presence of even one person who is not exquisitely attuned to the mother's feelings can stop some women's labors. All women are sensitive. Some are extraordinarily so. We learned this truth by observing many labors stop or slow down when someone entered the birth room who was not intimate with the laboring mothers' feelings. If that person then left the room, labor usually returned to its former pace or intensity.[14]

Fear and other negative emotions have been shown to stop labor, but even more, Ina May (and others before her) noticed that a woman's cervix can actually close down (reverse dilation) when the doctor comes in.[15] On the other hand, positive suggestions and true words spoken can open a "stuck" cervix. In Eireen Henderson's story, "Gently at My Side" (page 426), when her husband told her, "You are doing it. You're almost there! You are so strong," she was pushing within minutes.

More than anything, it is important to receive encouragement from your care provider. Suggestions from a person in authority, such as a doctor or midwife, carry extra weight in the mind. Rebecca Overson shared the following story about her midwife:

Some time after my birth, I was talking with my midwife, who told me about a birth she once attended. When she arrived, the woman had already been in labor some time and was only about two centimeters dilated. After checking her, my midwife announced that she was seven centimeters dilated and that this was going to be a fast and easy birth. What happened next was that the woman immediately dilated to seven centimeters and not long afterward, the baby was born, quickly and easily. . . . I had the strangest suspicion that she was talking about my birth.

It is important to begin early in your pregnancy—and even before—to notice how different thoughts, emotions, suggestions, and people affect your body. How do you feel during prenatal care visits? Do you feel comfortable opening up emotionally? Does your body tense or relax? How does your body react when people tell you their birth stories or birth scaries? Have you had any trauma or abuse in the past that your care provider should know about? Sexual abuse has lasting effects on the mind and body; however, a conscious, empowered spiritual birth can actually heal scars of sexual abuse, as you can read in Holly Young's story, "Helping Me Heal" (page 438), and Alisha's story, "Letting Go" (page 301).

From our ancient and recent legacy of birthing women, we learn how important it is to be surrounded by people who not only care for our bodies but also comfort and calm our minds. Make sure that during your pregnancy, birth, and postpartum days of rest you are surrounded as much as possible by people and things that uplift, edify, strengthen, and speak peace to your mind. (See "Unity with Providers of Care," on page 433.)

"You are not a human being in search of a spiritual experience. You are a spiritual being immersed in a human experience."[16]

—Perre Teilhard de Chardin

THE SPIRIT-MIND-BODY CONNECTION

After Adam and Eve partook of the fruit, thus gaining mortality, they realized their nakedness. In the scriptures, nakedness is metaphorical for awareness of our weaknesses, sins, flaws, fears, and vulnerabilities that we feel in our body-mind identified state.[17] For example, nakedness could include feelings of tiredness, fear, jealousy, not being good enough or strong enough, pride, insecurity, sensitivity, depression, impatience, anger, and clumsiness. However, as Phillip McLemore wrote, "the truth is we are not weak, vulnerable, afraid, and flawed. We have experienced these qualities outside of Eden, and unfortunately we have identified with them and made them real. But identification with our spiritual nature is the ultimate reality."[18]

Strong physical or emotional feelings may feel like reality; however, we are not our thoughts, emotions, or behavior. As I tell my daughter, there are no bad people, there is only bad behavior. Our spirits are still pure and perfect. When we are mind-body identified, we are "the natural man," who is "an enemy to God" (Mosiah 3:19).

However, we do not believe, as the mystics do, that the mind and body are a prison we long to escape. We know that before we came to the earth, we rejoiced at the chance to receive bodies (see Job 38:7). Our minds and bodies are intended to give us experiences, and are experiences are intended to be brought into harmony with the perfection of our spirits.

In Mosiah, King Benjamin taught that we can achieve this harmony by yielding to "the enticings of the Holy Spirit" (Mosiah 3:19). The Holy Spirit, which is different from our own spirits, is a member of the Godhead. It testifies of truth, binds, comforts, and reminds us of our own eternal nature. What is interesting about the Holy Spirit is that it works on all three levels: spirit, mind, and body. When a person is enticed by the Holy Spirit, it is the person's pure and perfect spirit that recognizes the Holy Spirit; a person is then said to feel the Spirit in the heart and the mind. If we did not have that perfect spiritual core, there would be no recognition, and without the mind and body, we could not act. It is through this three-part connection that communion with God is possible, that the Atonement is able to work in us.

In Luke, Christ is quoted as saying: "The kingdom of God does not come with observation: neither will they say, 'See here! Or See there!' For the kingdom of God is within you" (Luke 17:20–21). Christ was telling us that we are holy and divine in our essential being, just as Adam and Eve were in the Garden. When we accept and remember our spiritual nature as our true identity, our bodies and minds are no longer burdens obscuring our perfect spiritual nature; they become tools for glorifying God. The Apostle Paul taught us to "glorify God in your body, and in your spirit, which are God's" (1 Corinthians 6:20). It is through Jesus Christ's Atonement and our regular spiritual communion with God that we are able to rediscover our divine nature and glorify God. I can think of no better way to glorify God than to give life with all our body, mind, and spirit.

1   Dictionary.com, s.v. "might," http://dictionary.reference.com/browse/might
2   Dictionary.com, s.v. "strength," http://dictionary.reference.com/browse/strength
3   2 Nephi 25:29; Mosiah 2:11; Alma 39:13; Moroni 10:32; D&C 4:2; 11:20; 20:31; 59:5; 33:7; 98:47
4   Susan W. Tanner, "The Sanctity of the Body," *Ensign*, November 2005, http://lds.org/ensign/2005/11/the-sanctity-of-the-body.
5   Thomas S. Monson, "He is Risen," *Ensign*, April 2010, http://lds.org/general-conference/2010/04/he-is-risen?lang=eng
6   Socrates, in *The Writings of Plato*.
7   Ted J. Kaptchuk, John M. Kelley, Lisa A. Conboy, et al., "Components of Placebo Effect: Randomized Controlled Trial in Patients with Irritable Bowel Syndrome," *BMJ* 336, no. 7651 (2008): 999–1003.
8   Magne Arve Flaten, Terje Simonsen, and Harald Olsen, "Drug-Related Information Generates Placebo and Nocebo Responses That Modify the Drug Response," *Psychosomatic Medicine* 61, no. 2 (1999): 250–255, http://www.psychosomaticmedicine.org/cgi/reprint/61/2/250; Irvine Kirsch, "Specifying Non-specifics: Psychological Mechanism of the Placebo Effect," in *The Placebo Effect: An Interdisciplinary Exploration*, ed. Anne Harrington (Cambridge, MA: Harvard University Press, 1997), 166–186.
9   John Kappas, *Professional Hypnotism Manual* (Los Angeles: Panorama, 2009).
10 Ina May Gaskin, *Ina May's Guide to Childbirth* (New York, Bantam, 2003), 151.
11 D&C 38:30
12 Richard A. Dienstbier, "Exercise and Stress Tolerance," *University of Nebraska Faculty Publications, Department of Psychology*, April 1981, http://digitalcommons.unl.edu/psychfacpub/215.
13 Andrew Newberg, *How God Changes Your Brain* (New York: Balantine, 2009), 179.
14 Ina May Gaskin, *Ina May's Guide to Childbirth* (New York, Bantam, 2003), 138.
15 Ibid., 170.
16 Perre Teilhard de Chardin, *The Phenomenon of Man*, (USA: Harper & Brothers, 1959), http://en.wikiquote.org/wiki/Pierre_Teilhard_de_Chardin.
17 Phillip McLemore, "The Yoga of Christ," *Sunstone Magazine*, June 2007, 41.
18 Ibid.

THE PURPOSE OF LIFE

By Linda Burton King, RN, (CD)DONA

WHILE MY FAMILY AND I were watching the Winter Olympics at my parents' house, I started to feel a different kind of sensation than I had felt before with the previous "pressure waves" (a term we use instead of "labor pains"). In between the women jumping off the ski jumps and the men bobsledding, I knew I was entering my own physical endurance event.

My mother noticed that I had to pause every once in a while and take some deep breaths. She asked me if I was feeling anything. I casually said, "Oh, not really." After that evening's Olympic events were over, my husband Lance and I drove home to our small apartment. As a surgical nurse, I knew the mechanics and medical terminology of childbirth, but nothing is quite like the actual personal experience, especially for a first-time mother.

I informed Lance that the pressure waves were feeling stronger and were more frequent. He did not think that I was showing any significant change in my attitude or facial expressions but decided that he would time these waves by the clock and see if they had any pattern to them. To his surprise, they did. After about an hour or two, the waves were progressing to every minute and a half, lasting about sixty to sixty-five seconds.

I do not know what exactly caused me to feel an urgency to go to the hospital, but I decided that if I was going to get to the hospital at all I should go while I could still somewhat walk to the car. These intense feelings were becoming stronger but were not painful. It reminded me of when I used to run long distances. During the run, if I felt like giving up, I realized it was because I was tired, not because I was in pain. These pressure wave sensations were much like running up a hill and then back down again.

Lance and I made it to the hospital, which was only a few minutes away. It was the middle of the night, and we walked in calm, collected, and extremely relaxed. The nurses asked why I was there, and I said that I was in labor. They did not believe me. I leaned over every once in a while because I could not talk to them for longer than a minute at a time. They sent me to the triage room. To their surprise, I was opened to 7.5 cm and was 100% thinned. The nurse quickly said that I was staying at the hospital, and they called my midwife.

Lance and I walked to the next birthing room and sat on the chair, and that is where I stayed basically until our daughter Mariah was crowning. During the birthing process, I suggested to the nurses that instead of asking me about my pain level, it would be more effective to ask about my comfort level.

Lance was most helpful. He was involved with the whole birth process and applied counter pressure to my knees and sacrum, or tailbone. My birth water released all over Lance, and I appreciated him even more because of his dedication. Every moment that he was there made me feel like he was becoming the protector and provider I always knew he was.

After the release of water, I moved to the bed. Lance was there to hold my hand and support me the whole way. I knelt on my hands and knees, then switched positions to side-lying to give birth to Mariah. When I moved to my side, the birth waves spread out and I did not know what was happening. I started to become scared and prayed. I thought, "Please let my birth waves continue to progress."

This was the moment when I needed God the most. I did not know what to do. I knew that I was not in control of the outcome of my baby's birth. At the same time that this fear crept into my mind, another thought also came. My husband and I were co-creators with God. The terms Heavenly Father and Heavenly Mother had a whole new meaning.

This quiet confidence came by the Spirit and reminded me that we are all born with flesh, spirit, blood and water. What a most amazing and wonderful event to be part of. As I struggled to breathe deeply, I could see the look on my husband's face. He was going to receive the baby just after she was born. His expressions showed awe, concern, delight, anxiety, and anticipation as his eyes filled with tears of joy.

They say that seven is a "heavenly" number and Mariah's numbers were full of sevens. She was born at 7:07 in the morning, weighing 7 lbs, 7 oz and was born on the 17th of the month.

The sound of Mariah's first cry and small noises were the most pure and simple sound ever created. I felt wonderful! I held Mariah on my chest and looked into her eyes. She was awake and alert and beautiful. Lance and I did it together. We created this tiny, healthy baby girl, and I gave birth to this perfect child. Handing Mariah to Lance, I could see excitement and joy pouring out from his eyes. The moment I felt the Spirit the most was when my husband held our little daughter, Mariah, in his strong and loving arms.

At that moment I knew that the purpose of life is to bring life to others, to care for them, to teach them, and to love them. This experience truly felt like a rite of passage, our own Olympic athletic event, one that transformed a regular man and woman into real, loving parents. Our prize was more than a gold medal. It was a sweet and perfect, beautiful baby girl.

Thoughts on Morning Sickness

By Neoma Gould

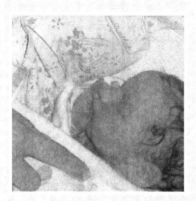

I DON'T GET AS SICK AS SOME WOMEN do when pregnant. My morning sickness is usually confined to the second half of the first trimester. I don't throw up daily, but I feel queasy most of the time. But I have learned that when I am busy helping someone else I don't notice the sickness as much.

About two months into my first pregnancy, my husband and I planned to go on a trip. We were going to travel from Seattle to Utah in a minivan with my pregnant sister and her four children. By this point in my pregnancy, I felt fairly nauseous most of the time, and I was nervous about being car sick during the fourteen-hour drive. At my request, my husband gave me a priesthood blessing the night before we left. We learned quickly that the Lord was looking out for us.

After driving for a couple of hours, the minivan broke down. I ended up spending all day watching the four children at the home of a friend of a friend who happened to live in that area while my husband and sister tried to get the car fixed. Miraculously, I wasn't sick all day. After the ordeal was over and we arrived safely home again, the morning sickness returned.

My second and third morning sickness "miracles" were remarkably similar stories. At about three months along during both pregnancies, I went to girl's camp as an adult leader. Both times I was in the middle of my morning sick period, but while at camp I felt fine. The first time I thought maybe I had just gotten past the third trimester and my morning sickness was over with, but lest I neglect to recognize the miracle in it, I was promptly sick again upon returning home. I have learned that ultimately Heavenly Father is in control of everything, even morning sickness, and He can help us when we really need Him to.

LIGHT, PEACE, AND JOY

By Brittany Cromar

DURING MY FIRST PREGNANCY, the Lord led me on a quest for knowledge. Since "the glory of God is intelligence" (D&C 93:36) and all light and truth come from God, I believe that my desire to find greater knowledge and truth about birth was directed by the Spirit. I believe the Spirit guided me to find more information on natural birth, since I had always assumed I'd get an epidural without giving it much thought. As a result of this research, I came to feel strongly that I wanted to avoid any medical interventions that I did not need. This led me to change care providers at thirty-four weeks of pregnancy to a practice that did not routinely use medical interventions, with whom I felt more comfortable overall, and who were able to give me the emotional support I needed when things went differently than I had hoped. Looking at it now, it's hard to see how the Lord could not be involved in such a drastic transformation of thought as the one I experienced.

For my first birth, I had been up all night with contractions and was only 2 cm when I got to the hospital. I ended up getting Pitocin because they discovered my amniotic fluid was leaking. After a few hours of little progress, I chose to get an epidural. I remember feeling kind of sad after the epidural was in because it wasn't what I planned. Even so, I realized that, under the circumstances, it was really a blessing that I could get it and get some rest.

I listened to my iPod after I got the epidural, and chose at that time to listen to a collection of instrumental arrangements of hymns arranged by Lex de Azevedo. I remember the soothing music giving me peace and helping me sleep despite my conflicted feelings about the situation.

Because the birth took place on a Saturday at a small hospital, we got our pick of the rooms on the floor and chose the one with a great view of the Mt. Timpanogos Temple from its large window. The drapes were open when I gave birth at 9:54 pm, and the temple was all lit up. I looked at the window while I held my daughter on my belly with the cord still attached. The delivery lights in the darkened room lit us up in the glass, and the temple glowed on the other side. I think it will be very special to tell my daughter that she was born under the glow of the temple.

During my second pregnancy, I did some journaling. In explaining why I wanted a natural birth, it came together to me that I feel that God designed the birth process with perfection, and that interference in the process causes trouble. I feel that the Lord has given us everything we need to create smooth and comfortable childbirth within our own minds and bodies. I used the Hypnobabies® hypnosis for childbirth method to prepare. I found ways to tie the philosophies of the program in with my religious beliefs and even found some hymns that had the word "peace" (a hypnotic cue used for comfort in this method) in them. These included "Be Still My Soul" and "Master, the Tempest is Raging." The latter was especially relevant because contractions in Hypnobabies® are "pressure waves." I thought about how Christ could calm the waves of the storm of my birth, saying, "Peace." I thought it would be a nice option to have hymns to sing during my birthing. I didn't end up doing that, but tying the hypnosis tools to a religious idea helped me integrate spiritual preparation into the preparation I was already doing that used the mind-body connection.

During my second birth, I focused on listening to my hypnosis tracks and using my hypnosis techniques. For much of my first stage, using hypnosis helped the atmosphere be more reverent because it kept me calm. Second stage was very intense, but I enjoyed experiencing the sudden change from feeling overwhelmed by the intensity to the complete joy of having my baby in my hands and knowing I had done it.

My second birth reminded me of Alma 36:17-20, where Alma describes his conversion as being "filled with joy as exceeding as was [his] pain." It made me think that maybe being "born again" is just as much like giving birth as it is like being born. I saw, in giving birth naturally, a metaphor for what it feels like when we allow Christ to take our burdens. Although I didn't recognize it at the time, I learned a lot spiritually by experiencing it.

Constant Nourishment

By Felice Austin, CHt

*"When a woman elevates her life for the better,
her entire family benefits, because she sets a new level
of awareness and clarity in the home."[1]*

GURMUKH KAUR KHALSA

In our worship, we are reminded of the need for constant nourishment to both body and spirit. *Constant nourishment* is a phrase that is incredibly deep significance during pregnancy. Every act of nourishing nourishes two bodies and two spirits—or more, if the mother is carrying multiples.

I can't think of a better example of constant nourishment than the umbilical cord. Through this channel, your baby always has access to what he or she needs. Even when you may not be able to keep any food down, your baby is still being nourished. I once told a friend that I wished I had an umbilical cord to heaven, to constantly fill me with God's love. I will never forget her answer. She said, "It is only an illusion that there is not."

In a revelation given to Joseph Smith, God promised that if we live righteously "the Holy Ghost shall be thy *constant* companion" (D&C 121:46; emphasis added). What an awesome promise to have a member of the Godhead as our companion. To qualify for this privilege, all we have to do is live righteously and nourish ourselves with things of the Spirit.

NOURISHING YOUR SPIRIT

There are many excellent ways to nourish your spirit during pregnancy, such as daily meditation, scripture study, affirmations, kind self-talk, uplifting music, art, great books, regular temple attendance, and modified fasting. Nourishing yourself spiritually may also mean avoiding certain things that you enjoyed before. In Japan, both anciently and today, pregnant women have been counseled not to look at anything unpleasant or view violent or dramatic movies. In some parts of Japan, there are huge billboards reminding pregnant women of this counsel.

This is wise advice. As we now know through modern science, what we consume, think, feel, and experience during pregnancy has an effect on our developing babies. Yet, modern science only confirms what was revealed anciently. In Judges 13, we learn from the story of Samson's mother (described later in this chapter) that a woman's choices while pregnant affect her child in the womb. Modern prophets and apostles have also taught this lesson. Elder Orson Pratt taught:

> Every good principle which you would have your children inherit should be predominant and reign in your own bosoms; for, though the spirits are pure and heavenly when they enter the infant tabernacle, yet they are extremely susceptible of influences either for good or for bad. The state of the parents' minds at the time of conception, and the state of the mother's mind during her pregnancy, will be constitutionally impressed upon the offspring, bringing with it consequences which, in a degree, have a bearing upon the future destiny of the child.[2]

Other ways to nourish our spirits are through learning and being creative. Learning invigorates our minds and makes us happy. When I was preg-

"If there is anything virtuous, lovely, of good report or praiseworthy, we seek after these things." —Article of Faith 1:13

nant, a man in my stake offered a Hebrew class through the institute of religion. I had never thought of learning Hebrew before, but I felt inspired to take the class. In it, I made great friendships and found an increased love for Jewish people.

Of the many ways to nurture the spirit, some of the most profound nurturing I have witnessed among mothers and mothers-to-be is the nurturing we give to one another by sharing wisdom and experiences, which is why so many personal stories are included in this book. On the following pages and throughout the book are examples of how women have nurtured their spirits during pregnancy and into motherhood.

NOURISHING THE BODY

In our information-rich society, there are so many different voices weighing in on physical health. The health section of the bookstore has thousands of books whose authors have all kinds of excellent credentials. Yet even with so much information available, many people are still floundering. As Latter-day Saints, we are blessed to have just a few straightforward pages on health, and we have the confidence of knowing that the author's credentials are that He is God.

The revelation that contains the Lord's law of health came to Joseph Smith in 1833. The Lord declared that alcohol and tobacco are not good for the body. In fact, we now have evidence that the use of alcohol and tobacco by pregnant women can cause physical and mental damage to their babies. It is hard to imagine a world where people didn't know that, but in 1833 such was the case.

God has always cared about the nourishment of His people, especially expectant mothers. In the birth story of Samson, in Judges 13, an angel appeared to the mother of Samson, told her that she was to bear a son, and gave her the following instructions: "Drink not wine nor strong drink, and eat not any unclean thing: For lo, thou shalt conceive, and bear a son; and no razor shall come on his head: for the child shall be a Nazarite unto God from the womb: and he shall begin to deliver Israel out of the hands of the Philistines" (Judges 13: 4–5).

A Nazarite was a man or woman who was consecrated unto God. The vow could be for the person's whole life or for a limited amount of time. A person who made a Nazarite vow was not permitted to drink wine, vinegar, or any other strong drink or to eat grapes or anything that came from a vine tree. Nazarites were also forbidden to cut their hair or touch a dead body or else their vow with God would be broken (see Numbers 6:1–9).

From the angel's words to Samson's mother, we learn that Sampson was foreordained to be a Nazarite "from the womb," and that what a woman takes into her body during pregnancy goes into the womb. This being true, in order for her unborn son to keep his vow, Samson's mother needed to keep the vow. We also learn from this story, among other things, that God gives personal revelation to women specific to the nourishment of their bodies and their babies during pregnancy.

Even though you may be familiar with the scriptures in Doctrine and Covenants 88 and 89, which contain the Lord's law of health, I invite you to read them again and reevaluate them to see whether you can live this law more faithfully. Here a just a few points that struck me as I read these sections from a mother-to-be perspective.

STRONG DRINKS

Strong drinks are any drinks that contain harmful substances. If you don't know whether your favorite drink contains harmful substances, do your research. Find out what those ten-letter ingredients are, and check the labels even on things you think only have one ingredient, such as milk. It is also important to understand what is meant by the terms *organic* and *conventional*. Sometimes, despite our best research, we may still be confused. Research changes often and may have opposing viewpoints. However, if you seek spiritual guidance, God will give you the answers you need for yourself and your baby.

DRUGS

From the Lord's law of health we learn that "we should not use drugs except when necessary as medicine. Some drugs are even more harmful than alcohol and tobacco, which are also drugs."[3] This means that we should carefully consider everything we put into our bodies. We should also define what the word *necessary* means. Is something medically necessary when there is a natural alternative?

In Alma, we learn that some people in the land were dying with fevers, but not so many "because of the excellent qualities of the many plants and roots which God had prepared to remove the cause of diseases"(Alma 46:40).

In the Word of Wisdom, God mentioned these plants and roots again, calling them "wholesome herbs," and said that He *ordained* them: "And verily I say unto you, all wholesome herbs God had ordained for the constitution, nature, and use of man" (D&C 89:10). When people are ordained, it means they are called of God and set apart through the priesthood with the laying on of hands. Pondering this thought has given me much more reverence for natural medicine.

"In Judaism, the purpose of eating is partly to fuel ourselves to serve God and partly to force us to enjoy what God has provided. This means that if you eat a chocolate bar or allow your children to have one, you must say a blessing before you eat it to remind yourself to celebrate its worth. If you eat too many candy bars, you can't celebrate because they are no longer special. If you eat and feel guilty at the same time, you demean the experience of pleasure and misspend the blessing. It's not a celebration anymore."[10] —Wendy Mogel

---

REST, WORK, EXERCISE, AND KIND WORDS

Also important in God's law of health are work, rest, and exercise. Doctrine and Covenants 88:124 states: "Cease to be idle; cease to be unclean; cease to find fault one with another; cease to sleep longer than is needful; retire to they bed early that ye may not be weary; arise early, that your bodies and your minds may be invigorated." Many people have heard and understand the wisdom in the "early to bed, early to rise" adage. What you may not have noticed in God's law of health, however, is something that is sandwiched in the middle of verse 124: "Cease to find fault one with another." This doesn't seem to have much to do with health, but if it is in the middle of this verse, it is no accident. Finding fault in others is contraindicated for health. In fact, research shows that spouses who display contempt for each other suffer more illnesses and diseases than respectful spouses.[4] And in the first book of the Book of Mormon we read that family discord brings

Lehi and Sariah down "even upon their sick beds."[5]

I discovered a visually stunning study when I found Dr. Masaru Emoto's book full of beautiful pictures that looked like individual snow-flakes. Dr. Emoto, a Japanese scientist, conducted experiments on water by speaking different words to it, playing music, and showing the water pictures. He then froze and photographed the crystals that the water formed. The water that was spoken words of love and gratitude formed breathtaking crystals. The water that was called unkind names, exposed to harsh music, or shown disturbing images would not even form crys-tals—the images looked like deformed blobs.[6] Dr. Emoto's findings are a powerful visual testament to the effect that words can have on the body, which is anywhere from 70 to 90 percent water, depending on your age. Babies start out in the womb almost 100 percent water.

MODERATION, SANCTIFICATION, CELEBRATION

God gave us all the beasts, fruits of the earth, and herbs for our use, but He also commanded us to use them "with prudence and thanksgiving" (D&C 89:11). To me, this means that we are to elevate the act of eating by eating consciously. It is only consciousness that sets us apart from beasts, who eat alone, on the run, only to survive, and without conscious grati-tude. Wendy Mogel, PhD, author of *The Blessing of a Skinned Knee: Using Jewish Teachings to Raise Self-Reliant Children*, suggested that setting a nice table, arranging food attractively on a plate, and saying a blessing raise the physical act of eating to a spiritual discipline.[8]

One of the many wonderful things my daughter and I have learned from Judaism is that food can be a medium for holiness and family unity. Mogel said, "At its core, Judaism is a table-centered religion. With the destruction of the ancient Holy Temple, each family's table serves to replace the original holy altar."[9] When we think of the table as an altar, it changes the way we think about what we put on it, how we come to it, and how we behave while there. Though I can't do it every day, at least once a week, on the Sabbath, I try to make my table an altar.

THE BLESSINGS

In D&C 29:34, the Lord tells us, "Wherefore, verily I say unto you that all things unto me are spiritual, and not at any time have I given unto you a law which was temporal." The promised blessings for living the Lord's law of health are therefore both temporal and spiritual. If we nourish our bodies and our babies in accordance with His law, Heavenly Father promises us health—"health in their navel and marrow in their bones . . . and [they] shall run and not be weary, and shall walk and not faint"—as well as spiritual knowledge: "wisdom, and great treasures of knowledge, even hidden treasures" (D&C 89:18–20). When we live the Lord's law of health, our senses are not dulled to celestial communication, which we need on this spiritual journey of motherhood.

Fasting While Pregnant and Breast-feeding

By Heather Farrell, CD(DONA)

The blessings of fasting are numerous, and they are both temporal and spiritual. Fasting is a wonderful way to nourish your spirit. In the Latter-day Saint Church Handbook of Instructions, it states, "A proper fast day observance typically includes abstaining from food and drink for two consecutive meals in a twenty-four-hour period, attending a fast and testimony meeting, and giving a generous fast offering to help care for those in need." [1] However, while pregnant or lactating, if you find yourself unable to observe a typical fast it is still possible to observe a proper fast by adapting it to your circumstances.

If completely abstaining from food or drink is not possible, consider choosing to fast from your favorite foods or to eat simple, small meals that satisfy your body's needs but don't indulge it. You may also choose to give up something other than food such as television, the Internet, or a negative behavior or habit. The purpose of fasting is sacrifice, and if you are making an earnest effort to "humble [your] soul with fasting" (Psalms 35: 13), it doesn't matter what you fast as long as you honor the spirit of the fast.

It is also important to remember that abstaining from food and drink is only one part of observing a proper fast. Attending a fast and testimony meeting and donating a generous fast offering are other components of a fast that will bless you and your family. Prayer is also another essential part of fasting. As you counsel with the Lord you will be able to find what constitutes an acceptable fast for your individual circumstances.

1   *Handbook 2: Administering in the Church* (Salt Lake City, UT: The Church of Jesus Christ of Latter-day Saints, 2010), 184.

1   Gurmukh, *Beautiful, Bountiful, Blissful* (New York: St. Martins/Griffin, 2003), 76.
2   Orson Pratt, *The Seer* (Salt Lake City: Seagull Book and Tape, 1993) 155.
3   The Church of Jesus Christ of Latter-day Saints, *Gospel Principles* (Salt Lake City, UT: The Church of Jesus Christ of Latter-day Saints, 2009), 169.
4   Poonam Sharma, "Marriage and Health," Holistic Living, http://1stholistic.com/reading/health/health-marriage-and-health.htm
5   1 Nephi 18:17
6   Masaru Emoto, *The Hidden Messages in Water* (New York: Atria, 2001), 8.
7   Thomas S. Monson, "That We May Touch Heaven," *Ensign*, November 1990, http://lds.org/ensign/1990/11/that-we-may-touch-heaven.
8   Wendy Mogel, *The Blessing of a Skinned Knee: Using Jewish Teachings to Raise Self-Reliant Children* (New York: Penguin, 2001), 164.
9   Wendy Mogel, *The Blessing of a Skinned Knee: Using Jewish Teachings to Raise Self-Reliant Children* (New York: Penguin, 2001), 160.
10 Ibid., 166.

FAIRER AND FATTER

By Felice Austin, C.Ht.

I HAVE ALWAYS BEEN A PRETTY HEALTHY EATER. I also have a metabolism that doesn't stop. This was a problem after my baby was born. When I lost all my baby weight in twelve days, I wasn't complaining, but I kept losing more. And more. When my baby was nine months old, I had lost so much weight that I was worried about my milk supply, feeling weak, and not liking the starvation victim look.

I wondered what more I could do. I was eating all the time. I ate whole grain food, plenty of vegetables, and good fats like avocados, nuts, fish, but for some reason I was still wasting away. One day I realized that I needed help. I knew God cared about my health and about my baby's milk supply, so I prayed to know what to do.

Immediately after I prayed, I opened my scriptures. They fell open to Daniel, Chapter 1, so I read. In verse 12, Daniel asks the prince to give him "pulse to eat and water to drink," and prove him ten days. At the end of the ten days, the prince compares him to the other men who have been eating meat and drinking wine. The result is that his countenance appears "fairer and fatter" than the others. I was shocked. This is what I wanted—to be fairer and fatter. I looked at the footnote for "pulse" and it said: foods made of seeds, grains, etc. I thought I had been eating that way, but as I sat there pondering, I realized that I had been mainly eating brown rice and whole grain bread and pasta, but I had forgotten about lentils, barley, oats, buckwheat, millet, mung beans, and so many other things.

I immediately went out and bought some lentils and other legumes and grains and learned how to cook with them. (I think it's funny that this same diet can help people lose excess weight, but God knew it was just what I needed to do the opposite.) It took a few months, but I gained the ten pounds I needed, my face became fairer and fatter, and my daughter nursed from an avalanche of milk for several more years.

ONE VERSE AT A TIME

By Mindy Colin

MY PREGNANCIES WERE DEPRESSION-RIDDEN ordeals filled with incessant puking and muscle atrophy, but they gave me something very positive: time. I had a lot of time to ponder the scriptures and listen to talks on the Internet or BYU TV. I could literally do nothing else. Because I was so weak and on anti-nausea medication that made me dizzy (better than the alternative), I was forced to stay in bed for many weeks during each pregnancy.

During my second pregnancy, President Hinckley issued the challenge to read The Book of Mormon from cover to cover. I was sick and depressed. I thought there was no way I could read that much of The Book of Mormon every day because I couldn't read more than one or two verses at a time before I would get dizzy from the eye concentration. I thought it was going to be a very difficult task to read even one chapter.

What happened was one of the most spiritual experiences I've ever had. Since I could only read one verse at a time, I had the opportunity to ponder the meaning of the words and themes of each verse in a very intimate fashion. Every verse became a treasure trove of gospel insights. When the eye strain got too intense, I would turn on BYU TV or the General Conference audio archives on LDS.org and close my eyes and just listen to the talks and programs.

During that time, I felt closer to the Sprit than I had ever felt before. I began feeling less depressed, and the Spirit helped me to love the baby I was carrying instead of resenting it for making me so sick. I'll never forget that experience and the intense joy and peace that the Spirit can bring when you spend quality time with the words of the prophets.

Nurturing My Spirit in the Barn

By Sara

I HAD A HARD TIME WITH MY FIRST BABY. I was new to being a mother, had just quit my job to be a stay-at-home mom, and discovered I had nothing for me. I had to get up every day and take care of everyone else, but I was not taking care of me. And the family suffered. I was stressed and tired and moodier by the day.

Then, when my son was thirteen months old, we got a horse. Horses have always been my life's passion, but I had never actually owned one of my own. That gave me the outlet I needed.

When I got pregnant with my daughter, I found myself at the barn more and more. Sometimes I would just sit on my horse's back and absorb the country sites and sounds. Then, after my baby came, it was so nice to have that bit of "me time" every day while I went to take care of the horse. I always came home happy and ready to be a mom. I had none of the stress and sadness I had after my son was born.

It's so important to have that spiritual nourishment. I definitely learned that if you don't care for yourself, you cannot take care of your family. For me, my horse feeds my spirit and it's wonderful.

CHAPTER EIGHT

Fear

There is no fear in love;
but perfect love casteth out fear.

1 JOHN 4:18

Three Categories of Fear

By Felice Austin, CHt

In a novel by Steve Martin, one of my favorite authors, a character named Daniel is crippled by fears and self-made neurotic behaviors. The story is a hilarious but tender-hearted portrayal of his journey to becoming functional in society once again. One of the first things that helps Daniel on this road to change is a child—an illogical but lovable toddler, whose presence requires Daniel to conquer his fear of stepping off curbs. By the end of the book, Daniel also finds true love, and it is the girl's love and influence that help him to complete his transformation: "With a cheery delicacy, she divided my obsessions into three categories: acceptable, unacceptable, and hilarious."[1]

I believe most human fears fit into the same three categories. An acceptable fear might be one that alerts you to danger, but fear is not always a sign of danger. Unacceptable fears are those that inhibit life or progression, such as fear of crowds or stepping off curbs. Hilarious fears are self-explanatory, and learning to laugh at oneself is a good thing to learn before having a child.

In this section, we are dealing with the fears that inhibit life or stop our progression. These fears may be deeply encoded into the subconscious, and even the collective unconscious, and are not always easy to let go of or, as Daniel tried to do, "convert them into a mistrust of icebergs."[2]

If you have fears about childbearing, you are not alone. Some women might be afraid of morning sickness, of losing their babies, of pain during birth, that their babies won't be healthy, or that they won't be good mothers. Other women aren't sure exactly what they are afraid of. I always tell newly pregnant women that is okay to be afraid—for a little while. I ask them to sit with their fear and see how it feels in their bodies and their spirits.

In John 4:18, we learn that "there is no fear in love; but perfect love casteth out all fear: because fear hath torment." "Fear hath torment" is one of the most accurate statements I have ever read. It is not just referring to emotional torment. Fear has a physiological component, too. If you're tuned into your body, you may have noticed that fear causes tension, and tension causes pain. This is called the fear-tension-pain cycle, which is referred to in depth in many childbirth education books and classes.

Fear can also hinder spiritual communication. President James E. Faust taught the following:

> Let us not take counsel from our fears. May we remember always to be of good cheer, put our faith in God, and live worthy for Him to direct us. We are each entitled to receive personal inspiration to guide us through our mortal probation. May we so live that our hearts are open at all times to the whisperings and comfort of the Spirit.[3]

Perhaps we can also convert our fears about childbirth into the less-used biblical definition of *fear*, which is to "honor, respect, reverence,"[4] as in Psalm 66:16: "Come and hear, all ye that fear God, and I will declare what he hath done for my soul." The scriptures also show us many different ways that we can banish fear, such as preparation, perfect love, faith, fasting, and surrender. In the stories that follow, you will see many of these principles in action.

---

1   Steve Martin, *The Pleasure of My Company* (New York: Hyperion, 2003), 161.
2   Ibid.
3   James E. Faust, "Be Not Afraid," *Ensign*, October 2002, http://lds.org/ensign/2002/10/be-not-afraid.
4   Topical Guide to the Scriptures, s.v. "Fear of God," 142.

GODDESS IN EMBRYO

By Rebecca Overson

I WAS THE ONLY ONE OF NINE CHILDREN born at home. I always felt special. My older siblings witnessed my birth, and it was impactful for them, such that my sisters all chose natural birth as well. I stood in awe of my sisters, and I couldn't wait until I could experience what it felt like to carry a baby and give birth.

I was almost twenty-nine when I became pregnant with my first. I interviewed doctors, nurse-midwives, and direct-entry midwives. One nurse-midwife listened to me so deeply that the only thing she had to say was, "Rebecca, it sounds to me like you really want a home birth. Why don't you do that?" The biggest obstacle to home birth was that my husband felt it was dangerous. However, after doing some research and talking to trusted friends, we chose and planned a home birth with a skilled professional midwife.

I finally went into labor at forty-two weeks after dealing with lots of pressure from well-intentioned people, asking, "When are you going to be induced? When are 'they' going to 'take the baby'?" I felt isolated, like I was an alien for choosing a natural approach to birth. Shawn was born after fifteen hours of slow and intensely painful labor. That experience was both terrifying and thrilling.

At one point, while I was nearing transition, I was crying, and I looked up at my mother and said, "Mom, I can't do this. I am going to die. I am going to die." She looked right back at me and said, "You know what, Rebecca? You *are* going to die. The carefree maiden you have been all your life is dying. You are giving birth to yourself, as a mother. It is the hardest thing you have ever had to do. And you *can* do it, because look at you—you *are* doing it!"

My mother always viewed birth as a rite of passage, a spiritual transition, an initiation into a new realm. She firmly believes that a woman must put her blood, sweat, and tears on the line for the child she is birthing; it is an opportunity to demonstrate that she has the strength to be a mother. It is not a time to avoid pain, because motherhood is painful at times. It is not a time to seek comfort, because motherhood is not comfortable. It is not a time to shrink back, because motherhood requires that a woman reach deep inside her soul and show what she really stands for. It is in birth, my mother taught me, that a woman must show her trust in herself, her trust in God, and be consciously involved in a deliberate act of creation by giving her heart, might, mind, and strength to what is before her.

Even though I felt the truth of my mother's teachings, there came a point during labor that if I had been offered drugs I would have taken them. Gratefully, I was surrounded by my mother, two sisters, and a supportive husband who saw me doing a beautiful job and birthing perfectly, even in all

---

When I was four months pregnant, I was at a retreat where I had the opportunity to write down and reflect on the things I feared in life.

---

my wailing. In the midst of my effort I heard a voice inside me say, "Rebecca, there is nothing you can do about this. It's not going to hurt any less, it's not going to go any faster. May as well go with it." That voice was calling for surrender, and in that moment I stopped fighting the pain and went *through* it. I focused. I worked really hard. I pushed for an hour, and finally Shawn was born, 8.5 lbs and healthy and beautiful. I cannot adequately explain how my view of myself changed that day. I knew that I had gone as far as I'd ever had to go and then went even beyond that. It was amazing.

My second pregnancy found me in the midst of a serious study in spiritual psychology for my program at school. I was doing a lot of work that focused on consciously cultivating a willingness to experience whatever was before me and to truly live in the present moment. When I was four months pregnant, I was at a retreat where I had the opportunity to write down and reflect on the things I feared in life. I made a list beginning with the seemingly harmless to the downright daunting.

I captured thoughts, such as, "What if I get a really bad sunburn? What if I have to go to the bathroom and can't find one?" all the way to "What if I get maimed? Raped? Lose someone I love? Lose the baby?" I meditated on each of them by opening up to the idea that I would be willing to experience those things, if it did in fact become "my turn" to experience them. I began to see the reality that any of these things could happen to me even if I did everything I knew to do to prevent them. As I let that awareness set in, I went one step further and began to try on the idea that I could be *willing* to experience any of these things if they were actually happening to me. Could I be *willing* to experience physical discomfort or embarrassment, if that was what I was feeling, or would I try to avoid it, suppress it, and hope that it never impacted me? My rational mind began to see times in my life where I had endured such things and survived, but what about the harder things, "Willing to be *raped*? To lose the baby?"

As I meditated on this, the wisdom that came to me said, "Yes." If it just so happened to be my turn to experience loss or violence, if I just so happened to find myself in the wrong place at the wrong time, I could simply remain sane and mentally intact in that moment and fully accept what had happened to me. The Buddhists say that pain is inevitable, but suffering is a painful feeling about pain. Pain is simply a sensation, but suffering comes from thinking that what is shouldn't be. I saw that no matter what happened to me in this life, I could trust that God had me in mind and that life happens *for* me, not *to* me. It's all for my good.

The words that the Lord spoke to Joseph Smith popped into my mind: "If the very jaws of hell shall gape open the mouth wide after thee, know . . . that all these things shall give thee experience, and shall be for thy good" (D&C 122:7). Could the same be true for me? Could it be that I truly could trust in God, *no matter what*? Even if the very jaws of hell gaped open after me in one way or another?

As I continued to reflect, more words from scripture came into my mind: "Here am I, send me" (Abraham 3:27). The words of Jesus became my words. I envisioned myself looking at all the possibilities for my earth life, accepting all the risks, and saying, "I am willing, send me. I am willing to be the one who is betrayed. I am willing to be physically uncomfortable. I am willing to lose a child. I am willing to be raped, lost, confused, hurt, offended, upset, in pain, maimed. I am willing, send me. I want to feel what it is to be alive, to love, to forgive. I am willing to face pain so that I might know true joy."

This took root in my heart powerfully, and I felt a change of heart, a melting away of fear, an acceptance of the inherent risk that life is and knowledge that I chose it this way. Then another phrase from scripture came to mind: "Willing to submit to all things which the Lord seeth fit to inflict upon [you]" (Mosiah 3:19). All things? I began to see that I do not know the mind of God. I do not know what He sees fit to inflict upon me, but I do know that His Son was willing to endure all kinds of discomfort in His lifetime. I do know that He loves me and He knows more about what I need than I do. But do I really trust that? I began to feel that trust open.

I had always said, "I want to be like Jesus," but did I really mean that? Was I truly willing? Another image flashed to my mind, the image of Christ pressing through a crowd, carrying His cross, people mocking Him, spitting upon Him. He was willing. I saw Him being fitted with a crown of thorns, shoved into His scalp. He was willing. I saw Him being flogged by a Roman soldier and simply receiving the beating. He was willing. At no point did He stop and fight back. He received what was being given to Him. He knew there was "no other way" (Helaman 5:9). He trusted God and knew God's plan must be fulfilled.

Tears streamed down my face as I realized I had lived my whole life in fear of bad things happening to me, things that could in fact be the very things that I *needed* to experience in this life to attain glory in the next. In this new awareness, I found myself saying, "Yes, I am willing. I am. So be it." My heart burst wide open and all those fears just slipped away as I said, "Yes," to all of life.

It was in this state of mind, this intense willingness to feel what it feels like to be alive, to intently receive everything that life has to offer me, that I gave birth to our second son. I was totally, completely willing to experience birth fully. I knew it was going to hurt, but I was willing to feel whatever it felt like. I knew I was going to reach that intense point during transition and have thoughts like, "I can't do this, I'm going to die," and I welcomed those thoughts. I was totally open to the possibility that this could be another fifteen hours of excruciating back labor.

As the contractions began in the morning, they were welcomed, and they even felt invigorating, like a good workout. Around 3 p.m., they jumped to three minutes apart but still were not painful. My midwife arrived at 4:45 p.m., and the contractions became much more intense. I could not talk through them, but again they were not painful, just lots of pressure.

My mind knew what to expect, and I opened to it. I even observed those thoughts of dread going through my head like, "I can not do this. Do I really

---

I repeatedly whispered to myself, "Just *feel* this. Just *feel* what this feels like." I just observed my body in the process, doing what it knows instinctively to do.

---

have to do this again? This is not happening already!" But because of my mindfulness focus, I was able to *simply* notice the thoughts, and I did not have to react to them. I surrendered to each contraction, much like one would surrender to contractions of the diaphragm when vomiting or sneezing. I repeatedly whispered to myself, "Just *feel* this. Just *feel* what this feels like." I just observed my body in the process, doing what it knows instinctively to do.

My body began shaking uncontrollably as the baby descended down the birth canal. I felt like I had to go to the bathroom, and I warned my midwife. She said, "Honey, that's the baby's head." I couldn't believe it. I reached down. Sure enough, there was his wrinkly little head beginning to crown. I wouldn't say I pushed because it actually felt effortless, like I was *being* pushed. His head was fully born in about two contractions, but his shoulder became stuck. After about thirty seconds, my midwife said, "Stand up," and she took both my hands and pulled me up so I could bend over the edge of the birthing tub. With one final intense push, he was born. I could not believe it.

He was born at 6:32 p.m., less than two hours after hard labor had begun. I sat back down in the birthing tub and clutched him to my chest. The experience was so ecstatic, so joyful, and so incredibly wonderful. The first thing I said was, "That was *awesome*." While the physical sensations I experienced were very intense, it was not painful. It was truly, truly transformative, and I attribute much of the wonder of the experience to my commitment to birthing mindfully and being willing to experience whatever was before me. I felt like a true goddess in embryo. I wish all women could feel what it is like to give birth without fear and to fully know what they are capable of.

CLOSE TO HEAVEN

By Kamille Larsen

WITH MY FIRST BABY, I really desired to have a natural childbirth, and I did my best to prepare myself for the experience. Although I was open to the option of an epidural, I hoped I could birth without it. I labored at home as long as I could and was dilated to 6 cm when I got to the hospital. Because I did not have the support I needed (neither my husband nor I were prepared enough to have a natural childbirth in a hospital setting), I could not find any relief. So I decided to get an epidural. At first, it was great, because I finally had relief from the pain. After pushing for thirty minutes, my son was born (posterior, I should add). It was a marvelous experience to meet my baby, but at the same time, I felt really disconnected from the experience. It was very surreal. I felt very, very tired after his birth and was disappointed in myself.

When I found out that I was pregnant with my second child, I was so excited. This time, I knew I wanted to do it differently. I did as much research as I could and chose an OB who supported birth as a natural process. I also hired a doula because I knew I would need that extra encouragement and support.

I had known a couple of women who had given birth at home, but (while I thought it was nice) I had never considered it for myself. Then we realized that, with the swine flu scare, my son would not be able to come visit me and the baby in the hospital. To me, that was too much. When I was about twenty-eight weeks pregnant, I started seriously researching home birth, weighing the pros and cons. I talked to my husband about it, and at first he was reluctant. Once we became educated on the safety of home birth, we both began to feel that it was the right decision.

Coming to a final decision was not easy at all. I was faced with a lot of negativity from my family and some friends. I prayed and prayed for guid-

As I prepared for my daughter's birth, I still had fears that I needed to release.

ance because I did not want to make the wrong decision. I wanted to do what was right for us, and I wanted to feel peaceful about it. There were times when I was in the decision-making process that I just wanted to give up and do what everyone else was telling me to do. It certainly would have been the easy choice. However, that didn't feel right to me.

With research and prayer, I was finally able to make my decision to birth at home when I was about thirty-two weeks pregnant. I knew that Heavenly Father was aware of me, and that He supported my decision. I also felt that He left the decision up to me; He would have been supportive of a hospital birth too. I think that was why it was so hard to make the decision—I had to make it, I had to decide. Once I decided, everything fell into place. We had financial concerns about the home birth, but with an extremely gracious midwife, we were able to afford it. I felt very comfortable and safe, and that made my decision easy in that regard.

As I prepared for my daughter's birth, I still had fears that I needed to release. All of the negativity surrounding our decision got to me at times. I wondered about the "what ifs" or the complications that could arise. Through educating myself about all aspects of childbirth, and especially the benefits of natural childbirth, I was able to put many of my fears to rest. I continued to pray that I would be able to feel peaceful when it came time to give birth. If I could rid myself of fear, I knew that I would be able to get through the pain of birthing my baby.

I remember one day, as I was pondering the upcoming birth, the scripture came into my mind—"If ye are prepared, ye shall not fear." I knew at that moment that I was prepared. I had done everything I could do. I had studied, researched, chosen a competent midwife, and kept my body and spirit healthy. Because of my preparation, I had no reason at all to be fearful. I knew Heavenly Father was in control of the situation and that He would be watching over me as I birthed my baby. I finally felt at peace.

My labor began on a Saturday morning. I had menstrual-like cramps, which felt identical to the beginning of my son's labor. My husband and I went on a long walk to see if they would get stronger. I continued to have crampy contractions that whole day, and they started picking up in the evening. Then, around 2:30 a.m., my contractions stopped, so we decided to try to get some rest. When I woke up the next morning, it was clear that my labor had stopped for a time.

My midwife came over in the afternoon and checked my cervix because I felt that something might be bulging into my vagina and wanted to be sure everything was okay. It turned out to be nothing, and I was dilated to 4.5 cm and fully effaced. She stripped my membranes and left. About an hour later, I began to have contractions that were five minutes apart and painful enough to have to breathe through them. We timed them for a while and decided to call the midwives. They came over, and I labored all night without much progress, but I was very relaxed and handling the contractions "beautifully," as my midwife said. I moved around, took a bath, ate, laughed, talked—it was very, very peaceful and calm.

In the middle of the night, my contractions began to really space out. I began to feel very down and hopeless. I felt like my baby was never going to come. I didn't mind the contractions; I just really wanted my baby to be born since I had been laboring so long. At about 5:00 a.m., my midwives decided to go get some breakfast, and my husband and I went to sleep. When they came back at about 6:30 a.m., we decided to call them when things picked up again.

At about 8:45 a.m., I woke up to a very loud pop! My water had broken! I hopped out of bed, excited and scared at the same time. I had my husband immediately call my midwife, Alison. I knew that things were going to go very, very fast because my baby was so low. I got very fearful at that point because I had not prepared myself to experience an unassisted birth.

It took about fifteen minutes before I began to have contractions that were very close together and incredibly intense. I asked my husband to say a prayer that everything would be okay and that I would not be afraid. After he said that prayer, I felt so much better. I was laboring on my hands and knees, but Alison told my husband over the phone to have me lie on my side. Doing so would slow things down in order for them to, hopefully, arrive in time.

As I labored on my side, it was very painful. I was feeling pressure, but I did not focus on that at all. I did not think about my baby moving down because I wanted to wait until the midwives arrived. There was a moment everyone told me I would experience in a natural birth—a moment where I would "walk through the valley of the shadow of death." They told me that was when the delivery would be so close. I truly experienced that moment, the moment where it was so intense, the tightening of my uterus so strong, that I almost felt like I could not do it anymore. That is when I relied on my Heavenly Father—I knew He was with me, and I knew I could do it.

It was in that next instant that I heard my midwives come in and throw their bags down, and I immediately felt my daughter's head shove down against my perineum and my body began to push. It did not take any mental effort to push as it had the first time with my son. I was amazed that my body just took over completely. It was an incredible feeling. I could no longer feel the pain of the contractions. I felt such relief.

After only a few pushes, my beautiful daughter, Maude Violet, was born! I reached through my legs to grab her. She was bigger than any of us thought. I held her down by my belly (her cord was too short to put her up to my breast) until the cord stopped pulsating. We cut the cord, and I brought her up to my breast. She immediately became quiet, and I marveled at what I had just done. I couldn't believe it was over and that I was holding my beautiful baby.

I was so amazed at how wonderful I felt after her birth. Although I was running on very little sleep, I had so much energy. I did not feel that after the birth of my son. After his birth, I was so tired and just wanted to sleep, but I couldn't because I was uncomfortable from complications caused by the epidural (I was not able to urinate). With Maude, I hardly felt like I had had a baby. I had a very small tear, but it was not enough to stitch up. I felt relaxed, energized, and in awe of what my body had just done.

My husband and I were brought closer together through this experience. We really had to rely on each other for support before my daughter was born. It was not easy for either of us to do something that was so different than what most people do. We had to trust in each other and depend on one another. It was the same in labor. My husband supported me the whole time. He was by my side. He was my strength. He had a calming presence. I knew he believed in me. I knew that he was proud of what I was doing to bring our daughter into this world. It was such an intimate experience to be in our bedroom, just us, together as I labored. Our home was sanctified by the birth of our baby and our marriage was strengthened.

My son's birth was a beautiful experience (first birth). He made me a mother. It was overwhelming, surreal, peaceful, calm... incredible. But the experience did not leave me spiritually changed. I would use the same words to describe Maude's birth: overwhelming, surreal, peaceful, calm... incredible. But I would add deeply spiritual. I believe that I was able to have such a deep spiritual experience with her birth because I felt everything God intended a woman to feel as she birthed her baby. That experience connected me with Him even more. I am grateful I was able to have the experience I desired, and I am grateful that I was guided by the Spirit as I made my decisions. Giving birth naturally was the most powerful, transformative experience. I emerged full of confidence in myself and in my body. I knew what it meant to sacrifice. I felt so strong and so very close to heaven.

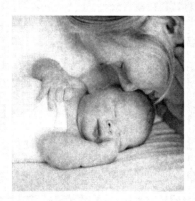

THE DREAM

by Tara M.

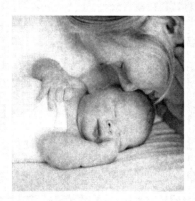

AFTER THE BIRTH OF MY THIRD SON, I was diagnosed with Crohn's disease and was living with constant pain and the fear of major medical problems in my future. While I had never envisioned stopping after three children, I was faced with the reality that my body was in no shape to have any more children in the foreseeable future. Thanks to the guidance of the Lord in changing my diet and much prayer and petitioning to the Lord to heal my body, several years later, I was in total remission of my Crohn's disease.

During that time of being sick, I often bargained with God, telling him that I would have another baby if I was healed. After almost a year of feeling healthy and well, I started to think about that promise. Yet I was really enjoying the freedom of having older children and had lost the hunger and desire to have a baby. Then I had the dream. I dreamt that I was at a swimming pool locker room, of all places, and that I was very pregnant. I was with a friend and was taking a shower and washing my hair when I started having contractions. Within a few contractions, I knew that the baby was ready to come, and I sent my friend away to go call someone. While I was there by myself, I started pushing and the baby just slid right out into my hands. I pulled the sweet little thing up to my chest and just sat there glowing with the feeling that only comes in that moment. Then I woke up, still glowing.

After that, I knew that I was ready to take the plunge and have another baby. I also had spent much of this time petitioning the Lord for a daughter. I always knew that I would have daughters. Yet here I was with three little boys and no girls. I prayed that the Lord would grant me this righteous desire of my heart. All through the first half of my pregnancy, I dreamed of pink nurseries, bows, and mommy-daughter activities that I would share with a daughter. I was sure it would happen this time. Then I went in for an ultrasound and that dream crashed down around me. I cried and cried and felt so alone. I wondered why the Lord would withhold something from me that I wanted so, so much.

After spending the first half of my pregnancy feeling so close to the Spirit and relying on my Savior to carry me through those long months of morning sickness, I was then distancing myself from the Lord. Looking back, I think of this as my tantrum phase. Just like my children throw a tantrum when they don't get what they want, I too was having my tantrum. But our Heavenly Father has a funny way of reaching out to us and taking care of us even when we don't deserve it. I finally poured out my feelings in prayer. After two months of anger, sadness, and depression over the daughter I would never have, I found peace. I knew that this little boy was meant to be in our family and that the rest would take care of itself.

When I was thirty-six weeks pregnant, I was having contractions very frequently. That was normal for me, and so I tried to ignore them and go about my normal activities. In mid-August I got a call from my friend telling me that she was in labor and was ready for me to come over. (I was planning to photograph her birth.) I got there as the midwives were arriving, and we all started to set up for the birth. I noticed that the apprentice had been listening with the dopplar for quite a while and was calling for the other midwife to come and try to find the heart tones. After ten minutes of finding nothing, the midwife could only conclude that the baby had no heartbeat. When she said this, I was truly in shock.

I went into my friend's closet and kneeled down and prayed. I started to pray that her baby would be alright but quickly knew I was praying for the wrong thing. So instead I prayed for strength for my friend, for her husband, the midwives, and for me. I knew this would be an experience that only God could carry her through. Thirty minutes later, her perfect daughter was born but never took a breath. I stayed with them till 2 a.m. taking pictures and

hand prints and footprints. The midwives found a hematoma in her umbilical cord, but otherwise she was perfect.

The weeks after the birth were like being in another world. I was sus-
pended in time and everything felt strange. I was waiting for my baby to
arrive, but I was also so focused on my friend and her grief and how I could
help her. Two weeks before my due date, I was having a day of especially
strong, frequent, and consistent contractions that had me convinced that
it was the big day. In the evening, I called my midwives and told them to
come. I set up the birth tub in my room and called my best friend to come
and take pictures. I labored into the night.

Around midnight, things started to slow down. I was tired and was falling asleep between contractions. I decided to go out and walk around the
neighborhood to try and get things moving. I got back and was throwing

After she left, I prayed. I prayed to be able to let go of my fears and have faith in God's plan.

up and thought I must be close but was still only 5 cm dilated, and the contractions were dying. Everyone went home, and I woke up the next morning
confused and in limbo.

After that, I didn't feel like I could go about my normal life. I was on
edge all the time and felt like I should stay close to home. Another week
went by and still no baby. I wondered why I had been so stupid to plan an
out of hospital birth. I wanted the option of the easy way out. I knew that
a doctor would have given me Pitocin that day two weeks earlier and my
baby would have been two weeks old by then. I didn't want to have patience
any more.

My due date came and went, and that night I started to get paranoid.
I hadn't been feeling the baby move as much as he normally did, and so I
used the doppler the midwives had left in the birth kit to listen to his heartbeat. It seemed slower than usual to me. I called my midwife and talked
to her, and she decided to send her apprentice over to check on the baby.
I knew that I was just being paranoid because of what my friend had gone
through, but I still couldn't shake how I was feeling. When the midwife

came she checked baby, his heart rate was a bit slower than normal but still in the safe range. While she was there, I talked to her about how I was feeling, my fears, and all the expectations I had had for this birth.

After she left, I prayed. I prayed to be able to let go of my fears and have faith in God's plan. I prayed to have my baby arrive when he was ready, and not when I wanted him to. I tried to let go of my preconceived notions about how this birth was going to play out. When I woke up in the morning, I felt a shift. I knew that it was time. I decided to go to the freestanding birth center that my midwives own. We arrived around 8:00 and found a lovely bath run with candles lit. It was a beautiful, safe cocoon there. I still had long breaks between, but the contractions were powerful. Around 10:30, my main midwife arrived and checked me. She said I was 8 cm dilated, everything was very soft, and the baby's head was very low. She suggested that I start to try and push and see if it would push my cervix out of the way. I went and sat on the toilet and started to push. Pretty soon I could feel his head bulging down and knew that I was fully dilated.

I got into the tub, since I wanted to deliver him in the water, and I pushed for about ten minutes. As I pushed, I could feel his head rotate as he was coming out. I was totally in control of his birth and the midwives just sat back and watched. Then I felt the rest of his body come out, and as he floated to the surface I grabbed him under his arms and pulled him up to me. It was the dream. I was exultant in that moment. This new person had grown inside of me for nine months, and I had given birth to him myself. There was no one else taking credit for "delivering" my baby—it was my accomplishment.

I learned two important things from this experience. First, that the Lord is in control and has a plan for our lives. We may not always like what he has in store for us, but he truly does know our needs and how to help us to grow. And secondly, I know that I wouldn't trade this experience of motherhood, with all it's pain, frustration, stretching, joy, and learning, for anything.

Faith

By Felice Austin, CHt

Your faith should not stand in the wisdom of men.

1 CORINTHIANS 2:5

I was recently at lunch with a woman who had devoted most of her life to studying birth. She said something that struck me: "I feel sad that women don't have faith in their bodies anymore. Where is their faith?"

In this essay, I would like to say something about faith that you may not have heard before. But there is nothing flashy and new about faith. Faith is the first principle of the gospel, the foundation upon which all other principles and ordinances are built. Since you have found this essay in the "Fear" chapter, you might be expecting to hear how faith is the opposite of fear—that faith banishes fear. This is true. But is it true for you? Is this your experience? As you know, believing something is true is not the same as making it your reality.

Faith and beliefs are not the same. Faith is not limiting, but beliefs often are. In the Bible Dictionary, it says "faith is more than belief, since true faith always moves its possessor to some kind of physical and mental action."[1] For example, I exercise faith that I can learn Spanish when I sign up for a Spanish class. I act in faith by following personal revelation. Examples of limiting beliefs can usually be found in statements that begin with "I can't . . . ," "I'm not . . . ," and "I'm the type of person who . . ." Limiting beliefs keep us from moving forward, from seeing our options, our potential, or our purpose. Satan is the master of limiting beliefs.

In fact, behind most fears is a limiting belief. To illustrate, below are some examples of fears and in parentheses are one or two possible limiting beliefs that could be behind the fears.

- I am afraid of being induced. *(My doctor is in control.)*

- I am afraid of pain. *(There will be pain. My body and mind are not powerful.)*

- I am afraid I will lose it and scream at people. *(I am not in control of my mind and body. Screaming is how people "lose it." I "have it" now.)*

- I don't want a cesarean section. *(Cesarean birth is substandard to vaginal birth. I cannot be happy if things don't go as I plan.)*

- My friends/doctor/family will think I am crazy for birthing out of the norm. *(People should like me and agree with me. Normal is . . . .)*

- I'm afraid I'll lose the baby. *(The baby is mine. I don't trust myself to make good decisions. I should have a say in when God takes spirits home.)*

Identifying limiting beliefs is not always comfortable, but it can be liberating. Whenever I hear one come across my mouth or a client's mouth, I ask, "Is that true?" Through a process called inquiry, we can examine beliefs and fears for distortion and begin to understand how believing certain thoughts pulls us away from happiness and peace. (Resources on the inquiry process are available on this book's website.) After exposing a limiting belief, I recommend creating a faith-based affirmation to replace the limiting belief. For example, "My body was made to give birth. I have faith in God's will for me." If inquiry or reframing is difficult, have faith that you will become better at it, and ask the Lord for help. You can increase your faith, and the Lord can show you how.

IF FAITH IS NOT BELIEF, WHAT IS IT?

In the Book of Mormon, we learn that "if ye have faith ye hope for things which are not seen, which are true" (Alma 32:21). Family is faith-based work. When you conceive a child, you cannot see into the future and know what your family life is going to be like. You are operating on hope.

Faith is also a principle of action. Just like the body without the spirit is dead, so faith without works is dead. First we must have faith, and then we must do. As Mosiah taught, " If ye believe all these things, see that ye do them" (Mosiah 4:10). This "doing" sometimes requires great effort. In

"As all have not faith, seek ye diligently and teach one another words of wisdom; yea, seek ye out of the best books words of wisdom; seek learning, even by study and faith." —D&C 88:118

the Book of Mormon, we can read Enos's experience: "And it came to pass that after I had prayed and *labored with all diligence*, the Lord said unto me: I will grant unto thee according to thy desires, because of thy faith" (Enos 1:12; emphasis added).

As we practice and try our faith, we will recognize the Lord's help. This is the witness that comes after the trial of faith. Often this trying of faith means taking a leap into the darkness—to the unknown. But as Goethe suggested, once we commit, providence moves too.

God has promised to help us achieve what is expedient: "If ye will have faith in me ye will have power to do whatever thing is expedient in me" (Moroni 7:33). The following example from Robyn Allgood shows the principle of faith in action:

I was looking forward to planning another peaceful, natural birth when the ultrasound revealed I had complete placenta previa. I remember the midwife calling me with the news and trying to explain that realistically it is unlikely for a complete previa to change position. I could tell it was hard for her to tell me this. She knew I had experienced a C-section before and this was also my first birth since my son had died. She didn't want to be the bearer of bad news.

I felt emotionless as I hung up and then the urge to cry. I know that it would have been okay to cry and mourn the loss of my plan for this birth, but instead I told God I was willing to have this baby in whichever way He saw fit, but that I also had faith in His power to work miracles. I invited His power to work through me. For two months we waited. I followed the restrictions I had been given and I visualized the placenta moving out of the way each day.

The night before the second ultrasound I asked for a priesthood blessing. I felt reassured of something I already knew but waited for it to be confirmed. The ultrasound technician happily reported that the placenta was no longer covering my cervix. I finally blurted out, "I knew it! I knew it!" I had already felt a confirmation of it as I had prayed.

David was born peacefully and naturally, my little miracle. I'll never know if I truly had placenta previa or not; I just know that I felt my faith tested. And my faith would be the same if a cesarean birth would have been necessary. But why not invite God to work miracles in us?

"Until one is committed, there is hesitancy, the chance to draw back, always ineffectiveness. Concerning all acts of initiative and creation, there is one elementary truth the ignorance of which kills countless ideas and splendid plans: that the moment one definitely commits oneself, then providence moves too. All sorts of things occur to help one that would never otherwise have occurred. A whole stream of events issues from the decision, raising in one's favor all manner of unforeseen incidents, meetings and material assistance which no man could have dreamed would have come his way. Whatever you can do or dream you can, begin it. Boldness has genius, power and magic in it. Begin it now."[2] —Johann Wolfgang von Goethe

---

All of the women who have shared their stories in this book have exercised faith. Because of that faith, they were granted power and wisdom and had their experiences consecrated for their good. I hope that as you read, their stories will brighten your hope for things that are not yet seen.

---

1. Bible Dictionary, s.v. "Faith," 670.

FAITH PRECEDES THE MIRACLE

By Martha Ware

IN ABOUT MY SIXTH MONTH OF PREGNANCY, I was at a baby shower for two ladies in the ward. Someone asked me, "So, are you going to get the epidural?" I said, "Pshhh. Yes. That seems like a no-brainer." The others laughed and agreed. About a week later, I started reading The Birth Book by William and Martha Sears as recommended to me by my friend. When she handed it to me months earlier, I thought, "What's there to know about birth? You just go to the hospital and the doctor takes care of everything." Three pages into the book, I had an epiphany: I wanted to have a natural childbirth. No one was more surprised than me to discover this.

I was on my lunch break reading the book. Martha Sears was recounting each birth story of her seven kids. Her last six were without medication. The way she talked about those births, in contrast to her first where the doctor definitely "took care" of everything, was something else. It moved me spiritually and emotionally. I remember walking back to the office with tears in my eyes. For the next months, I devoured that book and every other resource I could get my hands on.

The more I learned about natural childbirth, the more my testimony of God's greatest creation, the human body, grew. I had complete confidence in my body's ability to do what nature intended, and I knew God would not give me an experience I couldn't deal with.

I wrote up a detailed birth plan and presented it to my OB/GYN. She said it was all fine but she didn't understand why I'd want to experience all that pain. Neither did my cardiologist whom I'd been meeting with regularly (I have two heart diseases—aortic valve stenosis and hypertrophic cardio-myopathy). She and my cardiologist had no stats or studies to back it up, but they were also concerned about the risk natural childbirth might pose to my heart. I left their offices many times over the next couple months

The more I learned about faith, the more I knew it was my answer. Faith precedes miracles and I needed a major miracle.

sobbing all the way back to work. I was certain natural childbirth would pose no extra risk to my heart. I felt just the opposite, actually. I also felt trapped because I trusted them both to take care of the heart issues. They had worked together in the past on pregnant women with heart disease, and that was very important to me.

The final month was the worst. My amniotic fluid levels were all over the map, so I had to have extra fetal monitoring twice a week. Each visit threatened induction. I knew being induced would put a natural childbirth virtually out of my grasp, so I prayed more fervently than ever to be spared from induction.

I found great comfort in Ether, chapter 12. The more I learned about faith, the more I knew it was my answer. Faith precedes miracles and I needed a major miracle. Each time after fetal testing, I was sent home. Each time I knew it was a miracle. I still didn't know what the end would bring, but I just kept my faith fine-tuned, told God what I wanted, and left it up to Him.

I also had many pep talks with Sienna, my soon-to-be-born first baby. "Now, listen, little lady. We can't be induced. It's not an option. So, I need you to just stay inside as long as possible and keep showing the doctors what you can do." She was so obedient, I wanted to lean over and kiss her after every appointment but couldn't reach my belly with my lips. Adam had to take care of that for me.

The due date came and went. Due dates are a stupid, cruel thing. They mess with your mind and make everyone under the sun badger you about why your baby's not here yet. Poop on due dates. I'm not telling anyone mine next time. The following Monday night I had painful contractions all night long that allowed me little rest. I thought this was the beginning of the end and tried to rest as much as possible. Tuesday came. Nothing.

Wednesday at 2 a.m. I got up to pee for the umpteen bajillionth time and read my scriptures (Ether 12, I love you). At 2:30 a.m. I peed again and heard a little pop sound. Water breakage, folks! I woke up Adam and called my doctor's operator. She told me that the doctor's instructions were to come in when my water was broken *and* when I was in active labor. I thought this was odd because my doctor had told me several times that I'd need to come in if my water broke *or* if I was in active labor. Huh. The operator seemed pretty confident, so I agreed to call back when I was in active labor. Adam went back to sleep, but I couldn't.

Several hours later, Adam awoke when he heard me groaning in the front room and came out to help. I hadn't wanted to wake him up because I thought at least one of us should be well rested for the big day ahead. However, when he came in and started rubbing my back and encouraging me, it helped immensely. I was making quite a bit of noise through my contractions. I felt sort of cave-womanish which freed the inner natural childbirth hippie in me (which I liked).

I told him to call back the operator, and she gave him the go-ahead to come in. When we reached Labor and Delivery, the nurses stared at me as I leaned against the wall and did this thing with my feet like a bull does when he's getting ready to charge. Then they tried to put me in the wheelchair, but I declined. I didn't want to have my grand entrance be as an invalid and, more than that, I did *not* want to sit. Sitting did *not* feel good on my back.

After we got settled in our room, the nurse checked my cervix and announced, "You're dilated to 9.5!" I looked at Adam and said, "That is the *best* news I've *ever* heard." We were both shocked. So were the nurses. I am convinced that my doctor's phone operator was an angel sent from heaven and was the reason this natural childbirth was happening.

Meanwhile, my doctor came in, the nurses (about five or six of them), were bustling around the room, hooking me up to all sorts of things, or just staring for general amusement. A sweet middle-aged nurse came to my bedside and introduced herself as Cindy, a student nurse that was on her first day there. I loved her immediately and grabbed her hand. I made her hold it the whole time while Adam was on the other side, holding my other one. When she let go at one point I grabbed it again. There was no way she was leaving my side. I needed her cold, thin, strong fingers as much as I needed Adam's warm, bigger, strong fingers.

I pushed for about twenty-five minutes. Adam was tremendously helpful throughout it all. Long ago we had established that he would be my "focal point" during labor and delivery. Several times, when it seemed like I was losing it, he would say, "Martha! Look at me! You're doing great." He was very reassuring and my #1 cheerleader. He just kept telling me how wonderful I was doing, and I was believing it.

Anyway, the head did finally pop out, wouldn't you know it. Just one more push and out came the slithery little body. It was incredible. The doctor held her up, and I said possibly the dumbest thing ever, "It's a baby!" They put her on my chest, and the first thing I noticed were her long scraggly nails. Baby nails are tiny miracles unto themselves. I just looked down at her head of black hair while the nurses wiped her off. My doctor's comment after it all was, "Well, don't plan on it being that simple next time, young lady." Classic. I didn't care though. Nothing anyone could have said would have ruined that moment. They could have stuck her foot up my nose and I would have been thrilled. She was so perfect and big and warm and covered in blood and vernix. It was awesome.

Families Can Be Together Forever

By Amanda Hughes

I TOOK FOR GRANTED the idea that I would be a mother someday. I had a life plan that is probably similar to many girls. I pictured myself graduating from high school, attending college, meeting Mr. Right, getting married in the temple and ultimately having several children and living happily ever after. Being a mother was something I ultimately had to fight for, but that struggle only increased its value to me.

My husband, Andee, and I had been married for about two years when we felt it was time to really start "trying" to have children. We had about three unsuccessful years, during which time our efforts were intermittently interrupted by health issues. We knew that we were no longer satisfied with just trying on our own, but we didn't know if we should pursue adoption or look into medical treatments.

Eventually, we decided to dedicate a fast Sunday to seeking guidance, and we asked our families to fast with us. Shortly after the fast, both my husband and I learned of an infertility seminar hosted by one of the local fertility clinics. Andee and I attended the seminar together. Although anxious about all the information we were bombarded with, a feeling of peace settled over us. We knew that we were where we needed to be. We scheduled an appointment with one of the doctors who set up a battery of tests for us to complete.

After the testing was completed, we learned that neither my husband nor I had optimal fertility, and the doctor recommended that we try IVF. Although my heart sank when I heard this, I was again given a strong sense of peace regarding the matter. My husband and I went home and prayed, although we both felt that doing IVF was our answer, and we ultimately committed to doing the next cycle.

The IVF process was a difficult one for me, both physically and emotionally. Even though I felt we had received an answer to go forward with this process, I was immediately overwhelmed with feelings of doubt and discouragement. During this time, the temple became my refuge. I would escape to the temple any time I had a few extra hours in my schedule.

It was also during this time that I felt inspired to search the scriptures, particularly for other women's experiences with infertility. I was touched by the strength of these women and marveled at their trust in the Lord. I considered how difficult it must have been for them without the medical procedures or the adoption processes that we have today. During my studies, I was particularly impressed with the stories of Hannah and Rebekah. I was given comfort in knowing that noble women—even wives of great patriarchs—struggled with infertility.

There were two scriptures in the stories of Hannah and Rebekah that struck me. The first was Genesis 24:60. At the time, I had only cursory knowledge of Rebekah and her significance to the gospel plan. But I latched onto the blessing that her brothers gave to her before marrying Isaac: "Be thou the mother of thousands of millions" (Genesis 24:60). I clung to the hope that I would be blessed as she ultimately was. I was also impressed with Hannah's faith in the Lord during her struggle with infertility. I loved how when she had her son she, "called his name Samuel, saying, Because I have asked him of the Lord" (1 Samuel 1:20). I often felt that if I was blessed enough to have children, I wanted to somehow acknowledge the Lord's hand in giving them to us through their names.

One day, during a particularly difficult time, my schedule opened up and I was able to make another trip to the temple. I was feeling particularly distressed and felt that I needed special comfort. As I entered the temple, I was again overwhelmed with a sense of peace that remained with me through the duration of my visit. While in the celestial room, I sat in a favorite chair and prayed for strength to continue with the IVF process and to have peace throughout. As I was praying, I sensed two presences near me, one on either side. The spirit impressed me with the knowledge that these were my children, and that there was a male and a female. I also felt strongly that the names Rebekah and Samuel were appropriate for them. Before I left the Celestial room, I felt as though they whispered to me, "Everything will be okay."

Words truly cannot express my elation in hearing the words, "You're pregnant," from my doctor, followed shortly after with, "And it looks like there's a good chance you're having twins." An ultrasound a week later revealed that I was pregnant with two, and my husband's and my hearts were full as we watched them grow in the coming months. Eventually, we were able to learn "officially" that we were having a girl and a boy. Everything seemed to be falling into place, and I had never felt so happy and at peace with the world.

At one point I decided that I wanted to have a song that I played on the piano especially for the babies. I cherished a secret hope that after they were born they would remember the music and that the song would be special to them. I thought a great deal about what message I would want them most to learn, and ultimately decided that "Families Can Be Together Forever" was the perfect song for us. I began practicing the song regularly in order to perfect my ability to play it, and I made sure to play it regularly for them, at least once daily.

Shortly before I was six months along, I went for a standard doctor's visit. My husband came with me. After meeting with my OB for a few minutes, he took us to the ultrasound room. He picked up Samuel's image right away. Samuel was kicking and moving around happily. After a few minutes, the doctor moved on to Rebekah. As soon as I saw her image on the screen, I knew something was wrong. She was completely still, with no sign of a heartbeat. My doctor looked alarmed and made some adjustments to the ultrasound wand, with no change. Finally he said, "I'm very sorry. I can't find a heartbeat. I will need to send you to a specialist."

There is no way to explain the devastating heartbreak I felt, along with my sweet husband. As we drove to the perinatologist's office, I prayed for a miracle, but in my heart I knew that Rebekah was gone. The perinatologist confirmed that this was the case. I was heartbroken as I was informed that although the road would have been very difficult, Rebekah might have lived if she had been delivered. But the focus now turned to Samuel, and to delivering him safely. I was put on bedrest and was monitored closely by the perinatologist.

The next month was the darkest time of my life. I spent hours alone each day. I spent a good deal of time weeping and longing for my little girl. I noticed a distinct void in the place where she had previously kicked. I repeatedly asked the Lord why she had been taken from me. In my darkest hours, I found myself driven to my knees repeatedly. There were many times I felt irritated or saddened by the well-meaning comments of friends, family, and ward members. Ultimately I realized that the only one who could truly understand me would be my Savior. Many times I sat or knelt in prayer, weeping and pleading for comfort. And it was given me. The pain was never fully taken away, but I was given the strength I needed to bear it.

The doctors had informed me that I would need to have a C-section. Because of Rebekah's small size and the fact that she would be born first, the doctor was concerned that this would potentially complicate Samuel's delivery and safety. I felt frustrated that I would be unable to have a "normal" delivery, but I clung to the hope that I would be able to carry Samuel to term, and that he would be born healthy and strong.

Ultimately, I went into labor just under thirty-one weeks, two months before my son's original due date. My labor and delivery was nothing like the idyllic, strengthening experience I had envisioned when I first became pregnant. It was obviously painful, but the most difficult part was that no one would acknowledge that I was in labor. My water never broke, and the fetal monitors didn't pick up the contractions. I went to the hospital, only to be turned away and told that nothing was going on.

Finally, after hours of laboring at home and still experiencing a great deal of pain, my husband took me back to the hospital. This time, the nurses told me that I was already dilated to 5 cm and that I would be delivering soon. When I received this news, I burst into tears. I felt so unprepared for this moment—I knew Samuel was not fully developed, and I had not finished preparing for Rebekah's arrival (I had been crocheting a blanket for her to be buried with). I had not even packed a hospital bag. In addition, I had not done much research on labor and delivery because of the plan to have a C-section. In my moment of panic, I quickly said a prayer in my mind and was given the comfort and presence of mind to ready myself for the delivery.

I received an epidural, and my OB arrived and informed me that I was 9 cm dilated. Because my labor had gone so quickly and I was almost completely dilated, he felt I could have a vaginal delivery with little risk to Samuel. I agreed that this was what I wanted to do. Although the delivery was something of an ordeal at the time, I later realized I had been blessed. The fact that I had labored for so long on my own and without an epidural allowed me to dilate quickly, which ultimately allowed for a vaginal delivery— something for which I was extremely grateful.

Rebekah was delivered first. We were not able to attend to her much in the beginning because Samuel's heart rate dropped, and the focus turned to delivering him safely. He was very small (only four pounds), but quite healthy. Although he needed assistance breathing, I was able to hold him for a few moments before he was taken to the neonatal intensive care unit (NICU).

My doctor cleaned Rebekah and my husband and I were able to look at her. She was so tiny and fragile. Her body had deteriorated somewhat due to having stayed in the womb so long, but we could see that she had many of the same facial features as Samuel. Her feet were perfectly intact and, looking at the footprints we were able to get, I often remark that she and Samuel have the same feet.

Holding Rebekah for that brief time was one of the most difficult and beautiful moments of my life. My heart was very heavy, knowing that these moments would be the only time I would ever hold my daughter in this lifetime. I was also overcome with the Spirit and felt that she was there with us and had been with us during the process. My husband, father, and uncle were able to bless her and give her a name, Rebekah Noelle Hughes, as we had been told by priesthood leaders that she would be recorded on our family group sheet.

Late that night, as I was alone in my hospital room, I was overwhelmed with peace and felt the happiest I had since losing Rebekah. As I lay there, I felt that she was with me again. I also felt the Spirit telling me that Heavenly Father was pleased with my efforts and sacrifice to bring her into the world. Since that time, one of my greatest sources of comfort has been in knowing that my efforts were a worthy offering to the Lord.

Rebekah was buried in a local cemetery. We had a small memorial service for her, which was another beautiful and sacred experience. We sang "Families Can Be Together Forever," the song I had played for both of them. It is a song I still have difficulty singing without crying. On her marker, underneath her name, we quoted the scripture that had originally inspired her name, "Be thou the mother of thousands."

Samuel was in the hospital for five weeks. It was also a difficult time for us as parents as we watched him struggle to learn how to breathe and eat on his own. But the Lord's hand was evident a number of times. Throughout his stay in the NICU, there were several surgeries and procedures that the doctors believed he would need. But after many priesthood blessings and prayers, he was able to avoid every procedure and surgery and was able to come home just before Christmas. On his birth announcement, we quoted another favorite scripture, "For this child I prayed; and the Lord hath given me" (1 Samuel 1:27). Today he is healthy and active toddler, and we are daily grateful to have him in our lives.

When I look at the world and am concerned for my son's physical and spiritual safety as he grows, I am thankful to know that my daughter is safe from the cares of this world. I have also been blessed to feel her presence at times of extreme difficulty and trial. I recently had a miscarriage; while I was in the hospital and filled with despair, I suddenly received the impression that my daughter was there. I was immediately comforted, and later reflected that I find joy in knowing that she is on the other side, watching and waiting for us.

Nothing in the pregnancy went as I had planned or hoped for—from getting pregnant to the delivery. But from these difficulties, I learned that the Lord has a plan and trusting Him is the only true path to peace. Fertility is something that we continue to struggle with. We know we want to have more children but again are left uncertain as to the means. There are still times when I feel frustration at the inability to more easily fulfill what I know to be a righteous desire. But I have continued to find comfort in the stories of the faithful women in the scriptures who struggled.

I choose to view those of us who struggle with fertility as warrioresses who must fight to bring children into covenant homes. At times (not always, but sometimes) I am even grateful that the Lord has given me this challenge so that I can prove my willingness to help build up the kingdom. Although motherhood can sometimes be difficult itself, my experiences constantly remind me to never take it for granted.

I am so grateful for the gospel, and particularly for our Savior. During my darkest moments, I realized that He truly knows all my pains and that He will always be there to lean on. I am also eternally grateful for His sacrifice that I might live with my Rebekah again someday.

Power, Love, and a Sound Mind

By Sheridan Ripley, CD(DONA), HCHI

Often our first reaction to facing the unknown is fear. We can see this illustrated in Matthew, where Christ's Apostles witnessed something they had never seen before:

> And in the fourth watch of the night Jesus went unto them, walking on the sea. And when the disciples saw him walking on the sea, they were troubled, saying, It is a spirit; and they cried out for fear. But straightway Jesus spake unto them, saying, Be of good cheer; it is I; be not afraid. And Peter answered him and said, Lord, if it be thou, bid me come unto thee on the water. And he said, Come. And when Peter was come down out of the ship, he walked on the water, to go to Jesus. But when he saw the wind boisterous, he was afraid and beginning to sink, he cried, saying, Lord, save me. And immediately Jesus stretched forth his hand, and caught him, and said unto him, O thou of little faith, wherefore didst thou doubt? And when they were come into the ship, the wind ceased. (Matthew 14:25–32)

When Jesus told them to be not afraid, they let go of their fear. When Peter tried to walk on water, however, his fear returned, but Jesus helped him let go of his fear again.

The Apostles' experience can be similar to ours. There are so many unknowns when it comes to giving birth. Our first response to the idea of birth may be one of fear, and then, with faith and trust, we can overcome our fear and move forward.

Fears can certainly affect a mother during her birth, but fears usually arise earlier, when mothers are preparing for birth (or avoiding preparing for birth). Many mothers avoid thinking about birth because of fear. When a mother's fear causes her to separate herself from her birth experience, she may struggle to feel the spiritual power within the birth process. In contrast, women who prepare well and have good support teams they trust usually don't have fears arise during birth because they have dealt with the fears beforehand. When a mother thinks in advance about what she wants during her birth and makes informed choices along the way, she can have a more empowering experience. She has taken control rather than letting her fears take control.

I love that faith can help us let go of our fear. My favorite scripture is "For God has not given us a spirit of fear, but of power and of love and of a sound mind" (2 Timothy 1:7). Fear should not be our companion as we bring our children into this world. Many things can provoke worry during pregnancy and birth, such as birth-related television shows, birth horror stories, and scary comments from friends or even care providers (e.g.. "This is going to be a *big* baby!"). Luckily, God has given us physical and spiritual power, the emotion of love, and a sound mind to help us throughout our pregnancies and births.

POWER

Elder Dallin H. Oaks has said, "The power to create mortal life is the most exalted power God has given his children."[1] Elder Jeffrey R. Holland further described these sacred powers:

> One aspect of [God's] divinity given to virtually all men and women is the use of His power to create a human body, that wonder of all wonders, a genetically and spiritually unique being never before seen in the history of the world and never to be duplicated again in all the ages of eternity. . . . *The only control placed on us is self-control*—self-control born of respect for the divine sacramental power this gift represents.[2]

Conception, pregnancy, and birth are sacraments made possible through God lending some of His creative power to us, and He will give us power to move forward with faith instead of fear as we use those powers. He wants us to harness the tools He has given us.

Our Divine Mother also has powers, and, as Her daughters, we have inherited some of them. Elder Vaughn J. Featherstone reminded us, "Women are endowed with special traits and attributes that come trailing down through eternity from a divine mother."[3] Knowledge of and faith in a Heavenly Mother (and your creation in Her image) can help you overcome fears about your birthing journey and throughout your life.

Your powerful uterus helps your baby to be born. Welcome the power of your pressure waves! Your uterus is the strongest muscle in your body when you are pregnant. It helps to open up your cervix and get your baby in the ideal position to be born. Some moms feel overwhelmed by this power. One method of preparing to work with that power is training the mind to interpret it as pressure instead of pain, using techniques such as hypnosis. When we welcome our birthing powers, we can stay relaxed during pressure waves, allowing the uterus to do its job. Instead of fearing our power, we can harness it.

One of the best ways to use our God-given birthing powers is to change positions frequently, which allows your baby to move easily down through your pelvis and helps you feel more comfortable. If you prefer to stand, then stand. If you feel like walking, then walk. If you want to sit, then sit. Know that your body will tell you what position is ideal, and just follow what your body wants. Even if you are being monitored in a hospital setting, you can still be out of bed. The key is to really follow what your body wants and find a position that feels best for you. Your baby and body will work together to let you know what that is.

LOVE

It is important to feel loved in your birthing journey. Being surrounded by supportive people can significantly reduce a birthing mother's fears. As the scriptures instruct us, "There is no fear in love, but perfect love casteth out all fear" (1 John 4:18).

Hopefully you have a wonderful birth partner to be there by your side from the beginning to the end of your birthing journey. If you don't have the support of the father of your baby, find another family member or good friend to serve as your primary birth partner. It makes your journey go smoother to have one person who will be there by your side throughout your pregnancy and birth.

Think carefully about who you want present at your birth. Sometimes it is best to limit the support to just your birth partner. Sometimes having your mom or other family members there may distract you or make it difficult for you to relax. Think carefully about your family dynamics before inviting others to your birth. If you choose to invite others and find that during your birth you don't want them there, you can tell your nurse. The nurse is always willing to play the "bad guy" and kick people out of the room so you don't have to.

It is important that you feel respected during your birth, especially by your main care provider (doctor or midwife). Choose someone who is supportive of your birthing desires. You may also want to add a birth doula to your support team. A doula can start helping you early in your pregnancy by referring you to care providers, birth locations, and childbirth classes. She is available during your pregnancy to answer questions and help you create a birth plan. During your birth, she will be by your side continuously. She knows about normal birth and can help remind you of your options as things progress. She will support you in what you want. (To read more of the benefits of having a doula, see page 311.)

Having friends who support you in your desires for birth can be a great help as you prepare. It is challenging for mothers to feel misunderstood by friends who are not supportive of or simply do not understand their desires.

When a friend of mine was nearing forty weeks in her fourth pregnancy, all her other friends were asking when she was getting induced. She called me one afternoon and said her doctor was suggesting she get induced too and asked what I thought. Trying to be very diplomatic, I had my "You need to decide what is best for you" conversation with her. Finally, she said, "Sheridan, I just want someone to agree with me that I am not crazy for refusing the induction and waiting for my baby to decide when to be born!" Once I knew what *she wanted*, I was more than happy to let her know I totally supported her!

If you don't have any friends who can provide support, you still have options. Joining a local mothers group or going to a La Leche League meeting are some ways to meet mothers in your area. There are also many wonderful online groups where you can find support from women far and near.

SOUND MIND

I enjoy the story of the two thousand stripling warriors. They were young men who had every right to feel fear as they went forth to fight, yet they went forth with courage. Because they had been taught of God from their mothers, they had faith and firm minds and were able to move forward into battle, not fearing death: "Now this was the faith of these of whom I have spoken . . . their minds are firm, and they do put their trust in God continually" (Alma 57:27). Unfortunately, we may learn to fear birth from our mothers and society and move toward birth with trepidation instead of courage.

How can we make our minds firm and let go of any fears we have learned or inherited? Karl Menninger has said, "Fears are educated into us and can, if we wish, be educated out."[4] Hypnosis and meditation are great tools for harnessing the power of your mind and unlearning deep-set fears. To find out more about how these tools can help create firmness of mind, see the chapters titled "Meditation" and "The Spirit-Mind-Body Connection." (You can also visit our website for more info and a free meditation download.)

Learning how your body was designed by God to work during birth can also help you to trust that your body knows what to do. Reading positive birth stories and watching positive birth videos that show mothers having normal births is also a great form of education. As you learn about other mothers' experiences and that normal birth does happen every day, you will begin to see how it can happen for you.

Taking a complete childbirth class is another great way to strengthen the firmness of your mind. It is well worth the time and money to be educated about normal birth. The information presented in the class will go a long way in helping you trust your body and baby. There are many different choices for childbirth classes. Find one that fits with your desires for birth. When your mind is full of good information about normal birth, you will have the knowledge to make good choices for you and your baby on your birthing journey.

Flexibility is also a great mental tool for maintaining peace and a sound mind during your birthing time. Like skyscrapers that are designed to sway during earthquakes so they can stay standing, I find that moms who plan and expect the best, but remain flexible and open to whatever their births bring, tend to enjoy their births the most.

When we let go of our fears of birth, we can be more open to trusting our bodies, our choices, and the birth process. Strengthened with power, love, and sound minds, we can open ourselves up to the spiritual side of birth and move forward with faith, knowing that we are about our Father's and Mother's work.

Staying Flexible

Jennette was one of my doula clients. She was planning a home birth, and things started off great. After twelve hours of being at six centimeters with consistent, strong pressure waves, she chose to transfer to the hospital. She had been awake for over forty hours and needed a rest, so she chose to get an epidural. After two hours of resting, she was still at six centimeters, so she chose to get some Pitocin and rest some more. Two hours later, she was at ten centimeters and started to push. After an hour of pushing, her sweet baby boy was born.

When I went for our postpartum visit, I asked Jennette how she felt about her birth. She said she was very happy with her birth experience. She said her main goal had been to have a positive experience and, while her experience didn't go as she had planned, she felt supported every step of the way and made choices that were best for her. She said, "I feel like I have had an unmedicated home birth and a medicated hospital birth, so I had both experiences and they were both great."

If she had been fixated on a home birth, transferring to the hospital would not have been an easy transition for her. Because she was able to stay flexible and open to what she felt was best for her and her baby at the time, her experience—though not what she had anticipated—fulfilled her expectations.

1. Dallin H. Oaks, "'The Great Plan of Happiness'," *Ensign*, November 1993, http://lds.org/ensign/1993/11/the-great-plan-of-happiness.
1. Jeffrey R. Holland, "Personal Purity," *Ensign*, November 1998, http://lds.org/ensign/1998/11/personal-purity; emphasis added.
3. Vaughn J. Featherstone, "A Champion of Youth," *Ensign*, November 1987, http://lds.org/ensign/1987/11/a-champion-of-youth.
4. Qtd. in *Protecting the Gift*, by Gavin de Becker (New York: Random House, 1999), 58.

CHAPTER NINE

Pain

Cast thy burden upon the Lord,
and he shall sustain thee.

PSALMS 55:22

Categories of Pain

By Felice Austin, CHt

Come unto me, all ye that labour and are
heavy laden, and I will give you rest. Take my yoke upon you,
and learn of me; for I am meek and lowly in heart:
and ye shall find rest unto your souls.
For my yoke is easy, and my burden is light.

MATTHEW 11:28–30

I am not going to tell you that pain is an illusion. I work with people in pain, and I see that it is real to. I have been in pain. It was so real I could feel its hot breath on my neck. But I have come to understand a few things about pain that I'd like to share. In our language, there is only one word for pain—just as there is only one word for love. Anyone who has ever gushed "I love you!" to a friend or to the Thai food delivery man, followed by an awkward moment when they said they were married, can attest to the suffering caused by want of a few more descriptive words.

Just as there are many different kinds of love, there are also nuances of experience that are commonly called pain. As I have mentioned before, words have great power, and I think it is beneficial to break down and examine the different categories of pain. I have purposely not used birth examples in this chapter so that you can come up with your own insights and comparisons.

PHYSICAL PAIN

Physical pain is something you feel in your body. There are several different subcategories of physical pain. The first is is caused by something that is not supposed to happen in or to the body, such as broken bones, a burn, a bee sting, or a disease.

Then there are other physical sensations that are often mistakenly called pain. These may be intense sensations, but they are not incongruent with the body. A classic example is running a marathon. It involves challenging physical labor and training that lasts for months, but with proper mental and physical preparation, the body responds by producing the energy and endorphins needed to triumph. In such cases, everything is going right with the body. Not everyone calls these sensations *pain*, but many do. Other words might be *intensity, work, labor, travail, physical challenge*, or as Linda King explained in "The Purpose of Life," on page 228, it might be just *tiredness*.

A third kind of physical pain is real physical pain that is caused by emotional and mental overload. Basically, when mental/emotional pain becomes too much, the mind puts some of it into the body. This leads me to the next category of pain.

EMOTIONAL/MENTAL PAIN

It is widely accepted in complementary health care fields that approximately 90 percent of all physical pain is emotional/mental in origin. (I have described this in more detail in "The Spirit-Mind-Body Connection," page 220.) I have also seen this to be true with my clients. When I can help them reduce negative emotions or feel calm, their physical pain greatly diminishes. Examples of this can be found in thousands of medical studies on the placebo effect, hypnosis, and meditation for pain management.

But let us begin earlier. There are many different varieties of emotional pain, but the causes all distill down to one word: *attachment*—or to be more specific, attachment to anything other than God. To clarify what might be a confusing concept for some, being nonattached is not the same as being detached, the latter of which refers to not caring about people or yourself, or not assuming responsibility. (Also, attachment as stated here should not be confused with the psychological term as used in attachment parenting, which has many benefits.) Nonattachment is the basis of true love because it allows us to see from a divine perspective, free from the conditions and self-interest that are often tied to mortality. The principles of nonattachment have been taught for centuries. Jesus Christ taught nonattachment all through His ministry.[1] The following are some examples of things the Savior encouraged us to release attachment to in order to minimize the suffering we experience:

- Attachment to people, even our own family members, more than God: *"He that loveth father or mother more than me is not worthy of me. And he that loveth son or daughter more than me is not worthy of me"* (Matthew 10:37–39). Christ was not telling us not to love or be close to our family members. It is about loving God more and choosing Him first. Nonattachment in relationships is also about letting go of what we want/need someone else to be. It is seeing them through God's eyes, which allows for a truer love without suffering, neediness, or fear.

- Attachment to outcomes or the future: *"Take therefore no thought for the morrow"* (Matthew 6:34). It is good to research, plan for the future, and pray for what you want. God asks us to do this, but then we need to release attachment to the future and tend to the present. The present is what becomes the future and also the past. Most suffering comes from resisting *what is*. Suffering for not getting what you want is attachment to your own plan more than God's. In this example, *faith* is another word for nonattachment.

- Attachment to reputation, pride, and appearances: *"Take heed that you do not do your charitable deeds before men to be seen by them. . . . When you fast, anoint your head and wash your face, so that you do not appear to men to be fasting"* (Matthew 6:1, 17–18, New King James Version [NKJV]). This kind of attachment usually stops people from following inspiration because they are afraid of what others think. Maybe you've stated an opinion and feel that you can't change your mind in order to save face. This causes suffering.

- Attachment to the body: *"Do not worry about your life, what you will eat or what you will drink; nor about your body, what you will put on. Is not life more than food and the body more than clothing?"* (Matthew 6:25, NKJV). Christ was teaching us to let go of obsessions or anxieties about our bodies, their needs, and the sins to which they are easily beset. He was imploring us to remember what it is that truly sustains us—the living water of Christ.

- Attachment to or believing our own thoughts, distortions, judgments, and prejudices: *"Judge not, that you be not judged. . . . Why do you look at the speck in your brother's eye, but do not consider the plank in your own eye? . . . Hypocrite! First remove the plank from your own eye, and then you will see clearly to remove the speck out of your brother's eye"* (Matthew 7:1–5, NKJV). Jesus pointed out that we all have distortion. An example is when we misjudge another's positive intentions as negative and then feel rejected or offended. We also need to release attachment to being enlightened or perfect. This attachment is an easy trap for many religious people, high achievers, and people who like to do things right. However, this attachment causes much suffering and disappointment.

- Attachment to money, possessions, and so forth: *"Do not lay up for yourselves treasures on earth, where moth and rust destroy and where thieves break in and steal; but lay up for yourselves treasures in heaven . . . for where your treasure is, there your heart will be also"* (Matthew 6:19–21, NKJV). Jesus was telling us not to get attached to our possessions or anything that can be stolen. You can easily test your attachment/suffering level by imagining losing all your possessions.

- Attachment to the past, to your story, or to unconscious conditioning: *"No man, having put his hand to the plow, and looking back, is fit for the kingdom of God"* (Luke 9:62). Our stories are our histories. They make us who we are and can be valuable for learning and sharing with others. However, too many of us get caught in blaming the past or reliving similar stories. It is important to release attachment to stories (e.g., the story about being a victim or, being in pain or the story about sin or guilt) so that we can live new ones.

ADVERSITY

Adversity can include one or both of the above kinds of pain but doesn't have to include pain by definition. The definition of *adversity* is "adverse fortune or fate."[2] *Adverse* is defined as opposing one's interests or desires.[3] Therefore, based on what we know from the above, most pain that comes with adversity is caused by attachment to our own interests and desires. Every mortal will experience adversity. As we see in the life of Christ, awful things happen to good people. However, our response—our level of attachment or resistance to the adversity—will either lessen or deepen the emotional and/or physical pain. Here is an example: When I hold on to resentment or negative feelings, I don't sleep well at night. When I give people the benefit of the doubt and release attachment to being liked, I forget little slights almost immediately. I sleep well, too.

Sometimes, in a culture that looks favorably on transforming adversity, we unconsciously cause ourselves more pain or suffering. Transforming adversity is a good thing. However, while adversity provides opportunities for growth—often our greatest *opportunities*—adversity does not *cause*

"All souls can be healed by His power. All pain can be soothed. In Him, we can "find rest unto [our] souls" (Matthew 11:29). Our mortal circumstances may not immediately change, but our pain, worry, suffering, and fear can be swallowed up in His peace and healing balm."[4] —Kent F. Richards

---

growth. And we don't have to have adversity, pain, or suffering to progress. We can choose to grow. The scriptures teach: "Blessed are they who humble themselves without being compelled to be humble" (Alma 32:16).

For example, I am choosing to grow when I study my scriptures or meditate and receive insight. This is growth without suffering. Also, when we watch a friend suffer, we can learn and grow from their experiences without suffering or taking on their pain. There is always an amount of work involved, but work and pain/suffering are not synonymous. Also, we know that in the celestial kingdom, where there is no longer pain or suffering, we will still have opportunities to grow and progress. Revelation

The Power of a Word

In Genesis in the original Hebrew Bible, the same language was used when God spoke to Adam and when God spoke to Eve. After the Fall, God cursed the ground and said that both would have to *work* to survive. But after AD 200, translators, influenced by the horrible birthing conditions at the time, chose to translate God's words to Eve differently. Instead of bringing forth children by work, she would bring them forth in *sorrow*. This has become known as "the curse of Eve" and is now strongly embedded in biblical translations and in Western belief.¹

1 Marie Mongan, *HypnoBirthing* (Deerfield Beach, FL: Health Communications, 2005), 35–40.

21:4 states: "And God shall wipe away all tears from their eyes; and there shall be no more death, neither sorrow, nor crying, neither shall there be any more pain: for the former things are passed away."

THE GREAT AND LAST SACRIFICE

Nothing can be said about pain without mentioning Christ's suffering. The Atonement is called the great and *last* sacrifice because it has the power to relieve the pain of sins and suffering (physical and mental/emotional)—so that we don't have to suffer. This is true. But is it true for you? Talking about how the Atonement can free us from physical, mental, and emotional pain doesn't actually free us. As modern mystic Ekhart Tolle said, "A mere belief doesn't make it true.... What we are concerned with here is how you can *realize* this truth—that is, make it your own experience."⁵

Let me be clear in saying that experiencing any kind of pain does not mean that you are not enlightened enough. The beautiful thing about pain is that it forces us into the present moment—which is where our relationship with God exists. Elder Kent F. Richards said the following: "Pain brings you to a humility that allows you to ponder."⁶

When I feel pain, I am grateful for it. When I don't feel pain, I am also grateful. I testify that pain and adversity are not punishments. They are merely reminders (*remember* is the command given most often in the scriptures) and opportunities to try God, to try Jesus Christ and the Atonement. As Robyn Allgood explained in "Birth in Remembrance of Him" (see page 340), each woman, each pregnancy, and each birth is unique and can access the Atonement in its own different way.

Our Heavenly Parents didn't want us to have to suffer, and that is why They sent Their son, Jesus Christ. Joy is our divine birthright. The peace of Jesus Christ is your divine birthright. All of God's commandments were given to us that we might have peace and joy. But we must access this joy through grace and through our own best efforts.

So try fasting, meditating, and praying. Try surrendering your will to God's. Remember that this process is not a one-time event. This is why people call meditation a practice. So practice even when you are not in pain or experiencing adversity. It is only through Christ that we can release

---

"The main idea of the word [grace] is divine means of help or strength, given through the bounteous mercy and love of Jesus Christ. . . . However, grace cannot suffice without total effort on the part of the recipient."[7] —Bible Dictionary

---

our mortal attachments and become one with God. The more united we become with God's will, the more we become free. Listen to Christ's invitation: "My yoke is easy, and my burden is light" (Matthew 11:30).

---

1 For the following insights, I am heavily indebted to Phillip McLemore and his article "The Yoga of Christ." Phillip McLemore, "The Yoga of Christ," *Sunstone Magazine*, June 2007, 41.
2 Dictionary.com, s.v. "adversity," http://dictionary.reference.com/browse/adversity.
3 See Dictionary.com, s.v. "adverse," http://dictionary.reference.com/browse/adverse.
4 Kent F. Richards, "The Atonement Covers All Pain," *Ensign*, May 2011, http://lds.org/ensign/2011/05/the-atonement-covers-all-pain.
5 Ekhart Tolle, *The Power of Now* (Novato CA: Namaste, 2004), 38.
6 Kent F. Richards, "The Atonement Covers All Pain," *Ensign*, May 2011, http://lds.org/ensign/2011/05/the-atonement-covers-all-pain.
7 Bible Dictionary, s.v. "grace," 697.

MORNING SICKNESS MIRACLE

By Julie B.

WITH EACH PREGNANCY, I have experienced severe morning sickness lasting for seven months. I became so ill that I could not function at a normal level: I couldn't eat, walk, or function as a normal person. During my first pregnancy, I was given a priesthood blessing. I hoped for a complete and immediate healing. To my distress, this didn't happen. However, with each successive pregnancy, I was taught line upon line how to lessen the severity of the illness to where I had at least minimal functionality. I continued to seek healing as well as secular knowledge, but it wasn't until my sixth pregnancy that I was blessed with a miracle.

My husband and I had decided that we were done having children after our fifth. We felt our lives were full, and we questioned our ability to care for any more children. As I prayed for confirmation, the thought of having more kept coming to me. And the confirmation never came. One Sunday morning, after several months of prayer, the thought came to me, "The reason you don't feel a confirmation is that you need to have more children." All of the mixed up puzzle pieces in my brain suddenly slid right into place. It was clear to me that, because of my prayers, the Lord was alerting me of the wrong decision I had made.

So I testified to my husband of my experience. With just a little coaxing, we decided to have number six. The fear of the unbearable morning sickness returned. Just the thought of it filled my heart with dread and literal terror. I knew I would be doing the will of the Father, and so I trusted that he would give me the strength to get through this physical trial.

When the morning sickness set in earlier and with greater severity than in the past, I tried a strong medication I was never willing to use before. It didn't work. I used all the "tricks" I'd learned with prior pregnancies, and I prayed with what strength I could muster for help. Many times, my prayers consisted simply of: "Help. Please help me."

I committed to myself and the Lord that I would continue to pray (if only one word), read my scriptures (if only one verse), and go to church (even if I had to eat throughout the meetings to make it through) no matter how sick I got. I knew blessings were predicated upon obedience.

And then the answer came. The simple thoughts of the Savior's Atonement, that it applied to my sickness, that He bore my illness and suffered my pain so I wouldn't have to do so filled my being. With this new understanding, I prayed with all of the energy of heart, asking if He would bear my burden for me. Then came the tender reply, "Yes."

My morning sickness wasn't taken away, but it changed to an average case, and it went away after the first trimester. I know this was a miracle. I know that the Lord blessed me for my obedience to a command I felt I didn't have the ability to accomplish. He taught me an important lesson that has changed my life through this trial, and I can honestly say that even though it is the worst suffering I have ever known that it was worth it.

THE ORIGINAL SIN

By Heather Farley

BIRTH IS SUPPOSED TO BE PAINFUL. It was what I was told from every movie and TV show I saw. My mother never talked about her own birth experiences, but I knew she struggled with postpartum depression. And I felt I was blamed for her repeat cesareans. As the oldest, I had turned breech that last month, and I doomed my mother to cesareans. Birth wasn't a happy experience. Baby showers did nothing to mitigate the idea of pain. Women talking amongst themselves in hallways, in their homes, everywhere. Birth was painful. And you couldn't get away from it.

When I was engaged to my husband, McKay, I took an Anthropology class to fulfill the social science credit. We read a book, *The Spirit Catches You and You Fall Down*, by Anne Fadiman. It's not about birth, but there were two births described in it. In the first one, on the other side of the world in Laotia, a woman gives birth by herself without ever crying out. This struck me. Where was the inevitable pain? Why was she apparently exempt from what every other woman I had ever known had experienced? If she could have that, I wanted it too.

Upon marrying my husband, I gained a new family with new experiences. My husband's grandmother told of her labors—she didn't know she was in labor until she went to the bathroom thinking she needed to use the toilet and discovering, instead, that she was having a baby. Suddenly the idea was stronger—you don't have to suffer? But don't you? Shouldn't you have to?

Both the Hmong woman and my new grandmother-in-law had basically unassisted births. The Laotian woman was completely on her own. McKay's grandmother's children were caught by her husband who was a chiropractor. At that point in California medical history, chiropractors were licensed

---

There is no such thing as original sin. It seemed so obvious. This brought me relief the rest of my pregnancy. I could really believe now that I didn't have to suffer.

---

to catch babies. It was between her husband and herself. I decided that if that's how you can have a happy birth experience, that's how I would do it.

I got pregnant and prayed about the decision to have the baby on my own. I felt that God told me, "No matter what you choose, it will be alright." And I felt like He was almost challenging me, "Try me." So I would. That was the plan.

At thirty weeks along, I struggled with back pain. Being on my feet all day at work brought it on, and I asked my husband for a priesthood blessing. In it I was told that my back pain would go away, but that in my pregnancy my body would struggle, but it would be OK. I spent that entire night tossing and turning. I would struggle? I wouldn't get the happy birth I was hoping for? When McKay woke up the next morning, he saw me in obvious distress and asked me what the problem was. I broke down into tears, "McKay, I'm going to suffer!" He replied, "I said 'struggle' not 'suffer'."

A light had been turned on for me, but on a deep level I still didn't believe that I was free from suffering. While I'd like to think that Eve being punished with hard labors was just a Protestant concept, even our modern day revelation in Moses says, "Unto the woman, I, the Lord God, said: I will greatly multiply thy sorrow and thy conception. In sorrow thou shalt bring forth children" (Moses 4:22). And despite the assurances that going to the temple would bring me peace, even there I could not escape the sorrow of bearing children. Yes, in many Sunday School lessons it was pointed out that this could mean that simply raising children will mean we will have sad times, but no one ever discounted the idea that it also meant childbirth would be painful. I felt that even considering that I didn't have to suffer was an affront to the doctrine I had been taught. I felt guilty for challenging it.

While reading my scriptures, I tried replacing "man" with "woman" as I read. One day I was thinking about the second Article of Faith, "We believe that (wo)men will be punished for their own sins, and not for Adam's (or Eve's) transgression." I stopped and paused about that. I had grown up LDS and heard over and over that original sin did not apply to me, but the culture, my family, and even the experiences shared about childbirth between LDS women had not acknowledged for me that I was free from Eve's transgression. But I was. It was right there in the simplest of our doctrines.

The reason why that Laotian woman never cried out? That my grandmother-in-law never knew she was in labor until the baby was crowning? There is no such thing as original sin. It seemed so obvious. This brought me relief the rest of my pregnancy. I could really believe now that I didn't have to suffer. Even past forty-two weeks, I had no other complaints about pregnancy. But I wondered, "Wasn't I told my body would struggle?"

At 10:30 on a Thursday night, at forty-two weeks and five days, I went into labor. I spent some time in the bathtub with the warm shower. Eventually I decided to go to bed, remembering the many birth stories I had read. "Maybe I'll have a baby by morning," I thought. Friday morning came. That back pain I had felt at thirty weeks had returned, and I had intense back labor. My husband filled a birth tub with warm water, pausing to put counter pressure on my lower back as the contractions came. The day continued on.

As I was approaching twenty-four hours of labor, I asked my husband for another blessing. I was told that I would have the Spirit with me to tell me what I needed to do. I was also told to remember all the women who came before me and that their strength was my strength. I thought about Eve and her first labor. Was it just her and Adam there like it was with me and McKay? I also had the assurance that everything would be OK. I was told to try God, and so I told him many times in my mind, "Here, I am trying you. This had better turn out alright."

Saturday morning came, and there was still no baby. My back labor had kept me from getting a full night's rest, though I had received some sleep. I got up and prayed, wondering how I was supposed to feel the Spirit in this situation. I had been promised the Spirit, but I was in no position to feel it. Shortly after, I invited a friend over to help relieve my husband.

The day continued to pass. By mid-afternoon, the back labor was gone, but the contractions were still there and there was no baby yet. Evening came, and I started feeling pushy. But I did not doubt like I had that morning. This time, with each contraction, I pushed and I could feel when my baby moved down. If I had a contraction that didn't result in movement down, I resolved that the next one would, and I made sure of it. I was determined and focused.

Contractions were happening too slowly for my taste. At almost two days in, I wanted my baby out. My pushes would induce contractions, so I started pushing without waiting for them. In less than half an hour, I felt something crowning, but it was not the head. It was soft and squishy. My husband checked and it was my water bags, still intact. Upon the next contraction, I felt the head fully engage. A push later the head was out, still in the caul. There was a pause while the shoulders turned and with another push, the body to the middle was out. And in another push my whole baby was born and the water finally broke.

She was pink, breathing, and calm. We untangled the cord from around her arm, and I had a little girl. She nursed right away, and the placenta was released and out in ten minutes. In another priesthood blessing, I was promised that I wouldn't lose consciousness or hemorrhage.

I had tried God, and He had come through. And He was right—I had struggled. At now forty-three weeks, my daughter was born at 6:45 p.m.—over forty-four hours since the onset of labor. In fact, there was pain. But that wasn't the overriding feeling of my birth. The hardest part wasn't the pain, it was the feeling of abandonment I had felt around thirty hours during transition. But my birth wasn't about pain, and I don't associate pain or suffering with the labor at all.

I had brought another woman into the world. And I will make sure she doesn't feel the guilt I had felt in challenging the idea of original sin. Here she is in my arms: perfect and free from that. I didn't suffer. She won't have to either.

Letting Go

By Alisha

WHEN I WAS A SMALL CHILD, I truly believed in monsters, werewolves, ghosts and vampires. They existed in the form of people doing horrific things to my body and robbing me of the ability to feel safe and secure. There was never a moment when I was not wary of the world around me. As I grew, I came to realize that, while monsters don't truly exist, monstrous people do, and I didn't want to become one of them. Heavenly Father guided me to people who could help me unlearn some of the lessons learned as a child. He also began to gently teach me how to let go of the control I thought I needed to possess in order to survive in this world. Sexual abuse is about power and control and not necessarily about sexual gratification. The child who was sexually abused becomes the adult seeking the control that was lost.

When the test stick window showed a pink plus sign, four months after I was married, I was stunned. I was angry. I was terrified. This was the beginning of nine months of my body being completely out of my control. And yet I experienced a spark which eventually grew into a powerful source of light, along with my growing body. God began whispering to me, so gently and carefully, that I was more than my abuse. He began helping me to remember who I was—an eternal mother. I struggled those nine months to allow my body to do what it needed to do. I read everything I could and was determined to keep the "monsters" away from this child being entrusted to me. This child, who while in my womb radiated feelings of calm and peace, was reaching out to my spirit and helping recall feelings I thought were lost forever.

During labor, my body and my spirit wrestled for control. My body screamed that it was terrified, out of control, and was going to die. My spirit gently, but with eons of wisdom and strength, replied that all was well and this was an eternal process. My spirit and my body began to work together, and a healthy daughter was born. I looked into her deep eyes and saw the peace, innocence and trust I craved. I breathed and let it settle in my soul.

With each birth since then—there have been six more—I regain a little more of myself. I have discovered strength I didn't know I had. However,

God began whispering to me, so gently and carefully, that I was more than my abuse.

the Spirit reminds me of the strength I already had which allowed me to survive the "monsters" in the first place, and how that fortitude has shaped my mothering. I am the mother I am today in part due to what I experienced as a child.

Just as Heavenly Father knows us and our capabilities better than we do, so I believe does Satan. He remembers us and is trying to stop us from fulfilling our missions. I believe Satan knew of my potential for motherhood and tried to thwart my earthly mission early in my childhood. That being said, God is over all, and it is His plan and His will that will prevail. Heavenly Father knew my spirit and used my childhood experience for my good. He enhanced my endurance, strength, faith, and compassion for the suffering of others. All these qualities make me a better mother than perhaps I would have been otherwise.

My seventh baby was born in 2011. This labor was fantastic. It's a blessing to me to see how far I have come. With the first contractions came the familiar feelings of loss of control, fear, and doubt. Within a few minutes, I had asked God to help me remember who I was and to feel His love and strength. I was flooded with quiet confidence and knew I was being watched over. Since I was only having a contraction every fifteen minutes, I had a chance to ready my home and talk to my small children about what was happening. My mom and three older daughters, ages thirteen, ten, and seven, and I, drove to the birth center where my husband was waiting. Labor kicked-in with earnest and I knew the toughest part was yet to come, but I was ready. Through the process of birth, my desire to control has been transformed into the ability to let go. I am able to give in to the process of birth and let the contractions wash over me like waves in the ocean. Although they are painful, I revel in the strength and endurance of my body. I joy in experiencing the eternal nature of my spirit and feel a deep connection with the baby about to be born.

Within about forty minutes of contractions and five minutes of pushing, another beautiful daughter was born. Once again, she brought with her the peace of heaven and bestowed some of it into my hungry soul. I looked into the smiling eyes of my husband and three older daughters and knew the bond we had formed could never be broken.

I love being a mother more than anything else. I love to watch the wonder, joy, and pure innocence in my children's eyes. I try my hardest to create a place of refuge for my children and the children around me so they can feel safe and secure—at least for a while. I know my children will, and do, experience pain, disappointment, heartache and fear, but hopefully they will have the knowledge that their mother cared for them as best she could and gave everything she had—body and soul. I have taken that need for control and used it to propel me forward. With God's great mercy and love, He has guided me to a place of peace and happiness I didn't think was possible.

The Angel Standing By

By Elizabeth Day, CD(DONA), LCCE

And there appeared an angel unto him from heaven, strengthening him.

LUKE 22:43

I remember clearly the day I gave birth to my first son. It was a beautiful fall morning when I awoke to the sound and sensation of my water breaking. My excitement to finally receive my baby into my arms was second only to the exhilaration I felt at finally knowing what labor really felt like. I had supported many women as a labor doula, even though I had never given birth myself, and I remembered how difficult it was for them. Because of my doula work, I felt uniquely qualified to cope effectively with my own labor. I had a strange sort of overconfidence—a "bring-it-on" attitude— that made my husband and mother shake their heads.

Imagine my surprise when I transitioned to the second stage of labor about two hours later. I was amazed and shocked. I dropped to my hands and knees on the ground, as standing or sitting was impossible. Everything I had learned and taught other women about birth was gone. My hubris melted into helplessness as I screamed loud enough for all the women on the maternity floor to hear.

Then beside me, like an angel, my mother knelt, held my hand tight, and put her face close to mine. She smiled! Yes, in my moment of sheer agony, she smiled at me and whispered, "You're doing it, Beth! You're doing it just right! You know how to do this. You *can* do this." I locked my gaze with hers and started to breathe deeply and slowly. Two hours later, my son was born.

A few months after this surprising encounter with birth, I read the account of the Savior's Atonement in the Garden of Gethsemane with new eyes and a much-humbled heart. I caught my breath when I read the following words: "And he taketh with him Peter and James and John, and began to be *sore amazed*, and to be *very heavy*" (Mark 14:33). These words resonated with me. The Savior of the world was surprised by the weight of the burden He had long ago agreed to bear. That was how I felt. Sore amazed and very heavy described my exact emotional and physical state as I gave birth.

Further, this rite of passage into motherhood, which I had so long studied and anticipated, was so overwhelming that I just wanted someone to make it stop. I remember crying out, "Oh, my God!" Not to take the Lord's name in vain, but rather to call out and plead that He might somehow stop or ease my burden. Likewise, the Savior "went forward a little and fell on the ground, and prayed that, if it were possible, the hour might pass from him. And he said, "Abba, Father, all things are possible unto thee; take away this cup from me: nevertheless not what I will, but what thou wilt" (Mark 14:35–36).

What happened next is rarely mentioned, but it is extremely important. Luke was the only Gospel writer to include the following detail: "And there appeared an angel unto him from heaven, strengthening him" (Luke 22:43). Christ was uniquely prepared to withstand the pain and suffering of an infinite Atonement. He was half God and half mortal. He could walk on water. He could heal the sick and raise the dead. He could feed five thousand with only five loaves of bread and two small fishes. And yet, He came to a point in the Garden of Gethsemane where He would rather not have gone through with it. Yet, He humbly surrendered His will, and that is when His Father sent an angel.

God knows that when facing any great challenge—be it physical, mental, or emotional—the aid of another person, seen or unseen, who possesses greater vision and experience is essential in negotiating the path successfully. As I reflected on my own birth experience, I realized that in my darkest hour, I needed an angel standing by me to strengthen me. For me, that angel was my mother. For other women, their angels may be friends, sisters, aunts, husbands, professional doulas, midwives, compassionate nurses, or even unseen loved ones supporting them from the other side of the veil. But the need for a hand to hold, a kind word, a compassionate touch from a woman who understands is an almost universal necessity for women in labor.

As a doula, I often struggle to find the right combination of words, actions, and support to help each woman come out the other side of birth feeling positive and empowered by the experience. Some women need a lot of help and encouragement. Others want me in the room but prefer to labor alone in silence (except for an intermittent request for a drink of water and bite to eat).

However, as I reflect on the angel who supported the Savior, as well as the many women I have supported, I believe that there are a few key ingredients of labor support that make all the difference.

Ingredient 1:
An Understanding of the Laboring Woman's Strength and Potential

The angel in the garden knew of Christ's divine lineage and what He would become as a result of His great sacrifice. The angel knew that Christ had within Himself everything He needed to accomplish an infinite Atonement, and the angel knew of the glory that awaited Christ upon completion of the Atonement. The angel possessed a vision of Christ as the glorious, triumphant Messiah—not merely the mortal who suffered there in Gethsemane.

Likewise, your labor support person needs to know deeply and intuitively that you are strong and that as a woman you have within you everything you need to give birth. This understanding is an outcome of experience, but it is also a gift of the Spirit. I wish that every woman who believes she can't could see what I have seen. I have witnessed women who entered birth doubting their own strength but who emerged as strong, powerful mothers who knew they could do anything because they gave birth. I have seen women who, having peered into the darkness of the unknown, emerged transformed into joyful, exultant mothers in awe of their own power. I have known many wise women who have faced the challenge of pregnancy, birth, and new motherhood again and again and again; who have learned new lessons every time; and who have begun to savor that unique opportunity to fully submit their wills to that of the Father and thereby become one with the Divine.

Our culture tells women over and over again that they can't do it and it isn't worth it. Penny Simkin, founder of DONA International and mother of the doula profession, has often said, "Negativity is like poison to birthing outcomes." I weep for the women who believe the negativity and the lies because they never had anyone take them by the hands, look them deeply in the eye, and tell them that they are doing it and that it is indeed worth it. What if these women had just one person who stood by them and said, "You can because you are strong. Even if you don't know it yet, you are."

I remember one birth I attended as a doula about a year after I gave birth. The mother was progressing quickly. She was moaning and rocking and moving with the contractions that came wave after wave with very little rest in between. In my eyes, she was doing a wonderful job. But in her head, she felt that she was failing. The intensity overwhelmed her, and she began to panic. She began to cry over and over, "I can't do this! I can't do this!"

In that moment, I saw myself and I remembered my own mother's words to me. I grabbed her hands and held them tightly as I smiled and said, "Amanda, look at me." Reluctantly, she forced herself to open her eyes and look at me. I smiled and said, "You are doing it! You are so strong! You can do this! You were made to do this!" Like a climber on a mountainside who finally finds that elusive foothold, she clung to my words and dug deep. She began to breathe and to believe that she could.

Only moments later, she sat trembling on the bed, holding her new baby tightly in her arms. "I did it! I did it!" she exclaimed. Then she turned and said, "Thank you for telling me I could!"

Ingredient 2:
Knowledge of the Scope and Magnitude of the Plan as Well as the Great Importance of the Part the Laboring Woman Plays in That Plan

Jonathan Edwards, an eighteenth-century American theologian, wrote, "Christ seems to have a greater sight of his sufferings given him after this strengthening of the angel than before. . . . [H]e had greater strength and courage to grapple with these awful apprehensions, than before. His strength to bear sufferings is increased."[1]

I imagine that in the Savior's darkest hour, He may have momentarily lost sight of the big picture. I know I did. But when I imagine what the angel may have said to Christ, I imagine that he reminded Christ why He was doing what He was doing. "Remember the plan," the angel might have said. "There is only One who can save us all. Remember that this is only a moment. Remember that this is necessary and has a great purpose. It is only through this sacrifice that all humankind will return to the Father."

Reminded of the greater purpose of His sufferings, Christ no longer begged for a reprieve. He did pray more earnestly, but He prayed for the children of God and for strength and courage to finish His work. So, too, a laboring mother can benefit from a greater vision of how the moment fits into the big picture. She can be reminded that "You are the only one who can birth this baby. Your baby is coming down and will soon be in your arms. Think of your baby in your arms and breathe."

This big-picture perspective allows the birthing mother to gain context and an objective for her work, which in turn increases her ability to accept and cope with struggles and pain. Her resolve strengthens, she is empowered to confront her fears, and she ultimately discovers her own great power.

Ingredient 3:
The Holding Presence

Kathy McGrath, one of my hero doulas, described the traditional role of the labor support person as "the holding presence."

> The holding presence is one who acts as a support and a guide for a person who is facing a challenge, watches over the other person, creates a safe passage, allows others to do the work that needs to be done, and holds the waters back. [2]

The holding presence is usually not a loved one (although it can be). Many women have the expectation that the father will be all things during labor, including the coach. But the husband may be too close to the situation to remain objective in times of stress, struggle, or crisis. And if he has his own fears, he may be tempted to want to interrupt the process, thus adversely affecting the progress of the labor for both mother and baby. The holding presence, however, is usually one with greater perspective and experience, who can sense that fine line between too much and not enough.

My mind recalls again that moment when I cried out for relief. In my own minuscule version of Gethsemane, there appeared an angel unto me to strengthen me. My mother was my angel. She could have turned to worrying. But what did she do instead? She smiled. My mother understood that growth comes from working through challenge and that removing the challenge may very well have turned my refiners fire into a lukewarm bath. And because she knew me, she knew I needed this challenge to help me become a stronger mother. Kathy McGrath also stated the following:

> Labor was not designed to be easy. We don't find ourselves when things are easy. There will be many crossroads in labor when a mother must decide whether to stop or push forward. By presenting her with the opportunity to make discoveries about herself, we express our confidence in her and in her ability to stand on her own.

> That's what each of us must be: a "holding presence." We believe in the laboring woman. We trust that she can do it. We support her and encourage her and strengthen her so that she can do the work and cross the boundary. We don't cross it for her; instead, we provide her with the resources she needs to cross it herself. Our role is simply as a guide, to help her find her way.[3]

UNSEEN ANGELS

Not every woman will have that perfect support person helping her through labor. Some women will, for one reason or another, be alone during this momentous hour—even if there are people in the room. If you find yourself lacking support or feeling alone, know that you have the right and opportunity to call on unseen angels to assist you. You may not have a mother like mine who knows what birth should look like and who knows how to assist you. But you have mothers, grandmothers, and great grand-mothers on the other side of the veil who do, including your Heavenly Mother. Birth may afford you a unique opportunity to become acquainted with these noble and great women who have walked the path before you.

I became aware of these angels when I was pregnant with my

daughter, Eliza. Halfway through my pregnancy, I had not been able to find a midwife about whom I felt peaceful. I was five months pregnant and still had never had a prenatal exam. I had no idea who would support me. One day, frustrated and worried, I dropped to my knees and pled with my Father in Heaven, "Who is to be my midwife?" I asked. As I sat quietly on my bed, I looked to a framed print of Jesus Christ on the wall. Suddenly, a great calm swept over me and I heard the words in my head, "I will be your midwife." I felt a quiet sense that everything would be all right, and I wondered whether those words might have been spoken through the voice of the Spirit by a loving Mother in Heaven. I did find a midwife eventually. But this birth was unique in the sense that I felt the additional help and presence of others beyond the veil.

WHO WILL BE YOUR ANGEL?

As you prepare for your own birth, seek out your angel, whether an earthly angel or a heavenly one. Look for someone in whose presence you feel courageous, optimistic, and uplifted. Look for someone who knows when to step in and lend a hand and when to step back and let you walk your path with your own two feet. That angel can make all the difference.

1   Jonathan Edwards *The Works of Jonathan Edwards, A.M.: With an Essay on His Genius*, vol. 2 (London: John Childs and Son, 1839), 873.
2   Kathy McGrath, "Finding the Path," *Journal of Perinatal Education* 16, no. 2 (2007): 7–15.
3   Ibid.

Benefits of Having a Doula during Your Birth

What is a doula? A doula provides support to the mother and the father (as well as other family members) during the birth. The doula provides this support in many different ways.

- Ideas for comfort: Having a doula is like having your very own personal guide for your birth. Doulas know what can help during birth and how to do it. Your doula can either perform these comfort measures herself or help your family or friends support you with comfort measures. The father will feel more confident knowing that he is doing the right thing.

- Constant support and encouragement: A doula not only encourages the mother to keep going but also encourages the father to keep going as well. If a birth is long or even very fast, having an experienced person by your side to support you can help things go more smoothly.

- Reminders about your options: You may have learned about all the choices you would have before birth, but it can be difficult to remember all the pros and cons during birth. A doula can remind you of your choices and the benefits and risks of different interventions. She can also suggest good questions to ask so you can gather more information, which will help you to make the best choices for you and your baby during your birth.

Research shows that a doula's support can positively affect your birth experience in a variety of ways:

PHYSICAL
Fewer requests for epidurals (60%), narcotics (30%)[1-4, 7, 8]
40% decrease in use of Pitocin[1, 2, 4, 6, 7]
25% decrease in duration of labor[1-6]
41% decrease in forceps and vacuum deliveries[1, 2, 4, 5]
50% decrease in cesarean section rates[1, 7]
Decrease of neonatal hospitalization and rate of complications[2, 3]
Decrease of maternal fever and infection[2]
Decrease of maternal bleeding following birth[5]
Increase in chance of spontaneous vaginal birth[6]

PSYCHOLOGICAL
Increase in mothers' positive reviews of their birth experiences[4, 8,]
Decrease in anxiety level[4]
Increase in mothers' regard and sensitivity toward babies[4, 8]
Increase in mothers' sense of security and confidence[8]
Decrease in incidence of postpartum depression[4, 8]

1   K. D. Scott, G. Berkowitz, and M. Klaus, "A Comparison of Intermittent and Continuous Support During Labor: A Meta-analysis," *American Journal of Obstetrics and Gynecology* 180, no. 5 (1999): 1,054–1,059.

2   J. Kennel, M. Klaus, S McGrath, et al., "Continuous Emotional Support During Labor in a US hospital. A randomized controlled trial. *JAMMA*, 265, no. 17 (1991): 2197–2201.

3   K. D. Scott, P. H. Klaus, and M. H. Klaus, "The Obstetrical and Postpartum Benefits of Continuous Support during Childbirth," *Journal of Women's Health and Gender-Based Medicine* 8, no. 10 (1999): 1257–1264.

4   P. Keenan, "Benefits of Massage Therapy and Use of a Doula during Labor and Childbirth," *Alternative Therapies in Health and Medicine* 6, no. 1 (2000): 66–74.

5   D. Wand, X. Mao, and S. Qian, "Clinical Observation on Doula Delivery," *Zhonghua Fu Chan Ke Za Zhi* 32, no. 11 (1997): 659–661.

6   J. Zhang, J. W. Bernasko, E. Leybovich, et al., "Continuous Labor Support from Labor Attendant for Primiparous Women: A Meta-analysis," *Obstetrics and Gynecology* 88, no. 4, pt. 2 (1996): 739–744.

7   M. Nolan, "Supporting Women in Labor: The Doula's Role," *Modern Midwife* 5, no. 3 (1995): 12–15.

8   G. A. Manning-Orenstein, "Birth Intervention: The Therapeutic Effects of Doula Support Versus Lamaze Preparation on First-Time Mothers' Working Models of Care Giving," *Alternative Therapies in Health and Medicine* 4, no. 4 (1998): 73–81.

The Ultimate Form
of Compassionate Service

By Neoma Gould

WHEN WE FOUND OUT WE WERE PREGNANT, my husband Jason and I had been married a little less than a month. We were incredibly excited. The decision of which obstetrician to see was almost a no-brainer. Dr. B was a family friend who was a member of the Church and had been my home teacher when I was a little girl. I trusted him.

The pregnancy went well. I loved the feeling of carrying a child inside of me. I loved knowing that I was providing a body for one of Heavenly Father's choice spirit children. When I was pregnant, I could consecrate my whole self, twenty-four hours a day, to fulfilling God's plan. I looked forward to childbirth with full confidence that everything would go well.

Around seven months along, Jason began telling me that he had an impression that I would have the baby early. This seemed strange to me because ten of my mom's eleven babies had come late, but I trusted Jason. When my blood pressure was dangerously high at my thirty-seven week check-up, we were (mostly) prepared. I stayed overnight at the hospital to be monitored, and in the morning they scheduled me to be induced. I didn't want to be induced, but I finally resigned myself to the fact that pregnancy induced hypertension was a legitimate medical reason for induction.

I was excited for the baby to come, and I felt surprisingly calm about being induced.

We started on Friday morning with a minimally invasive prostaglandin induction at 10:10 a.m. At about 6 p.m. the nurse came in and said the doctor wanted to get labor going. I ended up receiving two of the interventions that I had specifically wanted to avoid, an IV and Pitocin. It took me a while to be okay with receiving Pitocin, but I felt like I didn't have much of a choice at that point. I had a complication that required an intervention. I was okay with it because I had to be. I hadn't failed. I could still have a safe labor and delivery without further medications.

After twelve hours of Pitocin and no real contractions, the nurse called Dr. B again. I was still at 3.5 cm, the same place I had been twenty hours earlier when the induction started. While Dr. B was doing the exam, my water broke. I guess the decision about what to do next was made for us. There was no going back. This baby was coming.

After my water broke, the contractions started in earnest. At first the contractions were bearable. I breathed slow and deep and concentrated on surrendering to the rush. I visualized relaxing and opening the muscles of my cervix. Because my blood pressure was still elevated, I had to lie on my side in bed most of the time. That was okay in the beginning but became more and more uncomfortable as labor intensified.

After hours of slow progress, Dr. B came back in. He expressed some concern about how slowly things were going and suggested that we may have difficulty delivering this baby vaginally—the other option being cesarean. Somehow that scared me and relieved me. I didn't know how I could go on. I felt like I was going to die. I told Jason that I really didn't know how I was going to continue. The only good news throughout this difficult part was that the baby's heart rate was fine. There was never any urgency on account of the baby.

The next sequence of events is somewhat of a blur in my mind. At that lowest point I think I would have agreed to anything, so I'm really glad no one offered me an epidural. I know I didn't want an epidural, but I didn't see any other way out. That is when I needed Jason the most, and he was there for me.

He remembered that I had talked about wanting to sit on a birthing ball. He asked about it and our new nurse agreed to let me get out of bed. The birthing ball was comfortable and allowed me to sit in a squat-like position. The contractions were still intense—if anything they were more intense—but sitting up and swaying back and forth helped me cope with them.

Jason also suggested that he and Dr. B give me a blessing. He spoke with the doctor, and together they gave me a blessing by the power of the Priesthood with holy anointing oil. I don't really remember what they said, but in essence they blessed me that I would relax and the baby and I would both be safe and the birth would happen according to the Lord's will.

Dr. B has mentioned this blessing several times since Sam's birth. He thanked Jason for thinking of it and for including him. He counts this as the turning point in my labor. This is where the miracle happened.

At some point while sitting on the birthing ball, I threw up. Jason had been feeding me snacks at my request through the labor, and out they all came. I was glad to vomit. I had read that throwing up was a good sign in labor. It means that you're in transition (the last stage before pushing).

Apparently sitting on the birthing ball helped the contractions be more effective because I was soon at 8 cm. Jason remembered that I had wanted to try the jacuzzi. I had thought that I wouldn't be allowed in the tub because my water was already broken, but the nurse said it was fine—I wish they would have told me that earlier. When I got tired of the ball, I moved to a hot bath. I found that the hot water really helped me relax between contractions, but when a contraction came the heat was almost unbearable.

I wasn't in the tub for very long before I felt the urge to push. The nurse and Jason helped me dry off. Then the nurse checked me and I was 10 cm—completely dilated! She said I could push if I wanted to. Boy did I want to. I really didn't know how to push, but it felt so good to do something—to be so close to the baby being born. At that point all breathing patterns went out the window. I made all sorts of moaning sounds. I tried to keep them low, like a cow mooing, just like I had read in Ina May's Guide to Childbirth.

The pushing went fast. Before I knew it the baby just slimed right out. I was surprised. I remember being amazed at how when the baby came out the pain relief was instantaneous and complete. It was all gone, and I felt wonderful—exhausted, but wonderful. Our baby was here. He was beautiful and perfect.

I was overwhelmed by feelings of awe at what my body had just done. It was so hard. It was so painful and yet it was incredibly fulfilling and empowering. I was so glad that I chose to experience all of it. I felt so close to God. I felt like I had just been inducted into a club. My husband would never experience this, but billions of women all over the world and throughout the millennia had experienced this same thing. They had all felt the contractions. We had all come nigh unto death to bring forth life.

Since then I've reflected on how going through a natural birth has helped me better understand Christ's Atonement. During the intensely painful part of labor, I remember wondering if there was any other way, but I knew the only way for this spirit to come to earth was through my body. I chose to submit my desires to God's will.

During my second birth, things progressed very quickly. The contractions were very hard and very close together. I felt like I was weaker than the last time I had a baby, but it turned out that I wasn't weaker. The labor was just going faster than my first time, but I didn't know that at the time.

At some point I started talking myself into an epidural. I remember thinking, "I don't care about the long needle in my back. I don't care about the IV. I don't care about being numb and not feeling my legs." I finally decided that I needed to think about something else. I reminded myself that no one dies from labor pains. I began praying, "Oh, Heavenly Father, help me!" That was all I could get out. I don't remember the contractions getting easier, but I did bear them, so I know He strengthened me. When I thought about it later, I felt that Heavenly Father sent ministering angels to bear me up. Spiritual midwives, if you will. I wonder who they were—maybe my grandmother or another ancestor. Christ had also been sent an angel to bear Him up at His weakest hour in the Garden of Gethsemane.

I know that God chose to have His children come to earth through pregnancy, labor, and delivery, with all its discomforts and joys. He must have designed it this way for a reason. Heavenly Father didn't do this to women as a punishment, but as a blessing. Through my experiences with pregnancy, labor, and delivery, and as a mother in general, I have learned about the selflessness of God. Motherhood is the ultimate form of compassionate service, of giving up your will to fulfill the needs of another.

Between Heaven and Earth

By Heather Farrell, CD(DONA)

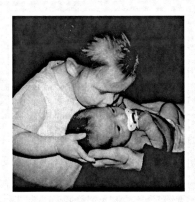

THE MORNING ROSE WAS BORN, I woke up at about 4:30 a.m. with several strong contractions. They were strange contractions because, even though they were strong and uncomfortable, after each one I would get a wave of pure pleasure sensation that rushed through my whole body and made me feel wonderful. For a while I just lay in bed and "rode" the sensations. I'd focus on making it through the strong contraction and then relish the feeling of pleasure and relaxation that followed. Eventually my legs really started to hurt, and I got up to go sit on the toilet.

Despite having a lot of trust in my body, in the birth process, and in God, in those moments in the bathroom, I got really scared. My contractions were stronger than I ever remembered having with my son's labor (two years earlier). If things went like his labor, I still had at least eight or nine more hours ahead of me. I was already having a hard time relaxing through the contractions and began to doubt whether I was going to be strong enough this time. After about fifteen minutes, my husband knocked on the door to see if I was all right. I told him that I was in labor. He got the biggest smile on his face. In my head, I thought, "Why are you smiling? This isn't fun."

After getting off the toilet, I put on my bathrobe and a bracelet that my family and close friends had made for me. It had beads and charms representing their faith in me, their confidence in my ability to access inner power and strength, and of God's love for me and my unborn daughter. Wearing that bracelet brought be so much peace and reminded me of all the birthing women who had gone before me and who would come after me.

Jon and I tried timing the contractions, but they didn't have any sort of pattern to them. I would get two or three incredibly strong contraction that were less than a minute apart, but then I would get several weak contractions that were about five minutes apart. I was also having pretty intense pain in my legs that didn't go away between contractions.

When we called the midwife, just a little after 5 a.m., she told us that it sounded like the baby's head was not in the best position and that was probably why my contraction pattern was irregular and I was getting leg pain. She told me to use the "polar bear position" (lying with your head on the ground and your pelvis up in the air) and to lean over the bed or a big ball to help open up my pelvis and let the baby move her head into a better position. She said that usually, when the baby is in a less than optimal position, labor doesn't progress as quickly because the contractions don't dilate the cervix as well. She told us that she would start getting ready and that we should call her in about an hour to let her know how things were progressing.

For the next hour, I spent most of my time leaning over the table or the couch, swaying my hips, in the "polar bear" position on the floor, or leaning over the birth ball. I also found myself talking and singing to the baby. I would tell her, "Move, baby move," and even made up a little song that went something like, "I love you baby, baby come to me, come to me, and I'll set you free." Not the most brilliant lyrics ever written, but singing to her helped me relax between the contractions and to feel safe.

Soon, however, I found that the only way I could make it through the contractions was to have Jon squeeze my hips while I bellowed "*Harder!* Squeeze *harder!*" at him. It was the combination of him pushing back against the contraction and my being able to bellow out some of the intensity that allowed me to emerge on the other side of the contraction still in control and calm.

It was about this point that I really started to get scared and to doubt that I was going to be able to make it through to the end. I remember leaning over the birth ball and telling myself, "I could handle this if I only knew that each contraction was doing what it is suppose to," and wanting to cry and give up.

It was then that I asked Jon if he would give me a blessing. In between contractions, I knelt in the polar bear position and he put his hands on my head and gave me one of the most beautiful blessings I've ever received. I was told that my Heavenly Father was aware of me, that everything would be alright, that I was not alone, and that He had sent angels to be with me and my baby. I wish I could remember everything that was said, but I distinctly remember the peace I felt.

As I labored on, my husband was there for me with his strong arms and his loving touch through almost every contraction. He didn't once get flustered or upset by my constant command of, "Squeeze *harder*," even though sometimes I could feel his arms shaking. There are only two times I remember having to go through a contraction without him. During one of those contractions I know for certain that I wasn't alone. Right at the peak of one of my hardest and longest contractions, when Jon wasn't able to be there for me, I looked down at my hand and felt that someone was holding it. I knew at that moment that what Jon said in the blessing was true, God was aware of me and there were angels with me.

It wasn't long after the blessing, probably around 6:30 a.m., that I felt the baby move down, the pain in my legs eased, and I knew that she had moved into a better position. We talked with the midwife again and told her that things seemed to become more consistent and that I had had a little bleeding when I sat on the toilet. She said that this was a good sign as it meant that my cervix was dilating, and she said that she would be there as soon as she could. She also said that it was okay for me to get in the birth pool as long as I got out if my contractions slowed down or stopped.

Jon helped me get into the tub, and the hot water relaxed my body all over. With all the commotion we were making, I think that one of our angels must have been upstairs keeping my son, Asher, asleep. When he woke up, Jon brought him down, and he was super excited that there was a swimming pool in the middle of our living room. He was really sweet to me and gave me several adorable love pats and kisses between my contractions.

I really only had five or six contractions in the birth pool before I felt like

I needed to start pushing. I called for Jon, who had just put Asher into his high chair and gotten him breakfast, and he came over and held my hands while I squatted. Jon called the midwife and I remember hearing, "Um... Heather [midwife's name], are you close? Because she is pushing." He was so incredibly calm and didn't seem panicked or worried in the least bit. He told me later that it was because he knew that I could do it and knew that everything was going to be all right. He told me, "That is what your body was made to do, and it did it. What was there to be scared about?" Yep, I married the world's most amazing man.

The midwife was still about twenty minutes away. Jon kept her on the phone as I held his hands and gave some more big pushes. I felt my water break in a little poof, and then, two pushes later, I felt her head crowning. I reached down and felt her head pushing against my hand and then on the next contraction I gave one really big push and her head flowed out of me.

Up until that point, I had been so engulfed in the sensations of birth, the intensity of the contractions and the all-encompassing urge to push, that the fact that my baby was coming right then and there, without the midwife, hadn't really penetrated my psyche. But once her head was out, I realized what was happening and had a couple seconds of anxiety. The midwife was still on the phone and was able to reassure me that everything was fine and that I just needed to be patient and the rest of the body would come out on the next contraction.

There is really no stranger feeling in this world than to look down and see that you have a baby half in and half out of you. It is a point all women reach when they give birth, but with my son's birth I wasn't as aware of it as I was this time. This time, I had a few minutes to look down at the head I was holding in my hands and appreciate what an amazing thing I was a part of. I realized that, for those few minutes, my baby was in between heaven and earth and that I was a wide open portal between them. I felt closer to God than I ever had before. I realized that He was working a miracle through me and that I was a beloved and cherished daughter of God. It was an incredible feeling and one of the most surreal experiences of my life.

With my next contraction, I felt the rest of her body flow out of me and I reached down into the water and pulled her up into my arms. She was really alert and peaceful. She didn't cry at all. She just looked up at me for a few moments with big eyes and then closed them and nestled into my arms.

The midwife asked us about her coloring, reflexes and appearance. She said, from what she could tell over the phone, the baby sounded healthy and strong, which she verified when she arrived a few minutes later.

Jon came over and put his arms around me, and we both just stared at our amazing little girl. Then we started to hear a sweet little "Mama? Mama?" coming from the high chair and Jon went and brought Asher over to meet his little sister. I can't even begin to explain the feeling that filled that room as we huddled there together as a family for the first time. There really are no other words but "sacred" and "holy" to describe how it felt. Even though we weren't planning on having Asher there for the birth, I am really glad that he was. I know that he felt and understood the intense amount of love and peace that filled our house. I know that we could all feel the presence of the angels who were watching over us. It has actually

There is really no stranger feeling in this world than to look down and see that you have a baby half in and half out of you.

been hard for me to share this birth experience with others because it was so sacred and beautiful and my words never come close to being able to describe what it felt like or what it meant to me.

Only about five or six minutes after the baby was born, my friend Elizabeth (we had called her to come pick up Asher before he woke up) came in the back door. I was still in the pool, and Jon and Asher were huddled around the baby, when we looked up and saw her tiptoeing into the room. She was shocked to see a baby in my arms and almost immediately started to cry. She told me afterward that, "The feeling in the room was incredible," and that she was honored to be a part of our special moment.

The midwife arrived about ten minutes after the baby was born and helped to deliver the placenta and get the baby and me all cleaned up. I was surprised by how good I felt. I felt like I could ride a bike to the moon and back. My body felt strong, my mind felt strong, and my spirit felt stronger than it ever had.

Even though things didn't go quite like we expected, Rose's birth was so amazing that I wouldn't change one thing about it. Her birth brought Jon and me closer together and made us stronger partners and parents. Every once in a while, we look at each other and get big grins on our face, remembering how together, here in our house, with no one to witness it except our son and the angels, we delivered our own precious little girl into the world.

Rose's birth has also given me so much more confidence in myself and in my body. I am simply awestruck by the amazing power my body has and when I look at myself in the mirror I think, "Wow, this is a body that has created, birthed and fed two other human beings." I understand now, more than I ever have before, how important it is to respect, honor, and love my body. I've also felt more confidence in myself as a woman and as a mother. I feel like if I can deliver my own baby then there isn't anything in the world that I can't do with God's help. During Rose's birth, I got a brief glimpse into eternity and realized who I am and what I am capable of, and that has made me a different woman.

Travail and Joy

by Heather Farrell, CD(DONA)

There could be nothing so exquisite and so bitter as were my pains.
Yea, and again I say unto you . . . that on the other hand, there can be nothing
so exquisite and sweet as was my joy.

ALMA 36:21

Travail isn't a word we use much in our modern vernacular, but it is commonly used in the scriptures to describe giving birth. It is an interesting word because even though it means work, effort, or struggle, in the scriptures it is often linked with joy. This joy is not *happiness* or *gladness*, but a richer type of emotion, such as the feeling you get after receiving the illumination of the gospel, gaining great knowledge, or being in communion with God. The joy a woman experiences after giving birth is one of the best examples of this type of feeling. Christ must have thought so as well because He used it to explain to His disciples how they would feel at His death and resurrection. He said:

> Verily, verily, I say unto you, That ye shall weep and lament, but the world shall rejoice: and ye shall be sorrowful, but your sorrow shall be turned into joy. A woman when she is in travail hath sorrow, because her hour is come: but as soon as she is delivered of the child, she remembereth no more the anguish, for joy that a man is born into the world. And ye now therefore have sorrow; but I will see you again, and your heart shall rejoice, and your joy no man taketh from you. (John 16:19–22)

Travail and joy are intricately linked. Barbara B. Smith, a former general Relief Society president, shared the following:

One thing is very clear in a study of joy in the scriptures. It is known to us only as we have practical knowledge of the dark and the light of human experience. . . . The significance of observing the light of joy is intensified by the darkness of sorrow through which a woman plods her way—or, as in the case of childbirth, the peaceful spirit that flows through her following the extreme exertion of childbirth—is that it brings the realization that joy is not easily won. Joy is not a momentary pleasure. The moments of joy have long-lasting, sustaining power in human lives.[1]

Our mortal experience is guaranteed to include travail, and pregnancy and birth are no exceptions. When God cast Adam and Eve out of the garden, He gave them two different stewardships but explained to them that both would require the same sort of work and effort. Just as Adam would have to labor to raise food from the ground, Eve would also have to labor to bring children into the world. It is beautiful symbolism that the fruit of both Adam's and Eve's travail is continuing life. God was teaching them, in a very powerful and unforgettable way, their first eternal lesson. He was teaching them that bringing forth life, in any form, involves effort but that this work can be filled with joy.

If we allow it, travail can help us develop our souls into the women and men God would have us be. In Ether 12:27, God said, "I give unto men weakness that they may be humble . . . for if they humble themselves before me, and have faith in me, then will I make weak things become strong unto them." Travail is a catalyst in which new life and new growth are created. To change something from one form into another requires a great amount of effort. For example, a chick must push and crack its egg to get out, and even the best ore must undergo extremely high temperatures before it becomes pure silver. It is through travail that our souls are stretched and pulled until at last—if we choose to allow it—we become reborn as stronger, more patient, understanding, and mature souls.

The scriptural birth story of Phineas' wife teaches us important lessons about travail and how we can choose to react to it. In the Bible, we read that during a war with the Philistines, Eli's daughter-in-law received terrible news. She learned that the ark of the covenant had been captured and that her husband and father-in-law were dead. At the time, she was very near giving birth:

324

When she heard the tidings that the ark of God was taken, and that
her father in law and her husband were dead, she bowed herself and
travailed; for her pains came upon her. And about the time of her death
the women that stood by her said unto her, Fear not; for thou hast born a
son. But she answered not, neither did she regard it. And she named the
child Ichabod. . . . And she said, The glory is departed from Israel: for the
ark of God is taken. (1 Samuel 4:19–22)

Even though the women aiding her encouraged her to "fear not"
because she had a new reason to live, she refused to be comforted. She
even named her son Ichabod, which means "no glory," because she felt that
everything in her life had been lost. What this woman failed to foresee was
that the capture of the ark and the deaths of her husband and father-in-
law would usher in the most glorious era of the Israelite nation, the years
of Samuel, David, and Solomon. Instead of looking with hope toward the
future, Phineas' wife allowed herself to become completely overwhelmed by
her present physical, emotional, and spiritual suffering and refused to live.

Compare Phineas' wife to Mary Fielding Smith, the wife of Hyrum
Smith, who was nine months pregnant when her husband and his brother,
the Prophet Joseph Smith, were taken violently from their homes and
imprisoned in Liberty Jail. Soon after her husband's imprisonment, Mary
gave birth to her son, Joseph F. Smith (who would later become a prophet
of the Church). After his birth, she became ill and for four months lingered
between life and death. She was unable to take care of her new son or
herself and was at the mercy of her friends and family.

During this time, the Saints were driven out of Missouri, and Mary
had to make the long trek to Illinois lying delirious in the back of a wagon.
She did not see her husband again until her son was nearly six months
old. Despite all this, she later wrote the following to her brother, who was
serving a mission in England:

O, my dear brother, I must tell you, for your comfort, that my hope is
full, and it is a glorious hope; and though I have been left for near six
months in widowhood, in the time of great affliction . . . if it had not
been for this hope, I should have sunk before this; but, blessed be the
God and rock of my salvation, here I am, and am perfectly satisfied and

happy, having not the smallest desire to go one step backward. The more I see of the dealing of our Heavenly Father with us as a people, the more I am constrained to rejoice that I was ever made acquainted with the everlasting covenant. O may the Lord keep my faith.[2]

It is beautiful that God teaches women lessons about travail and joy when they are young and bearing children. I can't think of a better way for God to illustrate the eternal principle that "after the trial of your faith" cometh the blessings (Ether 12:6) than through the experience of childbirth. By experiencing travail at the start of her journey into motherhood, a woman will know her inner strength and how to rely on the Lord. For God promises that with travail He will bless us with joy, the joy that "no man taketh from you" (John 16:22).

I have often wondered how Jesus could understand childbirth since He is a man. I knew that He had suffered and borne all of our grief, but childbirth is unique, and I couldn't quite see how He could relate to it. I was pondering this as I was pregnant with our fifth child, and the tune to the hymn "Jesus of Nazareth, Savior and King" (Hymn 181) came into my mind. I looked it up to read the words. When I came to the second verse, I got my answer. "Bruised, broken, torn for us on Calvary's hill, Thy suffering borne for us lives with us still." I knew then that He had felt what I had experienced in childbirth when He suffered and died on the cross. I knew that He understood and could truly succor me in my time of need. It really strengthened my testimony of Jesus Christ and His Atonement and this new found knowledge was very comforting to me as I gave birth to three more children.

–Valerie Sheldon

---

1   Barbara B.Smith, *Joy* (Salt Lake City, UT: Deseret Book, 1980), 11–13.
2   Leon R. Hartshorn, *Remarkable Stories from the Lives of Later-day Saint Women* (Provo, UT: Spring Creek, 2006), 142–144.

Swimming Through Adversity

By Natalie N. Willes

A YEAR OR SO AGO, when I was living in New York, I was incredibly over-whelmed with life in the city. However, my real adversity came after I gave birth to my daughter, Olive. I had a lovely and uneventful pregnancy, fol-lowed by a truly empowering natural childbirth. I remember feeling like I could jump off the bed and chest bump the midwife and the nurse after having accomplished such an incredible task. That was my high point.

In the weeks following Olive's birth, I felt a despair and anxiety so deep it nearly rendered me unable to function. I experienced insomnia, dif-ficulty concentrating, hypervigilance, jumpiness, nightmares, and feelings of intense distress—pounding heart, rapid breathing, nausea, muscle ten-sion, sweating. These emotions were so sudden and crippling, and so end-less that I had no idea how to deal with them. They simply would not go away. For the first several months of Olive's life, I endured these symptoms.

I'm a proactive person who can normally solve almost any problem, but I was absolutely unable to solve this one. As the weeks turned into months I realized this experience was robbing me of any feelings of love towards my daughter. I would care for her and her well-being, but I longed for feelings of warmth and affection. I prayed endlessly for this trial to pass, and some-times it would improve for a short time, only to come back again with the force of what seemed like a thousand bricks against my heart. I realize now it's because I was fighting against the adversity.

I have a close friend, Lauri, who is a successful physical therapist. I once asked her to explain to me as simply as possible how one's body builds muscle and endurance. She said that almost anything in our body (i.e: a bone, muscle, or tendon) responds to the stresses that are placed on them. If we are training for an event, like running a marathon, we are placing certain stresses on our body. By repeated use of these same muscles, you build up the muscle fibers that you are using daily as a response to these stresses. The actual muscle cells get bigger, and more efficient, to be able to tolerate increased training.

Now here is what I thought was more interesting. Lauri further explained that, when we are training, there are slight tears that occur in the muscle, however our body normally lays down scar tissue to repair these microscopic tears. When scar tissue initially forms it is kind of in an x or crisscross pattern. With training or repeated use of the muscle wherein the scar tissue lies, you can change the pattern of the scar tissue to be more regulated in a parallel pattern.

With the parallel pattern, the scar tissue can actually provide increased strength and in some cases the scar tissue is stronger than the muscle itself in this unilateral direction. However, if left in the x pattern, the scar tissue doesn't have a lot of strength. Essentially the body doesn't know which way

I had prayed a lot in the previous months for the Lord to comfort me, but that day it occurred to me to ask the Lord what he wanted me to learn from this trial.

it needs to strengthen itself. This is not unlike the "muscle-building" we experience as we progress through the challenges of life.

When you want to build muscle, you exercise. When you want to harvest the fruits and vegetables of a flourishing garden, you have to plant the seeds and spend hours nurturing them. When you want to build your career, you devote your time to learning and training. When we choose to undergo adversity in such endeavors, most of us accept the difficulties as the inevitable price to pay in order to achieve our desires.

What about when you want to build up your faith, your character, your moral integrity, and your charity? These are traits that we can strive to build on our own, but they are usually developed more effectively through the help of the Lord. Like a divine physical therapist, Heavenly Father prescribes courses of short- and long-term spiritual therapy—often in the form of adversity—to develop, refine, and maintain our most necessary spiritual "muscles." Unfortunately, when we receive an unexpected trial from Heavenly Father in order to strengthen those character traits, often we waste time asking why, wallowing in self-pity, and wondering what we did to deserve our suffering.

The Church manual, "True to the Faith" describes some who experience adversity as having the following reaction:

> They ask questions like 'Why does this have to happen to me? Why do I have to suffer this now? What have I done to deserve this?' But these questions have the power to dominate their thoughts. Such questions can overtake their vision, absorb their energy, and deprive them of the experiences the Lord wants them to receive. Rather than responding in this way, you should . . . consider asking questions such as, 'What am I to do? What am I to learn from this experience? What am I to change? Whom am I to help? How can I remember my many blessings in times of trial?'[1]

This very change in attitude was the answer to my debilitating postpartum anxiety struggles. It wasn't until I was swimming laps and thinking about my four-month-old daughter that everything changed. Those laps were long, quiet and solitary. I had no choice but to be alone with my thoughts. I also had to concentrate to avoid running into the lane line. This combined concentration and quiet surrendering to my thoughts really helped me to meditate. I had prayed a lot in the previous months for the Lord to comfort me, but that day it occurred to me to ask the Lord what he wanted me to learn from this trial. So I did.

I remember shedding tears as the Spirit told me that was what Heavenly Father had wanted from me all along—to ask Him what He wanted me to learn—to stop fighting and to start learning. As we read in the Doctrine and Covenants:

> And if thou shouldst be cast into the pit, or into the hands of murderers, and the sentence of death passed upon thee; if thou be cast into the deep, if the billowing surge conspire against thee; if fierce winds become thine enemy; if the heavens gather blackness, and all the elements combine to hedge up the way; and above all, if the very jaws of hell shall gape open the mouth wide after thee, know thou, my son or daughter, that all these things shall give thee experience, and shall be for thy good. (D&C 122:7)

I had a change of heart that day, and from that day forward I have been able to look to each potential challenge as a learning experience the Lord wants me to have for a specific reason. I have learned that there is little, if anything, in this life that is worth anything, that does not require work. Whether we bring it upon ourselves, others bring it upon us, or Heavenly Father places it on our shoulders, it is all truly for our good and progression.

---

1 *True to the Faith* (Salt Lake City, UT: The Church of Jesus Christ of Latter-day Saints, 2004) 8-9.

VBAC MIRACLE

By Deanna M. Lamadrid-Jensen

I PREPARED FOR A NATURAL BIRTH with my first baby using Hypnobabies®. After my water broke, I started having back labor and was not making much progress. Once I reached 4 cm, and after laboring for twenty-four hours, my midwife discovered that my daughter was breech. Because my water had already broken, I had an emergency cesarean. I was devastated. Right before finding out she was breech, my husband had given me a priesthood blessing saying that I would be able to have the natural birth that we had planned and practiced for. We talked about this later and feel that the Lord was referring to a future birth. I knew right away that I would try for a vaginal birth after cesarean (VBAC) for my second birth.

The disappointment of my birth coupled with a colicky baby led to postpartum depression. As I shared my experience with other women and helped influence them to make their own decisions regarding their births, I started to feel some closure from my own experience. I realized that had I not experienced the heartache and depression that I did with my daughter's birth, I might not have had the passion or motivation or empathy to help empower other women to feel good about their births. This quote by Elder Joseph B. Wirthlin helped me understand that my pain was leading to something greater:

> The Lord compensates the faithful for every loss. That which is taken away from those who love the Lord will be added unto them in His own way. While it may not come at the time we desire, the faithful will know that every tear today will eventually be returned a hundredfold with tears of rejoicing and gratitude.[1]

I knew that the Lord loved me and that there were things I could only learn through the disappointment of my daughter's birth. I am learning to trust in His will and timing.

With my second pregnancy, I again practiced with Hypnobabies® and envisioned the natural birth I had wanted the first time around. I found the only OB in my city who supported VBACs and hired a doula. Though I wanted nothing more than to have a VBAC, I had faith in the Lord's will and knew that He knew what I needed better than I did.

A week after my due date, I started having contractions. They were intense enough that I couldn't sleep through them. I felt them in my back again which alerted me that again my baby was not in an optimal position to be born. The next day I had an ultrasound to check my amniotic fluid level since I was "overdue." It was down to four and a half. Five is considered "normal." My doctor was concerned and could have scheduled me for a C-section right then but told me to come back in two hours to admit me to the hospital. Two hours later I was still at 1 cm.

After trying pelvic rocks and other positions suggested by my doula to turn my baby anterior to no avail, my doctor broke my water and gave me Pitocin. Of course that increased my back labor. It had been over twenty-four hours, and I could no longer take the pain in my back and the fact that I was progressing so slowly. I welcomed the epidural. I was still able to move around with the help of my doula and husband to try to get my baby in a good position. After about forty hours of labor, I was at 6 cm. I knew that my chances of having a VBAC were getting slimmer as time went on. I was also coming close to the twenty-four hour "deadline" that most doctors give to laboring women after their water breaks. I tried to prepare myself mentally for having another C-section, but the thought of that made me cry. It didn't seem fair, after having labored all that time, to just have another C-section.

My doctor was supposed to come back to check on me, but she got caught up in a surgery. During the time she was in that surgery, my baby finally turned. The back labor finally stopped, and I dilated to 10 cm. I know it was no coincidence that she was in the surgery for so long. Had she come back any earlier, I think she would have tried to force me to have a C-section. Never before in my life had I felt such intense power from the prayers of my friends and family.

I was able to have a VBAC! Being able to push my son out of my own body was a wonderful feeling. And I don't mind that I needed an epidural to be able to do that. I did it! The midwife, who also attended my birth, later told me that she had never seen any of her patients as determined as I was to have a vaginal birth. She said she was impressed with my stamina and determination. All of this empowered me and gave me such a feeling of accomplishment.

A few days after the birth, I read this scripture and felt the Lord speak directly to my heart: "And it came to pass that after I had prayed and *labored* with all diligence, the Lord said unto me: I will grant unto thee according to thy desires, because of thy faith" (Enos 1:12, emphasis added). My righteous desire was to have a vaginal birth. I'm so grateful He saw fit to grant me that desire not only because of my faith, but b ecause of the faith of my family and friends too. Together we all witnessed a miracle.

---

1   Joseph B. Wirthlin, "Come What May, and Love It," Ensign, November 2008, http://lds.org/ensign/2008/11/come-what-may-and-love-it?lang=eng.

Antepartum Depression

By Lani Axman

"I'M ALWAYS HAPPIER and more emotionally stable while pregnant," I used to say. In my first three pregnancies that had been true. But my fourth pregnancy changed that. As I entered my second trimester, I found myself swept away on a dark emotional roller coaster like nothing I had ever seen.

It wasn't until much later that I was able to identify what I experienced. It was antepartum depression. Postpartum depression is discussed extensively in the medical community and media, but I hadn't read or thought much about *pregnancy* depression until I experienced it myself. While the incidence of antepartum depression has been estimated at 12% to 16% of women, there are probably more.[1] Many cases are not reported, in part because women experiencing antepartum depression often see their symptoms as "just pregnancy hormones" and don't reveal to their care providers or loved ones that they're struggling to cope. My own depressive symptoms only became apparent to me because I had three previous happy pregnancies to serve as a stark contrast.

Antepartum depression felt like hell—like my mind and body had been literally hijacked by demons. I was bombarded with waves of oppressive darkness and misery, but it didn't make any sense to me. I was attending church, reading my scriptures, exercising regularly, eating more healthy foods than I had ever eaten before, I had an amazing husband and three wonderful children, so why was I so ridiculously miserable? I wrote in my journal a lot during that difficult time. One of those therapeutic entries reads:

> And now I'm losing it—again. It seems it doesn't matter how many epiphanies I have, how many priesthood blessings, how many times God reassures me. The demons, anger, and overwhelming gloom just keep coming back. They just won't give me more than the most brief rest. I am beginning to wonder whether I'll ever be able to love being a mother again.

During this time, I became quite reclusive. I rarely left the house except to go to church or grocery shopping. I excused myself from all but the most necessary social gatherings or activities. I felt guilty and horrible that many moments my thoughts were resentful and rejecting toward my special baby. I'm ashamed to admit that I shook my fists at the heavens on many occasions, crying from the depths of my soul, "Why? Why did you send this baby to me now if it was going to make me so miserable?" In my darkest moments, when it seemed that my cries toward heaven were going unheard, I even found myself questioning the existence of God. The adversary knows how to capitalize on our times of weakness. Fortunately, I have a rock of a husband who remained steadfast, never faltering, lovingly reminding me over and over that God really was there and really was aware of me.

I did a lot of reading during that time. Books brought me both an escape from my circumstances and insights into my struggles. One day, a little voice in the back of my head kept whispering, "Remember Viktor Frankl's book? Go get it off your shelf." So I finally obliged that whispering voice. And that little voice knew what it was talking about, as usual. These powerful words brought me temporary peace:

> If there is a meaning in life at all, then there must be a meaning in suffering. Suffering is an ineradicable part of life, even as fate and death. Without suffering and death human life cannot be complete.
>
> The way in which a man accepts his fate and all the suffering it entails, the way in which he takes up his cross, gives him ample opportunity—even under the

most difficult circumstances—to add a deeper meaning to his life. . . . Here
lies the chance for a man either to make use of or to forgo the opportunities of
attaining the moral values that a difficult situation may afford him. And this
decides whether he worthy of his sufferings or not.[2]

Writing my feelings in blogposts and in emails to friends and family was
also a key support as I struggled. Many times the comments and emails I
received from my loved ones gave me extra strength to endure.

There have been many times in the past when I have heard that someone I care about is experiencing a time of difficulty and wanted desperately
to do something to help. Sometimes all I could do was say, "I'm praying for
you." But it always felt so inadequate. I don't feel that way anymore.

I now know that our prayers in behalf of our loved ones absolutely do
make a difference. Sometimes I didn't find out until afterward that a friend
had put my name on the temple prayer roll or fasted in my behalf. But those
loving acts, many happening from very far away, lifted me out of my darkest
moments when I felt incapable of climbing out on my own. Several times,
I received a brief respite from my trial, feeling myself for several hours,
with no explanation other than the knowledge that many were praying for
me. Though the devil and his servants had been pummeling me with more
fierceness than I had possibly ever experienced, they were no match for the
prayers of those who loved me.

I had been so terrified that I would never feel totally "myself" again and
that my emotional hardships would linger until my baby's birth and morph
into postpartum depression. However, as I entered my third trimester, the
overwhelming gloom slowly began to dissipate until it was completely gone.

Looking back, as awful as that dark period was, I am grateful to have
experienced it. The lessons I learned about myself, life, God, friendship,
prayer, and happiness were invaluable. I can testify that these words from
Elder Richard G. Scott are true: "Even if you exercise your strongest faith,
God will not always reward you immediately according to your desires.
Rather, God will respond with what in His eternal plan is best for you."[3] I
know that the Lord allowed me to experience my trial in all its fury because
He knew it would refine me and those around me. And I know that Satan
tried to use my depression to destroy me because he knows the good we
are all capable of.

My fourth baby is sleeping on my chest as I write this. No words could describe the intense light, joy, peace, and love that this baby has brought into my family's life. She has been one of the greatest gifts I have ever received. Her sweet spirit was more than worth every moment of suffering I endured. And I would do it all over again for her.

1   Brenda M.Y. Leung and Bonnie J. Kaplan, "Perinatal Depression: Prevalence, Risks, and the Nutrition Link—A Review of the Literature," *Journal of the American Dietetic Association* 109, no. 9 (September 2009): 1566-1575, http://www.adajournal.org/article/S0002-8223(09)00768-8/abstract.
2   Viktor E. Frankl, *Man's Search for Meaning* (New York: Washington Square Press, 1985), 88.

CHAPTER TEN

The Atonement

I can do all things through Christ
which strengtheneth me.

PHILIPPIANS 4:13

Birth in Remembrance of Him

By Robyn Allgood, AAHCC

This do in remembrance of me.

LUKE 22:19

I remember rocking back in forth in the shower, repeating to myself, "God is with me," as warm water rolled down my back. I was still waiting for my husband, Jeff, to get home, and my two-year-old was asleep in her room. The contractions had become strong enough that I had abandoned the task of packing my hospital bag. I needed the reminder that I was not truly alone. I had my Heavenly Father to guide me. After Jeff arrived at home, I put him to work bringing me water and calling family. Things were progressing fast. I remember him asking me, "Robyn, can we get to the hospital now?" By then I was rocking on my hands and knees. I had retreated inward, concentrating as much as possible through the powerful contractions that my uterus was moving through my body. I was shaking and sweating even though it was a cold and snowy day outside.

I answered, "No." That was all I could say. Even with these signs of transitional labor, we were still surprised that my baby's head was already appearing. Jeff led me back to the bathroom. Oh, how it hurt. I felt as if I was being split in two. My mind turned to the Savior, who took upon Himself indescribable pain. I was sure that what I was experiencing could never rival what the Savior experienced for me, and I was humbled.

I asked Jeff whether his hands were there to catch the baby, because the baby was coming. Jeff had dialed 911 and barely had time to tell them what was going on before he had to put the phone down to put his hands in place. He told me his hands were ready, and it was then that I pushed for release. His hands were sure and steady. I will never forget the moment I first saw our baby, Kyle, as my dear eternal companion placed him in my arms. It felt as though heaven had opened and handed me one of its greatest treasures. There was no distracting me from the moment. Jeff had gone searching to find a clean towel to cover Kyle, and I was just taking it all in, alone but not alone with my son. I felt the power of God in that tiny room. I felt the vitality and strength of this little boy in my arms. I felt wonderful, divine, heavenly. My love hormones were soaring and everything felt right to me. Kyle's birth truly was a gift from God. It also allowed healing, because this birth was a vaginal birth after a cesarean birth. I felt at one with the universe, with heaven, with God, and with my miraculous feminine body. I felt the Savior's love and nearness.

Just as Kyle's birth was a gift of healing to me, the Atonement of Jesus Christ is the all-encompassing and infinite gift of healing to all mankind. In Moses 6:63, the Lord said that "all things bear record of me." As I have reflected on the births of each of my children, I have felt these experiences bear record of the Savior and His Atonement.

THE SACRAMENT

The sacrament is a sacred ordinance instituted by our Lord and Savior to bring to our remembrance His Atonement. In a more general sense, the word *sacrament* has also been defined as something regarded as possessing sacred character or mysterious significance.[1] As I reviewed this definition, I thought of childbirth. Many parents describe a child's birth to be one of the most significant events in their lives. As a mother of five children, I would agree. Childbirth is an event that is of sacred character and mysterious significance to me. Therefore, I would like to explain why I see childbirth as a sacrament of the Atonement.

Luke 22:19 describes the Savior offering the bread as His body: "And he took bread and gave thanks, and brake it, and gave them saying, This is my body which is given for you: this do in remembrance of me." Likewise, a woman in pregnancy offers her body for the sake of another. She may experience a variety of physical discomforts in order to give life to another. In any pregnancy, there is a certain level of sacrifice involved that in turn blesses the mother and her family. The bread Christ offered was broken as a token of His body being broken. Many women have likened the baby pushing through the birth canal as the rending open of her body. For nine months, a woman's body is expanded. Her hips widen and are given more flexibility from the hormone relaxin, which is released in increased amounts as she nears the birth of her baby.[2] Such a passage through the pelvis is a powerful experience, breaking a mother from maidenhood and initiating her into motherhood. She "breaks" away from her previous role into a new role. In a cesarean birth, this breaking also takes place as the layers of skin and muscle are cut and torn to make way for birth.

After breaking bread, Christ offered wine as a symbol of His blood, explaining that "this cup is the new testament of my blood which is shed for you" (Luke 22:20). During pregnancy, a healthy woman's blood volume increases by about 50 percent so that at birth she is prepared for the shedding of blood that is required.[3] Christ shed His blood for our sins, and a mother sheds blood in giving a physical body to her child.

In place of wine, water has been appointed to represent His blood. Not only is a woman's blood given, but water from the amniotic sac is spilled. Often, when left alone, the bag of water will remain intact until the transition of labor, which signals the breaking or change from first stage labor to second stage or pushing. The water in the amniotic sac keeps and strengthens the unborn baby. It prevents infection and bacteria from entering the uterus, acting as a protective barrier for the baby.[4] The water we partake in the sacrament is to remind us of the preserving power that the shedding of Christ's blood can be for us. If we repent and forgive, the blood of the Atonement will preserve us for our "birth" into a celestial being.

BAPTISM

As we partake of the sacrament, we are renewing our covenants of baptism. In Moses 6:59, we read:

> Inasmuch as *ye were born into the world by water, and blood, and the spirit,* which I have made, and so became of dust a living soul, even so ye must be born again into the kingdom of heaven, of water, and of the Spirit, and be cleansed by blood, even the blood of my Only Begotten. (emphasis added)

This scripture points out that birth and baptism are very closely related. There are two times in which we chose baptism: first, in the premortal existence through our birth into mortality, and second, when we partake in the ordinance of baptism by immersion and proper priesthood authority. Those who kept their first estate or premortal life (see Abraham 3:26) are those who chose Heavenly Father's plan of salvation as presented by His Son Jesus Christ, to come into this world by water, blood, and the spirit (see 1 John 5:6-8). Likewise, to keep our second estate of mortality (see Abraham 3:26), it is required that we be born again through choosing the ordinance of baptism (see John 3:3–8). Baptism is a symbol of new birth. Birth and baptism bring about new life, purity, innocence, and virtue. *Baptism* is also a word that is associated with being an induction or admittance to something.[5] Childbirth is an induction into motherhood, an event that marks a significant change in the mother, child, and family, just as baptism marks a significant change in a person's life. A past life is left behind to begin a new one.

THE ATONEMENT

After instituting the sacrament, Christ, "came out, and went, as he was wont, to the mount of Olives; and his disciples also followed him" (Luke 22:39). The phrase "as he was wont" means that He was accustomed to coming to this location. It was a place He went to often. The Savior wanted to be in a place He found familiar and where He could be secluded as He passed through the Atonement. Familiarity is something that can be very comforting to a laboring mother. An unfamiliar or uncomfortable environment can inhibit her ability to relax and can hinder the progression of her labor.[6]

It can be helpful for the mother prior to birth to tour the place she will give birth and visualize herself there. She could ask herself: How comfortable will I be here? What can I do to make it more familiar to me? Some women wear their own clothes, bring a favorite blanket or pillow, and even bring music or scents that are familiar to them to ease the transition of moving from home to hospital or birth center. Some women find it helpful to spend the majority of their labor at home or even birth at home. If seclusion and privacy are not available, a woman's labor can stop or become ineffective. Regardless of where a mother labors, it should feel safe to her. The Savior sought familiarity, privacy, and seclusion for the work He was about to do. Women find themselves doing the same as they labor.

In Mark 14:33, the Savior is described as becoming "very heavy." This condition of His mind and body were the result of the "exceeding sorrow" (Mark 14:34) He was experiencing. For a woman, this heaviness is most likely felt physically. Her body is expected to increase in weight to accommodate the growing baby. By the time she has reached full-term, her body feels the heaviness of the life created within her. Her back and other limbs may ache from carrying the extra weight on her frame. As her baby moves lower in the pelvis, the mother feels a new kind of heaviness that prepares her for birthing her baby. There is also a mental and emotional heaviness that may manifest itself at this time, giving the woman an increased desire to move on to the next stage: birth.

When Christ became heavy and sorrowful, He "was withdrawn from them [His Apostles] about a stone's cast, and kneeled down and prayed" (Luke 22:42). As labor progresses, a woman often withdraws, seeking privacy for this sacred event. A woman left alone to seek comfort as her body guides her will progress through labor much faster and easier.[7] It is also not unusual for a woman laboring naturally to fall to her hands and knees, signifying submission or surrender to the work that her body is doing. This position is quite favorable for labor and even birth. It reminds the baby to position itself anterior (facing the mother's back) so that the passage of the baby through the pelvis is much easier. It also relieves pressure on a woman's back and tailbone. Many women find comfort in calling upon God during their birth experiences, as the Savior did during His suffering. This call may be in the form of praying, repeating birth affirmations, or even singing a song.

THE LOVE OF GOD

We are told in Mark 14:32 that the Savior began to be "sore amazed." To be sore amazed means to be astonished or awestruck. What could cause the Savior to be astonished? It is likely that the reality of what He was bearing came upon Him and He felt the weight of it. He was taking upon Himself sins, sickness, infirmity, and all other dejection of humankind. The Savior, being holy and pure, had never experienced such anguish, and it astonished Him. For a woman experiencing labor and birth, the sensations she is having are new to her and can be startling. What is it about the Savior that carried Him through this difficult time? It would have to be His perfect and unconditional love for all mankind: "Greater love hath no man than this, that a man lay down his life for his friends" (John 15:13). President Joseph F. Smith said, "The love of a true mother comes nearer [to] being like the love of God than any other kind of love."[8] In any challenging or difficult circumstance, we can fill our hearts with love and find added strength in our own efforts. The power of love can provide the ability for a mother to endure as she gives life to another.

SUBMITTING OUR WILL

We read in Luke that Christ's words upon falling to His knees were, "Father, if thou be willing, remove this cup from me; nevertheless not my will, but thine, be done" (Luke 22:42). This suffering caused even the Savior to ask that it be taken away. A mother likewise may ask that this "cup" be removed. However, we know that the Savior knew it was His burden to bear and was ever willing to do His Father's will.

There are many different ways in which a mother offers her will to the Father when she enters pregnancy and childbirth. She is willing to let her body change. She may be sick or have to sacrifice a career. She can be ever patient, waiting upon the Lord's timetable instead of her own as she awaits the baby's birth. The scriptures remind us that a baby will come "at the time appointed . . . according to the time of life" (Genesis 18:14). There are also times when doing His will means abandoning the birth plan for what is medically indicated for the health of mother and baby.

The hymn "Jesus Once of Humble Birth" describes Christ's Atonement, stating "once He groaned in grief and pain."[9] It is not known for sure, but the Savior may have groaned as His body labored through the work of the Atonement. Some women find it helpful to moan or vocalize through contractions. It can be a way to release tension and to more fully relax.[10] Relaxation allows the body to avoid the fear-tension-pain cycle that can impede labor and childbirth. The more a mother can release and relax, the less pain she will experience. It is another way in which the mother can surrender as the Savior did, saying, "not my will but thine, be done" (Luke 22:42).

In the scriptures, blood is associated with life, humanity, and mortality, among other things.[11] In Luke, we read that "his sweat was as it were great drops of blood falling to the ground" (Luke 22:44). The blood that was squeezed from Christ for us has the power to give us eternal life, while the blood that a woman sheds for her baby gives physical life. The work of labor often causes a woman to sweat as she exerts pressure to push her baby out. As the baby moves through the birth canal, mucous and other fluids are squeezed from the baby's nose, throat, and other orifices. This squeezing or massaging of the baby prepares the baby to live outside of the womb.[12] In this way, the labor that a woman experiences is benefiting her baby, just as the labor the Savior endured for each one of us is for our benefit.

ANGELS

Certainly the phrase, "And there appeared an angel unto him from heaven, strengthening him" (Luke 22:43) is comforting. The Savior was strengthened by an angel in His moment of need. A woman also has access to this support when she births her baby. Elder Jeffrey R. Holland reminded us of the following:

> Usually such beings are *not* seen. Sometimes they are. But seen or unseen they are *always* near. Sometimes their assignments are very grand and have significance for the whole world. Sometimes the messages are more private. Occasionally the angelic purpose is to warn. But most often it is to comfort, to provide some form of merciful attention, guidance in difficult times. . . . I testify that angels are *still* sent to help us.[13]

I am sure I am not the only one to have felt the presence of unseen angels as I have given birth. The Lord has promised us: "I will go before your face. I will be on your right hand and on your left . . . my Spirit shall be in your [heart], and mine angels round about you, to bear you up" (Doctrine & Covenants 84:88). My first son, Kyle, whose birth I recounted, died when he was only two years old. I know that Kyle was able to see me through the birth of his brother, David. I like to think of Kyle sending his brother to us with his own "merciful attention." I know that others who have gone before me have been there to cheer me on, rejoicing in the growth of their posterity. Earthly angels can come in the form of a loving and supportive husband, the experienced hands of a doula, a mother, a sister, a friend, a midwife, a nurse, or other caregiver.

PRAYER

The Savior leaned upon prayer as He passed through this difficult time: "And being in an agony He prayed more earnestly" (Luke 22:44). Again, the Savior bent His will to the Father. In His agony, He prayed even more earnestly. Prayer can be a great comfort to a mother during her pregnancy and birth. A prayer can be offered by her or others in her behalf. She can also access the power of the priesthood through a blessing. The power of heaven stands ready to render aid to a life-giving mother.

CRUCIFIXION AND DEATH

Jesus endured physical brutality as the Atonement continued. It is written that Jesus was scourged (see Matthew 27:26), which means He was whipped with a lash that likely left the stripes referenced in Isaiah 53:5 with the promise "with his stripes we are healed." Many women have "stripes" or stretch marks as a reminder of the stretching her body experienced while being with child. Dr. Robert Bradley said they "should be worn as 'service stripes' of motherhood."[14] Christ's stripes are a physical reminder of His sacrifice for us, and a woman's stripes can be a reminder of the sacrifice she made for her child. Her body has changed. It bears the signs of service given in behalf of another.

347

Death was a necessary part of the Atonement. A perfect sacrifice had to be voluntarily offered for our sake: "And when Jesus had cried with a loud voice, he said, Father, into thy hands I commend my spirit: and having said thus, he gave up the ghost" (Luke 23:46). Initially, we may not like to think of birth and death in the same sentence, but the two are necessary and similar elements of the plan of salvation. Both involve passing through a veil. At birth, the woman's body toils and labors to bring forth life through the veil. At death, the body toils and labors to bring forth another kind of life through another veil. Both beings leave behind what is familiar to them. They leave behind loved ones. However, as they embark into another world, their arrival is celebrated. On one side of the veil it is a farewell, and on the other a joyous homecoming. Some of the most holy births are those in which a little one is called home after a short time on this earth.

RESURRECTION

The Atonement was not complete until after Christ voluntarily suffered and then demonstrated His power over the grave by rising from the dead. As the women approached His tomb, they said to each other:

> Who shall roll us away the stone from the door of the sepulchre? And when they looked, they saw that the stone was rolled away: for it was very great. And entering into the sepulchre they saw a young man . . . and he saith unto them, Be not affrighted: Ye seek Jesus of Nazareth, which was crucified: he is risen; he is not here; behold the place where they laid him. (Mark 16:3–6; emphasis added)

The empty tomb symbolizes the power of Christ and new life through the Atonement. It symbolizes joy and wonder and even possesses mysterious significance. In like manner, the mother's empty womb symbolizes the power of creation made possible through Heavenly Father. It is a sacred event, as are the Atonement and resurrection of the Lord and Savior, Jesus Christ. The empty womb symbolizes physical life offered to a spiritual being, offering joy, wonder, and mysterious significance—mysterious because it is easy to ask, "How is this done?" The only answer can be through God, through His infinite wisdom and power.

TEMPTATION

Let us not forget the Savior's pleading to His disciples: "Pray that ye enter not into temptation" (Luke 22:39). However, the scriptures say that "he found them sleeping for sorrow" (Luke 22:45). Is it possible that He wanted them to pay attention and understand the importance of what He was experiencing? Was He asking that His disciples not take these things lightly? I feel that just as we are not to take the Atonement lightly, we are also not to take the birth of a child lightly. Understanding birth's beauty requires study and preparation, both spiritual and temporal. The time and effort we give to it is important to the Lord and does not go unnoticed by Him.

A MESSAGE OF GLADNESS

While pregnancy and childbirth can be trying, as John 16:21 points out, "A woman when she is in travail hath sorrow . . . but as soon as she is delivered of the child, she remembereth no more the anguish, for joy that a man is born into the world." The pain and grief is swallowed up in the joy that childbirth is. Christ does want us to know what He endured for us, but He wants us to dwell on the joy and power of His Atonement. How would Christ want us to think of childbirth? Would He also want us to remember the sacrifice but dwell on the joy and power of the experience of bringing His brothers and sisters into the world?

UNITY

The word *atonement* in a more general sense is said to signify being at one, in harmony, or united.[15] Through pregnancy and childbirth, a woman can seek out unity with her Heavenly Father. She can leave behind selfishness and fear, replacing them with charity and faith. As a woman takes mother-hood upon herself through pregnancy and birth, she can become at one in her purpose with God's plan for her.

President David O. McKay described motherhood as making a woman a "co-partner with the Creator in bestowing upon eternal spirits mortal life."[16] The more in harmony she is with her Heavenly Father, the more unity she experiences in doing His will. Motherhood is a divine calling: "Motherhood is near to divinity. It is the highest, holiest service to be assumed by mankind. It places her who honors its holy calling and service next to the angels."[17]

THE ONE

At the heart of the word *atonement* is the word *one*. The Atonement can be personalized for each *one* of us. President Boyd K. Packer reminded us that "while the Atonement of Christ applies to humanity in general, the influence of it is individual, very personal, and very useful."[18] Just as each Nephite went "one by one" (3 Nephi 11:15) to feel the prints in Christ's hands and feet, we can connect with the Atonement one by one. The power of the Atonement can be accessed to provide comfort and to "succor his people according to their infirmities" (Alma 7:12). Christ can do that for a laboring mother because He took upon Himself our pains (see Alma 7:11). While what the mother is experiencing may still be present, the load is lighter with the help of the Savior's Atonement. Each woman, during each pregnancy and birth can access the power of the Atonement in her own unique ways.

It is my testimony that childbearing is a privilege and honor that can render our hearts more capable, more loving, more faithful, and more like the Savior. It can bring us to a greater understanding of the Atonement as we lean more readily upon its power. We can draw nearer to Christ and our Heavenly Father through the divine gift of giving life.

1   See *Oxford English Dictionary*, 2nd ed., s.v. "sacrament."
2   Richard Ivell, "Endocrinology: This Hormone Has Been Relaxin' Too Long!," *Science* 295, no. 5555 (2002): 637–638, http://www.sciencemag.org/content/295/5555/637.summary.
3   F. Hytten, "Blood Volume Changes in Normal Pregnancy," *Clinics in Haematology* 14, no. 3 (1985): 601–612, http://www.ncbi.nlm.nih.gov/pubmed/4075604.
4   Marsden Wagner, *Creating Your Birth Plan* (New York: Berkeley, 2006), 91.
5   Dictionary.com, s.v. "baptism," http://dictionary.reference.com/browse/baptism.
6   Barbara Harper, *Gentle Birth Choices* (Rochester, NY: Healing Arts, 1994), 15.
7   Ibid., 16–17.
8   The Church of Jesus Christ of Latter-day Saints, *Teachings of the Presidents of the Church: Joseph F. Smith* (Salt Lake City, UT: The Church of Jesus Christ of Latter-day Saints, 1998), 36.
9   Parley P. Pratt, "Jesus Once of Humble Birth," in *Hymns of the Church of Jesus Christ of Latter-day Saints* (Salt Lake City, UT: Deseret Book, 1985), no. 196.
10 Barbara Harper, *Gentle Birth Choices* (Rochester, NY: Healing Arts, 1994), 208–210.
11 Alonzo L. Gaskill, *Lost Language of Symbolism* (Salt Lake City, UT: Deseret Book, 2003), 29.
12 Ashwin Ramachandrappa and Lucky Jain, "Elective Cesarean Section: It's Impact on Neonatal Respiratory Outcome," *Clinics in Perinatology* 35, no. 2 (2008): 373–vii, http://www.ncbi.nlm.nih.gov/pmc/articles/PMC2453515/?tool=pmcentrez.
13 Jeffrey R. Holland, "The Ministry of Angels," *Ensign*, November 2008, http://lds.org/ensign/2008/11/the-ministry-of-angels.
14 Robert A. Bradley, *Husband-Coached Childbirth* (New York, Bantam: 1996), 149.
15 Oxford English Dictionary, 2nd ed., s.v. "atonement."
16 The Church of Jesus Christ of Latter-day Saints, *Teachings of the Presidents of the Church: David O. McKay* (Salt Lake City, UT: The Church of Jesus Christ of Latter-day Saints, 2003), 156–157.
17 David O. McKay, quoted in James R. Clark, comp., *Messages of the First Presidency*, 6 vols. (Salt Lake City, UT: Bookcraft, 1965–1975), 6:178.
18 Boyd K. Packer, "Washed Clean," *Ensign*, May 1997, http://lds.org/ensign/1997/05/washed-clean

My Angel in Gethsemane

By Carol Vezzani

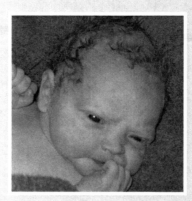

AFTER ENDURING THIRTY HOURS OF LABOR, I had dilated to 8 cm. Though I had an anterior lip of cervix that was still impeding the baby's head, I was still very excited at the great progress I was making. After checking me each time, my midwife would tell me the progression from the last time. Even if it was only that it felt softer than before, she never once told me there had been no progress. However, the next twelve hours were, I think, the longest of my life.

As wonderful as the midwives were, I was getting exhausted. My entire thought process during contractions by this point was reduced to "How can I lessen this pain so I can stand it? I can't stand it!" I prayed, I pleaded, and I begged. "Please! Please. Take this pain away. Take it away! Take it away!" I would cry through my contractions.

Finally, after hours of pleading, I began to realize that perhaps this pain wasn't going to go away. I stopped pleading for it to be taken away and started praying for strength to be equal to what God was asking of me. It was at this point, after more than a full day and a half of labor, that the most beautiful and sacred emotional experiences of my birth experience began.

As this mind shift came, and I gave myself up to whatever the Lord had in store for me, no matter what it was, I saw in it the Savior's pleading in the garden, "Father, if Thou be willing, remove this cup from me; nevertheless, not my will, but Thine be done" (Luke 22:42). I wonder how long He actually begged "remove this cup" before He said, "nevertheless." It took me hours to get to my "nevertheless" moment.

After that, the contractions were still just as utterly excruciating and exhausting, but, even in my utter fatigue, I had an increased measure of peace. I was carried along without feeling any need to control—at least beyond the innate and inexorable physical urge to create the position of least discomfort during contractions. My emotional struggles were gone. I was confident that the fatigue would not kill me, and beyond that, I could make it through anything else.

I think the most profound parallel to the Atonement that impressed itself upon me was not just suffering, but suffering for the sake of another. When I finally said, "I will drink this bitter cup. I recognize that it cannot pass from me, and I will drink it to the dregs," imbedded in that commitment was the realization that the purpose of this suffering had nothing to do with me. I knew that there was no benefit (beyond insight) that I could possibly derive from this experience. It would not make me healthier, it would not give me any skills, it would not lastingly affect my body in any positive way. But there was one entirely other person that would derive lasting and eternal benefit from my suffering: my child, my spiritual brother who was anxiously waiting to receive a body and come into this world. *Someone* had to do this so that he could receive a body, and he could not do it for himself.

Recognizing this gave me renewed focus between my contractions. I did not want the pain. I would run away from it if I could, but if that pain was there, waiting for someone to suffer it so that this child could receive a body, then I would voluntarily take it upon myself. I volunteered with every wave that wracked my body. I volunteered again and again, reminding myself, as I whispered to the life in my womb, "For you. For you. It's not about me. I will do this for you."

As I prayed and cried and swayed and squatted, my beautiful angel of a midwife was by my side every moment I wanted her. Countless times I leaned against her shoulder, and she would softly whisper, as she stroked my head, "It will take as long as it will take. It just takes as long as it's gonna take." As I say it now, it seems unhelpful, but at the time it soothed everything. I believe she was inspired in her comforting of me. That one simple phrase spoke volumes of, "I am here with you. I have seen this before. This has happened before. It will happen now. This is all the process. And this process will end. I promise that this process will end. And I will be with you all the way."

I cannot remember it now without recalling Christ suffering in the Garden of Gethsemane. Christ was left alone, but an angel was sent to comfort Him. It never made sense to me before what use an angel would be to the suffering Christ. This angel could not take the pain away. That would not be possible. Then why was the angel there? The presence of the angel was a very real reminder and comfort that although He was alone in the suffering, He was not alone in the process. I don't really know how He felt, or what

---

I stopped pleading for it to be taken away and started praying for strength to be equal to what God was asking of me.

He thought, but I do now understand, to some degree, how an angel in times of suffering can be a succor. My angel was my midwife. She was an anchor that reminded me of the larger picture that included my suffering, a reminder that this moment was not the whole picture.

The evening wore on, approaching midnight. There was still just a stubborn lip of cervix impeding the baby's progress. The midwife would check every couple of hours and tell me that it was a little softer, or a little thinner. Yet, hour after hour, endlessly, it was still there.

At this point, I was completely shut off from all sense and reason by each contraction, letting my body do whatever it wanted to ameliorate the pain to the greatest degree possible (which was usually rocking while on my knees, but sometimes standing and squatting vigorously up and down to distract myself). Slowly, I began to feel like I needed to use the bathroom—a bowel movement. I went a couple of times to the bathroom to sit and wait to feel it descend to the point that I could push it out, but it never did. (I didn't realize until later that it was the baby.)

One of the midwives had brought with her a birthing stool. It was low and horse-shoe shaped, about eight or twelve inches off the ground. It would provide support if you sat on it in a deep squat. We decided to try it, and this third midwife (who was the oldest and most experienced of the three) sat on the edge of the bed, and I sat in front of her on the stool. I was able to lean back against her for support and was cradled between her knees. I'm not sure where my husband was at this point, but I heard later that they had sent him to the other room to get some rest.

As the first contraction hit while I was on the stool, all of the blindingly unbearable pain of sitting during the contraction overwhelmed me, and I stood up to run away. The midwife behind me literally grabbed me and forced me back down on to the stool. She whispered to me, "Let the pressure go all the way down." Hearing through my pain-blurred senses, all I could assume was that this was an instruction of how to make the hurting stop without standing up. I focused all the energy I could muster into imagining the entire force of the contraction concentrated at the top of my womb and slowly falling down, off, out the bottom.

I imagined this over and over, blocking everything else out—the pain, my surroundings, the people in the room—until the contraction had passed. I dealt with contraction after contraction like this, squeezing the midwife's hands and pushing back into her, grasping at this visualization as my only hope of staying put during each wave of pain. I know at some point my husband came back in the room.

Finally, as I caught my breath between contractions, I stopped to ask my midwife, who was on her knees down between my feet, "Should I be pushing now?" She laughed as she looked up at me and smiled, "Honey, that's what you've been doing." I was dumbstruck. I had no idea. In fact, the last I knew there was still a lip of cervix that wouldn't let the baby's head come through. Apparently, the position my body was brought into by the birthing stool was exactly what I needed to open up the right way. As I focused on the baby coming, coming, closer and closer, I noticed the pain less. My midwife knelt in front of me massaging my perineum with oil while another midwife held a flashlight in the darkened room.

Progress in pushing was slow but came steadily. No one remembers what time I started pushing (I don't even remember starting to push), but at about 1:30 am, nearly two full days after the onset of labor, I pushed that little head all the way out. He just kept coming without my help and slipped right out into my midwife's hands. They wrapped him in a clean towel and laid him on my bare belly. I didn't notice the afterbirth because the pain in my back stopped as soon as he came out, and by comparison everything else was negligible.

They let me snuggle my son as long as I wanted. All I can remember as I continued leaning back against the midwife with my husband close by, taking pictures, was whispering over and over to my son, "I'm not having a contraction. I'm not going to have another contraction," with near delirious pleasure. It was the best news I could think of to share with him at the time. A few days later, our son had a name—Rhys Morgan.

From Darkness to Light

By Lara E.

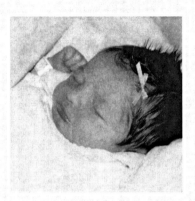

FOLLOWING MY PARENTS' DIVORCE when I was thirteen, I helped raise my five younger siblings. I knew from this experience that caring for children is very difficult. I had not liked the person I was when I tried to do this as an inexperienced teen. I had decided that it would be okay if I never had children. So it was not tears of joy I shed as I told my husband that we were going to be parents.

Only a few weeks later, as I started spotting and cramping, I had an internal struggle. Part of me was hoping that I would miscarry, and then I wouldn't have to be a mother. At the same time, the maternal instinct within me was holding on and terrified that this baby would not survive. It was an emotional two weeks while I rested, all the while wrestling with my emotions. I began seeing a counselor in an effort to quell them. With the help of the counselor, and lots of personal reflection, I finally realized that maybe this was God's way of letting me choose. Though I was not excited about being pregnant when I first found out, having that pregnancy threatened was causing me to consider what I really wanted. I ultimately decided that I did want this baby.

Now that I had accepted the fact that I was pregnant and had chosen to be a mother, I actually got a little excited about having a baby. I made blankets and clothes, smiling as I imagined my baby being wrapped in them. However, memories of my experiences as a teenager still haunted me.

In the last few weeks of my pregnancy, I became physically uncomfortable enough that I was ready for my baby to be born. I got my wish as he was born a few days early. I was in awe as I held this tiny child in my arms. I watched him as my husband held him, as he saw the world for the first time. I definitely had different feelings toward my own son than I had towards my siblings.

Once home, I found being a mother to a newborn to be overwhelming. In addition to the dramatic changes to my lifestyle, my son and I were struggling with breast-feeding. He could not latch on properly, and I experienced increasing pain as I tried to feed him. With bleeding nipples and in excruciating pain, I sobbed each time my child cried from hunger. After watching him lose weight and listening to his hungry cries, I gave up breast-feeding. I felt like a failure; I could not feed my child in the natural way that God had intended. Just like giving birth, women had been breast-feeding for centuries. Why couldn't I?

All of this sent me spiraling into despair. I was able to continue caring for my son's minimum needs, but I did not have energy to do much else. During the day, I sat in my home with the shades closed, feeding the baby and changing his diapers when needed, but I had little interest in doing anything else. Whenever someone would come to my house, I would hand them the baby to hold and go do something else.

Despite the darkness, there were moments when I felt intense love towards my son, an indescribable feeling that I had never felt before becoming a mother. I enjoyed making his blessing outfit and felt joy at his first smile. Those merciful moments helped to keep me going. I also continued to see my counselor who helped me tremendously. I returned to work which allowed me to escape from the demands of motherhood for a few hours every day, and I was able to pretend that everything was OK. It wasn't until much later that I even recognized that I was experiencing depression.

Although I was able to function, and even experience additional moments of joy occasionally, I continued to struggle with this depression for several years, riding a roller coaster of highs and lows as a second child was born and then a third, struggling to adjust after each birth. Through the continued help of my counselor, and several different prescription medications, I had periods of feeling good and coming out of the fog in which I was living.

Although I was receiving help from my counselor, I did not seek help from family or the other people in my life. I put on a good face and convinced many people that I was doing better than I really was. When my husband returned home each evening, he picked up the slack with cleaning and some of the cooking when I could not, but even he did not always know how bad it had been during the day.

It was during one of my low points that I realized just how much my depression had potentially damaged my marriage and my relationships with my children. I also realized that I had never actually prayed for help with my depression. I had been reading books and seeing doctors and my counselor and trying to heal myself. God had extended a myriad of tender mercies to me through my ordeal by sending my mother or mother-in-law

---

I began to feel the darkness receding as my life filled with light and the Atonement began working in my life.

---

to me unannounced when I really needed them. He also blessed me with several family members who babysat my children, when needed, or helped in other ways. He had also been the one to guide me to the counselor who had been so helpful. He had done all of these things without my asking.

I felt a symbolic light go on as I realized that I had never requested the help I really needed. I had also not allowed the Atonement to work in my life. The Atonement is not just for repentance of sin. Jesus Christ can heal all types of wounds and pain. What an epiphany that was. I couldn't believe that I had been relying on myself and other mortals to try to cure this ailment for so many years, without even considering the one Being who could actually do something about it. I immediately knelt down and prayed specifically for help with my depression. I then got up and went to work.

Just as I had invited Jesus Christ, the Light of the World, into my life, I also began letting in literal light. I forced myself to go outdoors into the sunshine and spent time sitting in front of a light box. I opened the blinds in my home every day to allow in more light and continued praying for help. I also opened my scriptures. I began to feel the darkness receding as my life filled with light and the Atonement began working in my life.

Although I cannot say that I am completely cured, my life is so much better now. Thanks to the healing and growth that I have experienced through the Atonement, the gospel, my counselor, and my social support network, my relationship with my children is much better. I do enjoy being with them. Being a mother is definitely the hardest thing I have ever done. It is still a constant struggle. I'm still trying to figure out how to be a mom. The difference is that now I know that, with the help of Heavenly Father and Jesus, I can do it. I have also learned that it's important to ask for help—from Heavenly Father and Jesus Christ and from others who are in our lives. We don't have to do it alone.

I thank God for tender mercies and for His patience while He waited for me to turn to Him. I'm so sad that I lost nearly a decade of my life (and the lives of my children) to depression, and that my memories of that time are so hazy. I wish that I had been more receptive to the promptings He was giving me so that I could have come out of the darkness sooner. I pray that I will not be so stubborn or suffer unnecessarily for so long in the future.

When my sister had her second baby, I had the opportunity to care for her oldest child. It was such a wonderful experience. I thoroughly enjoyed the day we spent together playing, shopping, and reading books. I also got to take her to meet her new baby sister. I cherish the memory of that day. I imagine that's how my early experiences as a mother could have been. Unfortunately, I can't change the past. However, I can make the best of the time I have left with my children. I also look forward to opportunities to create wonderful relationships with my future grandchildren.

Mary

By Heather Farrell, CD(DONA)

*Just as certain men were foreordained from before the
foundations of the world, so were certain women appointed to certain tasks.
Divine design—not chance—brought Mary forward
to be the mother of Jesus.[1]*

NEAL A. MAXWELL

Just like each of us, Jesus did not receive a fullness of knowledge at first but grew "grace to grace until he received a fullness" (D&C 93:13). We know He was taught by angels and by God, but he was also taught by his righteous mother. Elder Rex E. Pinegar said, "At Mary's bosom he was nurtured, at her knee he was schooled. It is not unreasonable to suppose that it was she who taught him of his divine birth and mission."[2] We don't know for sure whether Mary ever told Jesus the story of his birth, but it is beautiful that one of the most powerful stories in the Christian cannon is a birth story.

Mary was young (some scholars estimate she would have been about thirteen or fourteen) when she was visited by the angel Gabriel and told that, if she chose, she would become the mother of the Savior. She most likely knew that under Mosaic law it was Joseph's right to have her stoned publicly when he found out she was pregnant before marriage. She risked losing everything—her life, her social standing, and all her hopes for the future—however, Mary humbly and with faith replied, "Behold the hand-maid of the Lord; be it unto me according to thy word" (Luke 1:38). She was God's chosen vessel, and she was willing to be filled.

In Luke 2:22, we read that after Christ's birth, Mary observed "the days of her purification." Under the Mosaic Law a woman was physically unclean for seven days after the birth of a male baby and two weeks after the birth of a female. Being physically unclean meant that she was to be separated from other people for a prescribed amount of time. If she gave birth to a boy, then on the eighth day after the birth, her son would be circumcised. At this point, she was no longer physically unclean but was still considered ritually unclean. This meant she was unable to enter the temple or to touch holy things until forty days after the birth if she gave birth to a boy and twice that long if she gave birth to a girl. Once the days of her ritual uncleanness had passed, she then had to go the temple and offer a lamb (if she was poor, she could bring two turtledoves) to atone for her and make her clean again (see Leviticus 12).

It is difficult to imagine why Mary, or any woman, could be considered by God to be unclean or would require being separated from God after participating in something as sacred as creating life. Yet, when we recall that the law of Moses was given to bear testimony of the necessity of the Atonement and that all things are symbolic of Christ, things become clearer.

Giving life is a two-edged sword; every woman who brings life to a child must also accept that she has ultimately brought death, eventually, to that child. This is the paradox brought about by Eve—that one cannot know the sweet without tasting the bitter and that there cannot be life without death. While giving life was not a sin under the law of Moses, being the cause of death was. It may be that, under the law of Moses, a woman was unclean after giving birth not because her body was dirty or because she had sinned in conceiving the child, but because she had brought death into the world. Bringing a girl child into the world made a woman twice as unclean because each new girl meant more life and ultimately more death.

Under the law of Moses, each woman had to atone for her own sins, and she did that by being separated from the presence of God for a certain amount of time. Yet in symbolism of the Atonement that would one day be performed, she could be redeemed by sacrificing a lamb or a turtledove, once again becoming clean. Still, the sacrifice she offered was only symbolic, for until Christ completed his Atonement, bringing life still meant bringing death.

In accordance with the law of Moses, Mary took Jesus to the temple forty days after His birth and not only brought with her the required two turtledoves expected of the poor but also a much deeper and more valuable sacrifice—her lamb, the Lamb of God—as her offering to the Lord. She presented to the Lord the "great and last sacrifice" (Alma 34:13), the One who had the power to break the bonds of death and would ensure that every body created by women on this earth would live again.

While at the temple, Mary and Joseph were approached by a man named Simeon who recognized Jesus as the promised Messiah. Simeon held Jesus in his arms and prophesied many things about Him that caused His parents to marvel. Simeon told Mary that "a sword shall pierce through thy own soul also, that the thoughts of many hearts may be revealed" (Luke 2:34). We often talk about how much God loves us because He was willing to sacrifice His son, but Jesus was Mary's son just as much as He was God's son. It is humbling to think about the great love Mary must have had for all human souls in order to make the sacrifices she did.

Mary's one choice to consecrate her will to the Lord made all the difference. Without her willingness to conceive, bear, nurture, and sacrifice her son, the Atonement and resurrection would not have been possible. This has special significance for women because it means that no sacrifice they make of blood, labor, or love will be in vain.

Like Mary, it is one of our greatest responsibilities as women to sacrifice to bring children to this earth, to nurture them toward the light, and to give them the strength they need to accomplish their foreordained missions on this earth. Every conception is a gift from God and is, in essence, no less miraculous than Mary's immaculate conception. Each and every birthing woman is, as Mary, a chosen vessel of the Lord.

1 Neal A. Maxwell, "The Women of God," *Ensign*, May 1978, http://lds.org/ensign/1978/05/the-women-of-god.

2 Rex D. Pinegar, "Woman as a Teacher," in Woman (Salt Lake City, UT: Deseret Book, 1979), 30.

I Know Her

By Katy Rawlins

MY FIANCÉ AND I HAD ALWAYS FELT UNEASY about birth control. I suppose it had a lot to do with the fact that all I ever hoped to become was a mother. Suppressing my fertility for the sake of the legendary "adjustment" to marriage was never something that sat well with my heart.

There we were, weeks away from our wedding, kneeling together in my future in-law's living room, praying about our future family. Now or later? The Lord's will was clear. Now. Soon. Just like Mary, the knowledge of my upcoming pregnancy came *after* an engagement, but *before* my marriage.

We were married in the Salt Lake Temple and then enjoyed a precious week away from the world. The return home from our honeymoon brought with it an intense tenderness in my breasts. It was my body's first way of confirming we'd brought home quite the honeymoon souvenir—a baby!

Within a few weeks, we chose to share the news with our family. Their initial reactions left me feeling crushed. "Woah, that was quick!" came one reply. Eventually, everyone seemed to come around and be supportive, but we were sure it wasn't until after they'd carefully figured dates and accounted for our whereabouts for each and every day leading up to our wedding. A few months later, we were approached by a church fine arts director and asked to audition for the roles of Mary and Joseph in a pilot production of

"Savior of the World." My heart sunk as I realized my pregnancy had dashed the prospect of landing one of my dream roles in theater. "We're expecting," we told him. "When?" he asked. We shared. His eyes lit up, and he told us the production dates. I could rehearse up until my delivery date, take two weeks off, then finish out the tech and dress rehearsals. And they wanted our new baby to play baby Jesus at the end of Act I.

I spent the remainder of my pregnancy immersed in the role of Mary. I felt her humility as she knelt before the angel Gabriel, "Behold the handmaid of the Lord, be it unto me according to thy word." I sang with my

---

I sang with my whole heart as I shared what it was like for Mary to receive revelation—revelation that all those around her would doubt.

---

whole heart as I shared what it was like for Mary to receive revelation—revelation that all those around her would doubt. I looked into the eyes of my husband and felt the hurt and anger of Joseph as Mary told him of the immaculate conception. I saw the light in his eyes after the angel told him he would raise the Son of God.

My due date came and went. Due to a lack of knowledge and a full-on labor induction, I didn't exactly end up with an exalted-feeling birth experience. In fact, it was terrible and traumatic. Despite it all, I felt a great impression that although she may have been all alone, Mary was never traumatized through giving birth. Our new baby, a daughter we named Rachel, was welcomed by all our family and loads of dear friends. I felt the joy in Mary's heart as she welcomed guests from near and far with the words, "Then they shall see Him!"

Nearly eight years later, we still don't understand what all those newlywed "adjustments" are supposed to be, but having always consecrated our family size to the Lord, we are now happily raising four daughters. Through each of the subsequent pregnancies and births, I have fervently prayed to understand more about Mary. Each time, the Savior has taken more and more of my sorrows and disappointments from my first birth experience and filled my soul with assurances that the feelings, the heartaches and the joys, I feel as a mother are quite similar to what Mary experienced in her life in giving birth to and raising the Son of God. And in many of my mothering days, a song from "Savior of the World" brings the spirit of Mary into my whole being because I know her, and I sing:

> My Lord, My God
> Came to me that day,
> And His mercy on me has led me in His way.
> What I saw, what I heard,
> fills my heart to say,
> I will praise Thy name,
> I will praise Thy name,
> I will praise Thy holy name.
> Praise Thy name to all, alway.

Repentance and Forgiveness

By Felice Austin, CHt

"Forgive us our debts, as we forgive our debtors."

MATTHEW 6:12

Pregnancy can be a time of upheaval and reevaluation. During pregnancy, many women and their husbands find themselves with unexpected feelings about the past and contemplation about the future. Pregnancy and fertility issues can bring up sadness about old losses, old transgressions, guilt, shame, anger, and a number of other feelings. It is important to invite and allow healing, because unresolved issues may have a negative impact on pregnancy and birth. Ina May Gaskin, the nation's leading midwife, has noted that such thoughts and worries can powerfully "alter a woman's body's ability to perform a normal physiological function."[1] Unresolved issues may also affect her postpartum moods and future mothering. No matter how many pregnancies a woman has, each situation is unique and she and her husband may find a new opportunity to apply the Atonement.

FORGIVENESS

In Doctrine and Covenants 64:10, we read: "I the Lord will forgive whom I will forgive, but of you it is required to forgive all men." A mother or father may need to forgive self or others for things such as omissions, rejection, abuse, betrayal, scaring them about birth, wasting childbearing years, dishonesty, inconsiderate behavior, and breaking the commandments.

Forgiving others can take time, especially when the hurt is deep or the offenses are grave. Mothers should not feel defeated if they cannot forgive right away. If you leave a space in your heart for forgiveness and for the

Atonement to heal you, one day you may be surprised to find that it has. Also, forgiving someone doesn't mean that you will allow them to hurt you again. We can forgive and still make loving choices to protect ourselves and our children.

REPENTANCE

Repentance is the second principle of the Gospel of Jesus Christ. Repentance is the wonderful gift God gave us through the Savior, and it is an essential part of the plan of happiness. To invite peace and healing, a mother or father may need to repent. Repentance is for both small and large sins, such as selfishness, disobedience, poor care of one's body, bad decisions, bad behavior, contention, omissions, and pride.

If you feel that you need to repent, kneel down and allow yourself to believe that loving Heavenly Parents want to give you all the blessings they have. If you don't know where to start or what to change, take Elder Neil A. Anderson's advice: "Humbly petition the Lord, 'Father, what wouldst Thou have me do?' The answers come. We feel the changes we need to make. The Lord tells us in our mind and in our heart."[2]

Sometimes, even after we forsake our sins and forgive ourselves, we may still feel the sting or regret long afterward. This does not mean we have not been forgiven. Elder Anderson explained the following in his October 2009 general conference address:

> The scriptures do not say that we will forget our forsaken sins in mortality. Rather, they declare that the Lord will forget. The forsaking of sins implies never returning. Forsaking requires time. To help us, the Lord at times allows the residue of our mistakes to rest in our memory. It is a vital part of our learning.[3]

When life's issues come up during pregnancy, they give us a chance to heal and transform. No matter how small or large we feel our sins, flaws, or mistakes may be, Christ's hand is still extended to us.

Satan is a master at telling us that sin is no big deal, and then once we've sinned, he tells us it is such a big deal we could never repent and be whole again. Luckily, my two-year-old knew better. One sunny winter day, she and I were crossing a grassy field on our way to the beach. My heart was heavy because I had lost a measure of the Spirit and was still struggling with repenting. But she was joyful. She swung my hand and exuberantly sang these words, "Up from the ashes, grow the roses of success!" She grinned as she sang. I laughed, trying to figure out where she had learned this. Of course, one doesn't question a two-year-old, one must simply join in the chorus, so we marched as we sang: "Grow the roses! Grow the roses!"

Some time later, I realized she was teaching me a lesson I needed to learn. When we sin, we slide backward, and sometimes off the path completely, but we can come back. In fact, we can rise even higher and become even more beautiful—like the roses, or like the Phoenix, the beautiful mythic bird that is reborn from its ashes.

Though God does not want us to sin, He knows that we are going to. Lovingly, He prepared the Atonement for this purpose. It is amazing that if we return to Him and use the healing power of the Atonement, He consecrates our experiences—even our sins—for our good. When Joseph Smith succumbed to temptation and lost the first 116 pages of the Book of Mormon, he also "lost [his] gift" and his "mind became darkened" (D&C 10:2). This was a difficult time for Joseph. However, when the ability to translate was restored to him, he approached translating with renewed energy and vigor.

No matter what kind of ashes you may be sitting in right now, I invite you to remember the roses, the Phoenix, and the example of the Prophet Joseph—and then repent. In 1 Corinthians 10:13, God promised that He "will not suffer you to be tempted above that ye are able; but will with the temptation also make a way to escape, that ye may be able to bear it." I invite you to follow that exit and heed Christ's unceasing invitation: "I will be merciful unto them, . . . if they will repent and come unto me; for mine arm is lengthened out all the day long, saith the Lord God of Hosts" (2 Nephi 28:32).

---

1   Ina May Gaskin, *Ina May's Guide to Childbirth* (New York: Bantam, 2003), 134.
2   Neil L. Andersen, "Repent . . .That I May Heal You," *Ensign*, October 2009, http://lds.org/ensign/2009/11/repent-that-i-may-heal-you.
3   Ibid.

HEALING AFTER ABORTION

By Kristin

MY NAME IS KRISTIN AND I AM A BUTTERFLY. Every butterfly, before getting to spread its beautiful wings, must start out life as a caterpillar.

Just a few months after I turned eighteen and graduated from high school, my life was turned upside down. My parents were recently divorced, and my dad had remarried. The Church was the farthest thing from my heart. I had received a full-ride soccer scholarship at a local university and was only a few months into my relationship with a young man. During these emotionally turbulent times, I discovered that I was pregnant.

Never in my wildest dreams did I think I would, when placed in that situation, have considered abortion. Then again, I never imagined I would be in that situation in the first place. I remember running through my options a million times. All I could think about was my immediate future. I was just two weeks away from finally realizing my dream of playing soccer at the collegiate level. I didn't want to disappoint my coaches or my parents. I didn't know if I wanted to be with my boyfriend permanently and felt as though this pregnancy was an indefinite tie for better or worse. I certainly couldn't imagine being a parent or placing my baby for adoption.

In my teenage naiveté, I really thought having an abortion would be an isolated incident. I would move on, the boy and I would move on (or wouldn't), and life could continue to be lived just as it was. I significantly underestimated the abortion's permanence and continuing ripple effects. My decision was made. Unfortunately, the father's pleas to at least talk to someone else fell on a strong-headed, scared girl and went by the wayside. Despite this, he offered his support and was wonderful to me.

Two weeks after my abortion, I began college and had a successful soccer season. We were undefeated and won our division championship with me scoring the winning goal. My picture was in the paper, and the championship ring was on my finger. My dream was realized, but I no longer felt the same joy playing soccer. I would look at my ring that sat in a box and think about the heavy price I paid for something so insignificant in the big scheme of things.

Making the choice to end my pregnancy closed one chapter of my life and opened another. I ended up quitting the team and forgoing my scholarship. Over the next year, I moved to Florida to pursue wakeboarding and continued to make choices that made my life extremely difficult. I was hardened, I was tattooed, I was pierced, and I was exhausted.

I finally embarked on a quest to figure my life out. I wrote Heavenly Father a forty-page letter, ending it with: "If you think you can do more with my life than I can, go for it." I finally accepted my brother's offer to go to church with him. It felt so good.

After a few consistent weeks of church, I met with the bishop to start the repentance process. Due to the circumstances, a bishop's court was held. I met with four kind men, all of whom I had grown up with. After meeting and praying, they determined that the best course of action for me was to be disfellowshipped. Initially, there was not a sting to this because I had lived without the gospel by choice for so long.

My spirituality started to slowly be restored. My desire to take the sacrament and fully participate in church grew. I was a walking, breathing example of sanctification. The Atonement is real. I was being healed. My spirit was being restored. When I was asked to say prayers at meetings, it was very humbling to have to decline.

By the time the last two months came, I was like a thirsty wanderer in the desert who hadn't tasted water in months but could see the oasis. I was so ready, so excited, and so appreciative of the sacrament. Because I was given the chance to truly yearn for the sacrament, I will never forget what it was like the first time I was able to take it again. Never again will I be able to deny the power of the Spirit and the truthfulness of the gospel.

I was now twenty-one years old. I felt prompted to receive my patriarchal blessing. Through that blessing, the Lord told me that He knew me by name and that He loved me. He let me know that my experience with abortion was not in vain. I would help other women who had gone astray and let them know that the Lord lives and loves them. I truly was forgiven. An experience that was so ugly was transformed and made beautiful by our Savior Jesus Christ. It became my pearl and a very sacred experience.

Although I knew that I was forgiven, Satan continued to work on me.

I worried that I had taken away that spirit's chance to come to earth and get a body. I remember one therapy session when I was sobbing about this concern. A strong feeling came over me that agency exists on both sides of the veil—that this spirit knew what they were choosing and that was all the body they needed. I felt the impression of an older, wiser woman and learned that the Lord does not put the fate of another person's soul in a mortal's hands.

I graduated from BYU Hawaii and headed back to Utah for graduate school in clinical social work. When I was twenty-five, I received my endowment. I met my husband and got married to him in the Salt Lake Temple at twenty-six. I graduated from my masters program and started to embark on the second greatest journey of my life, being a psychotherapist. I was in a unique position as an LDS woman. The Lord knew the desire of my heart which was to reach women who faced similar circumstances and let them know hope and healing are possible.

At this point, my abortion experience was a part of me but didn't define me. I was comfortable having it be a part of my history and shared my story when prompted. However, when my husband and I decided to become pregnant a year and a half in to our marriage, I was filled with anxiety. I worried that because I chose to have an abortion, I wouldn't be able to get pregnant. I knew the Lord didn't operate that way, but I kept wondering. That year of trying to become pregnant was an emotional trial for me. Eventually, I became pregnant, but I worried that I would miscarry or that the baby would die. Each week of development caused me to reflect on my aborted child.

My midwife was very kind and reassuring the whole time. She offered to let me hear the heartbeat anytime I wanted to ease the anxiety. During the last month, I had to transfer care to a doctor. Little did I know that transferring care would be such a blessing because of my fear of my baby dying. I needed medical intervention so I could relax and bring my baby into the world. I was terrified of being a mother and this fear created tension that kept him in. And then my firstborn came into this world. Little Sam. What perspective I had to see this child in front of me. The miracle of it all.

During my next pregnancy, two years later, my anxiety of the baby dying crept in at various times but was manageable. I decided to birth naturally in a hospital setting. My baby was breech the majority of the pregnancy. I mentally prepared for whatever turn my labor would take, but hoped a cesarean birth would be a last option. Being optimistic, I hired my birth doulas and prepared to deliver naturally.

My thirty-eighth week came around, and my surges started in the middle of the night. They were relatively short and not terribly intense. By the early afternoon, we made our way to hospital. I walked the halls, my doulas by my side, having contractions every two or three minutes. About an hour and a half later, I was in transition. The last twenty minutes, I felt like I was going to die—not my baby, but me. I reached a point of surrender. I felt like I was truly walking through the valley of the shadow of death. Despite the chaos, there was a strong spiritual presence in the room. The veil was very thin and spirits that I knew were there. My daughter arrived. Little Penelope made her way into the world swiftly and was very alert from the minute she came. I felt like I tasted heaven and was changed forever.

I often ask myself if I would make a different decision about my abortion now, and naturally my answer is yes. However, you can't give your younger self the wisdom, perspective, and experience of your older self. You do the best that you can, given where you are in your life. My abortion experience will always be apart of me—my internal reminder of the power of the Atonement. This power is what caused my transformation from earthbound crawler to the beautiful butterfly that I am today.

Healing from Loss and Other Sorrows

By Robyn Allgood, AAHCC

Blessed are they that mourn for they shall be comforted.

MATTHEW 5:4

Nothing quite prepares you for the moment when time seems to stop. Just as the doctor was trying to tell us about the grave condition of my son Kyle, she received a message that we needed to come to his bedside right away. My heart started to race. I just knew. Somehow my feet moved me toward the ICU doors and then to his bedside. I witnessed the last-minute efforts of a team of highly skilled nurses and doctors as they tried to keep his heart beating. I felt his spirit leave his body. Then they stepped away, and I came to him. I told him I loved him and that I wanted him to go and perform the mission that God had for him. I knew, but did not want to admit it to myself before, that he was being called home.

I had joined that club. The one no parent wants to be a part of. The club made up of those who have had one of their precious little ones die. As I walked through those first hours, days, months, years, I learned how individual the grieving process is to each person. Not one of us experiences it in exactly the same way. Nevertheless, I am going to attempt to offer a few insights that I hope will provide healing to you or someone you care about. I have also included comments from parents who have experienced different kinds of loss. Though I can offer only a few thoughts on this subject, there are many books that address this issue in much more detail.

In Genesis 3:16, we read that God told Eve, "I will greatly multiply thy sorrow and thy conception; in sorrow thou shalt bring forth children." This sorrow came about because of the Fall of Adam and Eve. While in the Garden of Eden, Adam and Eve felt neither joy nor sorrow. When a family opens their hearts to experience an increase of joy and love through procreation, they are also opening their hearts to a greater capacity to feel sorrow. This sorrow can be experienced in different ways throughout childbearing. It may be felt because of miscarriage/pregnancy loss, infertility, stillbirth, death of an infant, or other similar circumstances. Most of the examples I will use will apply to birth and parenting; however, there may be other reasons to seek out the Atonement for the healing of sorrow, and it is my hope that my thoughts can benefit in those situations as well.

As much as we do not like it, death is an important part of the plan of salvation: "death hath passed upon all men, to fulfill the merciful plan of the great Creator" (2 Nephi 9:6). The scriptures explain the necessity that "there was an opposition; even the forbidden fruit in opposition to the tree of life; the one being sweet and the other bitter" (2 Nephi 2:15). The grief is a bitter but a necessary part of our mortal probation.

Grief often is experienced in a cycle of emotions, including shock/denial, anger, bargaining, sadness, and acceptance.[1] This cycle is not experienced in exact steps or in this exact order, but it is helpful to know them and allow yourself time to process what you have been through. A person can even go through some of the stages of loss more than once. (See "Healing from a Traumatic Birth," on page 396, for more information on the stages of grief.) It is important that you not expect yourself to heal on a certain schedule. One mother shared, "It was helpful for people to allow me to grieve in the way and time frame that I needed to grieve." Just as the Atonement is very individual, healing is individual.

It is essential that a family grieve and allow themselves to mourn their sorrow. Even though Christ knew He could raise Lazarus from the dead, the scriptures plainly tell us that "he groaned in spirit and was troubled" and then "Jesus wept" (John 11:33, 35). Of all people who have ever lived on the earth, Christ is the person who would have the greatest eternal perspective concerning death. Yet here we see that He mourned for Lazarus. He cried. He was troubled. He was sad. He loved Lazarus deeply, and so Christ mourned for Lazarus. Though the doctrines of the eternal family and the Atonement are very comforting, they do not change the fact that a deep and profound change has been experienced. Time is needed to grieve and adjust to a new normal. One father shared his thoughts after his baby girl passed away:

The loss and going through the grief has been one of the most challenging experiences that I have gone through during my mortal existence. It has really given me a challenge in ways that I would not have thought possible. It caused me to doubt my testimony, my belief in God, and even the purpose for this life. I did things because of expectation: attending church, doing callings, giving of time, talents, and abilities for the service of others. For the first part of the year, I often got mad but kept it bottled up in hopes that the anger and resentment would go away. Even to this day, I still have moments of anger, resentment, and doubts as to the purpose of life, God, and everything else in between. However, over time those moments have decreased. In fact, I could say that time has been the best healer of all.

The Savior taught us, "Blessed are they that mourn for they shall be comforted" (Matthew 5:4). The Savior did not try to minimize the experience of mourning. In fact, He proclaimed the mourner is "blessed." Mourning is an expression of love. We know that even the earth mourned for its Creator when He was crucified: "the earth did quake, and the rocks rent" (Matthew 27:51). Mourning is a part of the natural course of life. Because we love someone, we would be grieved at the separation of their presence from ours. One mother shared the following thought with me after her baby died of SIDS: "Grief is a product of love. If I didn't love my baby so much, I wouldn't be grieving her loss. Grieving is a normal part of life. While the gospel brings peace and comfort, it still doesn't make me miss my baby Naomi any less." God promises the mourner comfort. He provides this comfort through the Atonement and the Holy Ghost.

"The Lord takes many away even in infancy, that they may escape the envy of man, and the sorrows and evils of this present world; they were too pure, too lovely, to live on the earth; therefore, if rightly considered, instead of mourning we have reason to rejoice as they are delivered from evil, and we shall soon have them again."[2]

—Joseph Smith

THE ATONEMENT

The Atonement of Christ offers hope and the knowledge that there is always someone who understands and who cares. "He hath born our griefs, and carried our sorrows" (Isaiah 53:4). It is interesting that the words *born* and *carried* are used to describe how the Savior experienced grief and sorrow. The mother and father together have taken part in carrying a life and offering birth. Christ has suffered the sorrow of loss related to birth and carrying babies into childhood. He has truly "*born* our griefs and *carried* our sorrows." He knows your sorrow intimately and because of this He can offer "to heal the brokenhearted" (Luke 4:18). One mother commented the following:

> I am so thankful for the Atonement. That my Savior suffered, bled, and died so that I can return to the presence of my Heavenly Father. I can't help but think that Berkley must have been something special to not have to come to Earth. I often think of the work he must be doing and my loving Grandmother watching over him until I can hold him in my arms.

We can partake in the healing that the Atonement offers: "I will not leave you comfortless: I will come to you" (John 14:18). How is it that we can have Him come to us? The following are a few suggestions that will invite Him to come during whatever stage of grief you are in.

THE HOLY GHOST

Christ knew He would have to leave His beloved disciples. He knew they would still be in need of comfort and help, so He promised to send them "the Comforter, which is the Holy Ghost" (John 14:26). He explained to them how the Holy Ghost provides this comfort: "he shall teach you all things, and bring all things to your remembrance, whatsoever I have said unto you," (John 14:26). The Holy Ghost can teach us how to get through dark times. One mother said, "We were . . . on our knees. . . . A LOT. We were praying for the constant companion of the Comforter to lessen the sharp pains in our hearts." Following a miscarriage, a mother explained how the Holy Ghost comforted her:

> My husband gave me a blessing. While I don't remember a lot of the blessing, I do remember an extreme feeling of peace come over me, the same peace I had felt when I lost my mother. My Heavenly Father knows me and loves me and while it may not be easy it will be worth it. Our Heavenly Father has a plan for each of us and while we may not know His plan He will comfort us and guide us through each of these trials. I cried and was extremely upset, but I still felt an overwhelming peace.

It is natural and important to allow yourself to grieve. It is also just as important to allow for the *peace* that the Comforter can bring. The following are some of the ways that you can invite this peace in.

SCRIPTURES

The Holy Ghost is invited in every time we study the scriptures. "The words of Christ . . . carry us beyond this vale of sorrow" (Alma 37:45). After my son's death, I was drawn with even more interest to the doctrines of the gospel. I had previously read Alma 40:12, which states, "And then it shall come to pass, that the spirits of those who are righteous are received into a state of happiness, which is called paradise, a state of rest, a state of peace, where they shall rest from all care and sorrow." Reading it again after my son's death meant more to me. The verse told me where my son was and what it is like there. I was comforted. One mother shared how studying the scriptures helped her and her family:

> I was really drawn to scriptures that talked about the heart after Ian passed away. There are so many verses that talk about the heart and the sanctification of the heart, which is a process that I so strongly desired since the moment I realized my role in reuniting with Ian. In addition to the specific scriptures that have brought love into my heart, the act of obedience and reading daily brought peace into our home. It is one stepping stone that we can pave on our journey back to our Heavenly Father.

It is one way that as a family we show our love for our son and our desire to return to him someday.

PRAYER

The Lord has counseled us, "If thou art sorrowful, call on the Lord thy God with supplication, that your souls may be joyful" (D&C 136:29). Another mother, after experiencing miscarriage, shared the following: "Praying and just opening my heart to the Lord was very helpful, especially when I felt strong emotions coming on and I didn't want to take them out on my loved ones. I felt safe screaming at Heavenly Father because I knew He wouldn't be offended." One father shared how his prayers were answered:

> The thing that brought me the most comfort was the presence of one of my closest friends when he showed up at the hospital to help me give a blessing to Jill. I had felt all alone at the time, praying for our Heavenly Father's help when this friend showed up. We didn't have any family anywhere around; this friend was the closest thing we had to family.

After the death of an infant son, another mother noted the strength she received from the prayers of others: "I know there were many prayers said in my behalf, and I truly felt their power." Following the death of my own son, I was in awe of how tangible at times the strength from others was felt as they united in prayer in behalf of my family.

SERVICE

In the beginning of the grieving process, it is a blessing to have people offer service. Be willing to accept help. Service will bring healing to you and the people who offer it. In the midst of Christ's greatest trials, He reached out and healed His "enemy." When Peter cut off the ear of one of the high priest's servants who came to take Jesus away, He "touched his [the servant's] ear, and healed him" (Luke 22:51). When the time is appropriate, many families find comfort in finding ways to serve others:

We have a great desire to serve. We organized a donation to make in Ian's behalf on his first birthday, which ended up being huge. We have witnessed trial and grief bring out so much good in people. We try to do some service each year to celebrate his birth and return to the temple as close to his angel day as we can.

A close friend of mine found comfort in making blankets for nearby funeral homes to give families who have experienced the death of a little one. She also organized a local support group and started a blog. My son loved books, so we decided to choose a book each year to donate to our local library in his honor. I was touched when my brother told me his gift to Kyle was to set aside time early in the morning each day to read the scriptures.

COMPASSION

As the Savior neared the end of His ultimate sacrifice, in the midst of His greatest suffering, He pleaded with the Father, "forgive them; for they know not what they do" (Luke 23:34). When individuals are mourning, they are the recipients of many efforts to comfort and soothe. Sometimes they are even the recipients of unkind or thoughtless words and actions. Though I hope that a family not be subjected to anything that might further cause them pain, it is likely that someone, usually well-intentioned, will say or do something that might offend. Even having been through my own sorrows, I know that I could say or do the wrong thing when trying to offer help. When this happens, we can follow the Savior's example, who asks that we "forgive them for they know not what they do" (Luke 23:34).

Compassion for the actions of others will greatly further the healing process. Unfortunately, the adversary desires to take advantage of your vulnerability in grieving. He would have you hold on to the hurt and not allow peace. One mother shared, "I was victim to Satan's resounding discouragement, lack of hope, and failure." Satan would like to drive a wedge between you and loved ones and, more importantly, between you and the Lord. Satan wants you to be miserable like he is. On the other hand, the Savior stands resolute in his ability to offer His healing power.

He asks us to forgive and show compassion that we might allow His Atonement to soothe our souls. One father offered:

> At times of passing, we realize just how fragile and fleeting mortal earthly life can be. And so, we remind and encourage ourselves to be more kind and patient with those that we love who are still with us so that whenever separation happens we will have sweet memories to comfort us then too.

REMEMBER

The Savior intended that His life and sacrifice be remembered. He instituted the sacrament saying, "this do in remembrance of me" (Luke 22:19). He does not want us to forget what He has done in our behalf. He knows that His Atonement will bring us peace, healing, and ultimately power. He knows that our ability to remember His love for us will strengthen us in the hard times that will inevitably come. As we remember our loved ones, we are remembering Him and His Atonement because it is that very Atonement that makes it possible for us to be with our loved ones again. In 1 Thessalonians 1:2–3 we read: "We give thanks to God always for you all, making mention of you in our prayers; Remembering without ceasing your work of faith, and labour of love, and patience of hope in our Lord Jesus Christ, in the sight of God and our Father." As a family, we still mention Kyle in our prayers and we lovingly remember his faith, love, and hope in the Savior. One mother shared how her family remembers their angel baby:

> Shortly after Bella died, I spent a good week making her photo album. I so desperately needed that time to just look at pictures and remember. I wrote down memories in her photo book. I took the time to grieve over all the times we would not have together and the time to rejoice in the times we did have together. Every year for Isabella's birthday, I make a baby blanket with a crocheted border around it. It helps me to feel like I am doing something for her. And then since she was in the hospital her whole two months of her life, I find joy in giving the blanket to another baby struggling in the hospital. I usually try to find a connection

of someone I know who knows someone with a baby in the NICU. The blanket has not gone to the NICU every year, but it has most years. I think about how comforting it was for us when Bella was in the hospital and people were praying for her and gave us a blanket or some token of thoughtfulness, and it makes me hope that each year the blanket will somehow be helpful for the family it made its way to. I also find joy in visiting her grave with the family and talking about her and about being united together again someday.

Another mother shared how her family honors their baby's short life:

> Since Ella's life was so short-lived, it's a difficult time. We've decided to make the third of July (her birthday) her day of remembrance and celebrate her life. We host a family dinner and bake a cake and release pink balloons in her honor. We think about the traits we saw; her beautiful smile, dark hair, and feistiness. It's a sad and happy day, and we try to focus on the gospel teachings of eternal families. On the Fourth of July, we try to think of how much Ella would love the festivities and not focus on the day of her death. She would want her brothers to be happy and not sad, and that is easier for children than it is for us. It helps if we can leave town or enjoy a family vacation during that time.

Remembering is an action that is best accomplished by an activity. There are a variety of ways to remember the one who has died:

- Journaling, blogging, or scrapbooking
- Holding an annual birthday party
- Making art projects
- Planting a tree, bush, or perennial flower in your loved one's memory
- Going to a special place that has meaning to you and your loved one

The Spirit will help you know what activities will be appropriate for your family. Be mindful of any surviving children in your family, and involve them as much as you can. I am so grateful that my sister took the time to make a memory book with my daughter after my son died. I enjoyed making my two daughters Easter books that talked about their brother and how the blessings of the Atonement make it possible for them to be with him again someday. After a friend of mine experienced the stillbirth of her second child, she asked friends to take a picture of his name written somewhere. I waited for the weather to cooperate, and then I took a picture of *Aiden* etched in the snow. After I sent my friend the picture, she sent a picture back to me of *Kyle* written in the sand of a beach near her home. I love that she asked friends to take pictures. I know that pictures following a stillbirth may be hard to look at, and I felt that these pictures would be like receiving hugs.

MANAGING THE GRIEF

It is normal to experience feelings of guilt or blame. One mother shared with me her thoughts: "Things that were extra hard for me during this time were guilt, thinking that I must have done something wrong because he was in my body and something bad had happened to him. . . . What had I done that was so bad to deserve this?" I'll admit that I had an expectation of myself that I could handle the extreme emotions I was experiencing. People continued to comment on how well we were managing, and I felt the pressure to maintain the perception of managing my emotions. All the while, I could weep at the drop of a hat and cried myself to sleep each night. What is the difference between normal grief and abnormal grief? I'm not sure, but if you are having a hard time completing the normal tasks of the day, such as getting out of bed, getting ready, and eating, then it is a good idea to talk to someone who can help. One mother explained how she and her husband recognized their need for outside help after experiencing a stillbirth and two miscarriages:

> After seeing me crying day in and day out, my husband called the doctor and said that I needed something to help me get through this. I took some medicine for a few months. I didn't really notice a difference, but my husband said it was night and day. I was up and exercising, which was the one thing that made me feel the best. After I started exercising and getting out of the house, I didn't need the medicine anymore.

There are many resources available for families who are grieving. LDS Family Services is a good place to start. Depression is real and can be debilitating to the person experiencing it. Through prayer and study, you can discover what you will need to get to a place where you can function on a daily basis. (You can also read "Perspective on Postpartum Depression" and stories that follow it, on page 482.)

Helping Children Grieve

Remember that you are not the only one to have experienced this loss. If you have children, it is very important to be aware of their needs to mourn.

Do not deny your need to grieve. Your children will follow your pattern of grief. Involve your children as much as possible in the grieving process.

Avoid "buck-up therapy" that encourages children to suppress the need to cry, worry, talk, and so forth. They may not need to talk about it yet, but ensure the door is always open if they have questions or just need to talk. Children who are not allowed to grieve may struggle with bonding and intimacy in future relationships.

Dr. Sandra Fox identified four tasks that children use to mourn: *understanding* what caused the loss, *grieving* or experiencing the painful feelings associated with the loss, *commemorating* the value of the loss, and *going on with life* by accepting and integrating the loss psychologically and emotionally within themselves.

To ensure that children develop and master emotional skills as they process an initial loss and then face perhaps more profound losses in the future, caregivers have three major functions:

1 To foster honest and open relationships with children
2 To provide a safe and secure space in which children can mourn
3 To be role models of healthy mourning[1]

1 Maria Trozzi, *Talking with Children about Loss* (New York: Perigree Trade, 1999), 8–11.

GIVING LIFE AGAIN

There may come a time when you will be asked or *know* that it is time for you to welcome more of God's children into your home—be it through conception, birth, foster care, or adoption. Remember the Savior's words in John 14:27: "Peace I leave with you, my peace I give unto you. Let not your heart be troubled, neither let it be afraid." I have to admit that part of me feared bringing more children into my home for fear I would lose them and once again feel the pain of separation. I believe God asks that we be willing to reopen our hearts to more of His spirit children. One mother offered her experience in having more children following the death of her firstborn daughter:

> Having more children was such a blessing. None of our children have replaced her, and each time I have a baby, I go through a grieving process again—the grief of never having had those moments or milestones with Isabella. But each child has been so special, and I have loved talking about their older sister with them. I hope it gives them a reason to try to be good and continue on when things are tough. Having children is such a deeply spiritual experience to me that it helps me feel closer to my Isabella.

In reality, each life we carry within us is not ours; he or she is from God. We are only chosen as stewards for whatever amount of time He determines is appropriate. It is important that:

> We remember that each human being has a life of his or her own. We are only witness to that life. There is a greater, higher power that is in charge of life and death. . . . When we receive custodianship for a child (which is what we do when we accept pregnancy), we are surrendering to this mysterious co-creative power. Without the Creator, birth would not be possible. Without parents this particular child would have no way of incarnating, of embodying its spirit. Whether a child comes to full term, is born, and remains with us (for whatever period of time) is ultimately out of our hands. The moment of birth and the time of passing beyond this life are between the individual and the Creator.[3]

It helped me to know that "no righteous man is ever taken before his time. In the case of the faithful saints, they are simply transferred to other fields of labor. The Lord's work goes on in this life, in the world of spirits, and in the kingdoms of glory where men go after their resurrection."[4] There is a higher purpose to which we are subject. Ultimately, God has us and these little ones in His loving hands.

When You Don't Know What to Say

It is natural to feel awkward about what you should or should not say to someone who has experienced a loss of one kind or another. Saying something is better than saying nothing at all.

- Acknowledge the loss and that you care.

- Be prayerful in your approach.

- Try not to say something such as, "Aren't you glad we have the gospel?" or "Aren't you glad to know that you can be with them again someday?" Some people do not mind the reminder that they will be with their loved one again, and others do not need the reminder and merely need to grieve the separation. Saying that the family should be grateful for the gospel can be like saying they should not be sad when in reality they will need to mourn the loss.

- Resist the temptation to compare your experiences with theirs. There may come a time when they will ask you or it will be appropriate to share your experiences, but do not assume that your experiences are the same as theirs.

- Often it is enough to say, "I'm sorry. I care. I'm here for you." Sometimes just being there to listen is what is most needful. Sometimes flowers or offering to clean their home will be appropriate.

- Rather than saying, "Let me know if I can do anything for you," try to think of a specific way you can help, such as, "When can I bring you dinner?" or "Would you mind if I called you in a few days?" The important thing is let them know you care.

---

1   Lucia Capacchione and Sandra Bardsley, *Creating a Joyful Birth Experience* (New York: Fireside, 1994), 197.

2   Joseph Smith, *Teachings of the Prophet Joseph Smith*, sel. Joseph Fielding Smith (Salt Lake City, UT: Deseret Book, 1974), 196–197.

3   Lucia Capacchione and Sandra Bardsley, *Creating a Joyful Birth Experience* (New York: Fireside, 1994), 195.

4   Joseph Fielding Smith (in his remarks at the funeral service of Elder Richard L. Evans), qtd.in dedication page of *The Life Beyond*, by Robert L Millet and Joseph Fielding McConkie (Salt Lake City, UT: Deseret Book, 1986).

Hollowed or Hallowed?

By Krista Cole Frederico

ONCE AGAIN, IT IS HALLOWEEN. For most, this means grinning Jack-o-Lanterns, candy wrappers, and copious costume crafting. For me, by some nearly incomprehensible turn in life, my body is spending this Halloween week in the same process it engaged in last Halloween week: Miscarrying a baby.

This week has lent itself to great reflection. What might these twin experiences mean to me as I move on purposefully, with direction and insight to guide my life? In this trial, can I find a difference—can I seek the better part—between feeling hollowed and being hallowed?

You see, for a year I have felt that the miscarriage hollowed me. The symbolism of emptiness abounds following a loss like this. The empty nursery, empty time, and empty rocking chair echoed my physical emptiness. Where a heart had been beating, remained a hollow womb; when my due date arrived, my arms had nothing to gather and hold. The thought often crossed my mind that someone had invaded and robbed me of my greatest treasure.

As I turned for relief to church attendance, I felt spiritually and emotionally empty. In a church that focuses often on 1) The blessings in a woman's life of motherhood, and 2) Faith yielding blessings of healing and wholeness, I felt broken in every sense of the word. Like a shattered teapot with a piece subtracted, how could I be both reassembled and whole? Where was I remiss in my faithfulness? Were not my sobbing pleadings in prayer, priesthood blessings, and diligent searchings of scriptures, all on behalf of the high purpose of giving life, of being a co-creater with the divine, consistent with the path I was exhorted to take?

As an ultrasound yesterday confirmed that this difficult journey needs to be traversed yet again, I have recognized that rather than the hollowing, I should choose to see the hallowing, the opportunity "to make pure and holy" that the Lord has offered me for two autumn seasons.

I see the hallowing of myself begin as I accept that my body is not my own, that of its outcome I have little control. As we are often reminded, whosoever shall lose themselves for Christ's sake will find themselves. Pregnancy involves losing oneself—losing your energy, losing your sleep, losing your time, losing your body. In miscarriage, too, I lose possibilities and hopes for the future. But, when I choose to see it as losing myself for Christ's sake, for the sake of all I am to gain in this mortal experience, I find myself in newfound strength and courage, new appreciation for the majesty and mystery of life, and renewed compassion and capacity to aid those suffering around me.

C.S. Lewis teaches, "The moment you have a self at all, there is a possibility of putting yourself first—wanting to be the center—wanting to be God, in fact."[1] While on the surface, I focused this past year on the hollow-

---

I have recognized that rather than the hollowing, I should choose to see the hallowing, the opportunity "to make pure and holy" that the Lord has offered me.

---

ing, in retrospect, all I was truly focusing on was myself, my plans, and my future that was not meant to be. As I embark on this process again, I am reminded that God must be at the helm of my life. Not only will He direct me, but in His grace He gives me the peace that "all things shall give [me] experience, and shall work for [my] good" (D&C 122:7), that these miscarriages were not losses of life experience, but additions purposefully placed in my path. As I submit my own will, God will light the better way. In volunteering my plans, He will ennoble a greater purpose.

It is a delicate balance. The very act of my surrender feels like an emptying, the hollowing I fear. I must remain vigilant to prevent fear from filling what I viewed in the past as a void. As I leave that space for the Lord, for Him to fill me with His grace and purpose, I grow to be what He wants me to be. So rather than a hollow space I crave filling with another pregnancy, I know the Lord can make me whole and hallowed with whatever experiences He sees fit to bless me. Though I know that the physical pain will be great, I think of the beautiful insight I gained two weeks ago from this powerful prose I've sung hundreds of times, from "Nearer my God to Thee":

> Nearer my God to Thee, Nearer to Thee.
> E'en though it be a cross that raiseth me.

It is our personal crosses that raise us heavenward, that minimize the chasm between our ways and God's ways. Though the pain is often great to bear, it acquaints us with the divine—both that which is directing us and that which is within each of us. And with that acquaintance, born of the Spirit, I am never truly hollow. A beautiful knowledge to gain this All Hallow's Eve.

Prayer
and the Lord's Tender Mercies

by S. Westover

WHEN MY HUSBAND first started having health difficulties, I was four months pregnant with our second child. At the time it all seemed to happen so slowly, but in retrospect, it really flew past us. Before we knew it we learned we were expecting a boy a soon-to–be-born son. Never before had my prayers been so sincere as they were that summer.

I couldn't understand why Heavenly Father would take a good, hard working father from a happy family. I can't say that I understand it now either. However, through this I knew that I needed my Heavenly Father more than anything. People were so kind and loving but the only One who could bring me comfort was the Lord. I knew where I could turn for peace, and He was always there. It was in these trying times that I was humbled and blessed by my Heavenly Father.

I was given a lot of advice from caring people. One person gave me a book about a woman who had been in a similar situation. In this woman's book, she recounted several experiences where she saw and even had conversations with her late husband. This gave me hope. I kept waiting for my turn to have an experience like hers. I never did have an experience like that, but I did have an experience that let me know my Heavenly Father and then learned that my husband was in need of a bone marrow transplant.

We felt confident and positive throughout the process. Even up until the day he died, we were optimistic. Now I look back and see that we may have actually been in denial. I suddenly found myself a single mother of a twenty-one-month-old daughter and knew what I needed.

In the last moments of labor and pushing, I suddenly came to the realization that my late husband was there. I could feel his hand on my arm and I could feel his presence in the room. I knew if I turned my head to look I wouldn't see him. But I didn't need to see him because I could feel him and that was good enough for me. In that bittersweet time of my life, my Heavenly Father blessed me with the most tender of mercies.

Sixteen Pregnancies

by Sarah Bobo

WHEN ASKED WHAT I WANTED TO BE WHEN I GREW UP, I never had to think for a second. I wanted to be a mother, and I wanted many children. I was twenty and my husband was twenty-two when we got married. Many people tried to convince us that we should wait to have children and spend some time as just as couple. After much discussion, prayer and many blessings, we felt the Spirit strongly prompting us. We knew we should not prevent pregnancy.

Right after we married, I found out I was pregnant but immediately miscarried. It was devastating to us as newlyweds; however, because it was such an early miscarriage, I did not think of it as a problem. Yet as the months went on, I noticed that my periods were irregular. I was devastated as each pregnancy test showed only one line, reminding me that, yet again, the dearest desire of my heart was not mine. Everyone around me was pregnant or had young babies, and it was a difficult reminder of what I didn't have. I was truly happy for my friends and family members, but there were times that I was struggling too much to be around them.

That year was very difficult for me. I turned to the Lord to help me. I knew that His strength was the only thing that could get me through such a difficult time. When I felt discouraged, I would pray for help and every time I was granted peace and strength from my Heavenly Father. I also received blessings from my husband, my home teachers, and good friends. We prayed together as a couple, and it helped us to gain strength and feel at peace.

After that first year, we were so excited to be pregnant again. Shortly after we found out, the unthinkable happened, and I miscarried again sending me into a downward spiral. I was jealous, depressed, and angry. I cried and yelled. I didn't understand why this was happening to me.

Over the course of the first four and half years of our marriage, my husband and I suffered through nine miscarriages, some as early as five weeks and others as late as eleven weeks. I went through very dark times, becoming very depressed. I was just going through the motions of things. I shut everything and everyone—including the Lord—out. I went through the motions of being a wife, sister, daughter, friend, Primary teacher, student, everything that I was supposed to be. But I felt lost and desperate. I loved my husband, but I felt that I was failing him.

For the first three years, none of the doctors we saw could figure out what was wrong. They would write off my miscarriages and struggles to conceive as unexplained infertility. We felt prompted to move. We found an apartment in a small town just south of where we currently lived and knew immediately that it was where we needed to be.

Every time we drove up to our new apartment, we passed by a doctor's office. I was prompted to call and get an appointment with a doctor at that office even though all of the doctors there were family practice physicians. I wasn't sure what they were going to be able to do for me. When I called I was not sure which doctor I wanted to see. As the receptionist listed their names for me, one stuck out. It was John Taylor, just like the Prophet. I knew that was the doctor I needed to see. At my appointment a few days later, I explained my problems to Dr. Taylor. He listened closely. Then he said that he knew part of what was causing my fertility problems and pregnancy loss.

After four and a half years of infertility, I found out I was pregnant for the tenth time. I struggled with gestational diabetes, preeclampsia, and preterm labor during my pregnancy. With the help of medications, close monitoring, and bed rest, we had our first daughter not long after our fifth wedding anniversary. The spirit was strong as I labored and delivered my daughter. After all that we had been through we finally held our precious daughter in our arms. The Spirit was strong enough that even our doctor, who was also LDS, was touched. We finally were able to provide one of Heavenly Father's spirit children with a body and a family on this Earth.

Since that time, I have struggled through four more miscarriages but have also been blessed with two more beautiful children. My pregnancies are difficult, and my children have come at thirty-seven, thirty-three and thirty-one weeks, the last two spending many weeks in the NICU after they were born. Through all of our trials, my husband and I were constantly reminded of the amazing blessings our children are. We are grateful that we were able to grow stronger and closer to the Lord in our struggles to bring them into our family.

Healing from Traumatic Birth

By Sheridan Ripley, CD(DONA), HCHI

Women who have experienced a traumatic birth usually need special support. Friends and family are often not aware of how to provide this help. My first birth was an unexpected emergency cesarean section at thirty-four weeks. It was scary and traumatic for me, my husband, and my baby. Some of my friends felt that I was blowing things out of proportion. My baby was born, and my baby and I were both fine, so what was the big deal? I thought maybe I was crazy until I read a speech by Michael T. Hynan, PhD. He explained:

> During a high-risk birth the crazy, mixed-up feelings of . . . parents are a natural and normal reaction to incredible stress. When I talk to groups of high-risk parents, I feel like I am addressing a meeting of the veterans of the baby wars. If you have been in the life and death battlefield of the NICU, you are going to be disorganized and upset for months—some of us for years.

> We feel crazy, and we want to return to normal quickly. But that is the worst thing we can try to do, because we can't stop or reverse the natural, healing process of our emotional reactions without doing damage to ourselves. The only things that are normal for high- risk parents are terror, grief, impotence, and anger (plus assorted other feelings like guilt, frustration, jealousy, and intense fatigue). And experiencing these lousy emotions are signs that we parents are doing well, not poorly.[1]

What I had experienced was traumatic; therefore, it was natural that I would feel traumatized. It wasn't fun, but it was important to process what had happened to me. I found outside support and continued the healing process. I will be honest and admit that it took almost ten years to heal and to come to a point where I could completely enjoy his birthday without remembering it with sadness.

WHAT IS A TRAUMATIC BIRTH?

What may be traumatic to one mom might be okay to another. Some births are obviously traumatic. Other births may seem normal, but the mother is still traumatized by the experience. If a mother perceives the birth as traumatic, then it is traumatic. If a mother has a previous history of abuse, she may be more likely to experience a traumatic birth. She should get extra support and alert her care providers so that they can be sensitive to her situation.

Support will help a mother through the healing process and stages of grief, outlined below. Note that these stages do not always happen in the following order and a person may pass through the stage more than once.

1 Shock and denial: Sometimes during birth (or immediately after), a mother is in a state of shock, totally unable to believe what has just happened to her. She may even deny that the birth was traumatic at first. This is to help her survive the experience.

2 Pain and guilt: As the shock fades away, a mother may begin to feel overwhelmed by the pain (physical, mental, or emotional) from her birth experience.

3 Anger and bargaining: A mother may look for somewhere to place the blame for what happened—on herself or others. She may ask, "What if I had only done this?" or "What if the doctor had done this instead?"

4 Depression, reflection, and loneliness: Sometimes just when others think a mother should be getting past her birth experience, she might enter into a state of sad reflection, remembering with sadness the events that happened. She may feel very lonely, that no one under-stands or cares what she has been through. This stage is a normal part of grief, so it is important that a mother feels heard during this time. Listening and empathy will help a mother feel understood and help

her move to the next step on her own time.

5 Reconstruction and working through: It can be helpful for a mother to review her birth experience with someone who can help her see it from the perspectives of all of the people who were making choices for her and her baby. This review can help her work through the emotions she is feeling. Talking with others who were there or requesting copies of the medical records will enable the mother to process what happened. Be aware that revisiting the experience can bring some people peace but can be upsetting for other people.

6 Acceptance and hope: Even when we learn to accept and deal with what happened during a birth, it doesn't mean we will be happy about it. But it is a place to move forward from—hoping for a better experience for the next birth.

Traumatic births are on the rise as many mothers have less support from their care providers. It is important to honor and respect mothers as they birth their babies. Understanding that having a traumatic birth is something that may require extra support and time to heal can help both a mother and the people who surround her. If a woman has a traumatic birth, it is not her fault.

IF YOU HAVE HAD A TRAUMATIC BIRTH

- It is okay to feel sad or disappointed after a traumatic birth. It is okay to grieve the loss of the birth you desired.

- Talk—find a friend, family member, or therapist (trained in birth issues) who will listen unconditionally. If you are able to process your experiences, you will move through the stages of grief more quickly.

- Hypnotherapy and the emotional freedom technique are great tools for letting go of trauma.

- Use online resources to help you find other women dealing with similar emotions. You can easily find a group that can empathize with your experience.

- Don't put a time limit on your healing. Allow yourself to grieve, and know that if you continue to move forward and work through your experience, healing will come.

- Pray for help in healing physically, emotionally, and spiritually. Ask other people to pray for you.

- Ask for a priesthood blessing.

WHAT FAMILY MEMBERS AND FRIENDS CAN DO

- Remember that birth can be a life-changing experience, whether it be positive or negative. Supporting mothers with love will help them through a traumatic birth.

- Don't assume a mother is upset about parts of her birth or that she is happy about other parts. You could ask her, "How do you feel about your birth?" Or say, "Tell me what happened."

- Listen—don't verbalize your emotions. Even if her baby is okay, don't say, "At least your baby is okay." Of course the mother is happy that her baby is okay, but that doesn't make what happened to her okay. Certainly I would choose to have another emergency cesarean to save my child, but it was still the scariest day of my life.

- Be open to what the mother is willing to share. Don't judge her emotions or what she says. It is her reality, and she just needs support. What she experienced may not seem traumatic to you, but it was to her.

- Ask open-ended questions, and listen to the answers. Then paraphrase what she said to see whether you understand what she is trying to communicate.

- Let her know that it is okay to be sad, angry, or whatever she is feeling. Survivors of trauma just want to be heard and understood.

- Know that it can take a long time for some mothers to deal with their experiences. Don't put a time limit on their need to grieve. If you are concerned it is taking a long time, suggest some resources[2] where they can find additional support.

- Some things you can say:

  "I'm so sorry."

  "It sounds like you made the best choice you could given the circumstances."

  "I'm happy to listen whenever you feel the need to talk."

Why is it so important to be aware of mothers who have had traumatic births? Satan can use this vulnerable time to influence mothers. I know mothers who have had traumatic births and then refused to have another baby even when they felt prompted to have another. Their fear kept them from moving forward. Ideally, with proper education and support, very few women would ever have a traumatic birth. In the meantime, it is important to facilitate healing. Letting go of fear and moving forward with faith can be healing in many ways. It can allow a family to be open to the possibility of more children and more joy in their posterity. Please visit this book's website to learn more about what women can do to prevent a traumatic birth.

---

1   M. T. Hynan, "Helping Parents Cope with a High-Risk Birth: Terror, Grief, Impotence, and Anger (paper presented at meeting of the National Perinatal Association, Nashville, TN, November 10, 1996), https://pantherfile.uwm.edu/hynan/www/MINNAEP.html.

2   Helpful online resources include the Solace for Mothers website (http://www.solaceformothers.org) and the International Cesarean Awareness Network website (www.ican-online.org).

CHAPTER ELEVEN

Unity

I say unto you, be one;
and if ye are not one, ye are not mine.

D&C 38:27

Strengthening Marriage
during Pregnancy and Beyond

By Felice Austin, CHt

Husband and wife have a solemn responsibility
to love and care for each other.[1]

THE FAMILY: A PROCLAMATION TO THE WORLD

HELP MEET

When God created the earth and man, He said, "It is not good for the man to be alone, I will make an help meet for him" (Genesis 2:18). The phrase "help meet" (Hebrew *'ezer kanegdo*) is an interesting one. When I was pregnant, I felt inspired to take a Hebrew class, and from this introduction to Hebrew, I came to understand how much of the richness and the many-layered and poetic meanings of Hebrew words and phrases are lost in translation. For example, in the phrase "help meet," *'ezer*, which in this context is translated as "help" (or helper) has the English connotation of an assistant of lesser status. However, in Hebrew, the word implies an equal if not a superior status. In fact, in other places in the Old Testament, God is an *'ezer* to man. Jolene Edmunds Rockwood, in her article "The Redemption of Eve," stated, "A more accurate translation in this context would be 'strength' or 'power.'"[2]

The second part of the word, which is translated as "meet" in Hebrew means "fit for" and has roots in the Hebrew word for "equal to."[3] Thus, the phrase "help meet" could read "power or strength equal to." This translation is corroborated by the Joseph Smith Translation of Genesis 2:18, which reads, "A helper suited to, worthy of, or corresponding to him." Thus, we learn that men and women were created to be equal partners and strengths to one another.

If this is your first pregnancy, chances are that up until now, your and your husband's marital roles were similar. With pregnancy, however, many things may need to change or be reevaluated. These changes can put stress on the strongest relationships. Nurturing a marriage during this time is crucial to your future success and happiness.

"Men and women joined together in marriage need to work together as a full partnership. However, a full and equal partnership between men and women does not imply the roles played by the two sexes are the same in God's grand design for His children."[4]

—M. Russell Ballard

BONE OF MY BONE AND FLESH OF MY FLESH

Upon Adam being presented with Eve, I like to imagine that Adam's reaction was one of surprise and delight. He then said, "This is now bone of my bone and flesh of my flesh" (Genesis 2:23). Rockwood stated:

In Hebrew, these phrases indicate a closeness, a blood relationship between the two parties, and in this case a unified companionship between the man and the woman. But the phrases are also used in other places in the Old Testament to describe two parties who are not necessarily blood relatives but who have made a covenant with each other.[5]

What is also interesting is that *bone* in Hebrew symbolizes power, and *flesh* symbolizes weakness. Rockwood explained, "Bone of my bones and flesh of my flesh thus becomes a ritual pledge to be bound in the best of circumstances (power) as well as the worst (weakness)."[6] Adam's use of it here is similar to the words of the modern day marriage vow, which requires commitment "for better or for worse."[7] Depending on your circumstances, you may experience pregnancy in sickness or in health, for better or for worse. For many couples, pregnancy is the first true test of these vows.

Genesis 2:24 describes God laying out the marriage covenant for Adam and Eve's posterity: "Therefore shall a man leave his father and his mother and shall cleave unto his wife and they shall be one flesh." Cleaving to your spouse means not only remaining with him but also being unified in action and decision making.

The scriptures tell us that when Eve made her decision to partake of the fruit, Adam was *with her*. "[Eve] gave also unto her husband *with her*, and he did eat" (Genesis 3:6; emphasis added). Whether or not he was physically beside her when she took the fruit doesn't matter—what matters is that Adam and Eve were united. As we know, Eve's decision was not just to eat to become wise; hers was a thoughtful, brave decision to fulfill her mission on the earth—to be the mother of all living.

Though most of this book is about becoming parents and the importance of children in God's plan, Genesis 2:24 reminds us that the ultimate end of God's plan is about couples. Ideally, all of our children will find spouses and leave us to cleave unto them. And in the next life, though we may be bound through sealing powers, we will not be living in families of six or eight, but in married couples. This doctrinal foundation can also be found in D&C 49:16: "It is lawful that he should have one wife, and they twain shall be one flesh, and all this that the earth might answer the end of its creation."

Keeping sight of this goal amid the day-to-day struggles of raising a family may be a challenge but *can* be done successfully. Elder Russel M. Nelson stated that marriage brings greater possibilities for happiness than does any other relationship. In his April 2006 general conference address, Elder Nelson suggested specific actions to strengthen marriage and make it more joyful. I have chosen to elaborate on Elder Nelson's three action verbs—*appreciate, communicate,* and *contemplate*—to structure the information below.[8]

APPRECIATE

Elder Russell M. Nelson taught the following:

To say "I love you" and "thank you"—is not difficult. But these expressions of love and appreciation do more than acknowledge a kind thought or deed. They are signs of sweet civility. As grateful partners look for the good in each other and sincerely pay compliments to one another, wives and husbands will strive to become the persons described in those compliments.[9]

Returning to the Joseph Smith Translation of "help meet," in Genesis 2:18 we read "a helper suited to, worth of or corresponding to him." Notice that the translation does not say corresponding *with* him—which would mean they were identical—but rather corresponding *to* him. *Corresponding to* is defined as "associated in a working or other relationship: *a bolt and its corresponding nut.*"[10]

Often couples believe that their similarities far outweigh their differences. However, over time, couples may discover that they think and behave in opposite ways. While some of this may be gender related, it is not always helpful to generalize based on gender. The reality is that we are wired by God to be attracted to those who are most complementary

The Importance of Appreciation—The Rice Experiment

In response to the discoveries of Japanese scientist Masaru Emoto about the ability of words and pictures to transform the properties of water, one family in Japan decided to perform an experiment. This experiment was later published and repeated by families all over Japan with the same results.

The family placed rice in two glass jars, and for a month the entire family said, "Thank you," to one jar and, "You fool," to the other. "After a month, the rice that was told 'thank you' started to ferment, with a mellow smell like that of malt, while the rice that was exposed to 'you fool,' rotted and turned black."[1]

Later, a third jar of rice was added to the experiment, which was simply ignored. This rice actually rotted faster than the rice that was given negative attention.

1   Masaru Emoto, *The Hidden Messages in Water* (New York: Atria, 2001), 65.

to us, which can sometimes feel like oppositeness. If you could float up out of your body for a moment and view your relationship with perspective, you might see that your partner's strengths fill in areas you may lack and vice versa. For example, while one of you might be more logic ruled or have trouble expressing emotion, the other may be more emotionally ruled and love to touch and hug and express. Both logic and emotion are necessary in the relationship. The trouble comes, however, when we judge each other based on our own behavior and allow feelings of rejection to compound. When we learn to accept and appreciate our differences, frustrations decrease and joy can abound.

COMMUNICATE

Elder Nelson's recommendations about communication are in italics below.[11] Under each of his recommendations, I have included couples' comments that relate to continuing courtship and improving communication in the marriage relationship while preparing for birth.

"Good communication includes taking time to plan together. Couples need private time to observe, to talk, and really listen to each other."

- We were getting so busy, we sometimes didn't even see each other in a day. So, in addition to a weekly date, we scheduled in a fifteen-minute chat every day. Some days it is early in the morning, but we just do it. Only on certain days are we allowed to talk about money and scheduling. The rest of the time, we talk about ideas and feelings and we take turns listening.

- We take turns planning dates that are conducive to talking.

- We planned a last-hurrah "just us" trip when I was in my second trimester.

- My midwife told me that if I walked fives miles/day my baby would slide out of me, so I made my husband walk with me. The weather was nice, and in the evening it is somewhat magical. As we walked, we talked, and refell in love.

- My husband played along with me and made birth art. He actually really enjoyed it, and it was fun to hear his explanation of his art.

- We went to counseling to work on our communication. My sister is a therapist, and she said that too often people go to marriage counseling when things are beyond repair, so we decided to not wait till then. We learned great tools we still use.

- We spent time reading birth books to each other, especially when we had to spend a long period of time travelling in the car.

"They need to cooperate—helping each other as equal partners."

- My husband is not very handy, but I was so big I couldn't play carpenter, so he put the crib together while I read the directions, and we actually managed quite nicely. He had a great sense of accomplishment about it.

- When my husband saw how much there was to do, he just jumped in and did more. He knew I couldn't do it all alone.

"They need to nurture their spiritual as well as physical intimacy."

- When President Hinckley challenged everyone to read The Book of Mormon by the end of the year, it really got us motivated. Reading the scriptures together every day brought us so much closer.

- When I wasn't at all interested in sex, I was still interested in foot rubs. So, every night we took turns giving each other foot rubs—and the funny thing is, it usually got me more interested in sex. We also used the foot rub time to talk about our changing sexual identities and fears.

- At night, we lay together in bed and breathed in an out in unison, and many nights my husband would practice various relaxation techniques with me. Pregnancy turned out to be pretty doggone romantic.

"They should strive to elevate and motivate each other."

- We took a complete childbirth education course together that was highly recommended by a friend. It was a ton of fun, and we enjoyed practicing at home.

- We took turns writing in the baby journal we bought. It was nice to read what my husband wrote every other day. His words of love and encouragement uplifted me, and I think the baby felt them too.

- Serving each other and others motivates us. We made sure to always look for opportunities, especially while pregnant before the baby came. This got us ready to serve the new little spirit.

"Marital unity is sustained when goals are mutually understood."

- We keep a goals-and-dreams chart, where we list our goals and dreams and rate them by importance.

- We were both familiar with our list of birth preferences.

- One thing that helped us is when we realized that in order to reach our goals we needed to state them in positive terms. For example, rather than making our goal "to avoid traumatic birth," we stated it as "to enjoy a comfortable, peaceful birth experience that will promote even more love and intimacy."

"Good communication is also enhanced by prayer. To pray with specific mention of a spouse's good deed (or need) nurtures a marriage."

- We make sure to kiss after every prayer we say together.

- When we're traveling apart, we try to say prayers at the same time. It is strange, but I can feel when he's praying for me.

- I never get tired of hearing him thank Heavenly Father for his beautiful, amazing wife.

- In our own prayers, we expressed gratitude for each other and made specific mention of our needs and concerns regarding the birth of our child.

WHAT TO TALK ABOUT

Successfully transitioning from couplehood to parenthood requires more than just a hopeful wish. In a study of 250 couples from the wife's third trimester to the baby's third birthday, researchers Belsky and Kelly, who wrote *The Transition to Parenthood: How a First Child Changes a Marriage*, found that 51 percent of marriages declined after the first baby, 30 percent experienced no change, and 19 percent improved. The researchers identified several of the characteristics of the improvers: "Most important in facilitating a husband's and wife's smooth passage through the transition included the ability to surrender individual goals and needs and work together as a team."[12]

The researchers identified five issues about which new parents disagree most:

1 Division of labor
2 Money
3 Work
4 The couple's relationship (e.g., which spouse is to blame for disconnection or stress)
5 Social life (e.g., whether they are going out enough)

Pam England and Rob Horowitz, authors of *Birthing from Within*, added a sixth big issue, based on their clinical experience: *in-laws*. The hard truth is that one or both of you may need to reevaluate painful loyalty conflicts between your family of origin and your new family. If this is the case, you may want to contemplate the Lord's words to Adam and Eve: "Therefore shall a man leave his father and his mother and shall cleave unto his wife and they shall be one flesh" (Genesis 2:24).

In their chapter titled "Baby Proofing Your Marriage," England and Horowitz recommended making a postpartum adjustment plan, which includes brainstorming possible issues and solutions and listing small first steps. On The Gift of Giving Life website, you will find a simple example of such a plan, which we hope you will find useful. "Quite simply," summarized Belsky and Kelly, "couples who manage to resolve these issues in a mutually satisfactory way become happier with their marriage, whereas those who do not become unhappier."[13] Thus, good communication equals more happiness in marriage after the baby comes.

CONTEMPLATE

Elder Nelson taught the following about contemplation:

> This word has deep meaning. It comes from Latin roots: *con*, meaning "with," and *templum*, meaning "a space or place to meditate." It is the root from which the word *temple* comes. If couples contemplate often—with each other in the temple—sacred covenants will be better remembered and kept. Frequent participation in temple service and regular family scripture study nourish a marriage and strengthen faith within a family. Contemplation allows one to anticipate and to resonate (or be in tune) with each other and with the Lord. Contemplation will nurture both a marriage and God's kingdom.[14]

As Elder Nelson explained, contemplation is one of the many words that indicate meditation. Meditation in the Lord's house frequently is ideal, as is meditating in your home. As we learn in the Bible Dictionary, "only the home can compare with the temple in sacredness." If your home is not already a templum—a place or space to meditate—then join efforts with your husband to make it so.

As I described on page 199 of the chapter titled "Meditation," meditation is a set of principles and practices that invite the Spirit of the Lord. The power of this Holy Spirit should not be underestimated, especially as it relates to strengthening marriage. The Spirit is the binding agent in the universe. It is by the Holy Spirit of Promise that we are sealed in celestial marriage and eternal families. Elder Parley P. Pratt described the effects of making the Holy Spirit fully present in our lives:

> [The Holy Ghost] quickens all the intellectual faculties, increases, enlarges, expands and purifies all the natural passions and affections and adapts them, by the gift of wisdom, to their lawful use. It inspires, develops, cultivates, and matures all the fine-toned sympathies, joys, tastes, kindness, goodness, tenderness, gentleness, and charity. It develops beauty of person, form, and features. It tends to health, vigor, animation, and social feeling. It invigorates all the faculties of the physical and intellectual man. In short, it is, as it were, marrow to the bone, joy to the heart, light to the eyes, music to the ears, and life to the whole being.[15]

If the spark, passion, or tenderness has gone out of your marriage, it is time to invite the Spirit back in. There are many different ways to enjoy meditating as a couple. I highly recommend reading the "Meditation" chapter with your husband and instituting a daily practice of meditation. As Christ taught us, when we seek first to build up the kingdom of God and to establish His righteousness, "all these things shall be added unto you" (Luke 12:30–31).

OUR PERFECT EXAMPLE

As Latter-day Saints, we know that marriage is an essential part of God's plan of happiness, yet it is easy to become disheartened when couples you once admired split up. You may wonder who, if anyone, you can look to as an example. In Doctrine and Covenants 52:14, we read the Lord's answer: "I will give unto you a pattern in all things, that ye may not be deceived." The Lord *has* given us patterns to follow—they are in the Bible, the Book of Mormon, the Doctrine and Covenants, the Pearl of Great Price, "The Family: A Proclamation to the World," and the temple ceremonies. If you read the scriptures and attend the temple prayerfully, you will find the answers and patterns you need, so that you will not be deceived. This is a process that you may need to repeat over an over again as your marriage and family circumstances change.

Despite how well we know our spouses when we marry, we cannot predict what the journey will bring. Marriage is a condition of agency. If you are married to a nonmember or to a spouse who as become inactive, there is also a pattern for you. In 1 Corinthians 7:13–16, we read the following words of Paul:

> And the woman which hath an husband that believeth not, and if he be pleased to dwell with her, let her not leave him. For the unbelieving husband is sanctified by the wife and the unbelieving wife is sanctified by the husband: else were your children unclean; but now they are holy. . . . For what knowest thou, O wife, whether thou shalt save thy husband? Or how knowest thou, O Man, whether thou shalt save thy wife?

However, regardless of your spouse's status in or out of the Church, if you are being abused or think you are being abused (it is usually hard to tell because abuse turns us upside down in many ways), I invite you to read the resources on The Gift of Giving Life's website about abuse and to counsel with your bishop or Relief Society president immediately. They have resources that can help you. The most important thing is to make sure that you and your baby are removed from physical and psychological harm as soon as possible so that you may begin to heal. Heavenly Father has no tolerance for abuse. "The Family: A Proclamation to the World" warns that "individuals who violate covenants of chastity, who abuse spouse or offspring, or who fail to fulfill family responsibilities will one day stand accountable before God."[16]

As Elder Nelson and others have observed: "Each marriage starts with two built-in handicaps. It involves two imperfect people."[17] This

412

understatement returns us to the subject of our first parents. Adam and Eve made the unified decision and "fell" from their perfect state so that humankind might be. Flaws, fears, vulnerability, pain, and sin are conditions of mortal life—as are pleasure, victory, and love. Adam and Eve may have begun just as naive as any newlywed couple when they set out into the world outside of Eden. They looked forward to parenthood, but neither had earthly parents or previous experiences to draw upon and no books to read. Yet as they faced each new unknown, they had knowledge of the plan of happiness and the doctrine of the Atonement.

As followers of the gospel of Jesus Christ, we can use Christ as our ultimate example of how to have a happy marriage. Though we don't know much about Christ's marriage or about our Heavenly Parents' marriage, we know that Christ is the perfect example for both men and women in all things. Couples will achieve more and more happiness as they learn about the life of Jesus Christ and embrace the advice in 2 Nephi 31:12: "Follow me, and do the things which ye have seen me do."

1 The Church of Jesus Christ of Latter-day Saints, "The Family: A Proclamation to the World," *Ensign*, November 1995, http://lds.org/ensign/1995/11/the-family-a-proclamation-to-the-world.
2 Jolene Edmunds Rockwood, "The Redemption of Eve," in *Sisters in Spirit: Mormon Women in Historical and Cultural Perspective*, ed. Maureen Ursenbach Beecher and Lavina Anderson (Chicago: University of Illinois Press, 1992), 18.
3 Ibid.
4 M. Russel Ballard, "The Sacred Responsibility of Parenthood," *Liahona*, March 2006, http://lds.org/liahona/2006/03/the-sacred-responsibilities-of-parenthood.
5 Jolene Edmunds Rockwood, "The Redemption of Eve," in *Sisters in Spirit: Mormon Women in Historical and Cultural Perspective*, ed. Maureen Ursenbach Beecher and Lavina Anderson (Chicago: University of Illinois Press, 1992), 18.
6 Ibid.
7 Ibid.
8 Russell M. Nelson, "Nurturing Marriage," *Ensign*, April 2006, http://lds.org/general-conference/2006/04/nurturing-marriage.
9 Ibid.
10 Dictionary.com, s.v. "corresponding," http://dictionary.reference.com/browse/corresponding.
11 Russell M. Nelson, "Nurturing Marriage," *Ensign*, April 2006, http://lds.org/general-conference/2006/04/nurturing-marriage.
12 In Pam England and Rob Horowitz, *Birthing from Within* (Albuquerque, NM: Partera, 1998), 261.
13 Ibid.
14 Russell M. Nelson, "Nurturing Marriage," *Ensign*, April 2006, http://lds.org/general-conference/2006/04/nurturing-marriage.
15 Parley P. Pratt, *Key to the Science of Theology*, 9th ed. (Salt Lake City, UT: Desert Book, 1965), 101.
16 The Church of Jesus Christ of Latter-day Saints, "The Family: A Proclamation to the World," *Ensign*, November 1995, http://lds.org/ensign/1995/11/the-family-a-proclamation-to-the-world.
17 Russell M. Nelson, "Celestial Marriage," *Ensign*, November 2008, http://lds.org/general-conference/2008/10/celestial-marriage.

WORKING TOGETHER

By Jamie Wagner

MY HUSBAND, JOSH, wasn't present for the birth of his younger sister, but the way his mother talked about the birth as being a beautiful, powerful experience really stuck with him. So much that when I did get pregnant, he was the one to reassure me that birth wasn't something to be afraid of and that I could birth in whatever way we felt was best for me and the baby.

We wanted to go for an unmedicated birth with a midwife's assistance but that was, in reality, pretty frightening for me. I've always been afraid of the unknown to a huge extent—even to the point of literally shaking at dentist appointments. The idea was incredibly frightening, but Josh continued to show his confidence in me being able to give birth the way we wanted. I didn't realize at the time, but really he was telling me that it wouldn't be just me giving birth to our son, it would be *us*. I was not alone. This was our experience.

In the wee hours of the morning on April 14, I woke up in the hospital having contractions. (I had been prepped for an induction the previous morning due to preeclampsia symptoms.) I called for Josh, and he stayed by my side from that moment. He was always there, prompting me to relax and focus. He was the one I literally leaned on during each contraction. His voice was calm, and he quickly adjusted to my every request (more water, no whispering in my ear, stay there) and was always ready to give me a blessing should I request it. He just served me. I didn't feel smothered or captive to what he thought was best. I felt comfortable and loved and knew that, no matter what, he was there. All of his attention was on me and our son.

That hasn't changed. I believe that because we were both active participants in our son's birth, we have grown closer together in every family decision. We were both part of a significantly spiritual event, bringing our son into the world, welcoming him into our eternal family, and forging him into our family link. Happiness and unity in family life come from working together for a common purpose. Our son's birth is just one example, one that has changed our marriage and family forever.

A Sweetness I Never Expected

By Kelley B.

SEVERAL MONTHS BEFORE I GOT PREGNANT with my last child, a little girl, my then four-year-old son asked me where babies come from. I wasn't prepared with a pat answer, so I just shot from the hip and told it to him straight. I also told him that he'd be welcome to be there at the birth of our next baby. This really got him excited, and for the next several months I kept getting questions about when I was going to get another baby in my belly so he could watch it be born.

The pregnancy was not a pleasant one. I was miserably sick at the beginning (for the first time in four pregnancies) and in excruciating pain at the end. Around my sixth month, we moved to a different state, and I quickly found another midwife. We bonded immediately. She helped me cope through the last three very difficult months of my pregnancy, for which I was deeply grateful.

As I neared the end of my pregnancy, I began to worry about how I was going to handle having three rambunctious boys around me while I was in labor. I had never had my children present at my other births. I was also getting some really strange looks when I'd tell friends that my sons were going to watch the birth. I decided to brush off everybody else's opinions, and just focus on what I knew was right—that my boys needed to be there.

Finally the day we'd all been waiting for came. I started having contractions at about 3:00 in the morning, but managed to sleep through them off and on. They weren't too terribly frequent or intense by morning when everyone got up, so I took the kids to a birthday party at a nearby park.

Next came the part I had been mildly dreading—at home, taking care of my three kids by myself for a few hours while I was in labor. Fortunately, my boys took great naps, then played quietly (totally out of character for them, I should add) while I labored on a birth ball in our living room. My husband came home, and all four of them took very good care of me. They

---

My husband came home, and all four of them took very good care of me. They were gentle and kind, and I was truly surprised at how sweet the experience was turning out to be.

---

were gentle and kind, and I was truly surprised at how sweet the experience was turning out to be.

Fast forward a few hours. My boys were starting to get very excited, so my husband brought them to a nearby park. After my midwife showed up, I made myself a peanut butter smoothie, and we talked for a few minutes. After I finished, we went into the bedroom so she could check me.

What happened next was a total surprise to both of us. My cervix was positioned far enough back that she could barely reach it. I was about 4 cm and very stretchy. She lightly tugged on the edge during a contraction (they are inevitable when you're getting checked). I immediately opened up to about 10 cm and my baby's head came down right to her hand! She jumped up, and started getting things ready for the birth very quickly! I had her call my husband and tell him to get home immediately while I knelt on my hands and knees and vocalized through a few more contractions.

By the time they all arrived a couple minutes later, I was positioned on a birth ball at the side of my bed and pushing with all my might. My husband and our sons stood at the door of our room getting a full view of the action, but I didn't mind a bit. At one point, I remember my youngest son (the three and a half year old) telling his brother that the baby was going to come out Mommy's special hole in her bottom. Even though I was working hard, I just had to smile at that dear little voice saying such an innocent and funny thing. A few minutes later, my beautiful daughter was born, and my husband and boys saw every bit of it.

I will be eternally grateful that I trusted myself and my boys enough to have them at the birth. My almost six year old said some very special things about the birth later, even though he did admit to thinking it was just a little gross (boys *will* be boys!). All of them adore their sister. She was every bit as much their baby as she was my baby. I was pleasantly surprised at how delightful and sweet it was having my children there, and being able to hear their thoughtful comments and charming voices in the background. It is an experience I will always cherish, a moment when we truly became a family all together at last.

A Father's Sacred Support

By Lani Axman

In chapter 44 of the book of Alma, Moroni commanded the Lamanite leader Zerahemnah and his armies to cease attacking the Nephites and to go their way in peace. Moroni pled in the name of God, by their faith, by their religion and rites of worship, by their church, and "by the *sacred support* which we owe to our wives and our children" (Alma 44:5; emphasis added). While most modern husbands are spared the duty of protecting their wives from enemy armies and bloodshed, their sacred support is still a necessity.

As the adversary attacks marriages and families with increasing intensity, fathers have perhaps an even greater task before them than Moroni and his armies had. How can husbands protect their wives and marriages during the sometimes emotional and trying journey of pregnancy and parenthood? How can fathers provide the sacred support their wives and soon-to-be children need?

PRECONCEPTION AND PREGNANCY

Each of us is given personal revelation based upon our responsibilities and stewardships. Women's bodies were specifically designed to become sacred vessels for the Lord's spirit children. As such, women are entitled to receive revelation pertaining to the use of their bodies for childbearing. President David O. McKay counseled, "Let us instruct our young people who come to us . . . to know that a woman should be queen of her own body."[1] A father can provide sacred support to his wife by honoring the revelations she receives regarding her body's childbearing purposes.

Samson's father, Manoah, is a good example of this kind of support. Manoah's wife was infertile for some time. We don't know how long she was barren, but eventually an angel of the Lord appeared to her and said, "Thou shalt conceive, and bear a son" (Judges 13:3, 5). The angel also told her "the child shall be a Nazarite unto God from the womb" (Judges 13:5). After her visit with the angel, she ran and told her husband what she had learned. Manoah immediately started to entreat the Lord that He would

---

"Unity comes by following the light from above. It does not come out of the confusions below. While men depend upon their own wisdom and walk in their own way, without guidance of the Lord they cannot live in unity. Neither can they come to a unity by following uninspired men... The way to unity is for us to learn the will of the Lord and then to do it."[2] —Marion G. Romney

---

"teach us what we shall do unto the child that shall be born" (Judges 13:8). Manoah had faith that his wife had received divine revelation concerning her pregnancy and her baby, and he was supportive of what she had told him. Manoah provides an excellent role model for fathers seeking to provide sacred support to their wives in preparation for pregnancy and birth.

BIRTHING TIME

Fathers can play a unique and powerful role in the birth process. While most of the people tending to a laboring woman have her best interests at heart and are working to ensure her safety and the safety of her baby, a father is likely the only person present who knows her intimately and loves her deeply. He is also the only person who has contributed part of himself to give life to the baby in her womb and nurtured the beginnings of a relationship with that child he has not yet seen.

It's important for couples to discuss what role the husband feels comfortable filling during the birth. Society puts a lot of pressure on fathers (particularly first-time fathers) to be the sole support for their wives in labor, and this role can be overwhelming to many fathers. Some men just aren't comfortable taking on the coach role. Or they plan to fill the coach role but find themselves overwhelmed by the intensity and power of birth.

It's fine for a husband to be an observer if that's what he's comfortable being. However, husbands shouldn't sell themselves short. Some might think they aren't labor-coach material but fill the role beautifully after preparing themselves.

My husband was my greatest strength and help as I gave birth to my children, but I have also drawn on the support of experienced women and doulas and found added courage and comfort from their aid. Birth doulas are trained to assist women and their husbands in childbirth. (For more information about doulas and the importance of experienced, loving support, see "The Angel Standing By," on page 304.)

POSTPARTUM AND EARLY PARENTHOOD

There is, perhaps, no time when a father's loving support is more crucial than after a baby is born, particularly after the first child. The postpartum period of transition can be smooth and joyful, overwhelming and difficult, terrifying and unstable, or all of the above at different points throughout a given day. It is difficult to know just how a couple will weather that time of change and growth, but much of the hardship can be alleviated by the sacred support of a sensitive father.

My own eyes well up with grateful tears when I remember the night after my husband and I brought our first baby home from the hospital. With frequent visitors and my new heightened alertness and vigilance, I had slept only a few hours in the days since our daughter was born. Sometime around 3:00 a.m. on that first night at home, I was up again with my baby. My husband awakened with me, helping me change my daughter's diaper and get situated. As I sat on a very painful, stitch-filled bottom, fumbling and struggling to feed my new baby, tears soon streamed down my face. Nothing could have prepared me for how exhausting, overwhelming, and difficult that transition period would be.

I didn't say a word as I sobbed, but my husband somehow knew what I was feeling and what I needed. I can't even remember what he said, but I do remember how utterly lost and discouraged I felt before he spoke and how his few words were exactly what I needed to carry me through that night. I loved my husband when I married him, but going through pregnancy, birth, and new parenthood with him turned that fledgling newlywed love into something deeper and more profound than I ever could have imagined I would feel.

There is almost nothing more precious and sacred to me than the support my husband has freely given to me throughout my pregnancies, births, and mothering challenges. I'll never forget how my husband rubbed lotions on my first-time pregnant belly and spoke to our unborn daughter with excitement and anticipation. I'll never forget how his voice distracted me through the mild contractions of early labor, how he sprayed my back for an hour with hot water in the soon steamy and stifling hospital bathroom, how his presence and gentle touches kept me grounded when I felt like giving up, and how his eyes shone with tears the first time he held his baby girl in his arms. I'll never forget the way he lovingly and tenderly cared for me and our new daughter as we recovered from childbirth. Physically and emotionally comforting others was not a character trait that came naturally to my husband. But I watched in love and awe as "weak things" became strong unto him (Ether 12:27) in his efforts to support me through childbearing. I have a testimony that the Lord can and does qualify, aid, and strengthen fathers in this sacred call.

Labor Tips for Fathers

How can a father provide sacred support to his wife as she labors to bring forth their children? Remember the following six *Pr* strategies:

1. Preparation: Robyn Allgood teaches couples the Bradley Method of Husband-Coached® Childbirth. She encourages fathers to thoroughly prepare themselves for childbirth:

   Dads need to prepare just as much as moms through educating themselves, reading, going to a birth class, practicing, talking about birth options, and understanding the birth process. I fell in love all the more with my hubby as he took the time to study birth. It is our

actions that tell people we love them. His actions of practicing relaxation with me, actively listening in birth class, and letting me just
talk about my feelings became a strength to our marriage.

2. Presence: Sometimes all a wife needs is her husband's loving, physical presence. Be "present" in every way—don't let fatigue or fear take your attention
away from your wife's emotional and physical needs. Do not sleep unless
she's asleep or being given support and comfort by someone else. Do not
leave her alone unless she asks you to. Remember the Savior in the Garden
of Gethsemane—He simply asked His disciples, "Tarry ye here, and watch
with me" (Matthew 26:38).

3. Protection: You have been given a divine command to provide protection to
your wife and children. When you educate yourself about the birth process
and the possible complications and interventions that may arise, you will be
better able to ensure that your wife is not subjected to unnecessary harm.
Some interventions can potentially affect a woman's ability to bear children
in the future, so you should also consider yourself the guardian of your
wife's womb and powers of procreation, ensuring that those powers are not
jeopardized needlessly.

Be a buffer between your wife and the rest of the world. You can't protect
her from the intensity of childbirth or from the unexpected, but you can
protect her personal space and surround her with peace and calm.

- Close doors.

- Turn off/down the lights.

- If someone tries to talk to her mid-contraction, gently ask the person to
wait. Or, stand between the person and your wife until her contraction
and signal with your hands for the person to wait a moment.

- No matter what happens, ensure that your wife always feels safe and
secure. Try to emulate the Savior's calmness in the storm that frightened
His disciples. He comforted them, saying, "Peace, be still" (Mark 4:39).

- "Stand in holy places" (D&C 45:32; 101:22). Try to make whatever place
you are in a holy place.

4. Prayer: Just as the Savior asked His disciples to pray while He suffered in the Garden, you can pray when your wife is in her birthing time. Pray for her strength, pray for peace to fill her heart and yours, pray for her care providers to think clearly and calmly, pray for yourself that you will be able to stay alert and awake, and pray for guidance when you don't know what to do.

5. Priesthood: Elder Russell M. Nelson has said, "Your first priority in honoring the priesthood is to honor your eternal companion."[1] Giving your wife a blessing when labor starts can bring great peace and comfort. If complications or difficulties arise, don't forget that you have been granted a portion of God's power to aid your loved ones. The power of the priesthood can change the course of a difficult labor, bring about miracles, and help you make pivotal decisions. (See Neoma Gould's birth story on page 313.)

6. Praise: Elder Nelson offered more advice to husbands, saying: "As fathers we should have love unbounded for the mothers of our children. We should accord to them the gratitude, respect, and praise that they deserve. . . . Let your thoughts and actions inspire confidence and trust. . . . Let nothing in life take priority over your wife."[2] Elder Nelson's advice is especially crucial in the midst of childbirth. Ensure that all of your words instill your wife with hope, confidence, peace, comfort, pride, and power.

---

[1] Russell M. Nelson, "Honoring the Priesthood," *Ensign*, May 1993, http://lds.org/ensign/1993/05/honoring-the-priesthood.

[2] Russell M. Nelson, "Our Sacred Duty to Honor Women," *Ensign*, May 1999, http://lds.org/ensign/1999/05/our-sacred-duty-to-honor-women.

---

1 Qtd. in "Mature Intimacy: Courtship and Marriage," *A Parent's Guide*, by The Church of Jesus Christ of Latter-day Saints (Salt Lake City, UT: The Church of Jesus Christ of Latter-day Saints, 1985), http://lds.org/manual/a-parents-guide/chapter-6-mature-intimacy-courtship-and-marriage.

2 Marion G. Romney, "Unity," *Ensign*, May 1983, http://lds.org/ensign/1983/05/unity.

GENTLY AT MY SIDE

By Eirene Henderson

HE DECLARED HIS LOVE, he proposed, we married, we conceived. I was twenty-one, my husband Ben was twenty-two, and we were barely accustomed to the novelties of marriage before we were getting used to the idea of being parents. I had known my entire life that I wanted to be a mother. By the time I was in high school, I had chosen all twelve of my children's names. I never thought too much about the pregnancy and birth portion of child rearing, but as actual embryonic cellular division commenced within my womb, I realized that I didn't really know a uterus from a unicycle. It was time for information and decision.

I borrowed and checked out all the books on birthing that I could get my hands on, including *Birthing from Within* by Pam England and Bob Horowitz. I began attending La Leche League meetings. Nothing else, however, was quite so educational as a conversation I had with Ben about my birthing plans.

"Babe, I'm going to have the baby naturally."

"Why?"

"Because... it's better."

"Why is it better?"

"Because, it just *is*."

"Is it better just because your mom did it? Eirene, you don't have to prove anything to your mom."

"It has nothing to do with that!"

"Then why? Give me three reasons."

The conversation wasn't going in the direction I wanted it to. I had figured since it was by body, it was my choice, and Ben's job was to say, "Great! I know you can do it. Now who could use a foot rub?"

The first thing I needed to convince Ben of was why natural was what I wanted. I wasn't entirely sure myself, really. And to be honest, the fact that my mother had born nine children *au natural* had set a little bit of a precedent in my mind. I took a deep breath.

"Ben, it's kind of like this. Having a baby is sort of like a rite of passage for women. Kind of like... a mission is for men. It isn't easy. I don't think I understand now how hard it's actually going to be. I know I don't blame women for getting epidurals. But I do know that, like a mission, the more you put into it the more you get out of it. The more... rewarding it is." (For the record, the fastest way to relate anything to my Mormon male's understanding is to compare it to a mission.)

"Okay, I can see that. But why do you want to put yourself through so much pain when, either way, you get the baby in the end."

"I don't know. I feel like I owe it to womankind. I mean, they've been doing this for thousands and thousands of years, our bodies are made for it. It's hard, it hurts, it sucks, but it is a real part of life. And just like the rest of life, you dig in your heels, you do it, it becomes part of you, and you come to love it. And when I die, and look Eve in the face, I can say, I did it too."

"Well, then I'm going to be in the waiting room."

"No, because I want to have the baby at home."

"No. Absolutely not."

"Babe, it's not like we'll be boiling water, and tying off the umbilical cord with a string. There'll be a midwife there. It will be perfectly safe."

"Oh, right. We'll be safe because she'll chant some voodoo over your belly and finger-paint our faces, right?"

Clearly, there were going to be more roadblocks than one. We decided to just meet with a midwife and see how Ben felt about it. We scheduled my first prenatal exam with a certified nurse-midwife, who did hospital deliveries only (I could see that a compromise was necessary).

As it turned out, Ben loved the midwife. He was very reassured when her clinic was not inside a cave but looked and smelled in every way like a doctor's office. The appearance of the midwife herself was also reassuring. No beads, no tangled tresses, no gnarled staff, or wild look. She appeased Ben with her stylish pantsuit and technical vocab, and she appeased me with her gentle hands and listening skills.

Ben loved the midwife so much he began advertising for her everywhere we went. "Yes, our midwife is just the best. There is no going back once you try a midwife. You guys need a midwife." He was really coming around. Over the course of nine months, we read all my books together, studied and discussed various birthing techniques, conglomerated, and came up with our own kind of method. He listened approvingly as I read him my birth free-write, and he himself hung my birth art on the fridge (both exercises from *Birthing from Within*). At night, we lay together in bed, and breathed in and out in unison, and many nights Ben would practice various relaxation tech-niques with me. Pregnancy was turning out to be pretty doggone romantic. And little by little, before he even realized what was happening, Ben had become the staunchest disciple of natural childbirth that ever lived.

When our daughter Mae was born, all the reasons why I had thought I wanted a natural birth were rendered pretty much obsolete. Not that paying my dues to womanhood, rites of passage, Mother Eve, etc. weren't at the

He told me probably ten thousand times that I was doing a great job, that I was beau-tiful, that I was amazing. I never once grew tired of hearing it.

forefront of my mind. Of course they were. Or would have been, if I had had mind power to spare. I would have been philosophizing all about that stuff if it weren't for the distractions of labor and delivery. Mostly, it was the fas-cinating, frightening pain that truly monopolized my focus. I could not lose my concentration for even the tiniest instant.

Ben was truly the guardian of my concentration. Without speaking or distracting me, he seemed to neutralize the atmosphere and maintain my rhythm. He became an extension of me, for I could not breathe, or count, or moan without him doing the same, gently at my side. With every ounce of emotion I could spare, I loved Ben more than I ever had before.

He held water to my lips, he rubbed them with lip balm, he wiped my forehead with a warm wet cloth. He gently touched any part of my body that he could see tensing, and wordlessly cued me to relax and let go. He softly gave instructions to the nurses, (mostly asking them to leave, or use whispers), and he told me probably ten thousand times that I was doing a great job, that I was beautiful, that I was amazing. I never once grew tired of hearing it.

When my water broke, I felt my cervix spring open like a bear trap in reverse, and to keep myself from going completely wild, I began a sort of low chant (the sort of fiendish thing that Ben initially feared about natural childbirth, I'm sure). "Open... Oooooopen... Oooooopen," I repeated in a deep, controlled voice, going as low toward bass as I could. Ben jumped right in, and my midwife followed on his heels. We all sat there, forming a unified little triangle, lowing like cattle.

Then it happened. I lost my rhythm, I slumped down and writhed against the sheets of my hospital bed. I was exhausted and weak, and absolutely terrified. "I can't do it," I managed to announce. Ben grabbed my hand. His forehead was white with sweat, and his eyebrows contracted with compassion as he said, "Eirene, you are doing it! You're almost there! You are so strong. You can finish this." I suddenly sat forward. My midwife smiled, and said "Oooooopen." Minutes passed, and I was pushing.

I knew that baby had to get out of me somehow, and nobody could get it out but me. So by summoning energy from God alone knows where, I survived. And then, I had a baby. A tiny, warm life, right there at my heart. Wiggling, suckling, making unsure little sounds. Nothing else matters. Nothing else exists. I held that baby, who I knew and yet didn't know, but who I loved so intensely it made me breathless.

I never understood the Atonement better than when I held my new baby in my arms. I suffered for my daughter. Christ suffered for the world. Christ performed the ultimate selfless act. I did something truly selfless for the first time in my life. I thought that I couldn't finish. Christ asked his Father if there was any other way. An angel from heaven came to strengthen Him. My husband brought me back to reality and told me I could do it. I gave my child life. Christ gave the world life eternal. He finished it. I finished it.

This was the curious, beautiful moment, when all faculties both physical and psychological were completely spent, that I figured out why I had my baby naturally. I don't fully comprehend what Christ went through, for He suffered not only my pain but all pain that anyone has ever suffered. That was a burden that only a Son of God could bear, for I can't even wrap my mind around it. But I believe women are able to come as close to comprehension as is possible in this life. And that is a gift, and no mistake.

Catching my Son

By John D. Ellis

MAN, WITH THE GIFT OF AGENCY, is constantly defining himself by the meaning he makes and chooses to find for himself. Rites of passage are mediums for finding great meaning. I would like to share the meaning I found with my wife, Rachelle, as we passed into parenthood and experienced the rite of passage of our son Eli's birth.

My sister-in-law, Robyn, invited Rachelle and I to participate in the Bradley Method® childbirth classes. The knowledge was empowering for us. For the next nine months, Rachelle and I invested great time and emotion into preparing to pass through birth as a rite of passage. Rachelle and I drew closer together as husband and wife because of our mutual efforts.

We had our fears and doubts, but the knowledge and application of the Bradley Method® alleviated our fears. The midwives, along with Robyn, were supportive in our search for success and meaning in the natural birth of our son, Eli. I love technology. Rachelle and I were able to empower ourselves and make use of our local medical institution in a healthy way. We experienced the best of both worlds.

My feelings of inadequacy as a husband and a father had been subdued by my active participation in our process. I calmly and collectedly played my role in Rachelle's pregnancy and now her labor. My high school basketball team slogan repeated through my mind, "Fail to plan, plan to fail." We planned to succeed and were succeeding.

Rachelle and I worked together through her labor. Her contractions were irregular through the day as we shopped—doing daily tasks of living. Later, we found ourselves laboring in our bedroom and bathroom for about three hours. I helped her through her contractions with relaxation techniques and other comfort measures like the sacrum squeeze to alleviate pain.

Rachelle wanted to experience childbirth. I wanted her to experience childbirth. Rachelle was powerful, full of life and happiness, finding an inner strength I envy still. I loved and cared for my wife as I watched her sacrifice her mind and body for our son, as if the wife I love and cherish was a type and shadow of Christ and His Atonement. Everything, her whole essence, had and was giving life to our child. I witnessed her great strength and the tender mercies of our Savior, Jesus Christ. Rachelle took on the natural process of childbirth, trusting her body. God had accounted for everything. Her body created this life, and it could deliver it into mortality.

Robyn, my wife's sister and doula, helped us for about an hour of the three that was the more intense labor at home. Rachelle passed through the stages quickly after a certain point, and my calmness to avoid rushing to the "institutions" caused me to not realize she was in transition and soon would be pushing. We got to the hospital and to a room with the midwives. All was going smoothly.

Robyn took over as the main encourager and physical supporter. I was with the midwife behind my wife who was on the bed on all fours. The midwife was helping Rachelle not to tear. Pushing is a delicate process. Toughness and softness are required. I rubbed Rachelle's back as my child's head appeared. What I had invested in emotionally, mentally, spiritually, and financially was about to be birthed. The universe stopped for me. A brilliant silence came over me. I was at one with eternity. My son's head crowned. I gently held it in my left hand. It released, he turned and in an instant my right hand held my seven pound, twenty inch, little boy.

A new measure of my serenity arrived on that day. Eli was staring at me with deep blue penetrating eyes. I felt a voice, an idea, resonate in my person, "This is your child—my little boy." Eli J. Ellis, a divine mortal intelligence, with unique characteristics and attributes and a combination of Rachelle's and my DNA. He would echo our essence through eternity. Rachelle was connected with us as she observed me hold our child. This took only moments. I placed Eli in the arms of his mother. They bonded as I had been privileged to bond. Rachelle and I, along with Eli, had successfully experienced well the rite of childbirth together as a family. I don't share these things lightly for they are sacred to me. I wish to instill a desire in other fathers and mothers to experience well this sacred event.

Unity with Providers of Care

By Lani Axman

During my first year at Brigham Young University, I attended a devotional address by Elder Jeffrey R. Holland on the day after Valentine's Day. I entered that devotional with a heart heavy from the wounds of a borderline-abusive dating relationship. Elder Holland's words slashed through that destructive cloud of darkness like a ray of light straight into my soul: "I would not have you spend five minutes with someone who belittles you, who is constantly critical of you, who is cruel at your expense and may even call it humor. . . . [Y]ou deserve to feel physically safe and emotionally secure."[1] His words changed my life in a profoundly positive way. We cannot choose all of the relationships and people who will cross our paths, but there are some we can choose. As we enter the sometimes frightening new territory of pregnancy, childbirth, and motherhood, we deserve just what Elder Holland told us we deserve: "To feel physically safe and emotionally secure." The professionals we elect to oversee our physical and emotional well-being should be true care providers.

There are many ways to approach the selection of our maternity care providers. One of the most common is to ask friends and family members whom they recommend. Some women scan the list of providers who accept their insurance and choose the closest care provider. These methods can work well, but they can also result in frustrating incompatibilities. When we choose a doctor or midwife, we are entrusting our lives and our babies' lives to the individual's skills and expertise. And we are also choosing the person whose words and actions have the potential to affect us for the rest of our lives. This is especially important for mothers with histories of sexual, emotional, or physical abuse, who may feel especially vulnerable during their pregnancies and births. Old wounds and pain can be reopened and exacerbated by an insensitive care provider.

Research indicates that the treatment a woman receives by maternity care providers can have long-term positive or negative effects. Even many years later, women can remember with vivid detail and emotion the positive and the negative things that were done or said to them while giving birth. Author, physical therapist, childbirth educator, and doula trainer Penny Simkin has conducted research on women's long-term memories of their first births. She explained, "The women with positive feelings [fifteen to twenty years later] recall being well cared for and supported by the doctor and nurse, whereas those with negative feelings today tend to recall negative interactions with staff."[2] She urged caregivers to ask themselves the following question: "How will she remember this?" Having that question in mind at all times "will lead to kind and considerate actions, empowering and complimentary words, and consideration of her desires and needs during childbirth."[3]

Typically, we spend a great deal of time researching our options as we select a house, vehicle, or other important item to purchase. I suggest that an even greater degree of thought and research can enable us to feel true unity and comfort with our maternity care providers. As we work to bring children into this world, we deserve the kindest evidence-based care available. We should not settle for anything less.

Writing a birth plan or birth preferences list can be a helpful exercise. However, I think most women do it too late in the game. A birth plan will do little to help you if your care provider has policies or practice styles incompatible with what you have envisioned. Perhaps the best time to write your birth plan is before you ever choose a doctor or midwife. When you know your provider is comfortable with and supportive of your birth wishes, you'll be at ease when he or she arrives to catch your baby. In his book *Creating Your Birth Plan*, Dr. Marsden Wagner urged the following:

> Talk to the midwives and doctors available to you. Interview them at length, watching to see if they get restless or uncomfortable. . . . Don't be afraid to change care providers if after a few visits you don't like how one is caring (or not caring) for you. . . . Beware of any tendency to patronize you and suggest that you cannot possibly understand technical information about childbirth. . . . 'Be a smart shopper.'[4]

As you select several possible caregiver candidates, interview each, and hire the one whose philosophies and practice style are most unified with your wants and needs, you will increase your odds of a safe and satisfying birth experience. (There is more information regarding birth plans in the "Choice and Accountability" essay, on page 140.)

When the Savior was preparing His disciples for His death and resurrection, He told them, "I will not leave you comfortless: I will come to you" (John 14:18). He also spoke the words we know so well: "A new commandment I give unto you, That ye love one another; as I have loved you" (John 13:34). These two scriptures have brought to my mind the following question: "If Christ were our maternity care provider, what would He do?"

When Alma and his people were enduring the hardships and difficulties of bondage to Amulon, the Lord comforted them in their afflictions, saying:

> Lift up your heads and be of good comfort. . . . I will also ease the burdens which are put upon your shoulders, that even you cannot feel them upon your backs, even while you are in bondage; and this will I do that ye may stand as witnesses for me hereafter, and that ye may know of a surety that I, the Lord God, do visit my people in their afflictions. (Mosiah 24:13–14)

And the Lord did. Alma and his people were strengthened by the Lord "that they could bear up their burdens with ease, and they did submit cheerfully and with patience to all the will of the Lord" (Mosiah 24:15).

The Lord will do the same for us. Though we cannot literally have Christ as our maternity care provider, we can invite Him to attend in other ways. First, we can choose to let Him ease our pregnancy and birth burdens through the Atonement. Second, we can invite someone worthy to stand in His place as our caregiver. By the word worthy, I do not necessarily mean a temple-recommend holder. There are many wonderful maternity care providers both inside and outside the Church. While safety, experience, and skill are very important factors in our choice of provider, I feel certain that our loving older brother, Jesus Christ, wants us to be treated with the same respect He would give us if He were physically overseeing our births. We deserve, as Elder Holland said, to be both "physically safe and emotionally secure."[5]

The scriptures give us a description of the pure love of Jesus Christ, also known as charity (see Moroni 7:45, 47). As we choose our maternity care providers, we may want to keep the following list of attributes from Moroni 7:45 in mind:

- Suffereth long
- Is kind
- Envieth not
- Not easily provoked
- Thinketh no evil
- Rejoiceth not in iniquity
- Rejoiceth in truth
- Beareth all things
- Believeth all things
- Endureth all things

The words of one true care provider have been immortalized in holy writ. The biblical Rachel had a difficult labor as she worked to bring Benjamin into the world. It is clear from the context that Rachel was concerned that her child would not survive. She seemed to sense that something was amiss as she struggled. Indeed, her own life was hanging in the balance. The words her midwife spoke to her were important enough and powerful enough to be recorded and passed down from generation to generation for the next several thousand years. Even in the face of those difficult, precarious circumstances, this inspired midwife comforted Rachel, saying, "Fear not; thou shalt have this son also" (Genesis 35:17). And Rachel gave birth to a healthy baby boy.

The image of Christ with His disciples in the raging sea comes to mind. As the storm and waves threatened and frightened His friends, they cried out, "Carest thou not that we perish?" The travail of birth can feel, at times, like that frightening stormy sea, threatening to take our lives. But Christ, like Rachel's midwife, remained calm in the face of adversity, speaking to the waves and His disciples, "Peace, be still" (Mark 4:37–39).

In the end, it is not our doctors or midwives who deliver our babies to us. As Alma and his newly freed people rejoiced, pouring out their thanks to God for His tender mercies, they knew that "none could deliver them except it were the Lord their God" (Mosiah 24:21). We need not waste our time enduring disrespectful or belittling treatment from those to whom we entrust our care. Far too many women come away from their births suffering in body, mind, and spirit as a consequence of being mistreated in the labor room. We deserve much better. Finding providers of care who emulate the love of the Savior can be our ideal, and it can be our reality, if we seek it.

1 Jeffrey R. Holland, "How Do I Love Thee?" (devotional address given at Brigham Young University, Provo, UT, February 15, 2000), http://speeches.byu.edu/reader/reader.php?id=1618.
2 Penny Simkin, "Just Another Day in a Woman's Life? Women's Long-Term Perceptions of Their First Birth Experience. Part I," *Birth* 18, no. 4 (1991), 209.
3 Ibid, 210.
4 Marsden Wagner, *Creating Your Birth Plan: The Definitive Guide to a Safe and Empowering Birth* (New York: Penguin, 2006), 65–67.
5 Jeffrey R. Holland, "How Do I Love Thee?" (devotional address given at Brigham Young University, Provo, UT, February 15, 2000), http://speeches.byu.edu/reader/reader.php?id=1618.

Helping Me Heal

By Holly Young

AS A CHILD, I WAS SEXUALLY ABUSED BY MY FATHER. Following the break-down of my family, I was raised away from my siblings in foster care. I lived in a total of thirty families, two group homes, and one boarding school. I went through twelve years of therapy beginning at the age of seven. When I was fourteen, I became aware of my diagnosis: PTSD, depression, and generalized anxiety disorder. At sixteen, I attempted suicide. I was hospitalized and placed on anti-depressants. My longest foster placement was the last three years of high school with a lesbian couple. This is where I found the gospel and, at eighteen, joined The Church of Jesus Christ of Latter-day Saints.

I transferred to BYU so that I would have the most support in being a member as possible, but I still struggled with self-mutilation and prescription drug overdose. I was hospitalized three times while in college. I worked very hard during that time to feel Heavenly Father's love for me. I spent hours studying my scriptures, attending the temple, fulfilling my calling, and counseling with my leaders. After I graduated from BYU, I drifted from the Church. The social pressures triggered too much anxiety for me.

I had met my husband, Evan, three years before at BYU, but we had drifted. I studied abroad in China. He moved to Salt Lake City. When we re-met, he proposed after one real date, and we were married a few months later. We came back to the church while I was pregnant with Kyle. We wanted to be active. We both had testimonies and knew we wanted to raise our son in the Church. When Kyle was six months old, Evan blessed him. I was endowed shortly thereafter, and we were sealed when Kyle was nine months on May 14, 2009, in the Salt Lake Temple.

Having a baby and receiving womanly care compounded all my issues stemming from my physical and sexual abuse. I felt abused through my first pregnancy by several different OBs. I was re-traumatized through the way that I was treated and through vaginal exams that were painful, unkind, and clinical. The delivery was an induction that I felt was pushed on me through fear tactics. I did have an epidural with Kyle and was criticized for my pain management of that labor. I felt vulnerable and was placed in positions where things felt out of control. I didn't even realize how traumatized I was from my first pregnancy until my second pregnancy.

My husband was friends with a wonderful woman named Briana Black-welder—a midwife. I met her at thirty weeks into my first pregnancy. Bri gave me great books to read, like *Pushed*, and I watched "The Business of Being Born." Before my second child, Aiden, was even conceived, something which I waited and longed for, I knew that no one would be allowed to deliver my next baby but Briana. I knew I would have a home birth. Heavenly Father put Briana in my life at a time when she could help me heal. I met her right when I needed information at the end of my first pregnancy, and we were able to build a relationship so I was ready to let her in during my second pregnancy. I trusted her because of our friendship and my husband's long-term friendship with her.

I was a closeted sexually abused woman through both of my pregnancies until one particular prenatal appointment with Bri during the second half of my pregnancy. We spoke for three hours. Even though we had been friends through my first pregnancy, she'd heard the story of that birth, and she had my medical records, I recounted all the details to her and she listened. She validated. She was understanding. When I told her about the sexual abuse, she said she already knew. I know that for me a lot of my healing had to do with having someone who wanted to listen and was in tune enough to listen. I left that visit feeling powerful and ready to have my baby.

Bri gave me a book to read about sexual abuse and pregnancy. It contained a lot of horror stories and all the difficulties that women had birthing their babies when they suffered from previous sexual abuse. I devoured that book and then realized that I was not one of those women. I was going to deliver my baby surrounded by women who loved me and knew me, by my own things, in my own house. I knew my husband would be there, and he would not judge me.

My husband and I were attending the temple monthly as a couple all during my pregnancy. I also took a birthing class during the last month of my pregnancy, with Bri's partner midwife. We spoke of the power in our bodies, the divine design of our bodies, we spoke of being aware and letting go. We also did art (which made me uncomfortable) and made plans for the things that we needed in our space. Again, I found a woman who did not judge, who listened, who saw me for what I truly am.

Briana was kind and gentle. She only did a few vaginal exams at my request. No vaginal exam is comfortable, but Briana was always respectful by speaking to me about what she was doing before she did it, and it never felt like trauma. Briana acted out of love for me and my care was benefited with her knowledge of my sexual abuse history.

I birthed my Aiden at home in my own space with women that I chose who respected my body. They were guided by the Spirit and acted on their promptings to help guide me in my pregnancy. Giving birth was an experience in itself. I had to learn to accept what was happening to my body. Surprisingly, I felt comfortable with being so exposed. I was worried that I wouldn't be and kept telling my midwife during pregnancy that I wanted to cut a hole in my p.j. pants and just birth him through that. My midwife felt prompted to leave our house right when I was allowed to get in the pool at 6 cm. Almost immediately when Bri left, I went into active labor. For seventy-five minutes I was alone with my husband. That act, where I faced the most intense physical sensations, alone, and came through on the other side was an incredible act. I was powerful, my body was powerful, and I could not deny it. God orchestrated that. Briana gave me an environment where my body, created by Heavenly Father, was able to prove to me that it was capable, that it was strong, and that it was not a point of shame.

I believe that, with sexual abuse, finding a care giver is the critical part. I believe that is truly the way that I healed. Through people. Through people who have dedicated their lives to listening to women, to caring for women, to understanding women.

Briana passed away April 23, 2011, in a car accident. Too young to be gone—only twenty-eight—but I know she helped hundreds of other clients heal and give birth peacefully.

Unity with our Sisters

By Lani Axman

When and how we bring children into this world can be a very sensitive topic. It is not unusual for childbirth to come up in discussions among Latter-day Saints, highlighting the diversity of our choices and experiences. Far too often we pass judgment with very little understanding of one anothers' circumstances. I have been on both the giving and receiving end of too many of those spoken and unspoken judgments. Knowing how those "mommy wars" can be, I approached my third child's birth with a great deal of trepidation. The Lord had guided me to plan for a home birth, but I felt terrified of the potential opposition and criticism that often come with choosing an unpopular path. After praying for reassurance, I was given peace and personal revelation through a memory.

Two of my brothers, my sister-in-law, and their friend went fishing one cold November morning. What happened that day made November 8, 2006, a day I will never forget. The previously calm Strawberry Reservoir water became suddenly choppy. Waves began to overwhelm the boat. Before the group realized what danger they were in, the boat sunk out from under them. And the water was a frigid forty-one degrees. The human body loses heat faster in water than on land and will cease functioning and lose consciousness quickly in forty-one-degree water (generally within fifteen minutes to an hour), and death usually follows soon afterward. The group did what many of us would do under those circumstances. They prayed their hearts out, yelled for help, and swam as well as they could toward the marina.

Soon, my brother Kimball realized that they were swimming against the current and needed to turn around. He suggested the idea to my other brother, Steven, who said, "You think?" So Kimball and his friend turned around, and Steven went to where his wife, Catheryn, was swimming. Kimball thought Steven was just going to tell her the change of plans and follow them in the direction of the current. But Kimball never saw them again. Steven and his wife left mortality that day. And Kimball and his friend defied nature's laws and made it miraculously to shore over two hours later.

None of them were wearing life vests when the boat went down, and there were only three life vests in the boat. Once they were in the water, my brothers and sister-in-law quickly put their arms into the vests backward and started to swim. Their friend held onto a gas can to stay afloat. Later, Steven's and Catheryn's bodies slipped easily out of the life vests and into the deep reservoir water.

While search and rescue teams worked tirelessly to recover their lost bodies, my oldest brother, Paul, had a dream. In that dream, he saw spirits dancing in the bed of the reservoir. At first he looked and looked and couldn't see Steven and Catheryn. Then the other spirits began dancing their way into heaven, and finally he could see Steven and Catheryn dancing together. It wasn't until all the other spirits had danced into heaven that Catheryn and Steven, radiating joy, followed them. When Paul shared that dream with us at a late-night family gathering, we thought it was beautiful, but none of us understood its significance until later.

Within a few days, search and rescue teams found a body. And then more bodies. That reservoir had been holding the previously unrecovered bodies of four other accident victims whose families had lived for years without closure. The superior technology that was now available to search and rescue teams hadn't been available in previous years when the other bodies had been lost. All four of those bodies were recovered in the process of recovering the bodies of my brother and his wife. Four families were blessed and given peace. And then Catheryn and Steven danced their way into heaven.

We may look at the choices of that day as foolishness. We may say that they should have strapped themselves into those life vests before they took the boat out. But if they had been strapped into those life vests, their bodies would have remained afloat, never joining the other bodies held for years deep within the reservoir. Sure, it would have made finding them quicker and easier, but that wasn't God's purpose in choosing that particular place and time for their passing. No, He would bring about a beautiful blessing through their deaths. And Steven and Catheryn would have been thrilled to have aided in that beautiful blessing.

And what about swimming against the current? Was that a tragic mistake? I don't think so. Both of my brothers were praying. Steven would have had no trouble hearing and following the promptings of the Holy Spirit. The whisperings of the Spirit have told me that my brothers were *both* guided by the Lord that day. It's just that His plan was different for each of them. Kimball needed to go with the current so he could *live* and complete his mission on this earth. Steven needed to go the other direction to fulfill God's purposes for him and his wife and bring them to an important mission in the world of spirits. Neither path was wrong.

As the Lord brought these memories and insights to my mind, I felt at peace. I knew the path I had chosen was prompted by and approved of the Lord, so any dissenting voices were insignificant. God gives each of us unique directions, and we don't know what His purposes are for the people around us. Sometimes He says, "You need to swim this way," and that's the right way for you even if He tells the next person to swim the opposite way. Sometimes God's ways seem like foolishness to our mortal minds. But His ways are always exactly right. Sometimes even death is right.

When it came up in conversation that my husband and I were planning to give birth to our third baby at home, our home teachers were surprised. They were curious, naturally, why and how we had come to our decision. We mentioned a few of our reasons, and then I finished by saying, "But, most of all, it came down to personal revelation." One of the men, scratching his chin, said something like, "Wow. It's so interesting how we each get unique answers for our situations." Then he explained how his wife had delivered all of their three children by cesarean section and that he had given her a priesthood blessing in which she was told that she would need the advances of modern medicine to give birth.

This exchange reminded me how important it is to counsel with the Lord in such important matters, avoid assuming that *our* answer is for everyone, and respectfully support our friends in their own spiritually guided paths—regardless of whether we understand the paths or think we would choose those paths ourselves. It's so easy to look at the choices of others and say, "Are they *crazy?*" I fear that, far too often, we mistakenly become defensive or critical when our fellow sisters choose paths that contrast with our own. Those critical attitudes can become "shafts in the whirlwind" (Helaman 5:12) that may cause others to suffer needlessly. Unfortunately, "mommy wars" persist, even among those who have taken upon them the name of Christ and call each other "sister."

"Not war, not jangle, not contradiction, but meekness, love, purity, these are the things that should magnify us."[1] —Joseph Smith

---

A couple of years ago, in a fast and testimony meeting, a member of our ward bishopric recounted the story of the converted Lamanites who buried their weapons of war. The bishopric member asked us to consider what we might need to bury in our own lives. What were our weapons of war? I began to think about the emotional weapons I am prone to use. I thought about how often I judge others or make false assumptions that create a barrier to friendship and love. Wasn't it about time for me to bury those emotional weapons of war?

We are members of the world's largest women's organization—the Relief Society. While the Relief Society has many missions and purposes, we cannot forget the importance of the sisterhood and relief we can give to *each other*. As the Prophet Joseph Smith's mother, Lucy Mack Smith, urged, "We must cherish [and] watch over one another, comfort one another and gain instruction that we may all sit down in heaven together."[2] No matter how varied our paths or how diverse our perspectives, we can bear one anothers' burdens, rejoice in one anothers' joys, and sustain each other as we travel toward Christ together.

---

1   Qtd. in *Daughters in My Kingdom*, by The Church of Jesus Christ of Latter-day Saints (Salt Lake City, UT: The Church of Jesus Christ of Latter-day Saints, 2011), 18.
2   Qtd. in "The Enduring Legacy of Relief Society," by Henry B. Eyring, *Ensign*, November 2009, http://lds.org/ensign/2009/11/the-enduring-legacy-of-relief-society.

CHAPTER TWELVE

The Fourth Trimester

Bear ye one another's burdens, and so
fulfill the law of Christ.

GALATIONS 6:2

Line upon Line

By Sheridan Ripley, CD(DONA), HCHI

When my husband and I started our journey to parenthood, we thought we would have nine months before we would have to start parenting. I figured that with a baby in my tummy, how much work could it be? Well, I was in for a shock when I realized how many choices and how much responsibility I had before my baby was even born. These changes started when my changing body needed more and healthier food. I also realized I needed more structure in my day to function effectively. I started thinking about the upcoming birth and making choices regarding it. Taking a childbirth class answered many questions but also raised more. And then we faced the unexpected—preterm labor and complete bed rest—starting at twenty-five weeks.

My life was suddenly about keeping the baby safe inside me. I learned to trust my intuition and make educated choices. However, my care provider didn't really seem to listen to me and instead focused on medical tests, often belittling my intuition. I knew the situation was more serious than she thought, and I needed her to listen to what I was experiencing and feeling. Following my intuition, I changed care providers around twenty-nine weeks.

My first pregnancy was a stressful time. But with stress comes growth and learning, even though we may not realize it at the time. I never thought, "I will use all that I am learning now as I continue to mother my baby." But the experiences I had became a firm foundation that continues to influence the way I mother.

The choices you make during your pregnancy can start building the foundation you want to have as you parent. The Savior has taught us that we learn "line upon line, precept upon precept" (D&C 98:12). This principle is true in any calling and especially as we magnify our calling as mothers. What a blessing that we can take what we learn in pregnancy and birth and build upon it as we continue to learn more. The fun thing about being a parent, starting with pregnancy, is that the only constant is change. Once you think you know what you are doing, your child grows and things change. Parenting provides us with a wonderful opportunity for continual growth.

The following are examples of wisdom gained during pregnancy and/or birth that can help you build a good foundation for your future mothering.

PHYSICAL AND PRACTICAL

Meet Your Physical Needs

One piece of advice virtually all expecting moms hear is to sleep when the baby sleeps. Jane said, "During pregnancy and birth, I learned to listen to my body. If I am tired, I try to sleep. If [I am] hungry, [I] try to eat. [These are] important things to do as we parent a new baby." Your body knows what it needs. Sometimes the intensity of your physical needs increases with pregnancy, and it is good practice to listen to your body during pregnancy and after your baby is born.

Respect Your Body

One mother said, "I loved my body before, but now I really am in awe of it." I think that women often view their bodies negatively. The miracle of growing another person can help a woman's love and amazement of her body really blossom. That really happened for me with breast-feeding. I never liked my breasts and always thought they were too small. But once I realized how amazing it was that they could make milk and feed my baby, my attitude shifted.

Accept Help

Felice said, "I learned how to accept help." We may need more help than ever as we parent. Hopefully we can not only learn to accept help, but also learn to ask for it before we become overwhelmed. Whether we ask our spouses, our friends, our Church, or our Heavenly Father, asking for help is an important part of what we need to learn as mortals and as children of God. "Ask, and it shall be given you; seek, and ye shall find; knock, and it shall be opened unto you: for every one that asketh receiveth; and he that seeketh findeth; and to him that knocketh it shall be opened" (Matthew 7:7–8).

Some of us feel we are—or should be—so independent. Pregnancy and other circumstances may bring about occasions that force us to accept help. When I was on bed rest, the Young Women came over to clean my house. It was so hard lying there, watching my house get dirtier and dirtier, so I really appreciated the help. It was a great learning experience to be in a position of accepting help. I realized it wasn't that hard, and not only was I blessed but the girls were too. The experience helped me learn to ask for help and be willing to accept help when I needed it.

Establish Routines

Before I was a mom, I would sometimes skip breakfast, and if I forgot my morning prayer I could still function fairly well throughout the day. When I was pregnant, I had to eat breakfast every morning or I would feel faint by about 10:00 a.m. I did not have the same stamina as before, so I found prayer to become another essential part of my day. After my baby was born, I still needed a consistent, simple routine to function in a manner that was positive. I was so glad I already had one in place: get dressed, eat breakfast, read scriptures, pray, spend fifteen minutes doing basic chores. As I have followed this morning routine, I have been able to stay calmer and be more loving with my boys. If I miss any part of the routine, I find that I am not the kind of mother I want to be.

Make Educated Decisions

As I mentioned earlier, I changed care providers late in my pregnancy. After doing some research and educating myself, I knew that I needed better care. This decision was not easy, but I knew it was the right choice for me and my baby. So, with many prayers and tears, I pressed forward in finding a new provider. I learned that sometimes the choices I make as a mother are not easy. Yet when we educate ourselves, pray, and receive confirmation, we need to have the courage to follow through.

Robyn, mom of five, said, "I learned to research and make informed choices. It turns out there are years of additional choices ahead! So this is a good skill." Learning to make educated decisions during pregnancy has also helped Robyn to "think more about how my choices will affect my children in the short- and long-term." Indeed the choices keep on coming, and educating yourself on your options, combined with your intuition, can help in whatever issues come up.

EMOTIONAL

Embrace What You Have Been Given

While I was on bed rest with my first baby, my husband went out to watch a movie. When he came home, he told me that he ran into a couple we knew that were pregnant. I was so jealous that she got to go out and see a movie and I was stuck in bed. Yet, I also knew that in my situation, being in bed was the best choice for me and my baby. I did my best to embrace and make the most of the situation.

After my son was born, I noticed he had developmental delays. I tried hard not to compare him to other babies, though it was through some observations of others that I realized he needed some interventions to help him catch up. I decided to embrace the child I had. Yes, he was unique and not quite what I had expected, but embracing him as he is has made it more fun to parent him. Our attitude is an amazing tool. Thinking positively will help us enjoy our experiences much more.

Be Specific about Your Needs

During birth, I was pretty specific and direct with my husband about my needs: "Rub my back—to the left!" "Stop touching me!" "Rub my back!" I knew what I needed, and I knew he could give it to me. I needed to be specific so he could meet my needs effectively. This is important after your baby comes, too. After my second baby was born, I asked my husband to be in charge of the laundry for a while. He said, "Sure." Later, I discovered he had folded and hung up all of his clean clothes, but mine and the boys' were all thrown into a basket and were wrinkly. I realized I needed to not only tell him what I needed but to be specific. I then told him, "I need you to be in charge of washing, drying, folding, and putting away *all* of the laundry." He was just as happy to do this, and *I* was happy too.

Hold On—It Is Only Temporary

Breezy said:

> This too shall pass. Nearly nothing is forever; no feeling, no sensation, no circumstance is enduring. Stress clouds your vision and makes it harder to see the goal. I use this thought a lot when I feel I'm at the end of my rope with my children and struggle to be patient and kind.

Just as there are moments during pregnancy or birth that seem overwhelming, sometimes the enormity of being a new mom can feel a bit overwhelming. If you hang on and press through these moments, they are over before you know it. With my third pregnancy, I developed a horrible pregnancy rash called PUPPS (pruritic urticarial papules and plaques of pregnancy). I had to sleep with socks on my hands because I scratched in my sleep. It hurt to wear clothes, and I would want to cry when I had to take off my pajamas and get dressed to pick my big kids up from school. But I knew that the rash would go away once the baby was born, and remembering that kept me going. There are moments of motherhood like that, stages a baby is in that may be challenging, but remembering this too shall pass can help immensely.

Enjoy It—It Is Only Temporary

Shelly, mom of two, gave us the reminder to "relax and enjoy every minute because it all goes by so fast." I remember people telling me this when I had two small boys. I thought these people were crazy. One day could feel like a week. But now my oldest is twelve, and I have discovered these people were right. Time speeds up as children grow. My last pregnancy sped by so quickly, I found myself treasuring each thing (except that rash) because I knew it may be the last time I experienced it.

450

Develop New Skills

Felice said, "Learning to meditate and making it part of my life was the biggest thing I learned. It has changed my whole life and parenting. I learned in yoga classes and then found my own way with it. My daughter now meditates with me." Pregnancy is a unique time when you can find new tools to help you on your journey through motherhood. You can take any of the skills you learn and continue to use them in your life. I used hypnosis with my last two births. My youngest is now five years old, but I still find myself using my hypnosis tools at least once a month to help me stay calm and relaxed during stressful situations.

Stay Flexible

I certainly had an idea of how my pregnancy and birth were going to go. During each of my pregnancies, I took good care of myself and made the best choices along the way. Some births went just the way I wanted, but one did not—it went completely the opposite. Being flexible helped me to accept that drastic change in plans.

We all have hopes and visions of what our families will look like after we have children. Maybe you envision sitting down with your family every night for dinner. You know that it is important, so you work hard to make it happen. Then maybe your husband gets a different shift at work and isn't home until ten o'clock at night. This is when it is important to be flexible but still hold on to the important things. Maybe you'll need to switch to having a big family breakfast every morning. One thing that is helpful to remember is that there are different seasons in your family's life. Knowing that this too will pass can help.

Monica said, "There is no way to plan for everything. Just do the best you can, and go with the flow from there." Combining good planning with flexibility, you will be able to flow more smoothly along the journey your family is taking. Visualize what you want, and work hard to create it. Stand strong in what you believe are the important things, but be flexible along the way.

SPIRITUAL

Trust Your Intuition, and Follow the Spirit

Pregnancy is a special time when we are literally connected to our growing children. We have a wonderful opportunity to learn about them before we even meet them. During this time, we have to rely on our intuition. Be open to your intuition, and following the Spirit as you make choices along this journey.

Once your baby is born, you will be faced with many more choices. You can read many, many books. You can ask "experts," such as your pediatrician or your child's teacher, and you can ask your friends. But remember that you, teamed with God, are the expert for this child. You and God know your child better then anyone else. You can pray for inspiration, and you can be led as you make choices:

> I give unto you a commandment that ye shall continue in prayer and fasting from this time forth. . . . [Learn and] teach ye diligently and my grace shall attend you, that you may be instructed more perfectly in theory, in principle, in doctrine, in the law of the gospel, in all things that pertain unto the kingdom of God, that are expedient for you to understand; Of things both in heaven and in the earth, and under the earth; things which have been, things which are, things which must shortly come to pass; things which are at home, things which are abroad. . . . That ye may be prepared in all things when I shall send you again to magnify the calling whereunto I have called you, and the mission with which I have commissioned you. (D&C 88: 76–80)

One of our biggest missions in life is to mother our children. Following your intuition can start during pregnancy and birth and can help you to magnify your calling. The following two stories demonstrate the importance of following intuition.

Jenni was planning a home birth for her fifth baby, but said:

> When I went into labor, I just felt very panicked internally—something didn't feel normal to me—so off to the hospital we went. I asked for an epidural, a first for me. I also declined having my water broken, another

first for me; however, I felt very strongly that for some reason with this pregnancy and birth my water needed to be intact for as long as possible.

When Jenni started to push, her doctor discovered her baby was breech, but because Jenni continually followed her intuition, she was able to avoid a cesarean section.

Shelly, one of my former doula clients, really felt drawn to a home birth but never took the time to meet with a midwife. At thirty-seven weeks, she mentioned again to me the unease she felt about going to the hospital, and I suggested the idea of meeting with a home-birth midwife to explore that option. Shelly finally did meet with a midwife. After their meeting, she called me and said, "We are having a home birth, and I finally feel great about my plans." Shelly's birth was long, and the baby's head was tipped a little funny, but Shelly and her midwife trusted her body and her baby, and she birthed her little boy vaginally after thirty-five hours. When Shelly and I met for our postpartum visit, we both agreed that had she been at the hospital, she would likely have had a cesarean section.

You can see the power that both of these women gained as mothers as they followed their intuition through pregnancy and birth. Take the time to pay attention to your intuition, starting today, even if you haven't conceived yet. As you choose to follow your gut feelings, you will find that you will receive more and more of them, and intuition is a wonderful tool to use throughout your parenting journey.

Choosing home birth was really hard for me because it required taking so much responsibility for my birth experience—and the outcome—on myself. I couldn't pass the blame for how things went onto a doctor, a hospital or a nurse. I was the one who had made the choice, and I was going to have to accept the consequences for that choice, good or bad. That was scary for me. But making that choice really changed my life, and I see now that I am much more willing to take responsibility for things in my life. I have much more faith in my ability to listen to revelation. I've learned that God is always there for me."

—Heather Farrell

Following intuition may have saved my son's life. When Carson was a toddler, he had ten ear infections in ten months. My husband and I took Carson to an ear, nose, and throat specialist, whose advice was to do surgery for ear tubes. We figured the doctor was the expert, and that was fine. The surgery was a common procedure and low risk.

As the day for the surgery neared, I felt very nervous about it. I even reached the point that had Carson died during the surgery, I wouldn't have felt surprised. That really scared me. The day before the surgery, I finally told my husband about my fears. Why did I wait so long? My fear felt so irrational to me. Imagine my surprise when my husband explained he had been worrying about the same thing. We both knelt in prayer and received two answers. First, we had never given him a blessing of healing, and it was something we should have tried long ago. Second, Carson was not to have the surgery. This experience was powerful for both of us.

We cancelled the surgery immediately. We both felt immense relief after we cancelled. What if we hadn't talked to each other about our fears until after the surgery? Would Carson be with us today? I don't know what would have happened to Carson, but I do know I am glad we followed our intuition and that we used the power of prayer to confirm it. My husband did give Carson a blessing, and Carson hasn't had an ear infection since then. This experience has been an incredible teaching moment and one that has stayed with me as I continue to trust my intuition as I raise my boys.

I have found that mothers who are open to following their intuition, even if it takes courage and takes them where they don't expect, are able to grow in their capacity to do so. Meleah said:

> I really turn to the Lord for guidance and direction so much more as a parent because of the lessons I learned making educated, God-guided decisions during pregnancy. I am so grateful that I learned early on to use my intuition and to research different choices in child rearing.

God teaches us little by little. As we learn and follow His promptings, we are blessed with more wisdom. This principle applies in every aspect of our lives, including parenting. Even Jesus Christ, in His mortal life, had to grow and learn incrementally: "And he received not of the fulness at first, but continued from grace to grace, until he received a fulness" (D&C

93:13). I love what President Henry B. Eyring has said:

> When God communicates priceless truth to us, He does it by the Spirit of Truth. We have to ask for it in prayer. Then He sends us a small part of that truth by the Spirit. It comes to our hearts and minds. It feels good, like the light from the sun shining through the clouds on a dark day. He sends truth line upon line, like the lines on the page of a book. Each time a line of truth comes to us, we get to choose what we will do about it. If we try hard to do what that truth requires of us, God will send more light and more truth. It will go on, line after line, as long as we choose to obey the truth. That is why the Savior said that the man who obeyed His commandments built on a rock so solid that no storm or flood could hurt his house.[1]

Isn't it wonderful that Heavenly Father gives us ten months as our children grow beneath our hearts to start learning how to parent them? Little by little, we prepare our homes, our hearts, and our lives to welcome our children's sweet spirits. As we make choices along our journey to mothering our children, we are laying the foundation for our relationships with them. Now is the time to start creating that foundation as you learn and grow line upon line, starting during pregnancy and birth.

---

1   Henry B. Eyring, "A Life Founded in Light and Truth," Ensign, July 2001, http://lds.org/ensign/2001/07/a-life-founded-in-light-and-truth.

How the
Scriptures Helped Me Mother

By Rebecca Gustafson Williams

WHEN CALEB WAS EIGHT MONTHS OLD, we moved to a new ward. A few weeks later, my husband and I were asked to speak in sacrament meeting on the topic "Biblical mothers." I loved preparing for this talk. There were obviously too many women in the Bible to be able to address all of them, but I highlighted four: Eve, Sarah, Rebekah, and Rachel.

About two months before this, Caleb had started waking up one to three times during the night, after several months of sleeping nine to eleven hours straight. I didn't know how to help him return to the good sleeping habits he had originally acquired without any "sleep training." What was causing him to wake up all of a sudden? Was it teething? Was it hunger? Had he started waking due to a mild cold and then just continued waking out of habit?

My pediatrician told me to let him "cry it out," but I didn't feel good about that suggestion. I consulted various books, each providing a different approach for good sleeping and eating habits, and each seemed to shout, "This is the way to do it! If you don't follow this, your baby will never sleep well." Likewise, each friend and relative had a different method that they believed in.

Lost amid all these theories and philosophies, I began to feel much like Joseph Smith, when he was confused about so many religions and said, "In the midst of this war of words and tumult of opinions, I often said to myself: What is to be done? Who of all these parties are right; or, are they all wrong together? If any one of them be right which is it, and how shall I know it?" (Joseph Smith—History 1:10). I felt so inadequate as a mother during this time, not only in regards to sleeping, but suddenly about feeding, napping, and parenting in general. I wanted us all to sleep better, but not at the expense of Caleb's well-being. Was he going to be psychologically damaged, or hungry, or in pain if I chose to let him cry? Was he ever going to sleep through the night again if I continued to respond to his wakings? Was this all going on because I hadn't put my baby on a schedule? While each book had general theories and reasons for this behavior, none of them knew my baby and situation.

As I was working on my talk, I was reading about Rebekah in the Old Testament, who was the mother to twins, Jacob and Esau. While she was pregnant with these two boys, she felt them quarreling within her. She may have been anxious about her children, as most mothers are. The scriptures tell us she inquired of the Lord about this and received an answer. "And the children struggled together within her; and she said, If it be so, why am I thus? And she went to enquire of the Lord" (Genesis 25:22). As I read this, I applied it to myself, and understood that each mother should inquire of the Lord about how to raise her children. Each child is unique and has different needs for love and discipline.

Elder M. Russell Ballard spoke about this in the April 2008 General Conference talk "Daughters of God." He said, "There is no role in life more essential and more eternal than that of motherhood. . . . There is *no* one perfect way to be a good mother. Each situation is unique. Each mother has different challenges, different skills and abilities, and certainly different children."

After talking to my husband, I finally realized that discussing my concerns with the One Perfect Parent was the best way to address these issues. I began to believe that Heavenly Father gave me my baby because Caleb needed *my* mothering methods and not my friend's or anyone else's. If there was a parenting method that didn't seem right to me, then I didn't need to do it, even if a book (or doctor) told me otherwise.

This experience and realization gave me so much more confidence as a new mother. I prayed about my concerns with more faith that I would really receive an answer. I brainstormed ideas that might work to improve our situation. I chose one idea that seemed like a good compromise; it was something *I thought of*, not something I had read or heard about. After just a couple nights, Caleb's sleep habits began to improve. It took some time, but he eventually returned to sleeping through the night again.

I have come to believe, like Elder Ballard said, that there is no one perfect way to be a good mother. What works for one child in one family, may not work for another family (or even another child in the same family). It is, of course, important that we do our best to make sure our child is healthy and safe, loved and cared for, but *how* we do that is up to us with the guidance of Heavenly Father.

Forty Days of Rest

By Felice Austin, CHt

Traditionally, a honeymoon is a time when a newly married couple—a brand new family unit—remove themselves from the world and everyday life to relax and bond through physical intimacy. The "babymoon," though less common, has a similar function. It is a seclusion, a removal from the world for the baby's first forty days, and a time for a new family unit to bond. A child's first forty days in this world are very important. This is true in other mammals as well. When I spent time on a sheep ranch in Montana, I learned how important immediate secluded bonding time is for sheep and their new lambs. If the ewes don't get this seclusion and closeness, they are more likely to abandon or be inattentive to their lambs.

The term *babymoon* was coined in 1996 by Sheila Kitzinger in her book *The Year After Childbirth*, but the practice has been around for eons. Recently, the travel industry has tried to change the meaning to a trip one takes as a last hurrah before the baby comes. Although that sounds great, too, don't be confused—traveling is not part of the forty days of rest I'm talking about.

The spiritual practice of observing forty days of rest is widely followed in many cultures and religions, and a careful study of the scriptures can help us understand why the observance might be important. Forty is a significant and symbolic number that occurs many times in the scriptures. The following are just a few of the things that happened in forty-day periods:

- God sent rain for forty days and nights to cleanse the earth in Noah's time (see Genesis 7).
- Jesus fasted and meditated in the wilderness for forty days (see Matthew 4).
- Jesus taught His disciples for forty days after His resurrection (see Acts 1).

- Jonah gave Nineveh forty days to repent (see Jonah 3).
- Moses was on the mountain for forty days (see Exodus 24).
- The spies were in Canaan for forty days (see Numbers 13).

In each of the examples, forty days was a period of sanctification and transition from one state of being to another. Forty appears to be the number of change. For example, Jesus fasted for forty days right before He began His ministry, and the scriptures tell us that He was led by the Spirit into the wilderness to fast—separating Himself from the world. Christ also spent forty days at the end of His ministry, after His resurrection, with His Apostles, teaching them and preparing them to live in the world without Him. This teaching was also done in seclusion, away from the world.

Forty *years* is also a recurring theme in the scriptures, and there is a connection. In Numbers 14:34, we read God's explanation that the forty days the spies were in Canaan symbolized the forty years that Israel would wander in the wilderness. Using days to symbolize larger units of time is interesting when you consider that normal pregnancy is about forty weeks, and there is usually a maximum of forty days of bleeding afterward. God is a master of symbolism, and as He said, "all things bear record of me" (Moses 6:63).

Probably the most well-known reference to the forty days after giving birth is the forty days of purification that Mary observed after giving birth to Jesus. (See "Mary," page 361.) Many people think of purification today as taking something dirty and making it clean, such as tap water. However, in the dictionary, *purification* is synonymous with *sanctification* and *hallow*.[1] Thus, purification meant taking something ordinary and making it holy. In Leviticus, we learn more about this purification ritual:

> When the days of her *purifying* are fulfilled . . . she shall bring a *lamb* of the first year for a . . . sin offering, unto the door of the tabernacle of the congregation, unto the priest . . . and the priest shall make an atonement for her; and *she shall be clean*. (Leviticus 12:6–8; emphasis added)

I love the symbolism in these verses. The words *atonement, blood, purifying, lamb,* and *she shall be clean* stand out to me. Also, the woman makes the offering, but the priest, who "shall make an atonement for her," is symbolic of the Savior acting for us as our mediator. It is clear that God wanted our hearts turned toward the Savior and His Atonement as we give birth, and the forty days, with its symbolism, is one of the ways He hopes we will see it. Robyn Allgood, reflected on these verses:

> I have this theory that when a woman offers herself for another, she is rendered a certain amount of forgiveness, just as when we share our testimony we receive forgiveness. It is an offering of sacrifice that can be rewarded with sanctification. I don't think that someone automatically receives forgiveness, but it would be according to their "offering." What have I offered the Lord? What have I laid at the altar? The forty days are a time of meditation and pondering that can "hallow" us.[2]

The purpose of these ancient purification rituals was to turn the people's hearts toward Christ, who was yet to come. As we know, Christ's Atonement fulfilled the law of Moses, so women no longer have to offer a literal lamb. However, an offering is still required: "And ye shall offer for a sacrifice unto me a broken heart and a contrite spirit." (3 Nephi 9:19–20). Each woman's offering will be unique and should be governed by inspiration; however, there are some things that can make the first forty days a time of sanctification for your family.

Some women choose to observe their forty days of rest much like the Sabbath. For example, during my babymoon, I didn't work and didn't go to any stores or events. I bought everything online or sent willing friends and relatives to the store. I didn't cook much, thanks to friends and the Relief Society. I didn't even drive my car, because dealing with a car seat and traffic was too much of the world for me.

I did take easy walks with my daughter, I took a lot of baths, and I had only my favorite people over for short (or long) visits. My daughter and I mastered nursing. I read my scriptures and some other good books while she napped on my chest. I also kept the lights low and played soothing music. It was truly a honeymoon, a veritable love nest.

If you plan ahead and let people know what you are doing and that it is a spiritual practice, you may be surprised to find an amazing amount of support. My hairdresser volunteered to come to me during that time, and I had countless other offers of support. If you have older children, you can include them in some of the cuddling during baby time and also ask helpers to play with the older children or take them to the park.

Some women wonder how soon after having a baby they should go to church. This is a purely personal matter, but a decision should be made consciously and not because the mother feels pressure or wants to show off her new baby. As part of the ritual of purification, Mary was not allowed to go to the sanctuary for the forty days, which perhaps increased her desire to go. I know that I didn't feel ready until six weeks had passed, but I did miss the sacrament. I now realize that I could have asked to have the sacrament brought to me. Members of the priesthood often bring the sacrament to the sick, elderly, and public servants who can't come to church because they work on Sunday. The sacrament is a wonderful part of the sanctification process, and next time I will ask for it.

I can't express how fast my own babymoon passed. I have heard many people express the same feelings with surprise. Even fathers who at first thought the babymoon sounded like a forty-day sentence later described it as a much-too-short honeymoon. In fact, it's not just babies and mothers who benefit from this bonding time. Fathers need time to transition and bond too. Forty days of rest allows for plenty of time for intimate communication and transformation. Even if fathers have to return to work before the forty days is over, they can still help facilitate this time of wonder and amazement and remember to slip back into the love-nest state of mind when they come home.

Even though forty days felt like just the right amount of time, I was still sad the day I settled into my car to go to my six-week checkup and the grocery store. As I pulled out of my quiet neighborhood onto the large boulevard, I felt the world sweeping us into a fast current that would only take us further and further from those peaceful memories. Looking back, the babymoon was just a blink, but it set the tone for my daughter's whole life and my whole approach to motherhood. I am so glad I took the opportunity to bond, to build my confidence as a mother in the sanctuary of home, and to give my daughter a peaceful transition into the world.

---

1   Dictionary.com, s.v. "purification," http://dictionary.reference.com/browse/purification.
2   Robyn Allgood, private e-mail message, July 27, 2011.

ON MATERNAL BONDAGE

By Melissa Burns

WHEN I WAS PREGNANT, I worried a great deal about bonding. I wanted the Boy to bond to me. I wanted to bond with him. I wanted us to *bond*. And so I fretted about childbirth, and I breastfed as long as I could. I read to him and rocked him and cuddled him and sang to him. I nursed him in bed and napped with him. I walked miles with him.

I have days, particularly when he's teething (teething that will make you all run and cry, *"Save yourselves!"*), where I fantasize. About a PhD, an office, with a door I can close. Bookshelves lining the walls, filled with books. People who ask what I think and then *listen* to what I have to say. The pervasive quiet that allows you to hear the air conditioner and the hum of a computer. The ability to read at a desk without a solid head knock knock knocking against the bottom side of the desk, sturdy hands griping fistfuls of my pants to pull himself up on my knees, his expectant little face peering up at me as if to say, "But Mama, but Mama, *I am here*."

A tiny seed of guilt forms in my heart when I have these fantasies, and I shed that guilt and drop it into a little jar that I keep in a drawer in my mind. *Ping ping ping* go the seeds. One day when the Boy is grown, I will plant a garden with those seeds, and guilt flowers will bloom to be pollinated by butterflies.

And then, at night, when the house is quiet and dark—just the whirring of the fans—I think over the day in my mind. The things accomplished, others left undone, the books read and read and read again, the games played, the ringing of his laugh in my head, his expressions of puzzlement and delight. And as tired as I am, I smile and want to hold him. Some days are just like that. I want to put a stopper in time and say, "Nope. No progress for you today. Today is mine, to keep him small and funny."

I worried about bonding with him. How little I knew the ties that would bind me. I look at his little body. He is bone of my bone and flesh of my flesh—my body made his body, fed it, nurtured it, protected it. I am bound with living ties, in blood and nerves.

I wonder sometimes about those mothers who adopt. How much stronger their ties must be. I had forty weeks. They have been searching and working for that child for years.

He will grow up. Oh he will. Time is stubborn, and I cannot stop him. He will go out into the world and live. And that is what I want. I want him to live. I want him to experience life, even though I know that it means that he will be hurt. That is what it means to live, and I would not have him remain a child forever knock knock knocking to be let in to the world of adulthood. But I am curious. I wonder what he will see with his eyes that I have not seen with mine. I wonder what he will hear that I chose not to hear because I so loved the quiet. I wonder who he will love and lose and what he will learn from those experiences.

I know. I know that that time is coming. But today? Today is mine.

Blood, Breast Milk, and Living Water

By Robyn Allgood, AAHCC

Therefore with joy shall ye draw water out of the wells of salvation.

ISAIAH 12:3

I have always been grateful to have been able to breast-feed each of my babies, particularly my first baby. My daughter and I struggled after a difficult labor and birth. Because of the effects of epidurals and other interventions,[1] we had some obstacles to overcome that made breast-feeding harder than it had to be. I remember crying as the nurse took my baby girl from me and fed her a bottle because she was not latching on. She had been given a bottle while I was in post-op following a cesarean section. The bottle of sugar water granted my baby instant gratification. She did not have to work for the milk and, as a result, she became impatient and unwilling to latch on and work for the colostrum I had to offer her.

I will forever be grateful for the two nurses who sympathized with my desire to make breast-feeding work. My husband and I decided to make some changes to allow us to get breast-feeding established. Our baby would no longer go to the nursery. She would room-in with us constantly. We also banned bottles and had a breast pump brought in. After many hours of working with our baby with the help of these two special nurses and help at home from my younger sister, mother, and sister-in-law, we were able to finally establish breast-feeding. I still cry when I think about their loving service.

I learned many lessons from that first experience with breast-feeding. Thankfully, each of my subsequent babies latched right on without any interruption in the breast-feeding relationship and had the opportunity to work for their nourishment. Every time I sit down to nurse my newest little baby, I express gratitude to the Lord for this blessing.

LIVING WATER

My early struggles with breast-feeding brought me to a greater appreciation for it. It was something I had to work and sincerely pray for. As I sat nursing my fifth baby one day, I pondered this miracle once again. I thought about how breast milk is made from the mother's blood, which in turn becomes sweet living water full of antibodies and immunities that cannot be replicated artificially. As one author has points out:

> In the last 50 years, medical science has learned a great deal about human milk, particularly in the area of immunology. We now know that colostrum is loaded with antibodies that protect newborns from disease, that mature milk has a perfect balance of nutrition for infants, and that toddler milk becomes more concentrated with immune factors as the toddler begins to nurse less. Milk that is produced after a premature birth is different from the milk of mothers whose babies are born full-term, and those unique properties are beneficial for fragile premies. . . . Human milk is a complex, living substance that is the key to good health and optimal development for human infants.[2]

As I pondered the living nature of breast milk, I then thought of the living water that Christ offers us, available because of the blood Christ shed for us. *The Guide to the Scriptures* tells us that living water is "a symbol of the Lord Jesus Christ and his teachings. As water is essential to sustain physical life, the Savior and his teachings (living water) are essential for eternal life."[3] In fact, Jesus taught the woman of Samaria that "whosoever drinketh of this water shall thirst again: But whosoever drinketh of the water that I shall give him shall never thirst; but the water that I shall give him shall be in him a well of water springing up into everlasting life" (John 4:13–14). Though breast milk mainly consists of water, it really is more than that:

> Mother's milk, a *living liquid*, contains just the right amount of fatty acids, lactose, water, and amino acids for human digestion, brain development, and growth. It also contains many immunities a baby needs in early life while her own immune system is maturing. One more instance

of mother extending her own power, (love) to her developing child.[4]

PATIENCE

Patience has never been my virtue, and breast-feeding requires a great deal of patience in establishing the relationship and then continuing it. Heather Farrell explained this need for patience well:

> It has always really impressed me that a baby has to work pretty hard to get its milk. It has to learn how to latch on, and then they have to suck and suck for a while before anything gets flowing. It can be frustrating and slow at the start. Yet the more they suck the more milk their mother produces. If they were to stop sucking, the milk would go away, but when they ask for more, it comes in abundance.

> I think that is just like our Father in Heaven. He has told us, "ask and ye shall receive, knock and it shall be opened unto you." He has living water for us, but we have to be willing to ask Him for it, over and over again. Sometimes we even have to work, and it takes a while before anything comes.

> If we give up and scream and cry because what we want isn't coming fast enough, then we miss out. We have to keep working and asking, and soon His living water begins to flow—like a river. It amazes me that this is one of the very first lessons that we are taught when we come to this earth. God could have made breast-feeding a much different process, but I think He knew that His children needed to learn this right away.[5]

LOVE

Hormones play an important role in the process of breast-feeding. Oxytocin and prolactin are integral in releasing and stimulating milk production and ejection. Oxytocin is known as the love hormone and causes the ejection of the milk.[6] French researcher and obstetrician Michel Odent pointed out that "it is noticeable that whatever the facet of love we consider, oxytocin is involved."[7] Right after the birth of the placenta, we have a high level of prolactin, the mothering hormone. While we are nursing, we continue to have elevated levels of prolactin, with the level decreasing over time. The entire process is triggered by love. Love is also at the root of what brought about the Atonement. "For God so loved the world that He gave His Only Begotten Son" (John 3:16). Author Cory Young has said:

> The altruistic oxytocin is part of a complex hormonal balance. A sudden release of oxytocin creates an urge toward loving which can be directed in different ways depending on the presence of other hormones, which is why there are different types of love. For example, with a high level of prolactin, a well-known mothering hormone, the urge to love is directed toward babies.[8]

It is no mistake that this first meal is sweet. This experience in life is a powerful symbol. God intended for the first taste in life for each and every one of His children to be pleasing and full of love. Babies go through a lot being born. How powerful for them to know that life, from the very first mouthful, is intended to be sweet. In 2 Nephi 2:25, we are reminded that men, women, and babies are born "that they might have joy." God's symbolism never ceases to amaze me.

SACRIFICE

It is a blessing to nurse our babies, but there is a measure of sacrifice involved. To continue a successful breast-feeding relationship, there is a need for the mother to offer her body to benefit her baby. It can be hard to adjust to feeling that your body does not just belong to yourself anymore. All of a sudden, your schedule is determined by someone else's needs for nourishment. Mother will be on call day and night. This fact reminds me of the constant availability of our Savior when we have needs. We are reminded that "his hand is stretched out still" (Isaiah 9:16). He does not turn us away, whether it is 3:00 p.m. or 3:00 a.m.

Along with losing a bit of independence, sometimes breast-feeding is a trial for mother and baby. Just ask the mother who has had to deal with thrush, breast infections, cracked nipples, or other difficulties. She has had challenges to overcome that require sacrifice. Some women sacrifice greatly to pump and then feed their baby, making the process twice as long. And some mothers must sacrifice what they had so desired to give their babies when, for whatever reason, breast-feeding cannot be established or continue. We are all called upon to "sacrifice in the similitude of the great sacrifice of the Son of God" (D&C 138:13). Nursing our babies is one of the ways in which mothers can sacrifice for the benefit of others, as the Savior did.

UNITY

It is easy for me to get busy and forget that it is time for my baby to nurse again. When this happens, she gently rubs her head into my chest until it dawns on me, "Oh, you're hungry!" I have become distracted from her needs. I savor the reminder, and we go to our comfy glider to enjoy a feast of sorts. I think of her gentle reminders and wonder how often the Savior is quietly and gently nudging me to come to Him and drink of living water. Breast-feeding has provided me an opportunity to become aware of this need to come to Him frequently, becoming one in purpose. In Isaiah 49:23, we are reminded, "And kings shall be thy nursing fathers, and their queens thy nursing mothers: they shall bow down to thee with their face toward the earth, and lick up the dust of thy feet; and thou shalt know that I am the Lord: for they shall not be ashamed that wait for me." I think of those who wait for Him as those who continue to come to Him for the living water and nourishment He can provide. They come again and again (just as a baby does) to partake of His living water through repentance, forgiveness, service, and submission of their wills to His.

The other side to the unity we experience through breast-feeding comes from the mother. When a baby has not been fed for a while, a mother will likely experience physical discomfort. Her breasts may become engorged and full, and she'll *want*, almost with desperation, to feed her baby. It is almost impossible to forget to feed your baby when your chest is full and hurting. This is also symbolic of the Savior: "Can a woman forget her sucking child, that she should not have compassion on the son of her womb? yea, they may forget, yet will I not forget thee" (Isaiah 49:15). The Lord doesn't want to be away from us anymore than we want to be away from Him. He wants, with desperation, to give us the life that He is overflowing with. Unity works both ways—the mother and child are bound to each other through need and necessity, and the same is true of our relationship with our Heavenly Father.

Pondering this subject has caused me to be more in awe of the miraculous feminine body that God created to give His children life. The female body is a powerful symbol of God's love for His children. Nursing has become more to me than a way to nourish my baby. It has also become a time for quietly communing with my Savior and for partaking of *His* living water.

1 Della A. Forster and Helen L. McLachlan,"Breast-Feeding Initiation and Birth Setting Practices: A Review of the Literature," *Journal of Midwifery and Women's Health* 52, no. 3 (2007): 273–280, http://www.medscape.com/viewarticle/558119.
2 Anna Edgar, "Anatomy of a Working Breast," *New Beginnings* 22, no. 2 (2005): 44–50, http://www.llli.org/NB/NBMarApr05p44.html; emphasis added.
3 The Guide to the Scriptures, s.v. "living water," http://lds.org/scriptures/gs/living-water.t1.
4 Cory Young, "The Science of Mother Love," Babies Online, http://www.babiesonline.com/articles/baby/scienceofmotherslove.asp; emphasis added.
5 Heather Farrell, the GOGL Google group discussion.
6 Michel Odent, *The Scientification of Love* (London: Free Association, 2001), 10–11.
7 Ibid.
8 Cory Young, "The Science of Mother Love," Babies Online, http://www.babiesonline.com/articles/baby/scienceofmotherslove.asp.

ONE MORE TRY

By Julie M.

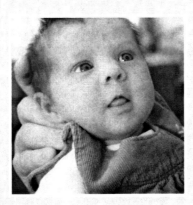

I HAVE ALWAYS STRUGGLED with nursing my children. However, nursing has always been very important to me. So when my daughter, Elise, was born (our fourth baby), it was no surprise to have some struggles in the hospital. It was typical, so I didn't think that much about it. By the time we got home, it was getting harder and harder and more painful, and I began to see why it was getting worse.

My first three kids were boys, but my Elise's mouth was much smaller than her brothers' had been. Her mouth was too small to be able to latch on properly. This is because I am (unfortunately) very large busted, and so she just simply couldn't do it. By the time I finally figured this out, I was in tons of pain every time she tried nursing. My face would just run with tears. I began bleeding every time, and when she would let go, she would have blood around her mouth, and that of course just made me cry more and feel like I was failing her.

We went to see the doctor because we were afraid I was going to develop mastitis. The doctor let me know that I was fine. He then told me that it's no big deal not to nurse and that I should just give up and not worry about it. Well that wasn't going to work for me. I got a really good pump and began pumping for her. I pumped and pumped and pumped. I pumped everything she ate. I kept a log of how much milk I pumped, what she ate, and how much I had in reserve. I also had a system to make sure the milk was being rotated properly.

My family and I prayed and prayed that Elise would be able to nurse. After a couple of weeks and then months, I pretty much gave up on that idea and just accepted the fact that she wasn't going to. I would try from time to time to get her to nurse, but she didn't like it. It would just make her mad. My oldest son Jake (he was five and a half at the time) was not willing to give up. He continued to pray. He was very faithful about praying for us everyday.

There were some blessings I gained from pumping. My husband, David, was able to help feed his little girl. He really enjoyed taking part in this. The boys also enjoyed helping out their new little sister. I think it helped them realize how special she was. They are so close to her and absolutely adore her, and she really looks up to them a lot. Also it forced me to be more organized. Pumping to that degree takes a lot a time, and so I needed to be very careful with my time. Plus my milk supply is very sensitive. If I missed a pumping or was more than fifteen to twenty minutes off my schedule, I could see the effects of it the next day. So this experience really taught me several things.

Then one day, when Elise was about four and a half months old, David asked me if I had tried nursing her lately. I said no, because I had just accepted that I was going to pump and that nursing wasn't going work. Now, like I said, Jake would not give up on praying for us. He was very diligent. David encouraged me to go ahead and try one more time. So I did, and she took right to it! I couldn't believe it. My little girl was four and a half months old and started nursing. To us it was a miracle and a true answer to prayer. I am so incredibly grateful that Jake never gave up. After that, we didn't have any more struggles with nursing. But I did have one other problem. I had 432 ounces of breast milk stocked up in my freezer!

FINDING MY MOTHERLY INTUITION

By Meleah Ekstrand

BREAST-FEEDING WAS NOT GOING TO BE A PROBLEM for *me* and *my baby*. We had the perfect recipe for a breast-feeding relationship: he was born at home without drugs, given immediate skin to skin contact, and quickly offered the breast. But he wouldn't latch, and I was shocked.

I tried everything I could think of, but he just was not interested. My doula tried a few tricks and then my midwife, but still no luck or suck for that matter. Within the first three days, he lost one pound. We finally used a nipple shield, and he latched right on. However, at his two-week check-up he had not reached his birth weight by almost seven ounces. He was gaining weight, but very slowly. My midwife became concerned and immediately suggested I contact a lactation consultant as well as my baby's doctor to work on a plan of action.

She quickly located a lactation consultant in my area, and the following morning I had an appointment. I arrived at the consultant's small office with about eight other moms, all crammed in for a breast-feeding session. I am not sure if it was the fact that my baby was born at home, but I was immediately not comfortable with the large group atmosphere. Despite my discomfort, I decided to sit down and try it out. After she weighed my baby, she gave me a "goody bag" with several freebies including a small ice pack, a cooler, and milk storage bottles for my breast milk (that just so happened to have a formula company's name on them).

Then we each sat nursing so that the lactation consultant could evaluate how we were doing. While watching the other moms nurse, I noticed one beginning to stroke her baby's back while she cradled her head as she nursed. I admired this mother and the outward love she was showing her baby. Then it was suddenly disrupted by the lactation consultant telling her to stop—she was "agitating her daughter" and making her "not want to nurse." I should have left then, but I stayed.

After the lactation consultant made her rounds, it was my turn. She watched me nurse, began correcting my form, and then began to talk supplementation. She began to offer formula. (Over half of the women in the class were supplementing with either formula or their own breast milk.) I declined. She then offered my breast milk via a bottle. I declined this option as well. She then offered my breast milk via a syringe. If there was one thing I knew, it was that my baby did not need supplementation. My breasts and my baby were doing their job, but they just needed a little more time. As I sat and contemplated this, she then said, "You want your baby's brain to grow, don't you? We need to get him something to eat." I immediately began to cry. She tried to comfort me but then started pushing the syringe again, adding "I have seen babies suck and suck, not get anything, and starve themselves to death." I wanted to leave, but I stayed, allowing her to give my son a syringe of my breast milk. After we finished, she gave me a stock of syringes and a long list of instructions on what to do until next time.

As soon as I walked out of the class carrying my baby, my strength and motherly protection over this little baby started to come back. As I left in the elevator, I knew without a doubt that there wouldn't be a "next time." As soon as I got home, I threw the syringes in the trash. I knew that my baby was OK. I was not worried about his health or his breast-feeding. I felt an amazing sense of peace that he just needed a little more time to gain his weight back.

The following morning, we had an appointment with my baby's doctor. I'll admit that I was nervous about what he might say. I had been warned that doctors admit babies to the hospital for not re-gaining their birth weight. However, as I discussed the situation with the doctor, my motherly intuition was confirmed. He was not at all concerned about his weight, felt that the quantity of diapers and weight gain were the right indicators he was looking for, and that in a week or so he would reach his birth weight.

Just like all babies are not all born on their due dates, not all babies hit their birth weight at two weeks. As my baby's mother, all along I felt a calming presence I had never felt before—that my baby was fine, that we would figure out breast-feeding, and he would quickly recover his weight. Against all of the experts' advice (with exception of my pediatrician), I knew that my baby was OK. I knew that allowing him a little more time was just what he needed. Even though that day with the lactation consultant was so upsetting for me, I consider it my defining day—the day I discovered my motherly intuition.

Babywearing: Carried from the Womb

By Robyn Allgood, AAHCC

Hearken unto me . . . which are borne by me from the belly,
which are carried from the womb:
And even to your old age . . . will I carry you.

ISAIAH 46:3–4

One of the earliest memories from my early childhood is of lying on my mother's chest, listening to her heart and trying to match my breathing to hers. The rhythm of her heartbeat would relax me, and I would eventually find myself falling to sleep with her. Now I find myself carrying my own babies close to my heart.

Caring for a baby is demanding work. A baby has a constant need to be near his or her mother for nourishment, comfort, and warmth and a longing to be integrated into the mother's daily activities. One of the ways we can meet all of these needs is through babywearing. So what exactly is babywearing?

"Babywearing" simply means holding or carrying a baby or young child using a cloth baby carrier. Holding babies is natural and universal; baby carriers make it easier and more comfortable, allowing parents and caregivers to hold or carry their children while attending to the daily tasks of living. Babywearing helps a new dad put a fussy newborn to sleep. It allows a new mom use both hands to make a sandwich. It lets an experienced parent or caregiver carry a baby on her back and wash the dishes, do the laundry, take a hike, or weed the garden, all while keeping the baby safe and content.[1]

Babywearing is not new. It is a very old practice used in many cultures.

Anthropologist Ashley Montague pointed out that our babies are actually born nine months early, meaning that because they are not mobile and cannot seek food without our help it is obvious that they require additional gestational time in our arms. They are born when they are small enough to fit through the birth canal, but they still require a great deal of care.[2] Many babies prefer being near their mothers' hearts rather than being in car seats, bouncy chairs, swings, cribs, or other mechanical devices. While these devices have their time and place, we can easily overuse them. Even so, the truth of the matter is that our arms can get tired. This is where baby-wearing comes in. When done correctly, babywearing can be a wonderful way to aid your baby's contentment and development.

As I have pondered the benefits of babywearing, several passages of scriptures, provided below, have taken on special meaning to me and brought me closer to the Savior.

COMFORT

"As one whom his mother comforteth, so will I comfort you" (Isaiah 66:13).

Because your baby is near you, your baby is more likely to be happy. If he or she requires comforting, you can meet your baby's needs quickly.

REASSURANCE

Who comforteth us in all our tribulation, that we may be able to comfort them which are in any trouble, by the comfort wherewith we ourselves are comforted of God" (2 Corinthians 1:4).

I know that my babies have felt more confidence when near me. An alarm seems to go off in babies' little hearts when they do not know where their mommies are. When they are in our arms, they are reassured with love and safety.

LOVE

"In all their affliction he was afflicted, and the angel of his presence saved them: in his love and in his pity he redeemed them; and he bare them, and carried them all the days of old" (Isaiah 63:9).

To a little baby, mother is the "angel of presence" who teaches love. Baby-wearing promotes love because of the proximity of the baby to the mother and the availability to give and receive love.

TRUST

"I will abide in thy tabernacle for ever: I will trust in the covert of thy wings" (Psalm 61:4).

Because your baby feels reassured and comforted "in the covert of thy wings," your baby is taught how to trust and in whom to trust. Your baby understands whom to go to when scared or in need of reassurance.

ACTIVITY

"Verily I say, men should be anxiously engaged in a good cause, and do many things of their own free will, and bring to pass much righteousness" (D&C 58:27).

Integrating our babies into our activities early on teaches them to appreciate work and to be active as we are. If we are always trying to entertain them, then entertainment will be their focus.

EXAMPLE

"He . . . shall gather the lambs with his arm, and carry them in his bosom, and shall gently lead those that are with young" (Isaiah 40:11).

Carrying our babies enables us to gently lead them as they are taught by our examples. They will be able to go about life with more confidence because they have had time watching and learning from their parents. Through emulating our examples, our babies learn to identify "the power within them" and become "agents unto themselves" (D&C 58:2).

NOURISHMENT

"That ye may suck, and be satisfied with the breasts of her consolations; that ye may milk out, and be delighted with the abundance of her glory for thus saith the Lord, Behold, I will extend peace to her like a river, and . . . ye shall be born upon her sides, and be dandled upon her knees" (Isaiah 66:11–12).

One of the remedies for problems in establishing breast-feeding with a newborn is to wear the baby skin-to-skin. Babies can't help but learn where nourishment comes from when they are so near it. Some mothers become so comfortable with babywearing that they are able to breast-feed while wearing their babies.

HUMAN INTERACTION

"A child left to himself bringeth his mother to shame" (Proverbs 29:15).

Babies worn close to our hearts learn to be stimulated by social interaction instead of by mechanical, electronic, or digital means. In this day and age of technology, it is important that our children learn to interact in face-to-face social situations. There is something lost in relying too much on technology. Babies also learn to regulate their breathing and temperature by being held in our arms.

Studies show that babies who have their needs quickly met are happier and cry less.[3] A happier baby means a happier mother, father, and family. Babywearing is not just for mothers. It is a great way for fathers to bond with their babies too! I cherish the memories I have of my husband with a baby strapped on while he went about his business working in the garage or vacuuming the floors. I also love that my daughters have enjoyed wearing their "babies" in a sling. One daughter in particular proudly and lovingly wore her three baby dolls all at the same time.

Wearing your baby also has undeniable health benefits. In addition to preventing ear infections,[4] it also aids in other areas of development:

> Babies' brains . . . expect closeness and proximity—to be held— for their safety, their psychological growth, physical growth, mental growth, to aid and stabilize their physiological processes and keep their immune systems strong.[5]

Babies were made to be held, loved, and nurtured in close proximity.

As I have pondered the needs of my babies to be carried and worn near my heart, I am inclined to think of the Savior. The scriptures tell us that "surely he hath borne our griefs and *carried* our sorrows" (Isaiah 53:4; emphasis added). Just as our babies are best nurtured in close proximity to us, the Savior can only nurture us as much as we are willing to be close to Him. It is not a mistake that the imagery used to describe the mission of our Savior is often filled with images of motherhood. We are to be reminded of the Savior and how He carries us as we carry our babies. Carrying our babies near our hearts allows us to create a strong bond with them, remaining their guides through life. Babywearing allows us to emulate the Savior, who desires that we and our babies be "encircled about eternally in the arms of his love" (2 Nephi 1:15).

---

1 "What Is Babywearing," Babywearing International, http://www.babywearinginternational.org.

2 Ashley Montagu, *Touching: The Human Significance of the Skin*, (New York, NY: Harper & Row Publishers, 1986), 75, 57.

3 William Sears and Martha Sears, *Christian Parenting and Childcare* (Nashville, TN: Broadman & Holman, 1997), 243–244.

4 Regine Schon, "Natural Parenting-Back to Basics in Infant Care" *Evolutionary Psychology 5*, no. 1 (2007): 102–183, http://www.epjournal.net/filestore/ep05102183.pdf.

5 Tiffany Field, *Touch* (MIT Press, 2003), 69–74, http://books.google.com/books?id=1fBdoaBC9-YC&printsec=frontcover&source=gbs_ge_summary_r&cad=0#v=onepage&q&f=false.

Babywearing Safety

There are a variety of ways to carry your baby. There are ring slings, pouch slings, Asian baby carriers, and wraps, to name just a few. You can even make your own sling with a long piece of fabric. Just as breast-feeding takes practice, so does babywearing. It is also necessary to find out how to wear your baby safely. Be sure to do research regarding the type of sling you are using and how to use it properly according to the age and weight of your baby or toddler. The Tummy 2 Tummy DVD is a great resource. You can also visit this book's website for more information and resources on baby wearing.

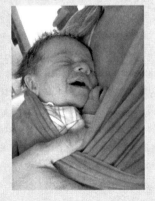

Perspective on Postpartum Depression

By Amy King

Know thou, my [daughter], that all these things shall give thee experience, and shall be for thy good.

D&C 122:7

"Is she a good baby for you?" I asked a friend. She had given birth to her first baby just four weeks prior. This is my automatic question of mothers with new babies. You can tell a lot from their answers, especially how they are feeling about motherhood. "Oh, yes," my friend responded enthusiastically. "She's perfect . . . I can't even believe how easy it is." When I hear those words, I can't believe it either. *Just be happy for her*, I have to remind myself time and time again. You would think after seven years and three babies I would be over my own postpartum experiences. You would think that I wouldn't twitch just a little every time a new mother tells me that all her newborn ever does is eat or sleep. Or that her labor was just too easy. Or that recovery was a cinch.

For me, having babies was traumatic, exhausting, chaotic, painful, frustrating, overwhelming, and depressing. Colic. Colic. Colic. C-section. C-section. C-section. Three babies. Three times. Only, the first time I didn't realize that I was suffering from postpartum depression (PPD). I didn't want my baby to wake up. I didn't want to wake up. Sleep? When was the last time I slept? When was the last time my newborn ate or *stopped crying*? When was the last time I got out of the house? Or had a minute to myself? Nursing wasn't working; he cried too much. All the techniques to swaddle and soothe didn't work. Wasn't all this supposed to come naturally to me? Wasn't this what I wanted? What I had always hoped for? What was wrong with me? Why was it so easy for other women? Failure. I was a failure. Guilt. My baby hated me. Alone. Oh, so alone. It all became a big blur, rolled into one nightmare that seemed to last forever. This was supposed to be the most special time of my life. I loved my baby, no question about it. I had always considered myself a very sane and functioning individual. Why, then, was I feeling and acting this way?

About 10 percent of women who have babies experience postpartum depression, which typically occurs within four weeks after giving birth but can occur anytime during the following year. . . . Mothers experiencing postpartum depression may have one or more of the following symptoms:

• Struggling for perfection.
• Feeling overwhelmed or feeling a sense of failure.
• Experiencing shattered expectations.
• Plunging into despair.
• Having difficulty focusing and concentrating.
• Feeling lonely.
• Panicking.
• Having difficulty sleeping.
• Lacking appetite.
• Feeling as though she is losing her mind.
• Struggling to survive.

"Family members and close friends can help mitigate postpartum depression by watching for its symptoms and offering help and support."[1]

—**Lynn Clark Callister** PhD, RN, FAAN,
Brigham Young University professor, College of Nursing

[1] Lynn Clark Callister, "Managing Postpartum Depression: A Gospel Perspective," *Ensign*, August 2009, http://lds.org/ensign/2009/08/managing-postpartum-depression-a-gospel-perspective.

My husband had *no* idea what was going on—just that he was living with a different person, who cried almost as much as the new baby (he was really suffering from his own type of PPD). I certainly didn't know what was going on. People would often tell me that it would get better. "This too shall pass," they would say. "The baby will grow out of this, and it will be wonderful." This is all very true. But, in the moment, it was difficult to see past the situation I was in. Though I was struggling deeply, it didn't occur to me to ask for help.

I later read a story about some villages in Africa. When a new baby is born, the village women come in to care for the mother and baby for the first four weeks. They do all the cooking and cleaning and even take care of the older children. The mother is pretty much left alone to bond with her baby and recover. Although the article didn't say it, I don't doubt that if the mother had major surgery and an extremely fussy baby, those village women would be right there, taking turns soothing the baby and making sure the mother had plenty of rest so she could make a full recovery. I'm convinced this would have made a world of difference in my case.

Unfortunately, our culture rarely resembles the village model. If someone is coming over, our house needs to be clean, and we want to show that we are handling things just fine. We are independent women and not used to asking for help. Some women don't even realize they need help. As Brigham Young University nursing professor Lynn Clark Callister pointed out in her article about managing PPD, "Women might have unrealistic expectations for themselves at a time of great transition, feeling that they should be able to do everything immediately for themselves and their newborn because they should be 'super-mom' and 'super-wife.'"[1] As women, we naturally put a lot of pressure on ourselves.

This is where good friends, family, and the Relief Society come in. We need to be more proactive in recognizing PPD. It is *real*. It can happen to *anyone*. But different mothers experience PPD on different levels and for varying lengths of time. What doesn't vary is that they need love, support, intervention, and resources. I had no idea that there were a lot of resources out there to help me, including other women who had felt what I was suffering. As with most trials in life, women with PPD must endure it and overcome it. But how much easier it can be to endure when a mother is surrounded by people who are willing to lift her burden, to not judge her, to just love and support her. The scriptures remind us to be willing to "bear one another's burdens, that they may be light . . . and comfort those who stand in need of comfort" (Mosiah 18:8–9). Words can indeed be comforting, but actions are divine.

Not long before I had my second baby, our family moved from Arizona to Indiana. I was reluctantly leaving my parents, siblings, and security network. My husband was starting a full-time master's program, and I knew I would be alone most of the time. Realizing I had three months to make new friends before our baby arrived, I made an extra effort to be social and to put myself out there. I knew from my first bout with PPD that I would need the support. I was blessed to make friends quickly, and I became very close to one neighbor in particular. Janel lived in the apartment just above mine. She (and her actions) would be the major reason I quite literally survived my second round of PPD.

I had my daughter, Addisyn, in January. My son, Connor, was twenty-two months. We were stuck in our tiny little basement apartment for a long, cold winter with a screaming newborn who was failing to thrive because she wouldn't nurse. It was an intense semester for my husband, so he was rarely home. I needed him, and he needed me, but emotionally and physically we could not be there for each other.

This is where Janel stepped in. She would bring her nine-month-old down to my apartment and try to help me nurse my newborn. She even went to the lactation consultant with me. After she put her baby down at night, she would bring the monitor down to my apartment and do my dishes, fold my laundry, or hold the baby while I had a break. She would bring me lunch or dinner and actually feed it to me while I nursed. She would feed Connor and even bathe him. She arranged for friends in the ward to take him a couple hours a day for the first few weeks, so he could get away from the chaos at home.

Although I still suffered from PPD, and it was a very dark time in my life, the Lord provided a way for me to endure. He succored me by allowing another person to serve. What a tender mercy I will remember for the rest of my life. Janel's actions were inspired. President Spencer W. Kimball taught, "God does watch over us and does notice us, but it usually through someone else that he meets our needs."[2]

Tender mercies are all over the place when we stop to look around. Just when I thought I couldn't take it anymore, someone would call or stop by or say something kind. Or the baby would cry just a little less or sleep a little longer so I could get that shower I desperately needed. In those moments when I felt as though no one understood, the Spirit reminded me of Jesus Christ. The Savior truly did understand my pain and sorrows. He has taken upon himself all our "infirmities, that his bowels may be filled with mercy, according to the flesh, that he may know according to the flesh how to succor his people according to their infirmities" (Alma 7:12). He has the power to help us cope in our times of trial and lift us to a higher place.

I have come to realize that, as unpleasant as my experiences with PPD were, good did come out of them. I am more compassionate toward those who have similar struggles. I now have true empathy for them. I have had the opportunity to comfort those who stand in need of comfort. I am able to lend an understanding ear to other mothers and reassure them that they are not alone, even when it seems so. I am a stronger woman for my experiences.

---

1   Lynn Clark Callister, "Managing Postpartum Depression: A Gospel Perspective," *Ensign*, August 2009, http://lds.org/ensign/2009/08/managing-postpartum-depression-a-gospel-perspective.
2   Spencer W. Kimball, "Small Acts of Service," *Ensign*, December 1974, http://lds.org/ensign/1974/12/small-acts-of-service.

DIMINISHING DARKNESS

By Tori Gollihugh

I WAS BROUGHT UP in The Church of Jesus Christ of Latter-day Saints. However, I began to rebel when I was about sixteen, and I was officially "off the
path" by the time I was eighteen. I stayed off the straight and narrow for
nearly ten years.

While in rebellion, I married my husband, and we had our first child. A
girl. She was a sweet, wonderful, quiet, smart baby girl. Postpartum depression set in almost immediately. By the time my baby was five weeks old,
I was having horrible thoughts about how to kill her and myself. At the
time, in my inactivity and lack of understanding, I thought I was having the
thoughts of myself. In actuality, I was clearly discerning the whispers of the
deceiver's angels and accepting them as my thoughts.

The darkest days of that experience of postpartum depression lasted
about seven months. I chose not to seek help with the depression because
I was deeply concerned that I would not be trusted to mother my child. But
I knew I could be trusted. I also believed that I would be unable to refuse
medication. Regardless of how the medical community professes that it
does not affect the child of a nursing mother, I knew it was wrong for me.

I began attending church, finally, when my little girl was about four
months old. It was very difficult to keep going to the ward I was meant to

attend because I was not greeted nor spoken to at all. After two months of that, I came home from church and decided not to return. My husband was not a member, my baby was a handful, and I just knew nobody there cared. The difficulty I experienced in my effort going back to church was exacerbated by the horrible thoughts that accompanied my experience of PPD.

That Friday night I had a dream. In that dream, my eldest daughter was a full-grown adult talking to me. We talked for a few hours, but the only part of what she said that I could remember when I woke up was, "You're going to be my Mom. You have to make sure you're going to church so I don't have to find it." The next day I did go to church. Regardless of the trials I have faced since then, I have continued to go to church. It was soon after that dream, after making a real commitment to myself to go to church regularly, that the PPD began to abate in earnest.

I became endowed when my first daughter was one year old. When my second baby was three weeks old, we moved. My temple trip travel time went from a minimum of eight hours round-trip down to four. When someone else mentioned their monthly temple trips, I felt the Spirit whispering to me that I should make a concerted effort to get to the temple monthly.

We had gone to the temple while my Mom was in town during the first month of my newborn baby's life. But I knew I couldn't go to the temple on my own with a two-month-old unless I pumped, and I refused to pump unless I was in dire straits. So I asked my non-member husband to help me make monthly temple trips by going with me, caring for our children, and enabling me to nurse before and after my time in the temple. He agreed.

So we went to the temple every month from the time my second daughter was three-and-a-half weeks old. I fell into PPD when she was about three months old. It was a difficult time, in general. I had more emotional tumult unrelated to the PPD, but the overall experience of PPD was not the horrible deep dark of my first experience. Additionally, the darkest days of that PPD "only" lasted five months.

We continued to attend the temple every month from our move until after our third daughter was born. When she was five months old, PPD came to visit. By this time I had, for sure, figured out where those horrible thoughts originated. So, when they flitted into my brain, I pushed them right out. The PPD this time around was a "hazy gray" instead of the inky blackness of #1, or the dark-cave in which some things are discernable of

#2. The darkest days of the PPD this time around lasted only three months.

When my third daughter was about eighteen months old, we moved closer to the temple. I felt that we should begin making twice-monthly temple trips. I proposed it to my hubby. He agreed, but in a way that caused me concern. I did not press. We continued our once monthly temple trips. The next month, I reminded my hubby about the twice-monthly idea and asked if we could do two temple trips each month for the rest of the year (two months). He agreed, so we did.

By December, my hubby had been unemployed for a month, and we were six months preggie with #4. When a sister I knew through an LDS homeschooler group challenged me to attend the temple weekly, I pooh-poohed the idea initially. After a couple weeks of stewing on it, I decided I'd at least see what my hubby thought. He thought it could be good for me and encouraged me to do it. So I did.

I went to the temple three times in December. My hubby got a job after being completely unemployed just under a month. I attended the temple four times in January. I went to the temple three times in February, and my hubby started an even better paying job the last day of that month. I was able to make it to the temple once in March before baby arrived.

During those few months, I came to understand that the sister who challenged me to weekly temple attendance had been inspired of the Lord. Heavenly Father wanted me to attend the temple as often as possible so that I could build up a store of spiritual "oil," ensuring that any PPD would be significantly less than my past experiences.

As of this writing, baby #4 is ten weeks old. I have had only three bluesy/weepy days. According to the medical literature I've been able to find on this subject, once a woman has had PPD after giving birth, it becomes more likely that she will have PPD and that the experiences of it will worsen.

I know, I bear testimony, that the decreasing intensity and duration of PPD that I have experienced after each of my children is one of my personal miracles. I know that the Lord has provided this awesome miracle and gift to me because I have desired and worked to draw nearer to Him. I truly believe that I will not have any PPD at all after my next baby (and may not have any bluesy days at all either). I also believe that, by the time my quiver is full, I will not have any depression issues at all. I believe this to be true and possible because of what I have already experienced and because of the whispers of the Spirit of the Lord to my mind. I know that this same miracle is possible for all who will draw nigh unto the Lord that He may draw nigh unto them.

HEALING FROM SEXUAL ABUSE

By Shantel Gardner

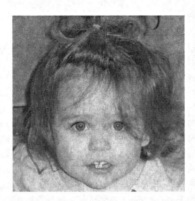

I WAS SEXUALLY ABUSED. There was never a time when I did not have a memory of it. I thought I had dealt with it. I thought I had forgiven. My third pregnancy went great until I reached the end. I was at thirty-six weeks, and I was so miserable and tired. I started having anxiety and horrible dreams. I would wake up with horrible memories of being sexually abused, and they would make me throw up and trigger a lot of contractions. I started begging my midwife to break my water so I could have the baby. She refused, of course, since I was only thirty-six weeks.

At my thirty-seven week exam, my midwife again refused to break my water. I started crying and sobbing, and she said "Were you sexually abused as a child?" I said, "Yes." She rolled her eyes and said, "I knew it. I always end up with these patients. That is why you are having such control issues. You need to deal with this before you give birth or you are going to have a horrible experience." I cried harder.

Finally, at thirty-eight weeks, my water broke on its own, and I gave birth to a 9 lb 4 oz baby boy in two hours. Afterward, I hemorrhaged and went into shock. A few hours after I gave birth, I fell asleep. I had lost quite a bit of blood, so I was very weak. I had a dream that I was standing at the doors of a building. It was a school. I was holding the hand of a little boy. There was a huge storm swirling around me. The sky was black, the wind was blowing, lightning crashed, and it was raining very hard. I had this strong feeling that I needed to go into the school to seek refuge from the storm. I tried the doors, but they were locked. The storm was getting worse, and I was concerned not only for my own safety, but the safety of my son. I started crying, and I woke myself up crying. That was the beginning of my release.

Recovering from my birth was horrible, and I spiraled into a sexual-abused-triggered postpartum depression. I realized I had to deal with being abused and heal before I was going to feel better. I remember kneeling at the toilet one day, and I looked to my right and saw an angel standing there. She looked like a sweet Relief Society sister. She smiled, and I had these words come into my mind. *This is going to be hard—maybe the hardest thing you will have to do—but I will be there every step of the way. The Lord loves you, and he will be here too. Everything will be fine.* She faded away, and I started to throw up. I did not stop for seventeen hours.

After this incident, I called a hypnotherapist I had worked with before and asked to see him right away. He had me see a medical doctor, and they put me on two different medications three times a day. I did not want to take them. I felt like I was giving-in, and I had anxiety about what it would do to me. I knelt down and prayed about it, and I heard a voice *loudly* say, "*Shantel, take the medication!*" That was it. I needed to have my answer that way, or I would not have taken it.

I had so much anxiety, I was unable to do anything on my own. Showering was a monumental task, never mind caring for my home or my other children. Luckily my husband worked from home and took over. I saw my therapist twice a week. My therapy with him can best be described as going through a giant closet filled with boxes. I would pull one out, open the lid and examine what was inside in detail, and then I would decipher what was truth and throw out the rest. The truth I would turn over to Heavenly Father and asked for healing through the power of the Atonement.

My turning point was one day when I was standing in the shower, and I felt that I understood why someone would want to kill herself. This scared me, and I realized I was at rock bottom. Then I heard a voice say, "Remember who you are." From that point on, things began to change. I became diligent about scriptures and prayer.

Gradually, over time, I was healed. Bit by bit, line upon line, the anxiety began to leave. Through my process of healing, I realized I had been severely abused. I grew to understand that Porter (my baby) was a Savior to me. He was sent to trigger those things so I could get them out and heal them.

THE BIRTH OF A MOTHER

By Erica England

A FEW DAYS AFTER O WAS BORN, I lay in the hospital bed next to TJ who was asleep on his couch pull out. I stared at my sleeping husband and started to cry. I felt really scared inside and suddenly wasn't sure about having a baby any more. He awoke, he calmed me down, and I didn't have those feelings again until the second day we were home from the hospital.

The first two weeks of O's life are a complete blur to me. I went from crying in the shower, to crying in my bed. I didn't eat. I didn't really sleep. I just cried and felt scared. It wasn't that I lacked love for my little man, I just felt very, very, extremely overwhelmed. I wanted to run away.

I had heard women talk about it before but had no clue I would experience postpartum depression first hand. It hit me like a ton of bricks. I didn't want to hold O and at times didn't even want to be in the same room with him. It makes me feel awful and sick inside thinking about those days. I knew that the way I was acting was not me. My emotions and hormones took over, and I was a mess.

I prayed daily for strength. My family called multiple times a day to talk me through things. I had friends come over and sit with me, cry with me, and hold Baby O while I took some time for myself. My husband gave me countless blessings, and I, in turn, leaned on him like I never had before. All my shields fell down, and he became my rock because I could no longer function as myself. TJ became the caretaker—he did the feedings, the changings, and was so understanding of every little emotion I was having. He listened, he talked, and he held me close when I needed it.

Everyone told me it would get better, things would get easier and to just hold on, and that is what I did. I held on for dear life and puttered through the days as best as I could. TJ would hurry home from school or work and slowly things did get better. I am very fortunate that, with the help of modern medicine, the depression didn't last much longer than a month or two.

At this three month mark, I look back and have learned so much about myself. I am *not ashamed* or *embarrassed* about those first two weeks because I know that it wasn't my fault that I felt that way. I have stepped back and realized that this small trial is something that I can learn from. I have learned that I can do anything. I have learned patience. I have learned that family and true friends are key in my life. I have learned that I couldn't get through things without my husband. I have learned to trust in the Lord.

Last night, as I put my baby to bed, we read stories and said a small little prayer together. As I prayed, he squirmed in my arms and drooled all down his jammies. After I said "Amen," I looked down to see him grinning from ear to ear at me. It felt as if my heart would explode with pure love. For the first time in three months, I finally realized that it is okay to *enjoy* being this new person called Mom.

The Society for Relief

By Felice Austin, CHt

We are going to do something extraordinary.[1]

EMMA SMITH,

At the first meeting of the Relief Society

Sometimes when you hear a word too often, it loses its meaning and power. But if you were to allow yourself, magically, to hear again for the first time the words *Relief Society*, think how meaningful you might consider them. The name of our women's organization is unique. Most churches call their similar organizations the "Women's Auxiliary." *Auxiliary* means "reserve or supplementary." One of the less common definitions of *auxiliary* is "giving support, helpful."[2] Though the purpose of an organization named Women's Auxiliary can be ambiguous, there can be no doubt about the mission of an organization called the Relief Society.

As Latter-day Saint women, Relief Society is one of our most important resources, especially during pregnancy, the transition to motherhood, and after each subsequent baby. According to many studies, being a loving mother has more to do with the stability of resources than with the number of resources. Studies on animals show that youngsters in a stable environment with plenty of food get the most nurturing from their mothers. Animals who receive scarce but consistent amounts of food receive almost as much nurturing. But animals in an unpredictable environment (at times they have an abundance, and sometimes food is scarce) not only receive the least amount of nurturing but are also subject to abuse or aggression from their mothers.[3]

In humans, the stability of resources includes not just money and food but also consistency in social and emotional resources, such as support, friendship, love, energy, sleep, space, and time. According to Sarah Hardy:

"We know that the purpose of Relief Society as established by the Lord is to prepare women for the blessings of eternal life by helping them:

- Increase their faith and personal righteousness.
- Strengthen their families and homes.
- Serve the Lord and His children." [1]

---

1 Julie B. Beck, "Relief Society: A Sacred Work," Ensign, November 2009, http://lds.org/ensign/2009/11/relief-society-a-sacred-work.

Mothers have always relied on allomaternal care from others. So whatever a mother does and others do to help her, inside or outside the home, to ensure the predictability and availability of resources—financial, emotional, and social—may ultimately secure her children's future well-being.[4]

Ensuring the predictability and availability of physical as well as emotional and spiritual resources for mothers and families has been the Relief Society's primary occupation for more than 150 years. In the early Church, the Relief Society "owned livestock, real estate, and dress shops, the proceeds of which helped the needy."[5] Through two world wars and the Great Depression, the Relief Society sewed, assembled, and donated thousands of items for Saints in the United States and in Europe. In times of physical need, the Relief Society has always been first to provide relief to its members and other children of God.

Lucy Mack Smith, in contemplating the future of the Relief Society, said, "We must cherish one another, watch over one another, comfort one another, and gain instruction, that we may all sit down in heaven together."[6] This is exactly what the Relief Society has done. Most of the women I know in the Relief Society have been benefactors of some kind of emotional or spiritual nurturing from other women.

Studies show that an allomother, or substitute mother, can help break the cycle of inattentive nurturing. Louann Brizendine, MD and author of *The Female Brain*, said that "females 'inherit' their mothers' maternal

497

behavior, good or bad, then pass it on to their daughters and granddaughters."[7] This inheritance is not passed on genetically, but through what is called "epigenetic imprinting." Women who were born to inattentive mothers but then raised or influenced by nurturing allomothers tend not to behave like their genetic mothers.[8]

Any woman in a child's life can be an allomother. Even into adulthood and becoming mothers ourselves, we need other women, and each woman brings something unique. In my teen years, I needed the hip Beehive teacher who rolled down hills with us as much as I needed the strict Laurel advisor who blushed every time she said the word *bottom*.

After I had my baby, I needed allomothering more than ever. If it weren't for a friend who stayed with me in the hospital, I would have been alone. If it weren't for an aunt who had a knack for picking out great drawstring skirts, I wouldn't have had anything to wear during the first six weeks. And God bless the widow in my ward (also my visiting teacher) who volunteered to be my daughter's surrogate grandmother and stayed with me a few of those first sleepless nights.

The saying that "it takes a village to raise a child" is not just a cliché. It's true. Unfortunately, many people today are cut off from their extended family by distance or other factors and don't have the benefit of this kind of community. We are lucky to be part of a divinely inspired organization of women who love and serve each other and all of God's children. As Elder Jeffery R Holland reminded us, "Relief Society service is not limited to serving members of the Church. We all try to take care of our own, but the great sisterhood of Relief Society—and specifically compassionate service—knows no borders."[9] Pregnancy and childbearing and rearing are times that women everywhere need both society and relief. Relief Society is something you can draw on to provide service for your friends and neighbors, even if you are not in a position to help yourself. The following comment posted on The Gift of Giving Life blog by Pam in April 2010 is a wonderful testament to the great work of the Relief Society:

> I am not a member of The Church of Jesus Christ of Latter-day Saints (I am another type of Christian), but I am very close friends with many women in my local ward and serve them as a doula and childbirth educator. I love and honor the LDS faith so much in so many ways. . . .

I appreciated your post that pointed out the goodness of Relief Society. Two years ago my youngest son was diagnosed with leukemia, and our local Relief Society brought our family meals and cleaned our house for thirty days. I have never received such Christ-like service ever before—my friends tease me about how much I keep telling them I love RS.[10]

The Relief Society has a great history of sustaining women through child bearing. As you can read on page 22, midwifery was once a spiritual church calling. Women were set apart as midwives for life, and they were sustained and supported by the Relief Society. Later the Relief Society established birth centers and maternity chests. Women in the Relief Society also held washing and anointing ceremonies for women who were approaching their birthing times (see page 165.)

Though the world has changed significantly, the Relief Society has continued to flourish during more than 150 years of change, upheaval, and transition. Relief Society is now the largest and oldest women's organization in the world. As I mentioned earlier, consistency is a key ingredient to success in motherhood. Belle S. Spafford, the ninth Relief Society general president, said, "In the midst of all this change . . . Relief Society has been just as constant in its purpose as truth is constant. The purposes that were important for a handful of women in Nauvoo are still important to women worldwide. That is the miracle of Relief Society."[11] Elder Holland said, "It's not a program per se. It is the gospel—the gospel in action in the lives of our remarkable women. In difficult times we realize it offers its members, and by extension the whole Church, just what we need to help us right now."[12]

While we no longer sustain midwives in Church meetings, we still have a duty to sustain our fellow sisters in their callings, namely their chief calling of motherhood. In order to sustain or allow others to sustain us, it may be helpful to ponder the definition of sustain. Here are a few of the word's meanings:

1 To support, hold, or bear up from below
2 To bear (a burden, charge, etc.)
3 To undergo, experience, or suffer; endure without giving way or yielding

4 To keep (a person, the mind, the spirits, etc.) from giving way, as under a trial or affliction

5 To keep up or keep going

6 To supply with food, drink, and other necessities of life

7 To provide for by furnishing means or funds

8 To support by aid or approval

9 To uphold as valid, just, or correct, as a claim or the person making it

10 To confirm or corroborate, as a statement [13]

As you can see, there are many ways to sustain our sisters during these important years. Below are a few things that we as sisters and as an organization can do.

INFORM, EDUCATE, EDIFY

Emma Smith felt strongly that women needed to be spiritually self-sufficient and that Relief Society was the place for women to become such. The emphasis on education continued while Emmeline B. Wells was general Relief Society president (1910–1921). "She felt passionately that Latter-day Saint women should be 'the best informed of any women on the face of the earth'."[14]

In many ways, Relief Society women have become some of the best-informed women in the world. Within my ward's Relief Society are women with MFAs, MDs, PhDs, JDs, and certifications; there are also self-taught gurus of all kinds. However, the combined body of knowledge about pregnancy, childbearing, breast-feeding, and other basic female processes in that same group of woman is very limited. This ignorance about our own bodies is part of Satan's subtle plan. Any time we can inform, educate and edify women about childbirth in loving ways, we are fulfilling the mission of the Relief Society and our Heavenly Parents. The visiting teaching program is one way to do this.

MEET TEMPORAL NEEDS

I am the oldest child, but I grew up in awesome hand-me-downs thanks to someone in our stake who had a daughter. When my mother had cancer, the Relief Society brought my family meals for months. Sometimes this kind of support is organized, but many times it is spontaneous and impromptu—sisters serving sisters for no other reason than they see a need.

The visiting teaching program is your greatest opportunity to serve regularly. It is an inspired program rooted in love and friendship in which you and a companion are given a stewardship over one or several women. Ideally, every woman should have a visiting teacher. As a visiting teacher, you can pray regularly to know the needs of the sisters you are assigned. There are many ways to give. Even my own mother, when cancer was having a party in her body, still found ways to serve others by making baby dolls or clothes or delivering homegrown herbs.

BE VIGILANT ABOUT MOODS

Everyone in the Relief Society should know the signs of postpartum depression and be vigilant about new mothers' moods. Many women can put on a happy face at church, but it is important to ask questions such as "How are your moods?" more than once during the first year after a woman has her first child and all subsequent children.

PROVIDE CHILDCARE

Babysitting or allowing your children to be cared for by another mother or young woman will give children the wonderful opportunity to learn from and bond with other women (allomothering). It will also give you much-needed rest.

SUPPORT

Sometimes we just need someone to talk to. Someone who has been there. If you have all the friends you need, pay attention to who might be lacking and give them a call. If you are isolated, then find an online group of women who can support you. You would be surprised what close friendships can grow "virtually."

Sister Holland said:

> I think it could be said that, given the challenges facing women and families, no other organization in the world is going to be more helpful in the future than Relief Society. We need to rally the women of the Church to their calling as leaders and as "captains" of the welfare of children, especially now as we see families crumbling. We have to march together, hand in hand, to be able to get the work done.[15]

SHARE TALENTS AND SPIRITUAL GIFTS

There are many ways we can share our talents to sustain our sisters in the calling of motherhood. Some can sew. Some can cook. Some can use power tools. Some can organize. Some can listen. Some can teach. Some can bear testimony. Some can make people laugh. Discovering and sharing your spiritual gifts can be very rewarding for you and others. President Boyd K. Packer said: "Service in the Relief Society magnifies and sanctifies each individual sister. Your membership in Relief Society should be ever with you."[16]

ENCOURAGE OTHERS TO ACCEPT HELP

Sister Holland said:

> I think in the hearts of women is the desire to serve others in need. It doesn't matter if a woman is young or old, married or single. Relief

Society provides the perfect opportunity for her to serve because there are always others in need. Likewise, every woman at some time or other will need to be served.[17]

BE AWARE OF SINGLE MOTHERS

Single mothers are more common than you think and will probably continue to be so. If you are single, you aren't alone. There were also women in this situation in the Lord's Church anciently and in the early days of the Restoration. For example:

> Emmeline B. Wells [who later became the fifth general Relief Society president] lost her first son when he was five weeks old, and shortly thereafter her husband deserted her. Heartbroken, she later recorded, 'How dreadful when I remember my agony at that time, my utter loneliness.' Later she married Daniel H. Wells. Similar scenarios were common. The sisters' association with each other kept many women going.[18]

Don't let your identity as a single mother stop you from asking for and partaking in the blessings of the gospel, such as priesthood blessings and temple attendance. We learn in Matthew chapter 15 that when the Gentile woman approached Jesus and asked Him to heal her daughter, Jesus referred to her, a Gentile, as a "dog" (v. 26), yet He did not send her away as His disciples suggested He should. The woman answered Jesus humbly: "Truth, Lord: yet the dogs eat of the crumbs which fall from their masters' table" (v. 27). The Savior, who may have been testing her, was pleased. He said, "O woman, great is thy faith: be it unto thee even as thou wilt. And her daughter was made whole from that very hour" (v. 28). The woman did not let her identity as a Gentile interfere with her faith and the blessings she knew could be given her.

PRAY FOR EACH OTHER

Through the course of writing this book, my collaborators and I have all had to occasionally shout for help and prayers from each other. We are all

503

mothers, struggling with similar concerns about home and children. Even though we are spread across the United States, the combined prayers and inspired words from our society have provided each of us at different times with great relief. I have been spiritually uplifted by their words daily. Sister Holland described this type of sisterhood as essential:

> Relief Society is needed now more than ever before because of the challenges we face in the world today. The women of the Church have a greater need to be righteous, to live close to the Spirit, and to be faithful. And women need each other too, in order to keep and sustain their faith.[19]

The history, purpose, and work of Relief Society are unique among all women's organizations. At the centennial of the Relief Society in 1942, the First Presidency of the Church said, "No other woman's organization in all the earth has had such a birth."[20] I propose that no other women's organization can have such an *influence on motherhood and birth*. It is my prayer that we continue to uplift and sustain one another on the journey of motherhood. We are indeed doing something extraordinary.

1 Qtd. in "Charity Never Faileth," by Elaine L. Jack, *Ensign*, May 1992, http://lds.org/ensign/1992/05/charity-never-faileth.
2 Dictionary.com, s.v. "auxiliary," http://dictionary.reference.com/browse/auxiliary.
3 Study cited in *The Female Brain*, by Louann Brizendine (New York: Broadway, 2006), 114.
4 Louann Brizendine, *The Female Brain* (New York: Broadway, 2006), 110.
5 Sheri L. Dew, "Something Extraordinary," *Ensign*, March 1992, http://lds.org/ensign/1992/03/something-extraordinary.
6 Qtd. in *Daughters in My Kingdom*, by The Church of Jesus Christ of Latter-day Saints (Salt Lake City, UT: The Church of Jesus Christ of Latter-day Saints, 2011), 25.
7 Louann Brizendine, *The Female Brain* (New York: Broadway, 2006), 110.
8 Ibid., 111–112.
9 Jeffrey R. Holland and Patricia T. Holland, "'Charity Never Faileth': A Discussion on Relief Society," *Ensign*, March 2011, http://lds.org/ensign/2011/03/charity-never-faileth-a-discussion-on-relief-society.
10 Pam, comment on "Cow's and Chicken's," The Gift of Giving Life (blog), April 30, 2010, http://www.thegiftofgivinglife.blogspot.com.
11 Belle S. Spafford, "Reaching Every Facet of a Woman's Life: A Conversation with Belle S. Spafford, Relief Society General President," *Ensign*, June 1974, http://lds.org/ensign/1974/06/reaching-every-facet-of-a-womans-life-a-conversation-with-belle-s-spafford-relief-society-general-president.
12 Jeffrey R. Holland and Patricia T. Holland, "'Charity Never Faileth': A Discussion on Relief Society," *Ensign*, March 2011, http://lds.org/ensign/2011/03/charity-never-faileth-a-discussion-on-relief-society.
13 Dictionary.com, s.v. "sustain," http://dictionary.reference.com/browse/sustain.
14 Sheri L. Dew, "Something Extraordinary," *Ensign*, March 1992, http://lds.org/ensign/1992/03/something-extraordinary.
15 Jeffrey R. Holland and Patricia T. Holland, "'Charity Never Faileth': A Discussion on Relief Society," *Ensign*, March 2011, http://lds.org/ensign/2011/03/charity-never-faileth-a-discussion-on-relief-society.
16 Boyd K. Packer, "The Circle of Sisters," *Ensign*, November 1980, 109–110.
17 Jeffrey R. Holland and Patricia T. Holland, "'Charity Never Faileth': A Discussion on Relief Society," *Ensign*, March 2011, http://lds.org/ensign/2011/03/charity-never-faileth-a-discussion-on-relief-society.
18 Sheri L. Dew, "Something Extraordinary," *Ensign*, March 1992, http://lds.org/ensign/1992/03/something-extraordinary.
19 Jeffrey R. Holland and Patricia T. Holland, "'Charity Never Faileth': A Discussion on Relief Society," *Ensign*, March 2011, http://lds.org/ensign/2011/03/charity-never-faileth-a-discussion-on-relief-society.
20 Julie B. Beck, "Relief Society: A Sacred Work," *Ensign*, November 2009, http://lds.org/ensign/2009/11/relief-society-a-sacred-work.

Elisabeth:
Go before the Face of the Lord

By Heather Farrell, CD(DONA)

Elisabeth, the wife of Zacharias, was the mother of John the Baptist, who was born only six months before his cousin, Jesus. Before John the Baptist was even born, Zacharias prophesied that his son would "go before the face of the Lord to prepare his ways" (Luke 1: 76). In the same manner that John prepared the way for Christ to accomplish His divine mission, John's mother, Elisabeth, helped prepare the way for Mary to accomplish her divine mission.

Elisabeth and Zacharias were childless and both "stricken in years" (Luke 1:7). When Zacharias was visited by an angel, who told him that Elisabeth would bear a son, Zacharias doubted, and so the angel struck him dumb. Yet just as the angel promised, Elisabeth became pregnant in her old age (see Luke 1:11–25).

Six months later, the same angel visited Mary, Elisabeth's young cousin, with similar miraculous tidings. When Mary asked, "How shall this be, seeing I know not a man" (Luke 1:34), the angel explained that the Holy Ghost would overshadow her. The angel also told her that her cousin Elisabeth was six months pregnant, perhaps as proof that "with God nothing shall be impossible" (Luke 1:37). After the angel left, Mary went "with haste" to visit Elisabeth (Luke 1:39).

When she reached Elisabeth, Mary saw that Elisabeth was indeed more than six months pregnant. I imagine they greeted each other with affection. Then, at the sound of Mary's voice, Elisabeth and the babe within her womb were filled with the Holy Ghost:

> And she spake out with a loud voice, and said, Blessed art thou among
> women, and blessed is the fruit of thy womb. And whence is this to

me, that the mother of my Lord should come to me? For, lo, as soon as the voice of thy salutation sounded in mine ears, the babe leaped in my womb for joy. (Luke 1:42–44)

Elisabeth knew, even before Mary told her, that Mary was carrying the Savior and Redeemer of the world.

The story of Elisabeth and Mary demonstrates beautifully that when God gives us a commandment or personal revelation, He often give us multiple witnesses to proclaim the truthfulness of His word. Although Mary humbly submitted to her destiny, she may have felt unsure about how she was to explain her situation to others or how her family would react. What a blessing for her to have Elisabeth, who through the power of the Holy Ghost was able to discern the truth and give her added support. If Mary had any lingering fears, they surely evaporated, enabling her to state with surety that "all generations shall call me blessed" (Luke 1:48).

Just as He did for Mary, God usually sends people into our lives to help pave the way for us to accomplish our divine missions on this earth. He sends people to us who will guide us, who will bear testimony to promptings, dreams, visions, and revelations that we have received from the Lord.

My sister-in-law was my "Elisabeth." It was her faith, strength, and encouragement that guided me and sustained me on my path toward becoming a mother. After a struggle with fertility, my sister-in-law gave birth to her first child just six months before I gave birth to mine. I was terrified of motherhood and doubted my ability to handle pregnancy, childbirth, breast-feeding and all the other responsibilities that came with having a baby. Yet as I watched my sister-in-law blossom in her pregnancy and saw her make faith-filled and conscious decisions about birth, breast-feeding, and motherhood, I was in awe. I took strength from her example, and I began to look forward to childbirth and breast-feeding with joy. She bore testimony to what I knew the Lord had told me and gave me the courage to go forth in faith. I will be forever grateful for her.

As we venture into motherhood, let us not forget that God has given us wonderful women in our lives we can look to for examples and strength. And may we recognize the many opportunities to be another woman's "Elisabeth."

Author Bios

FELICE AUSTIN is a mother, writer, certified hypnotherapist, Hypnobabies® Childbirth Hypnosis Instructor, prenatal yoga teacher, and spiritual childbirth educator. She enjoys long walks on the beach, quantum physics, twirling in circles, spiritual chats, writing, reading, and anything else that blows her hair back. Felice's passion for creativity and helping others create positive change drives her in her daily life and in motherhood. She has planted her tree of life in the rich, beautiful soil of Los Angeles, where she can be found with her daughter inhaling and exhaling deeply.

You can download Felice's free hypnosis MP3: "Relaxed, Peaceful, Divine" at TheGiftofGivingLife.com. You can also download her "Peaceful Parenting Affirmations" on itunes or from www.treeoflifehypnosis.net.

LANI AXMAN finished her studies in English and editing at Brigham Young University in 2003. Following the birth of her second daughter, Lani put her pen to work for her new-found passion—childbirth advocacy. In 2007, Lani created her blog, Birth Faith (http://birthfaith.org), where she continues to share her thoughts and research and is followed by thousands of readers each week. Lani became trained as a birth doula through DONA International in 2009 and in neonatal resuscitation in 2011. She looks forward to serving through birth work when her children are older. Lani now resides near Phoenix, Arizona, with her husband, four children, and many beloved houseplants.

HEATHER FARRELL is a certified birth doula (DONA International) and is addicted to seeing babies be born. She is a graduate from Brigham Young University and received her bachelors of science in Public Health and a minor in Women's Studies. Heather is a self proclaimed scripture nerd and loves to study about the lives of the women in the scriptures. She authors the blog Women in the Scriptures (womeninthescriptures.blogspot.com) which is read weekly by thousands of people around the world. Heather and her husband live in Utah and are the parents of three beautiful children.

ROBYN ALLGOOD is a doula and childbirth educator affiliated with the Academy of Husband-Coached Childbirth. In addition to teaching and learning from the moms and dads in her childbirth classes, she leads a local ICAN chapter (International Cesarean Awareness Network) offering support to moms after cesarean birth, supporting vaginal birth after cesarean, and offering information to prevent unnecessary cesarean sections.

After serving a mission in the Dominican Republic, she married the "boy down the street." Robyn completed a bachelors degree in Speech Communication at the University of Utah. She also loves to read, write and reflect.

Serving in the gospel has been a constant source of growth for Robyn. She treasures her calling as a mother. With five beautiful children to chase after, she spends way too much time searching for matching little shoes so they can leave for their next adventure.

SHERIDAN RIPLEY has always loved all things pregnancy, birth and babies. Even when she was in high-school she would cut class and go to the library to read pregnancy books. After graduating from Vanderbilt University she served a mission in Bordeaux France. Soon after returning home she married a boy she had been dating before her mission. Within two years her dream of being pregnant became reality.

Her first son was born by emergency cesarean at 34 weeks. Her second son was born by VBAC (vaginal birth after cesarean) in the hospital with an epidural. Her third son was also born via VBAC in the hospital naturally using Hypnobabies®. She had a doula for her third birth and that is what inspired her to become a doula.

As a DONA certified doula, she assists women and their partners during their birthing time. She is also a Hypnobabies Childbirth Hypnosis Instructor and loves to help expecting parents prepare for a positive birth. You can download her free e-book The Top Three Tips to Enjoy Your Birth at her blog, www.Enjoy Birth.com.

Photo Credit

Tiffany Bergsjo 213, *317,*
Jackie Brethen Leishman *28*
Shawna Bryan *509 (Lani Axman)*
Shanan Durda *334*
Shannon Flores *cover, 509 (Felice Austin)*
Chelsey Gines *134*
Eric Gordon *168*
Shannon Harris *510 (Heather Farrell)*
Brooke Mayo *179*
Andee McDonald *10*
Amy Morgan *263*
Olya Nelson *211, 252*
Cali Stoddard *510 (Robyn Allgood)*
Brittney Warburton *297*

Index

513

477, 480, 486, 493, 503, 507
scriptures, xvii, 12-13, 60, 63, 71, 86,
121-122, 144-145, 163, 186, 202,
205, 218, 220-221, 225, 239, 244,
246, 251, 273, 276, 280, 283, 292,
294, 296, 299, 323, 324, 334, 345,
346, 349, 360, 368, 375, 378-380,
388, 404, 407, 412, 435-436, 438,
448, 456-458, 459-461, 466, 477,
480, 484, 492, 510,
service, 42, 158, 160, 162, 165, 176, 186,
194, 220, 279, 313, 316, 347, 350,
376, 379-380, 384, 410, 465, 469,
498, 499, 502,
sexual abuse, 225, 301, 438-440,
491-493
Sheri L. Dew, 65
Sheridan Ripley, 107, 190, 281, 398,
446,
Sheila Kitzinger, 459
Shiphrah, 71-73
Socrates, 221
Spencer W. Kimball, 49, 63, 72, 485
Spirit, xiii, xiv, 4, 12, 14, 15, 32, 33, 35,
41, 46, 48-52, 57, 61, 62, 64, 68-69,
79, 81, 86-89, 91, 96, 99, 102, 106,
116-117, 120, 123, 124, 128, 140,
142, 154, 157,166, 169, 172, 173,
177, 178, 188, 191,193, 201, 205,
208, 213-215, 220-226, 229-230,
233, 236-237, 242, 246, 247, 251,
260, 262, 264, 269, 276, 279, 281,
282, 297, 299-300, 302-303, 306,
310, 316, 321, 324, 329, 337, 342,
347, 348, 366, 369, 371-372, 374,
375, 382, 385, 390, 393-395, 411,
420, 437, 440, 443, 452, 455,
460-461, 486, 488, 490, 504
Steve Martin, 250
stewardship, 61, 63-66, 501
stillbirth, 108, 375, 383,
subconscious/unconscious, 45, 202, 204,
222, 250, 291

support, xvii, 6, 7, 8, 10, 14, 22, 32, 33,
45, 79, 93, 94, 100, 111-113, 125,
137, 147, 153, 156, 163, 166, 169,
183, 192, 196, 209, 229, 233, 258,
262, 282, 283, 284, 304-312, 336,
346, 355, 360, 370, 380, 396-400,
420-425, 438, 443, 461, 483, 484,
485, 496, 499-505, 507
Tad R. Callister, 109, 144
temple, 13, 19, 26, 38, 43, 48, 53, 80, 97,
158, 165, 166, 168,214, 234, 236,
241, 275, 276, 299, 336, 362-363,
364,372, 380, 410-413,435,
438-439, 488-489
The Giving, 76
Thomas S. Monson, 144, 203, 221
transformation, 201, 211, 233, 250, 373,
462
transition, 33, 68, 97, 106, 155-156,
160, 187, 253, 256, 286, 300, 315,
342-343, 373, 409, 422, 431, 460,
462, 484, 496, 499,
travail, 22, 289, 323-326, 349, 436
tree, 2, 3, 8, 13, 28, 59-60, 64,162,
171-172, 238, 375, 382
trust, 15, 37, 39, 76, 83, 88, 89, 91, 97,
101, 111, 121, 125, 166, 253-255,
262, 268, 276, 281-282, 285, 302,
309, 317, 331, 425, 446, 452, 454,
478, 495
ultrasound, 55, 56, 82, 98, 104, 129-130,
134, 264, 269-270, 276-277, 332,
388,
unconscious (see subconscious),
Valerie Hudson Cassler, 64
Vaughn J. Featherstone, 283
VBAC, 107, 110-111, 143, 157, 193,
331-333, 511
veil, 46, 61-66, 68-70,137, 169, 172,
188, 205, 305, 309, 310, 348,
372-373,
Viktor Frankl, 335
visiting teacher, xiv, 124, 168, 498, 501

CPSIA information can be obtained at www.ICGtesting.com
Printed in the USA
LVOW131851070612

285126LV00011B/58/P